Medieval Muslim Historians and the Franks in the Levant

Medieval Muslim Historians and the Franks in the Levant

Edited by

Alex Mallett

BRILL

LEIDEN | BOSTON

Originally published in hardback in 2014 as Volume 2 in the series The Muslim World in the Age of the Crusades – Studies and Texts.

Cover illustration: The Umayyad mosque in Damascus, where many of the historians examined in this volume studied or taught. Image by Istock/Getty Images. Design by Pieter Kers (with brown and gold background).

The Library of Congress has cataloged the hardcover edition as follows:

Medieval Muslim historians and the Franks in the Levant / edited by Alex Mallett.
pages cm. — (The Muslim world in the age of the Crusades ; v. 2)
Includes index.
ISBN 978-90-04-27741-0 (hardback : alk. paper)—ISBN 978-90-04-28068-7 (e-book) 1. Crusades—Historiography. 2. Historians, Arab—Islamic Empire. 3. Islamic Empire—Relations—Latin Orient. 4. Latin Orient—Relations—Islamic Empire. I. Mallett, Alexander.

D156.58.M434 2015
909.07—dc23

2014026905

This publication has been typeset in the multilingual "Brill" typeface. With over 5,100 characters covering Latin, IPA, Greek, and Cyrillic, this typeface is especially suitable for use in the humanities.
For more information, please see brill.com/brill-typeface.

ISBN 978-90-04-73343-5 (paperback, 2025)
ISBN 978-90-04-27741-0 (hardback)
ISBN 978-90-04-28068-7 (e-book)

This book is printed on acid-free paper.

Dieses Buch ist Cornelia Lenz gewidmet

Contents

Acknowledgements ix
List of Abbreviations x

Introduction 1
Alex Mallett

Ibn al-Qalānisī 7
Niall Christie

ʿImād al-Dīn al-Iṣfahānī 29
Lutz Richter-Bernburg

Ibn al-Athīr 52
Françoise Micheau

Sibṭ Ibn al-Jawzī 84
Alex Mallett

Kamāl al-Dīn ʿUmar Ibn al-ʿAdīm 109
Anne-Marie Eddé

Ibn Wāṣil: An Ayyūbid Perspective on Frankish Lordships and Crusades 136
Konrad Hirschler

Taqī al-Dīn Aḥmad ibn ʿAlī al-Maqrīzī 161
Frédéric Bauden

Index 201

Acknowledgements

The realisation of any edited volume primarily depends on the good will and hard work of a number of people. It has been some time since the idea of a project such as this first occurred, and since then I have had the good fortune to work with a group of contributors who have been fantastically patient, enthusiastic in their support of the project's aims, and who have produced excellent pieces of scholarship. It is only because of their generosity of time and energy that this volume has been completed. I must also mention other scholars who helped through their suggestions for contributors to this volume, particularly Daniella Talmon-Heller and Evrim Binbas, as well as to Olivier Berrou, who kindly translated a French article into English.

At Brill this volume has been warmly received from the beginning, and this enthusiasm has been carried on throughout the editorial process. Over the course of production Kathy van Vliet, Nienke Brienen-Moolenaar, Teddi Dols, and Kim Fiona Plas have all helped greatly in bringing this project to fruition. Also to thank are the series editors Suleiman Mourad, Paul Cobb and Konrad Hirschler for accepting the project. It would be remiss of me not to also thank Carole Hillenbrand, Jenny Grene and Louise King for their useful advice.

Finally, to Conny, who was such an inspiration. Du fehlst mir.

List of Abbreviations

EI2	P.J. Bearman et al. (eds), *Encyclopaedia of Islam, Second Edition*, 11 vols (Leiden, 1954–2002)
EI3	K. Fleet et al. (eds), *Encyclopaedia of Islam Three* (Leiden, 2007–); http://referenceworks.brillonline.com/browse/encyclopaedia-of-islam-3
EIr	E. Yarshater et al. (eds), *Encyclopaedia Iranica* 16- vols (London, 1982–)
EMC	G. Dunphy (ed.), *The Encyclopaedia of the Medieval Chronicle*, 2 vols (Leiden, 2010)
Gabrieli, *Arab Historians*	F. Gabrieli, *Arab Historians of the Crusades*, tr. E. Costello (Berkeley/Los Angeles, 1969)
Hillenbrand, *Crusades*	C. Hillenbrand, *The Crusades. Islamic Perspectives* (Edinburgh, 1999)
RHC Or.	*Recueil des Historiens des Croisades: Historiens Orientaux*, 5 vols (Paris, 1872–1906)

Introduction

Alex Mallett

Writing the history of the Crusades and of the Latin states of the Levant in the period of Frankish settlement in that region requires the utilisation of source material written in a variety of languages and a multitude of social and religious milieux, including Greek texts written in the Byzantine Empire, Syriac works written under Muslim rule, and Armenian histories written in Armenian Christian lands, among others. Yet the main languages in which evidence for the history of the crusading period is written are Latin, Old French and Arabic.[1] Modern historians of the Crusades and the Latin East, for reasons which extend far back into the cultural and educational history of Europe and North America, almost exclusively come from a background of, and have been trained in, one or both of the first two of these languages and the cultures of western Europe which nurtured them. Although very recently some studies have attempted to employ Arabic sources to the same extent as the Latin ones, Arabic texts have, traditionally and regrettably, been used almost exclusively only in as far as they back-up what the western ones say, and ignored if they disagree.[2]

Although the Arabic sources for the history of the crusading period are of the highest importance for scholars studying the subject, there has been little attempt to analyse them, or even to provide translations for some of this material. For example with regard to the former, the translations provided in the *Recueil des Historiens des Croisades: Documents Orientaux*[3] are of some use, but are marred by poor editing and translating of the texts in question, and the selective nature of many of the passages chosen means the medieval historians' overall agendas are unseen, while there is also no attempt to place the works into their wider context. Another oft-employed selection of translations is Francesco Gabrieli's *Arab Historians of the Crusades*[4] and, while the

1 A useful introduction to the majority of sources for the crusading period, at least for the Levant, is provided in M. Whitby (ed.), *Byzantines and Crusaders in Non-Greek Sources* (Oxford, 2007).

2 One good example of the full incorporation of Arabic sources into the crusading narrative can be found in the account of the siege of Damascus in 543/1148 in J. Phillips, *The Second Crusade: Extending the Frontiers of Christendom* (New Haven CT, 2007), pp. 218–26.

3 *Recueil des Historiens des Croisades: Documents Orientaux*, 5 vols (Paris, 1872–1906).

4 F. Gabrieli, *Arab Historians of the Crusades* (Berkeley and Los Angeles, 1969).

 | DOI 10.1163/9789004280687_002

translations provided by this work are extremely useful, there are also significant deficiencies with them, particularly that the English version was translated from Italian rather than directly from Arabic, and again there is no attempt to contextualise them. There have also been a number of brief studies devoted to the rather inaccurate idea of the 'Arabic Historiography of the Crusades', although these are now generally rather dated.[5]

Despite these problems, there are some scholarly outputs which remain useful; these include translations into English such as Broadhurst's rendering of al-Maqrīzī's *Kitāb al-sulūk*,[6] and the selected translations into French by Eddé and Micheau.[7] Other studies remaining important include Cahen's old yet still informative analytical passages at the beginning of his *La Syrie du nord*[8] and Richards' studies of Ibn al-Athīr and 'Imād al-Dīn al-Iṣfahānī.[9] There has also, in the last decade or so, been a renewed attempt to provide translations of significant Arabic texts from the crusading period into English, although rather disappointingly these have, in general, simply re-translated works which have already been available in western translation for some time, leaving numerous other extremely important works un-translated in full, or even lacking a decent edition.[10] The last ten years has also seen a number of quality studies of historical writings relevant to the crusading period, but their conclusions

---

5 See, for example, F. Gabrieli, 'The Arabic Historiography of the Crusades', in B. Lewis and P.M. Holt (eds) *Historians of the Middle East* (London, 1962), 98–107.

6 Al-Maqrīzī, *Kitāb al-sulūk li-ma'rifat duwal al-mulūk*, tr. R.J.C. Broadhurst as *A History of the Ayyūbid Sultans of Egypt* (Boston, 1980).

7 A.-M. Eddé and F. Micheau, *L'Orient au temps des croisades* (Paris, 2002).

8 C. Cahen, *La Syrie du nord à l'époque des croisades et la principauté franque d'Antioche* (Paris, 1940).

9 D.S. Richards, "Imād al-Dīn al-Iṣfahānī: Administrator, Littérateur and Historian', in M. Shatzmiller (ed.), *Crusaders and Muslims in Twelfth-Century Syria* (Leiden, 1993), 133–46; idem, 'Ibn al-Athīr and the Later Parts of the *Kāmil*: A Study of Aims and Methods', in D.O. Morgan (ed.), *Medieval Historical Writing in the Christian and Islamic Worlds* (London, 1982), 76–108.

10 Foremost among the new translations (although all of these have been translated into a western language previously) are those by D.S. Richards: Bahā' al-Dīn Ibn Shaddād, *The Rare and Excellent History of Saladin* (Aldershot, 2002), and Ibn al-Athīr, *The Chronicle of Ibn al-Athīr for the Crusading Period from* al-Kāmil fi'l-ta'rīkh, 3 parts (Aldershot, 2006–8); another useful work is Usāma b. Munqidh, *The Book of Contemplation*, tr. P.M. Cobb (New York, 2008). However, as some of the articles below demonstrate, important texts remain only partially translated or are poorly edited, such as the chronicles of Sibṭ Ibn al-Jawzī and Ibn Wāṣil. Important texts which remain unedited include large sections of Ibn al-Furāt's *Ta'rīkh al-duwal wa'l-mulūk*; I am currently working on an edition of the third volume of this text, which covers the years 544/1149–562/1167.

have not generally been placed within the field of crusader studies.[11] Given this overall state of research it is hoped that the studies within this volume will act as both an introduction for students and scholars studying the crusading period to some of the main Arabic historical texts and a spur to further investigation in this area by Arabists.

This study does not aim to bring any new source material to the overall corpus of Arabic works available in translation. Such a contribution is certainly valuable, and it is a future aim to bring Arabic sources into the field of crusader studies by providing new translations and highlighting the relevance of material already well-known in other fields of Islamic Studies, such as religious texts. However, it seems that it would be rather imprudent to bring new source material to bear without first providing some information on the social, cultural and religious atmospheres in which those texts already available in translation were written, or on the authors' historiographical approach.

This volume contains seven studies, each of which focusses on one Muslim historian and the work or works they wrote containing information relevant to the crusading period, and each of the seven follows a broad template. Approximately the first third of each study is devoted to a summary of the author's life and influences, as far as they are known, in order to allow for an understanding of the milieu in which he lived and worked. This will, in turn, allow for a greater appreciation of why the Franks and the events of the crusading period are presented as they are. Following this, there is a short assessment of the author's total written outputs, in order both for his overall agenda in writing to be understood and for his specific historical works relevant to the crusading period to be placed within that agenda. Following this, the work(s) relevant for the history of the Crusades and the Latin East are examined in detail. While each of the modern contributors has been given the freedom to explore the text in the way they regard as being most effective, each textual study aims to: describe the history of modern studies, editions and translations of the text; highlight the reason for writing the text, its agenda and overall narrative framework; and demonstrate how the Franks of the Levant and the various Muslim rulers from the crusading period are presented and why. It is hoped that this will help modern scholars of the crusading period to cut through the rhetoric within these texts and so utilise them in a more effective manner. As far as possible, this has been carried out using examples from within the texts which are already available in western language translation

11 See, for example, K. Hirschler, *Medieval Arabic Historiography: Authors as Actors* (London, 2006) and F. Micheau, 'Le *Kitāb al-kāmil fī l-ta'rīkh* d'Ibn al-Athīr: Entre chronique et histoire', *Studia Islamica* 104–105 (2007), 85–106.

in order to allow scholars without Arabic to locate them; sometimes, however, this has not proved possible, particularly with texts only partially translated, and so previously non-translated sections have had to be employed.

The texts and their authors examined in this volume have been chosen for two main reasons. Firstly, it is intended that the studies should primarily examine chronographical historical writings rather than biographical, autobiographical, or any other genre which may contain evidence for the crusading period, as chronography is the genre which is most often employed by modern historians to write the history of the time. Furthermore, an attempt to include multiple genres across the volume could cause confusion on the part of the non-expert reader.[12] Secondly, as this volume is aimed primarily at scholars and students reading these texts in translation it is only natural that it should focus on works which have been translated into a western language, and in this context this primarily means English or French. It is felt that the seven authors and their works which are examined in these studies best fit these aims.

At this point, it may be useful to highlight some of the authors who have been excluded from this volume, and the reasons why. There are a number of writers whose works cover the events of the Crusades and have been translated into western languages, and which can contribute greatly to modern understanding of the period in question. These include Ibn Jubayr's *Riḥla* ('Travels'),[13] Usāma b. Munqidh's *Kitāb al-iʿtibār* ('The Book of Instructions'),[14] Abū Shāma's *Kitāb al-rawḍatayn fī akhbār al-dawlatayn* ('The Book of the Two Gardens on the Reports of the Two States'),[15] and Bahā' al-Dīn Ibn Shaddād's *al-Nawāḍir al-sulṭāniyya wa'l-maḥāsin al-yūsufiyya* ('The Sultan-ly Rarities and the Joseph-ly Merits');[16] these have been omitted because they are not chronicles but are instead, respectively, a travel narrative, a series of 'memoirs', two biographies and one biography. A number of other important chronicles, some of which are mentioned in passing in this volume, have been excluded because they have not been translated into a western language. These include al-Nuwayrī's

12 It is hoped that a future volume will contain studies of other types of Islamic historical writings.

13 Ibn Jubayr, *Riḥla*, tr. R.J.C. Broadhurst as *The Travels of Ibn Jubayr* (London, 1952).

14 Cobb, *The Book of Contemplation*.

15 Abū Shāma, *Kitāb al-rawḍatayn fī akhbār al-dawlatayn*, ed. and tr. in RHC *Or*. Vol. IV, pp. 3–522 and vol. V, pp. 3–206.

16 Bahā' al-Dīn Ibn Shaddād, *al-Nawāḍir al-sulṭāniyya wa'l-maḥāsin al-yūsufiyya*, tr. D.S. Richards as *The Rare and Excellent History of Saladin* (Aldershot, 2002).

Nihāyat al-arab fī funūn al-adab ('The Ultimate Goal in the Field of Culture'),[17] and al-Birzālī's *al-Muqtafī 'alā kitāb al-rawḍatayn* ('The Continuation of the *Kitāb al-rawḍatayn*').[18] Other Arabic writers have been excluded because it is the aim of this volume to focus on Muslim historians, and so Christians who wrote relevant material in Arabic are not included; one such example is Ibn al-'Amīd and his *al-Majmūʿ al-mubārak* ('The Blessed Collection').[19]

The writing of history in the medieval Islamic world followed a rather different path to that of history writing in contemporaneous western Europe. There had been no tradition of writing history among the pre-Islamic Arabs, and during the first centuries of Islam it held little respect amongst the majority of the Muslim *'ulamā'*, the religious classes, as it was believed to add nothing to the understanding of religion (i.e. Islam), being at best frivolous and at worst dangerous. The only history which was, in general, believed to be permissible to write was the history of the life of Muḥammad and the early 'Rightly-Guided' caliphs (the Rāshidūn), as their almost-perfect examples of rule could be of use to later generations through attempts to emulate them. There was also no such thing as a 'professional' historian in the medieval Islamic period. All historians were instead primarily employed in some other respect—usually in a religious or bureaucratic position of some sort—and for them the writing of history was a hobby, albeit a serious one.[20]

With the exception of al-Athāribī, who wrote a now-lost account of the crusading movement, no Muslim history of the Crusades and the Latin presence in the Levant was written. Thus, the historians on whom we rely for information were not the equivalent of Latin historians such as William of Tyre, Walter the Chancellor or the author of the anonymous *Gesta Francorum*. Instead, they followed a historiographical approach more related to writers such as Orderic Vitalis or Matthew Paris—including accounts of the events of the crusading period but in a wider context, presenting those occurrences in a manner which

17 Al-Nuwayrī, *Nihāyat al-arab fī funūn al-adab*, ed. M.M. Amīn et al., 28 vols (Cairo, 1923–92).

18 Al-Birzālī, *al-Muqtafī 'alā kitāb al-rawḍatayn*, ed. 'U. Tadmurī (Sidon, 2006).

19 Ibn al-'Amīd, *al-Majmūʿ al-mubārak*, partial ed. C. Cahen in 'La "Chronique des Ayyoubides" d'al-Makīn b. al-'Amīd', *Bulletin des Études Orientales* 15 (1955–57), 109–84, pp. 127–77; tr. A.-M. Eddé and F. Micheau as *Al-Makīn Ibn al-'Amīd, Chronique des Ayyoubides (602–658/1205–6–1259–60)* (Paris, 1994).

20 For general assessments of medieval Arabic-Islamic historiography, see, among others, C.F. Robinson, *Islamic Historiography* (Cambridge, 2003); T. Khalidi, *Arabic Historical Thought in the Classical Period* (Cambridge, 1994); F. Rosenthal, *A History of Muslim Historiography*, 2nd ed. (Leiden, 1968); and B. Lewis and P.M. Holt (eds) *Historians of the Middle East* (London, 1962).

fits with the broader message and agenda of their chronicle. It is these messages and agendas which these studies will attempt to highlight.

One question which has exercised modern historians of medieval Islamic historiography concerns the extent to which the source material can be trusted in terms of the 'facts' contained within it. As Meisami has commented in the context of medieval Persian historical writing, 'the medieval historian's primary interest lay less in recording the "facts" of history than in the construction of meaningful narratives'.[21] One of the most extreme examples of this can be found in a study by El-Hibri, whose argument surrounding accounts of the 'Abbāsid caliphate in the second/eighth-third/ninth centuries is that almost all the information contained within the chronicles was, in essence, invented by the authors in order to make a political point.[22] While most modern scholars consider this to be too extreme a position, the extent to which historical writing was moulded to suit political circumstances in the late fifth/eleventh and early sixth/twelfth centuries has been amply demonstrated by Safi in his important deconstruction of the mechanisms created by the Seljūqs to legitimise their rule.[23] With these ideas in mind, it is hoped that not only will this volume prove useful to crusade scholars, but, through a deconstruction of the circumstances surrounding the composition of these works, that it will also enable those working in Islamic history and Arabic/Islamic historiography to further knowledge in their respective fields as well.

21 J.S. Meisami, *Persian Historiography* (Edinburgh, 1999), p. 3.

22 T. El-Hibri, *Reinterpreting Islamic Historiography: Hārūn al-Rashīd and the Narrative of the 'Abbāsid Caliphate* (Cambridge, 1999).

23 O. Safi, *The Politics of Knowledge in Pre-Modern Islam* (Chapel Hill NC, 2006).

Ibn al-Qalānisī

Niall Christie

The Author

Abū Yaʿlā Ḥamza ibn Asad al-Tamīmī, better known to modern historians by his family name of Ibn al-Qalānisī (c. 465–555/1073–1160), is an obscure figure, which is somewhat surprising given that he was a member of a prominent family in Damascus, held important positions in the city's administration, and that his chronicle is such a well-known source for the first sixty years of the crusading period. Even though Ibn al-Qalānisī's work is widely employed by scholars the amount of modern scholarship devoted specifically to the author and his work is relatively limited—usually only forming part of wider studies—presumably as a result of the paucity of contemporary information about him.[1] There has been only one book-length study of Ibn al-Qalānisī and his work, Nadā ʿAbd al-Razzāq Maḥmūd al-Jīlāwī's *Ibn al-Qalānisī: Sīratu-hu wa manhaju-hu fī kitābi-hi* ('Ibn al-Qalānisī: His Biography and his Method in his Book'), which focusses primarily on the author's biography, historical methodology and literary technique.[2]

The main source of information about the life of Ibn al-Qalānisī is the biographical notice found in the prosopographical work of his contemporary, the religious scholar and preacher Ibn ʿAsākir (d. 571/1176), entitled *Taʾrīkh madīnat Dimashq*.[3] This reports that Ibn al-Qalānisī had the title of *ʿamīd*, indicating that he reached a high rank in the city's administration.[4] It also notes that Ibn

1 See, for example, C. Hillenbrand, *The Crusades. Islamic Perspectives* (Edinburgh, 1999), *passim*; H.A.R. Gibb, 'Notes on the Arabic Materials for the History of the Early Crusades', *Bulletin of the School of Oriental and African Studies* 7 (1935), 745–54; and F. Gabrieli, 'The Arabic Historiography of the Crusades', in B. Lewis and P.M. Holt (eds), *Historians of the Middle East* (London, 1962), 98–107, pp. 102–3.

2 N.R.M. al-Jīlāwī, *Ibn al-Qalānisī: Sīratuhu wa-manhajuhu fī kitābihi* (*Dhayl taʾrīkh Dimashq*) (Baghdad, 2008).

3 ʿAlī ibn al-Ḥasan ibn ʿAsākir, *Taʾrīkh madīnat Dimashq*, ed. ʿU.Gh. al-ʿAmrawī, 80 vols (Beirut, 1995–2000), vol. XV, p. 191 (no. 1749).

4 Gibb suggests that this term means that Ibn al-Qalānisī was head of the correspondence bureau of Damascus; see Ibn al-Qalānisī, *The Damascus Chronicle of the Crusades*, partial tr. H.A.R. Gibb (London, 1932; repr. Mineola NY, 2002), p. 8. However, al-Jīlāwī suggests that the position actually involved representing the Seljūq sultan in a broader range of administrative fields and hence also encompassed a wider range of powers; see al-Jīlāwī, *Ibn al-Qalānisī*,

 | DOI 10.1163/9789004280687_003

al-Qalānisī was an *adīb* who was also devoted to calligraphy, at which he was particularly skilled. By describing Ibn al-Qalānisī as an *adīb* Ibn 'Asākir indicates that he was a master of *adab*; in its broadest interpretation, this term indicates cultural refinement and good breeding, encompassing encyclopaedic knowledge of etiquette, customs and a range of literature including religious texts and doctrine, historical traditions and poetry. Probably the best-known exponent of such a range of knowledge in the crusading period was Usāma ibn Munqidh (d. 584/1188), whose 'memoirs' are well known to historians of the Crusades.[5] In a more narrow sense, *adab* indicates expertise in poetry, prose and grammar. Whichever Ibn 'Asākir means in this case, it is clear that he regarded Ibn al-Qalānisī as a literary as well as political figure.[6]

When describing his political life Ibn 'Asākir notes that Ibn al-Qalānisī twice held the position of *ra'īs* of Damascus.[7] A number of towns in Syria maintained this position which, between the fourth/tenth and sixth/twelfth centuries, meant being the head of the urban militia known as the *aḥdāth*, who occupied themselves principally with maintaining public order and firefighting. They were also involved in urban defence and, as a focus for local sentiment, could be influential in resisting or seeking to influence the Seljūq rulers or their appointees who governed the city.[8] As Zakkār notes, Ibn al-Qalānisī is rather reticent about his own activities, and he tells us nothing about his time in office, with the exception of one hint that he may have held the position in 540/1145–46,[9] while other sources do not furnish any more details. However, he was

pp. 33–37. It is here worth underlining that Gibb's translation of the text is partial; only episodes related to the struggles with the Franks are rendered into English, while those to do with the internal politics of Damascus and the rest of the Muslim world are ignored. This means it is not possible to fully understand the situation in the city from his translation, and so scholars should refer instead to the full French translation for this period by Le Tourneau: *Damas de 1075 à 1154*, tr. R. Le Tourneau (Damascus, 1952).

5 Usāma ibn Munqidh, *Usāmah's Memoirs Entitled* Kitāb al-iʿtibār, ed. P.K. Hitti (Princeton NJ, 1930; repr. Beirut, 1981); tr. P.M. Cobb as *The Book of Contemplation: Islam and the Crusades* (New York, 2008).

6 Cf. F. Gabrieli, 'Adab', in *EI2*. For a useful discussion of the origins and development of *adab*, see M.G.S. Hodgson, *The Venture of Islam: Conscience and History in a World Civilization. Volume 1: The Classical Age of Islam* (Chicago, 1977), pp. 444–72.

7 Ibn 'Asākir, *Ta'rīkh*, vol. XV, p. 191.

8 On the *ra'īs* and the *aḥdāth* in this period see T.K. El-Azhari, *The Saljūqs of Syria during the Crusades, 463–549 A.H./1070–1154 A.D.* (Berlin, 1997), pp. 303–7 and P.M. Holt, *The Age of the Crusades: The Near East from the Eleventh Century to 1517* (London, 1986), pp. 71–72.

9 In his account of this year, in a section beginning with 'The *ra'īs* … Abū Yaʿlā Ḥamza ibn Asad ibn Muḥammad al-Tamīmī said …', the writer notes explicitly that he is providing a

not the only member of his family to hold this position, and it was subsequently held by a number of his sons and other relations.[10] Perhaps most notably, his nephew ʿAbd al-Munʿim ibn Muḥammad was installed as *raʾīs* of Damascus in Dhu'l-Qaʿda 548/February 1154 and, along with the city's *aḥdāth*, was involved in the final negotiations with Nūr al-Dīn (d. 569/1174) that led to the handover of Damascus to the latter in Ṣafar/April of that year, despite the ongoing determination of its Būrid governor to retain power.[11] Ibn al-Qalānisī does not mention his nephew's involvement in the handover, suggesting that despite his description of Nūr al-Dīn's assault on the city as being 'for the good fortune of the king Nūr al-Dīn, and the people of Damascus, and all men together',[12] he may have had mixed feelings about the negotiations and the takeover. However Ibn al-Qalānisī himself felt, the incident reminds us of how influential the *raʾīs* and *aḥdāth* could be in the fortunes and politics of their communities in Syria at this time. However, Nūr al-Dīn's takeover led to a decline in the influence of the *raʾīs* and *aḥdāth*, as under his rule power was transferred into the hands of the *shiḥna* (military governor) and the *ṣāḥib al-shurṭa* (chief of police), and the *raʾīs* and *aḥdāth* would disappear completely during the Ayyūbid and Mamlūk periods. In being involved in the negotiations to hand Damascus over to Nūr al-Dīn, members of Ibn al-Qalānisī's family were instrumental in altering the power structures within Damascus, and as members of the *aḥdāth* and former *raʾīs* were actually helping to bring about the downfall of those institutions through which they had wielded power.[13]

Returning to Ibn ʿAsākir's biography of Ibn al-Qalānisī, the notice returns to the theme of Ibn al-Qalānisī as a littérateur, providing three examples of his poetry. The first of these is a love poem, but the second and third are exhortations to steadfastness in the face of calamities, and while the third is directed at an unspecified reader, the second is aimed at the *nafs* [self or soul] of the poet himself:

---

contemporary account. The dating of Ibn al-Qalānisī's time as *raʾīs* therefore hinges on whether the opening statement of this paragraph is the work of the copyist or of Ibn al-Qalānisī himself, with the latter referring to himself in the third person. Ibn al-Qalānisī, *Taʾrīkh Dimashq: 360–555*, ed. S. Zakkār (Damascus, 1983), p. 441; idem, *Damas*, p. 271. On the unusual nature of Ibn al-Qalānisī's reticence see page *lām* of the introduction to Zakkār's edition.

10 Al-Jīlāwī, *Ibn al-Qalānisī*, pp. 42–47.

11 Ibn al-Qalānisī, *Taʾrīkh*, pp. 501–2; idem, *Damas*, p. 339; El-Azhari, *Saljūqs of Syria*, p. 368; Holt, *Age of the Crusades*, pp. 71–72.

12 Ibn al-Qalānisī, *Taʾrīkh*, p. 504; idem, *Damascus Chronicle*, p. 319; idem, *Damas*, p. 341.

13 El-Azhari, *Saljūqs of Syria*, pp. 298–99 and 306–7; and Holt, *Age of the Crusades*, p. 72.

> O *nafs*! Do not worry about calamities that have increased, nor put more faith in [earthly] joy than the God of mankind.
>
> How many calamities have appeared and become great, but their effects on wealth and the heart have passed away afterwards?

Given that Ibn al-Qalānisī lived through periods of war, political unrest and economic hardship, including the Second Crusade's siege of Damascus in 543/1148 and the blockade of the city imposed by Nūr al-Dīn in 548/1154, we might see in the Damascene author's words an attempt to console himself in the face of the hardships that he personally had experienced.

Ibn ʿAsākir then notes that Ibn al-Qalānisī was also a historian who compiled a chronographical work covering events from 440/1048–49 to the year of his death, although he fails to give a title or further details regarding what this history covered. On the basis of statements in later sources, however, it is safe to assume that he is referring to the *Dhayl ta'rīkh Dimashq*. Ibn ʿAsākir concludes his biography with the date of Ibn al-Qalānisī's death (7th Rabiʿ I 555/17th March 1160), notes that he was buried the following day on Mt. Qāsiyūn outside the city of Damascus, and records that he was present for the prayer over the deceased.[14]

Such is Ibn ʿAsākir's biography of Ibn al-Qalānisī. A small amount of additional information can be gleaned from scattered references in later works; for example, it is from Ibn al-Qalānisī's Aleppan contemporary Muḥammad ibn ʿAlī al-ʿAẓīmī (d. after 556/1161) that we learn that the former's work was known to others in his own time as the *Dhayl*, and likewise we learn from Muḥammad ibn Aḥmad al-Dhahabī (d. 748/1348) that Ibn al-Qalānisī was in his eighties when he died, allowing us to place his birth in about 465/1073. However, he remains an enigmatic figure.[15]

Intellectual and Political Context

Ibn al-Qalānisī wrote his history in a complex political and intellectual environment. Like many Muslim chroniclers, he augments his account of each year with notices on important figures of his time. As a key to the context in which

14 Ibn ʿAsākir, *Ta'rīkh*, vol. XV, pp. 191–92.

15 Muḥammad ibn ʿAlī al-ʿAẓīmī al-Ḥalabī, *Ta'rīkh Ḥalab*, ed. I. Zaʿrūr (Damascus, 1984), p. 343; Ibn al-Qalānisī, *Ta'rīkh*, page *lām* in Zakkār's introduction. For a fuller study of Ibn al-Qalānisī's biography, see al-Jīlāwī, *Ibn al-Qalānisī*, pp. 17–69.

he was working, his account of the year 548/1153–54, the year of Nūr al-Dīn's successful attempt to take Damascus, provides an instructive example. In this account he notes the arrival in the city of the famous poet Muḥammad ibn Naṣr ibn al-Qaysarānī and the philosopher-*shaykh* Abu'l-Futūḥ ibn al-Ṣalāḥ (both of whom died in the same year), and also reports the death of Burhān al-Dīn 'Alī al-Balkhī, the head of the Ḥanafī school in Damascus.[16] The reader's attention is thus drawn to a poet, a philosopher and a religious scholar, a cross-section that highlights the diversity of intellectual activity in the city at the time, and provides an indication of the types of person in whom Ibn al-Qalānisī took an interest. Ibn al-Qaysarānī was one of a number of Muslim poets who wrote on the topic of the military jihad against the Franks.[17] Although originally an enthusiastic satirist, he eventually found his talents more profitably employed writing panegyrics at the courts of 'Imād al-Dīn Zengī (d. 541/1146) and Nūr al-Dīn; his arrival at Damascus was probably also a case of the lure of patronage, as he was invited there by its last Būrid ruler, Mujīr al-Dīn Ābaq (r. 534/1140–549/1154).[18] Damascus was home to other poets, including Aḥmad ibn Muḥammad ibn al-Khayyāṭ (d. btw. 513 and 523/1120s), who has also been studied for his compositions on the military jihad.[19] As has been seen, Ibn al-Qalānisī himself also seems to have been known for his poetry, and his work is periodically enhanced by quotations of such material written both by himself and others.[20]

Turning to the topic of religious and philosophical speculation, it is worth noting that Damascus was a centre of considerable ferment in these fields during Ibn al-Qalānisī's lifetime. In 488–89/1095–96 the city had received a visit by the great philosopher and religious thinker Muḥammad ibn Muḥammad al-Ghazālī (d. 505/1111), who stayed at the Great Umayyad Mosque and gave a number of lectures.[21] The city and its surroundings also witnessed numerous calls to the jihad against the crusaders. For example, it saw the promulgation of *Kitāb al-jihād* ('The Book of the Jihad') of 'Alī ibn Ṭāhir al-Sulamī (d. 500/1106), who publicly pronounced his work in the mosque of Bayt Lihyā in the

16 Ibn al-Qalānisī, *Ta'rīkh*, pp. 498–500; idem, *Damas*, pp. 334–36.

17 See, for example, Hillenbrand, *Crusades*, pp. 75, 114–15 and 150–51.

18 Ibn al-Qalānisī, *Ta'rīkh*, p. 498; idem, *Damas*, p. 334.

19 Hillenbrand, *Crusades*, pp. 69–70 and 298.

20 For one example of this see Ibn al-Qalānisī, *Ta'rīkh*, p. 370; idem, *Damascus Chronicle*, p. 209; and idem, *Damas*, p. 198.

21 D. Talmon-Heller, *Islamic Piety in Medieval Syria: Mosques, Cemeteries and Sermons under the Zengids and Ayyubids (1146–1260)* (Leiden, 2007), p. 78; and E. Sivan, 'La génèse de la contre-croisade: Un traité damasquin du début du XIIe siècle', *Journal Asiatique* 254 (1966), 197–224, p. 223.

agricultural suburbs of the city in 498–99/1105, and did so again in public the same year; the work was dictated yet again in the city's Great Umayyad Mosque in 506/1113.[22] By the same token, the city's chief *qāḍī* Abū Saʿd al-Harawī issued an impassioned plea for aid that moved his listeners to tears in the wake of the fall of Jerusalem, and it was also the context for the activities of Ibn ʿAsākir, who was instrumental in the composition and dissemination of propaganda on behalf of Nūr al-Dīn at the end of Ibn al-Qalānisī's lifetime.[23] Religious concerns were also prominent as the city saw considerable tensions between the Sunnīs, who formed the majority of its inhabitants, and the Nizārī Ismāʿīlī Shīʿīs (the Bāṭinīs, or 'Assassins'), who were tolerated by Ẓāhir al-Dīn Ṭughtegīn (r. 486/1093–522/1128), the atabeg and then official ruler of Damascus, but were violently purged from the city by his son and successor Tāj al-Mulūk Būrī (r. 522/1128–526/1132), an act which Ibn al-Qalānisī clearly approved of.[24]

The presence of Nizārīs in the city draws attention to a further factor that undoubtedly had an impact on Ibn al-Qalānisī's writings: the political position of Damascus, for the Nizārīs were a political as well as a religious movement. Damascus occupied a difficult political position, caught in a web of opposing forces, including the Fāṭimid caliphs in Egypt, the ʿAbbāsid caliphs and Great Seljūq sultans in Iraq and Persia, the Franks with their states based in Jerusalem, Tripoli and elsewhere, and the Zengids of Mosul and Aleppo (from 522/1128), not to mention smaller forces including the Nizārīs and other local rulers and dynasties. Thus, in order to maintain its independence and to flourish the city was forced to engage in a delicate balancing act, forming alliances with one power or another as circumstances dictated, the overall goal of which was to preserve Damascus' autonomy and influence in the face of repeated attempts by others to take control of it, most notably the Franks and Zengids. This independent spirit is reflected in Ibn al-Qalānisī's own writings, which celebrate rulers who contribute to the success of the city and criticise those believed to have acted in a manner which put the city's independence at risk.

---

22 N. Christie, *The Book of the* Jihad *of ʿAli ibn Tahir al-Sulami (d. 1106): Text, Translation and Commentary* (Farnham, in press).

23 ʿAbd al-Raḥmān ibn ʿAlī ibn al-Jawzī, *al-Muntaẓam fī taʾrīkh al-mulūk waʾl-umam*, ed. M.A. ʿAṭā and M.A. ʿAṭā, 19 vols (Beirut, 1992), vol. XVII, p. 47; E. Sivan, *L'Islam et la croisade: Idéologie et propagande dans les réactions musulmanes aux croisades* (Paris, 1968), p. 63; and S.A. Mourad and J.E. Lindsay, 'Rescuing Syria from the Infidels: The Contribution of Ibn ʿAsakir of Damascus to the *Jihad* Campaign of Sultan Nur al-Din', *Crusades* 6 (2007), 37–55.

24 Ibn al-Qalānisī, *Taʾrīkh*, pp. 350–56; idem, *Damascus Chronicle*, pp. 187–95; idem, *Damas*, pp. 178–83.

Ibn al-Qalānisī was certainly well placed to make comments on this subject. As noted above, he filled a number of high-ranking administrative positions, including twice being *ra'īs* of the city. This latter role is a reminder of another factor in the political life of the city: the relations of the rulers with its people. The rulers of Damascus were, to its inhabitants, foreigners, Turks imposed on the local population from outside (or at least tacitly approved) by distant figures like the Great Seljūq sultan. Figures like the *ra'īs* were representatives of the people in an uneasy relationship with their foreign rulers, a relationship that the rulers neglected or abused at their peril; Ibn al-Qalānisī notes, for example, the involvement of the people of Damascus in the deposition of Shams al-Mulūk Ismā'īl (r. 526/1132–529/1135), who had engaged in arbitrary arrests and confiscations as well as threatening to hand the city over to Zengī or the Franks.[25] However, on the whole the people tended to support their rulers, provided that they maintained the autonomy and welfare of Damascus as major priorities.

This does not mean, however, that we can take Ibn al-Qalānisī's depictions of the rulers of Damascus and other figures as being objectively accurate portraits; he was, like any author of the time, strongly aware of the need to maintain the goodwill of the rulers about whom he wrote, particularly those who were still alive. Thus, for example, he frequently describes Nūr al-Dīn in positive terms, despite the latter's having repeatedly deployed forces against Damascus and eventually starved the city into submission. While it could be suggested that the Būrids had by then ceased to be effective rulers of the city, and thus the possibility of a ruler who would prove more so was something to be welcomed, Ibn al-Qalānisī's favourable presentation of Nūr al-Dīn still smacks of concern to avoid attracting the ire of those in authority. His position and experience would certainly have made him sensitive to the limits of free speech at the time.

The Chronicle entitled *Dhayl ta'rīkh Dimashq*

Ibn al-Qalānisī's chronicle *Dhayl ta'rīkh Dimashq* or *Mudhayyal ta'rīkh Dimashq* ('Continuation of the History of Damascus') exists only as a single, incomplete manuscript held in the Bodleian Library in Oxford (Hunt. 125), which is itself a copy made in 629/1232.[26] Two editions have been published of this text, the

25 Ibn al-Qalānisī, *Ta'rīkh*, pp. 387–90; idem, *Damascus Chronicle*, pp. 228–32; idem, *Damas*, pp. 217–20.

26 Ibn al-Qalānisī, *Ta'rīkh*, p. 549; idem, *Damascus Chronicle*, p. 7.

first by H.F. Amedroz in 1908 and the second by S. Zakkār in 1983.[27] There have also been two partial translations, the first by H.A.R. Gibb, presenting selections from the text covering the years 490/1096 to 555/1160, and the second by R. Le Tourneau, a full translation which covers only the years 468/1075 to 549/1154.[28] A full translation of the whole work remains a desideratum, for it contains a wealth of illuminating material about the history of Damascus in particular and the Middle East in general in the 4th/10th to 6th/12th centuries that deserves to be made more widely available to historians.

The chronicle is a *dhayl* ('continuation'), but what it is a continuation of is unclear. Ibn al-Qalānisī tells us that the actual continuation begins in 448/1056, but he does not state which work he is extending.[29] Amedroz asserts that it is a continuation of the now mostly-lost universal chronicle of the Baghdad historian Hilāl ibn al-Muḥassin al-Ṣābi' (d. 448/1056). This assumption is based on a comment to this effect by Ibn Khallikān (d. 681/1282), the coincidence of the start of Ibn al-Qalānisī's continuation and the death of Hilāl al-Ṣābi', and a resemblance between some lines written by the two authors.[30] However, this view has been challenged by Claude Cahen, who does not regard these factors as sufficient evidence to support Amedroz's case. Cahen demonstrates that the differences between Ibn al-Qalānisī's work and the surviving parts of Hilāl al-Ṣābi''s, both in terms of content and methodology, outweigh the similarities, and proposes that while Ibn al-Qalānisī may have used Hilāl al-Ṣābi''s chronicle as a source, his continuation is instead of another unknown work.[31] The question will probably only be answered if another manuscript, including the 11 folios that are missing from the beginning of the extant manuscript, is found, for if the Damascene chronicler does indicate which history he is continuing, it is likely to be at the start of his own work.[32]

Turning to the question of Ibn al-Qalānisī's sources, it is striking that the author rarely names his sources of information; one of his favourite phrases is *warada al-khabar min ... bi ...* ('News arrived from ... about ...'), which gives very little guidance as to who his informants were. However, as Gibb notes,

27 Ibn al-Qalānisī, *History of Damascus, 363–555 A.H.*, ed. H.F. Amedroz (Leiden, 1908); and idem, *Ta'rīkh*.

28 Ibn al-Qalānisī, *Damascus Chronicle*; idem, *Damas*.

29 Ibn al-Qalānisī, *Ta'rīkh*, p. 140.

30 Ibn al-Qalānisī, *Ta'rīkh*, pp. 3–6 of Amedroz's introduction; idem, *Damascus Chronicle*, p. 9. Al-Jīlāwī is of the same opinion; see al-Jīlāwī, *Ibn al-Qalānisī*, pp. 49–66.

31 C. Cahen, 'Note d'historiographie syrienne: La première partie de l'histoire d'Ibn al-Qalānisī', in G. Makdisi (ed.), *Arabic and Islamic Studies in Honor of Hamilton A.R. Gibb* (Leiden, 1965), 156–65.

32 Ibn al-Qalānisī, *Ta'rīkh*, p. 3 of Amedroz's Introduction.

Ibn al-Qalānisī claims to have made the utmost effort to ensure that his work is accurate:

> I have completed the narrative of events set forth in this chronicle, and I have arranged them in order and taken precautions against error and rashness of judgment and careless slips in the materials which I have transcribed from the mouths of trustworthy persons and have transmitted after exerting myself to make the fullest investigations so as to verify them, down to this blessed year 540 [1145–46].[33]

By the same token, occasionally Ibn al-Qalānisī comments on the trustworthiness of his sources. For example, when describing Nūr al-Dīn's defeat of the Franks at al-Mallāḥa in Jumādā I 552/June 1157, he notes 'none of them escaped, according to the report of a reliable informant, save ten men whom destiny had respited'.[34] Thus, he again seeks to emphasise the *quality* of his source, even though he does not name the informant in question. However, Ibn al-Qalānisī's dedication to the anonymity of his sources is not entirely complete. For example, he notes that his account of the victory at Inab in Ṣafar 544/June 1149 by a joint force of troops from Damascus and the army of Nūr al-Dīn, along with the subsequent operations around Antioch, came from the emir Mujāhid al-Dīn Buzān, though he admits 'it is from his own words and description that this narrative has been written, but with a view to abridgement and avoidance of prolixity'.[35] However, such cases are few and far between.

It is likely that Ibn al-Qalānisī's professional position enabled him to make use of a wide range of sources, including earlier histories (we have already mentioned the chronicle of Hilāl ibn al-Muḥassin al-Ṣābi' above), official correspondence, and other government and archival documents. Cahen notes that Ibn al-Qalānisī's written sources seem to have been principally from Egypt and Syria, with his information on Iraq and places further east being rather more patchy.[36] As has been seen, he also made use of the spoken testimony of eyewitnesses and contemporaries, and to this we can also add his own personal observations, since he lived in Damascus during a significant portion of the

33 Ibn al-Qalānisī, *Ta'rīkh*, p. 441; idem, *Damascus Chronicle*, p. 10; idem, *Damas*, p. 271. Such comments could, however, be a literary *topos*; investigation into such is required before these can be taken at face value.

34 Ibn al-Qalānisī, *Ta'rīkh*, p. 523; idem, *Damascus Chronicle*, p. 336.

35 Ibn al-Qalānisī, *Ta'rīkh*, p. 475; idem, *Damascus Chronicle*, p. 294; idem, *Damas*, p. 307.

36 C. Cahen, 'Ibn al-Ḳalānisī', in *EI2*; Cahen, 'Note d'historiographie syrienne', pp. 158–63. On Ibn al-Qalānisī's sources, see also al-Jīlāwī, *Ibn al-Qalānisī*, pp. 151–86.

period covered by his work. It is unfortunate that we know so little about the author and his day-to-day life, since that would give us more insight into the extent to which his personal experiences have informed his narrative.

Despite its limitations, Ibn al-Qalānisī's chronicle received considerable recognition for its importance as a historical work about the Levant in the Middle Ages; we find the *Dhayl* used as a source by numerous other Muslim writers, including Ibn al-Athīr (d. 630/1233), Sibṭ Ibn al-Jawzī (d. 654/1256), Abū Shāma (d. 665/1267) and al-Dhahabī. It is also held in high esteem by modern historians of the Crusades, for a number of reasons. It is one of the few extant works by a contemporary Muslim historian covering the early crusading period, and, within that, it is one of the even fewer works that have been translated into western languages. It is also of immense significance as an account that reflects close experience of the events of the time, written by a Muslim and thus providing a view that gives some balance to the perspectives of the western sources; as an illustration, Ibn al-Qalānisī literally gives us an insider's view of the attack on Damascus made by the Second Crusade in 543/1148. Consequently, his work is valuable because it is both rare and intimately acquainted with many of the events described within its pages.

Ibn al-Qalānisī's Concerns

The question of how Ibn al-Qalānisī presents the Franks in the *Dhayl* will now be examined in more detail. In order to achieve this the way in which the Damascene author presents both them and the three forces that arguably had the greatest influence on the development of the city in the early sixth/twelfth century—its Būrid rulers, Fāṭimid Egypt, and the Zengids—will be examined.

The Franks

Unsurprisingly, Ibn al-Qalānisī presents a largely negative image of the Franks, an attitude which is mostly founded on the religious differences between them and the Muslims. He is aware that they are Christians, but like most Muslim authors of the crusading period he focuses on the differences rather than the similarities between the two faiths. The Franks are frequently described as *mushrikūn* (polytheists), thus accused of the worship of multiple deities rather than adherence to the one true God, a traditional Muslim accusation against Christians which has its basis in the Christian doctrine of the Holy

Trinity, which is itself specifically refuted in the Quran.[37] This terminology also links the Franks to the pagan idolaters who opposed Muḥammad and his Companions, thus underlining this unfavourable image. Wars against the Franks are normally described as jihad, further marking the Franks as a religious enemy against whom Muslims are obliged to fight, and victories against them are described as gifts from God, thus proclaiming that He is undoubtedly on the side of the Muslims in the openly religious struggle.[38]

However, it is not only religious differences that characterise the Franks in Ibn al-Qalānisī's account. Another commonly-mentioned feature is their untrustworthiness, for they frequently break agreements made with the Muslims. One illustrative example is the account of the Frankish conquest of Jubayl in 497/1104, in which the author records 'They attacked and blockaded it, and gained possession of it by capitulation, but when they had taken possession, they dealt treacherously with its people and did not observe the promises of security which they had given to them, but confiscated their property, and deprived them of all their possessions and money by penalties and various torments'.[39] It is clear that the motivating factor in such instances is usually greed, which Ibn al-Qalānisī seems to regard as an inherent trait of the Franks, along with a general predisposition to violence; he notes, for example, in the case of another broken truce in 503/1109, that the Franks returned to what he calls their 'customary ravaging and destroying'.[40] Treachery, avarice and aggression are, in Ibn al-Qalānisī's eyes, what can normally be expected from the Frankish foe.

In Ibn al-Qalānisī's account of the Second Crusade we see these features combined with Frankish arrogance. He notes that the Franks' 'malicious hearts were so confident of capturing [Damascus] that they already planned out the division of its estates and districts'.[41] Arrogance, a vice criticised in the Quran, further differentiates the Franks from Muslims, who are urged in the holy text to adopt an attitude of humility; in this case Ibn al-Qalānisī may have been thinking in particular of the first *āyas* of Q. 23: 'The believers must (eventually) win through—those who humble themselves in their prayers,

37 Q. 4:171 and 5:73.

38 For example, Ibn al-Qalānisī, *Taʾrīkh*, p. 473; idem, *Damascus Chronicle*, p. 291; idem, *Damas*, p. 305.

39 Ibn al-Qalānisī, *Taʾrīkh*, p. 231; idem, *Damascus Chronicle*, p. 60; idem, *Damas*, p. 53.

40 Ibn al-Qalānisī, *Taʾrīkh*, p. 265; idem, *Damascus Chronicle*, p. 93; idem, *Damas*, p. 89.

41 Ibn al-Qalānisī, *Taʾrīkh*, p. 463; idem, *Damascus Chronicle*, p. 282; idem, *Damas*, p. 294.

who avoid vain talk'.[42] In Ibn al-Qalānisī's narrative the Muslims do indeed win through, and the arrogance and 'vain talk' prove to be of no benefit to the Franks, who are eventually forced to 'retreat in disorder ... and to flee, broken and forsaken'.[43] In this way Ibn al-Qalānisī continues to accentuate the differences between the Muslims and their Frankish opponents, using religious associations to emphasise the negative qualities of their 'otherness'.

Yet Ibn al-Qalānisī's presentation of the Franks is not always entirely negative, and at times he expresses what seems to be a grudging respect for some of them. For example, when recording the death of Baldwin 'the Little' (Baldwin II, r. 511/1118–526/1131) he notes, 'On many occasions he fell into the hands of the Muslims as a prisoner, but he always escaped from them through his famous devices and historic stratagems. After him there was none left amongst them possessed of sound judgment and capacity to govern'.[44] However, it is striking that his most effusive descriptions of Franks are normally linked to records of Muslims defeating them; thus, for example, in his account of the Muslim victory at Inab mentioned above, he notes that the Frankish leader Raymond of Antioch, who was killed by the Muslim forces, was 'amongst the Frankish knights who were famed for their gallantry, valour, power of cunning, and great stature, and had acquired a special repute by the dread which he inspired, his great severity, and excessive ferocity'.[45] Of course, by praising their enemy so highly, Ibn al-Qalānisī makes the Muslims who defeated him all the more impressive, and in this way his apparent respect for the Franks actually serves as a mirror intended to demonstrate the virtues of his own co-religionists.

Given Ibn al-Qalānisī's clear hostility to the Franks, this does call into question how he would have reacted to the various truces and alliances that a number of Muslim rulers made with them. As indicated above, by the time of Nūr al-Dīn's last siege of Damascus he seems to have become unhappy with the city's dependence on Frankish support, and it is striking how Nūr al-Dīn's treaties with the Franks, at least, are presented as being made out of necessity rather than desire, suggesting that the author sought to excuse Nūr al-Dīn for making such agreements with them. Other than in these cases, however, Ibn al-Qalānisī is on the whole studiously neutral in his descriptions of negotiations conducted between Muslim rulers and the Frankish enemy. This suggests

42 Q. 23:1–3.

43 Ibn al-Qalānisī, *Taʾrīkh*, pp. 465–66; idem, *Damascus Chronicle*, p. 286; idem, *Damas*, p. 298.

44 Ibn al-Qalānisī, *Taʾrīkh*, pp. 369–70; idem, *Damascus Chronicle*, p. 208; idem, *Damas*, p. 197.

45 Ibn al-Qalānisī, *Taʾrīkh*, p. 474; idem, *Damascus Chronicle*, p. 292; idem, *Damas*, p. 306.

that he may have been personally opposed to treaties with the Franks but was either practical enough to realise that such dealings were unavoidable or hesitant to avoid voicing his opposition too loudly in case he attracted the disapproval of the rulers of Damascus.

The Būrids

If there is a hero in Ibn al-Qalānisī's chronicle, it is the first Būrid ruler of Damascus, Ẓāhir al-Dīn Ṭughtegīn. Ibn al-Qalānisī frequently seeks to draw the reader's attention to his good conduct, even at one point juxtaposing his hospitality with the avarice of the Seljūq sultan in Baghdad to emphasise the former's laudable qualities.[46] It is striking that unlike other Muslim authors of the period, Ibn al-Qalānisī consistently refers to the Būrid atabeg using his Arabic honorific title, 'Ẓāhir al-Dīn' ('Revealer of the Faith'), a title that emphasises his credentials as a good Muslim ruler. For the Damascene author Ṭughtegīn is an ideal figure: upright, honourable, and supported in his position by the favour of God.[47] He is also a fighter in the military jihad who takes the lead in the struggle against the Franks, and an acknowledged authority on good governance who is consulted by the rulers of other territories.[48] While at times he might come to negotiated agreements with the Franks at others he refuses their requests, giving greater priority to the military jihad against them. In his treatment of Ṭughtegīn Ibn al-Qalānisī does not express a strong preference for one approach or the other, though later in his work it is clear that he dislikes the Damascenes' periodic dependence on the Franks for aid, noting that 'all believing and right-minded men were filled with distress of mind and increasing aversion to such a hateful and repulsive state of affairs'.[49] In some senses Ibn al-Qalānisī's view of Ṭughtegīn and the good qualities that he showed in ruling Damascus are summed up in the last speech that Ibn al-Qalānisī describes him giving, on his deathbed, to his retinue as he designated his son Tāj al-Mulūk Būrī to succeed him:

46 Ibn al-Qalānisī, *Taʾrīkh*, p. 226; idem, *Damascus Chronicle*, pp. 52–53; idem, *Damas*, p. 47.

47 Ibn al-Qalānisī, *Taʾrīkh*, pp. 236–38; idem, *Damascus Chronicle*, pp. 66–68; idem, *Damas*, pp. 58–59.

48 Cf. Ibn al-Qalānisī, *Taʾrīkh*, pp. 318–19 and 302–3; idem, *Damascus Chronicle*, pp. 157–59 and 146–47; idem, *Damas*, pp. 147–48 and 131–32, respectively.

49 Ibn al-Qalānisī, *Taʾrīkh*, pp. 263–65, 293–94 and 586; idem, *Damascus Chronicle*, pp. 92–93, 133–34 and 304; idem, *Damas*, pp. 88–89, 120–21 and 320.

> I have no doubt as to the uprightness of [Būrī's] conduct, his desire to do what is best, and his love [of justice], nor that he will follow in my footsteps in preserving the hearts of the amīrs and troops and act according to my example in dealing equitably with the notables and subjects. If he accepts this my testament, and walks in the way of approval in extending justice and fair dealing to all, and removes from them by his good government all causes of anxiety and fear, that is what is expected of such an one as he and hoped for from his uprightness and good action. If he turns aside from this conduct to follow any other way, and inclines from the uprightness which is sought of him in secret and in open, he will now himself call you to witness against himself in such a case, and declare sentence against himself in such a turn of events.

Ibn al-Qalānisī then enumerates some of Ṭughtegīn's good deeds, including restoring properties that had been confiscated by unjust officials, cancelling unfair taxes, and seeking the permission of the ʿAbbāsid caliph to sell abandoned lands around Damascus for re-cultivation in order to raise funds for the military jihad against the Franks.[50] In this way the writer draws attention to what he sees as the major features of a good ruler: just treatment of all his subjects, protection of them from oppression by their superiors, restoration of the economic prosperity of Damascus and its surroundings, obedience to the caliph, and dedication to the holy war. One can see how many of these concerns would be of direct relevance in the mind of a *raʾīs*, a representative of the people of the city.

It is against this yardstick that Ibn al-Qalānisī seems to measure the other Būrid rulers of Damascus. Ṭughtegīn's son Būrī is probably the figure who receives most approval in this regard; as indicated above, he receives particular praise for his expulsion of the Nizārī Ismāʿīlīs from Damascus, an episode that Ibn al-Qalānisī reports in detail and with considerable relish, closing his account with the comments 'So disaster came upon the evildoers and rejecters of God, and felicity to the upright and heedful of admonition … so this district was rid of them and purified from their uncleanness'.[51] Ibn al-Qalānisī also draws attention to Būrī's generosity and efforts in the military jihad, noting for example that he did not hesitate, when he heard that the Franks were

50 Ibn al-Qalānisī, *Taʾrīkh*, pp. 347–49; idem, *Damascus Chronicle*, pp. 183–86; idem, *Damas*, pp. 174–77.

51 Ibn al-Qalānisī, *Taʾrīkh*, pp. 351–56; idem, *Damascus Chronicle*, pp. 187–95; idem, *Damas*, pp. 178–83.

preparing to attack Damascus in 523/1128, to prepare to confront them, including summoning aid from the Turkmen tribes in the surrounding region:

> He was joined by all the men of valour and might in battle from their various tribes, eager to perform the obligation of Holy War and hastening to raid the infidel antagonists, and he hastened to deliver to them what they required for their food and fodder for their horses.[52]

We thus see Būrī demonstrating concern for the welfare of both his subjects and the *mujāhidīn* (fighters in the holy war), as well as, implicitly, the good of his religion, that echo those of his father.

The start of the reign of Būrī's son and successor Shams al-Mulūk Ismāʿīl is described by Ibn al-Qalānisī as having been similarly praiseworthy but, as noted above, Ismāʿīl eventually turned into an erratic tyrant who

> went to every excess in the indulgence of immorality and in doing the acts which, being prohibited by religion, indicated the corruption of his intelligence, his love of injustice, and the transformation in his character from the impetuous zeal for the interests of the Faith which formerly marked him, and the eagerness to prosecute the Holy War against the heretical foe.

Ibn al-Qalānisī goes on to enumerate Ismāʿīl's misdeeds, including unjustly confiscating property and falsely accusing his deputies, threatening to hand Damascus over to Zengī or the Franks, and having 'a constant inclination towards low and unworthy actions'. As indicated, Ismāʿīl was eventually deposed and killed on the orders of his mother, with the result that 'everyone was rejoiced at his overthrow and pleased to be rid of him, and gave abundant thanks to God Most High'.[53] Thus Ibn al-Qalānisī presents Ismāʿīl as a figure who transformed from being a ruler who, like his predecessors, was concerned with the wellbeing of his subjects, justice, generosity and the good of the faith to one who was precisely the opposite, and in the process the Damascene author further highlights the marks of good rulership that he has drawn attention to previously.

The remaining Būrid rulers are, on the whole, presented by Ibn al-Qalānisī as having been somewhat lacklustre, something that reflects the fact that

52 Ibn al-Qalānisī, *Taʾrīkh*, p. 357; idem, *Damascus Chronicle*, pp. 195–96; idem, *Damas*, p. 185.

53 Ibn al-Qalānisī, *Taʾrīkh*, pp. 387–90; idem, *Damascus Chronicle*, pp. 228–32; idem, *Damas*, pp. 217–20.

soon afterwards the balance of political power in Damascus shifted away from its nominal rulers and into the hands of their subordinates, principally the military leaders. Probably the best known if these is Muʿīn al-Dīn Unur (d. 544/1149), who was instrumental in leading the defence of Damascus from the Second Crusade and is praised by Ibn al-Qalānisī for his 'valour, steadfastness and gallantry such as was never seen in any other, never wearying in repelling [the Franks] nor taking respite from the struggle against them'.[54]

The Fāṭimids

In a perhaps appropriate reflection of the political situation of Damascus in the early sixth/twelfth century, Ibn al-Qalānisī's attitude towards the rulers of Fāṭimid Egypt initially seems somewhat ambiguous. His evident animosity towards the Nizārī Ismāʿīlīs would seem to suggest that the Damascene author was a staunch Sunnī Muslim, but he does not demonstrate the same outright hostility towards the form of Islam promoted by the Fāṭimid rulers; indeed, he repeatedly refers to their activities against the Franks as jihad and does not seem to question the idea that they should be seen as legitimate Muslims, unlike the Nizārīs. At the same time, like many Sunnī writers he subtly disparages the Fāṭimid claims to be the rightful caliphs, using other titles such as *ṣāḥib Miṣr* ('the lord of Egypt') to designate them.[55] It is also clear that he seeks to present the Fāṭimid caliphs as having lost much power to their viziers by this period, something that was a source of periodic tension between the two. He notes, for example, that it was the constraints placed by the vizier al-Afḍal Shāhanshāh (d. 515/1121) on the Fāṭimid caliph al-Āmir (r. 495/1101–524/1130) that led the latter to arrange the vizier's assassination. Thus the Damascene author emphasises the idea that the caliph was largely under the control of his theoretical subordinate, though in this specific instance the caliph eventually found a way to escape it.[56]

54 Ibn al-Qalānisī, *Taʾrīkh*, p. 464; idem, *Damascus Chronicle*, p. 284; idem, *Damas*, p. 296.

55 See Ibn al-Qalānisī, *Taʾrīkh*, p. 336; idem, *Damascus Chronicle*, p. 171; idem, *Damas*, p. 162. The incidence of the word 'caliph' on p. 163 of Gibb's translation is here a problematic rendering of *amīr al-muʾminīn* ('commander of the faithful', a title admittedly used by caliphs but not, strictly-speaking, the term designating the caliphal office); see Ibn al-Qalānisī, *Taʾrīkh*, p. 324.

56 Ibn al-Qalānisī, *Taʾrīkh*, pp. 323–25; idem, *Damascus Chronicle*, pp. 163–64; idem, *Damas*, pp. 153–55. The degree of powerlessness of the caliph has been exaggerated by Ibn al-Qalānisī; see, for example, P.E. Walker, 'Al-Afḍal b. Badr al-Jamālī', in *EI3*.

In his description of al-Afḍal's death, Ibn al-Qalānisī also notes that the vizier was 'a firm believer in the doctrines of the Sunna', which suggests that he sees (or wants his readers to see) al-Afḍal as having been an orthodox Sunnī who was working for a Shīʿī pretender.[57] In this is perhaps the key to understanding the ambiguity in Ibn al-Qalānisī's presentation of the influence of Fāṭimid Egypt; while the Fāṭimid caliphs themselves might be heretics, as far as the Damascene author was concerned their subordinates were both the major wielders of power and Sunnīs. Thus it is these latter figures who had the most influence in the formation of his image of the Egyptians. As may be inferred from the above comments, al-Afḍal is a figure whom Ibn al-Qalānisī greatly admired; he notes the vizier's leadership in the holy war against the Franks, and his comment on al-Afḍal's adherence to Sunnī Islam forms the start of a wider eulogy in which he states the following:

> [Al-Afḍal was] upright in conduct, a lover of justice towards both troops and civil population, judicious in counsel and plan, ambitious and resolute, of penetrating knowledge and exquisite tact, of generous nature, accurate in his intuitions, and possessing a sense of justice which preserved him from wrongdoing and led him to shun all tyrannical methods. All eyes wept and all hearts sorrowed for him; time did not produce his like after him, and after his loss the government fell into disrepute.[58]

Thus it seems that, in the eyes of Ibn al-Qalānisī at least, Egypt experienced a decline in leadership similar to that which would be experienced later in Damascus, after the deaths of Ṭughtegīn and Būrī.

This does not mean, however, that Ibn al-Qalānisī sees Egypt as having ceased to be an important force in the region. He gives a detailed description of one successful Egyptian naval expedition against Byzantine and Frankish shipping around Tyre in 550/1155, attesting to the continued importance of Egyptian naval power.[59] In addition, he provides a particularly intriguing account of diplomatic correspondence between Damascus, Baghdad and Cairo in 542/1147, in which he notes that Muʿīn al-Dīn Unur received diplomas of investiture from both the ʿAbbāsid caliph and Great Seljūq sultan, and the

---

57 Ibn al-Qalānisī, *Taʾrīkh*, p. 325; idem, *Damascus Chronicle*, p. 164; idem, *Damas*, p. 155. Walker questions this understanding of Ibn al-Qalānisī's statement; see 'Al-Afḍal b. Badr al-Jamālī', in *EI3*.

58 Ibn al-Qalānisī, *Taʾrīkh*, p. 325; idem, *Damascus Chronicle*, p. 164; idem, *Damas*, p. 155.

59 Ibn al-Qalānisī, *Taʾrīkh*, p. 510; idem, *Damascus Chronicle*, pp. 323–24.

rulers of Egypt.[60] This suggests that even as late as a mere seven years before Nūr al-Dīn's takeover of Damascus, and despite their waning influence in the area, the rulers of Egypt still felt that their authority should be recognised in Damascus. It is striking that even after the takeover the Egyptians engaged in diplomacy with Nūr al-Dīn, continuing to seek to make their influence felt in the region, as an embassy from Egypt brought gifts for Nūr al-Dīn to Syria in Ramaḍān 553/October 1158, fighting its way through a Frankish force *en route*. Ibn al-Qalānisī immediately follows his account of this with a report of yet another Egyptian victory over the Franks at al-ʿArīsh, which he describes as 'a great victory and highly-esteemed success—to God be given praise and thanks therefore'.[61] Clearly Egyptian participation in the military jihad against the Franks was, in Ibn al-Qalānisī's view, an ongoing and important element.

The Zengids

It must have been particularly hard for Ibn al-Qalānisī to decide how he was going to present the Zengids. As noted above, a significant portion of his work was written while Damascus was under the rule of Nūr al-Dīn, and so he had to be careful not to write anything that might attract the latter's ire. Yet at the same time both Nūr al-Dīn and his father had periodically attacked Damascus or threatened its interests, and Zengī in particular had lived up to his reputation for uncompromising ruthlessness in his dealings with the city. The result of this dilemma is that we see Ibn al-Qalānisī seeking to strike a careful balance between transmission of information and diplomatic phrasing in his discussion of Zengī and Nūr al-Dīn.

Consequently, Ibn al-Qalānisī's depiction of Zengī presents the latter as an enigmatic figure, on the one hand devoted to the faith and to righteousness but on the other driven by ruthless ambition, capable both of acts of great piety and justice and contrasting acts of treachery and viciousness. One example epitomising this dual character is found in the description of events following the assassination of Shihāb al-Dīn Maḥmūd (r. 529/1134–533/1139), the Būrid ruler of Damascus. Zengī had married Shihāb al-Dīn's mother, Ṣafwat al-Mulk, the previous year, and when her son was killed she wrote to Zengī asking him to take revenge. Ibn al-Qalānisī writes, 'On learning this news, he was moved with the utmost detestation of the crime and was not one to be content with the

60 Ibn al-Qalānisī, *Taʾrīkh*, pp. 458–59; idem, *Damascus Chronicle*, pp. 279–80; idem, *Damas*, pp. 289–91.

61 Ibn al-Qalānisī, *Taʾrīkh*, pp. 539–40; idem, *Damascus Chronicle*, p. 348.

continuance of such actions'.[62] Zengī set out towards Damascus, where preparations were made to resist him. Thus Ibn al-Qalānisī presents the Turkish sultan as acting out of a desire to exact justice for the murder of his son-in-law, leaving unspoken the fact that this incident also provided an excuse for Zengī to try to take control of the city. In the continuation of his account Ibn al-Qalānisī records that Zengī diverted his march to Baalbek, in Damascene territory, besieging and taking the city. He also notes, as part of this, that Zengī took a number of the defenders prisoner, with sworn guarantees of safety

> but when the fortress was in his hands he violated his pledge and went back on his guarantee of security, owing to a personal grudge and irritation against its defenders which he nursed in secret. He ordered them all to be crucified and none of them escaped except those whose destiny guarded them. The people were horrified at his action and at such an unheard-of breach of oath on his part.[63]

Thus in one page Zengī transforms from a pious agent of justice to a treacherous, vindictive tyrant, suggesting that the Damascene author sought to present him as a character who wavered between extremes.

Zengī's contemporary reputation was made by his conquest of Edessa in 539/1144, and in Ibn al-Qalānisī's version of the events we again see two sides of Zengī. His account begins by noting that Zengī 'had long been desirous of [Edessa], ambitious to possess himself of it, and on the watch to seize any opportunity against it. The thought of it never ceased to revolve within his mind and his ambition for it was ever present in his memory'. It is striking that the author does not mention the jihad at this point. It is only after Joscelin II's departure from the city and the start of Zengī's advance on it that the word is used, in connection with Zengī's call to the Turkmen tribes of the region to 'give support and assistance against [Edessa] and to carry out the obligation of the Holy War'. Ibn al-Qalānisī then describes the siege and fall of the city, and notes that Zengī stopped his forces from plundering the city and killing its people, ordering that it should be rebuilt and defended, and reassuring its citizens of good and just treatment.[64] Thus in this case we see Zengī presented as ambitious for territorial expansion but also a clement and merciful conqueror, with

62 Ibn al-Qalānisī, *Taʾrīkh*, p. 422; idem, *Damascus Chronicle*, p. 254; idem, *Damas*, p. 252.

63 Ibn al-Qalānisī, *Taʾrīkh*, p. 423; idem, *Damascus Chronicle*, pp. 255–56; idem, *Damas*, p. 253.

64 Ibn al-Qalānisī, *Taʾrīkh*, pp. 436–37; idem, *Damascus Chronicle*, pp. 266–68; idem, *Damas*, pp. 266–67.

an ambiguous attitude towards the military jihad that suggests either genuine piety or cynical use of religious propaganda.

What Nūr al-Dīn would have thought of this rather mixed depiction of his father is of course impossible to tell. We do not know how well Nūr al-Dīn got on with his father on a personal basis, and it may be that Ibn al-Qalānisī felt that Nūr al-Dīn would see it as a fair depiction of Zengī. Alternatively, it is likely that Zengī's less-attractive traits were so well known that the Damascene chronicler felt that it was safe to draw attention to them in his work.[65] Or he may have felt that Nūr al-Dīn simply would not care, being more concerned with how he himself was depicted by contemporary writers.

This last interpretation dovetails with Ibn al-Qalānisī's depiction of Nūr al-Dīn, which is almost entirely positive. Ibn al-Qalānisī is careful to depict Zengī's son as just, pious and dedicated to the jihad against the Franks. He dutifully records that one of Nūr al-Dīn's first actions after his father's death was to retake Edessa from Frankish occupiers, riding night and day to get there, defeating the enemy and taking the fortification within which the Frankish leader had taken refuge 'in less time than it takes to tell'.[66] Thus Ibn al-Qalānisī sets the tone for his numerous later depictions of Nūr al-Dīn as a holy warrior who fights enthusiastically against the Franks and prioritises the welfare of Islam and the Muslims above anything else.

Ibn al-Qalānisī is also careful to emphasise Nūr al-Dīn's other positive characteristics. For example, he notes that the latter showed remarkable forbearance in the face of the Damascenes' refusal to join him in an alliance for the military jihad against the Franks in 544/1150, a refusal resulting from a preexisting treaty between the Franks and the rulers of Damascus. Although Nūr al-Dīn then advanced on Damascus, he prohibited his troops from causing damage to the villages around the city even after hearing that the Damascenes had called in their Frankish allies, to the point that 'prayers were continually being offered up for him by the people of Damascus and its provinces, and all the cities and their districts'. Ibn al-Qalānisī also notes that Nūr al-Dīn's arrival in the region coincided with the end of a drought there, with the result that people claimed 'this is due to [Nūr al-Dīn's] blessed influence, his justice, and his upright conduct'.[67] In this way the Damascene author highlights Nūr al-Dīn's

65 On Zengī and his reputation, see C. Hillenbrand, '"Abominable Acts": The Career of Zengi', in J. Phillips and M. Hoch (eds), *The Second Crusade. Scope and Consequences*, (Manchester, 2001), 111–32.

66 Ibn al-Qalānisī, *Taʾrīkh*, pp. 449–50; idem, *Damascus Chronicle*, pp. 274–75; idem, *Damas*, pp. 280–81.

67 Ibn al-Qalānisī, *Taʾrīkh*, pp. 478–79; idem, *Damascus Chronicle*, pp. 296–97; idem, *Damas*, pp. 311–12.

restraint and concern for the welfare of the common people of Damascus, as well as using the story of the drought to subtly imply that Nūr al-Dīn enjoyed divine approval.

Both the desire to avoid shedding Muslim blood and the theme of divine favour noted above make more obvious appearances elsewhere in Ibn al-Qalānisī's depictions of Nūr al-Dīn. For example, the victory at Inab in 544/1149, referred to above, is described as 'the favour conferred upon [Nūr al-Dīn] by God, to Him be the praise, in giving him victory over the deluded muster and broken host of the Franks', a clear assertion of God's support for the Zengid ruler.[68] Meanwhile, Ibn al-Qalānisī notes that Nūr al-Dīn restrained his troops from attacking during his siege of Damascus in 546/1151 'out of a scrupulous aversion to the slaying of Muslims, saying, "There is no need for Muslims to be slain by the hands of one another, and I for my part will grant them a respite that they may devote their lives to the struggle with the polytheists"'.[69] Thus he again emphasises the idea that Nūr al-Dīn preferred to direct his aggression against the Franks and was only seeking to refocus the efforts of Damascus on the jihad.

As part of his creation of a positive image of Nūr al-Dīn, Ibn al-Qalānisī is normally careful in his description of instances when the Zengid ruler behaves in ways that could be criticised. Treaties that Nūr al-Dīn makes with the Franks are usually described as 'necessary' to avoid suggesting that Nūr al-Dīn may have adopted anything other than a hostile attitude towards the enemy.[70] As indicated above, his final attack on Damascus is depicted as having been made not for his benefit, but for the benefit of the people of the city and all Muslims. Ibn al-Qalānisī does mention one case in 550/1155 when Nūr al-Dīn broke an alliance with the Seljūqs of Rūm and took control of some of their territories, but he does not dwell on it and notes only that Nūr al-Dīn responded to the Seljūqs' protests with 'polite excuses and smooth words'.[71] There is only one point in the narrative when Ibn al-Qalānisī seems to let his guard down slightly: when describing the hardships suffered by the people of Damascus as a result of Nūr al-Dīn's economic blockade in 548/1154, which he seems to have recorded as they happened, he comments, 'It was said that Nūr al-Dīn was determined to proceed to the siege of Damascus and hoped to capture it by this means, since it was difficult for him to break down its resistance owing to the strength of its sultan and the number of its troops and auxiliaries—we

68 Ibn al-Qalānisī, *Ta'rīkh*, p. 473; idem, *Damascus Chronicle*, p. 291; idem, *Damas*, p. 305.

69 Ibn al-Qalānisī, *Ta'rīkh*, p. 489; idem, *Damascus Chronicle*, p. 309; idem, *Damas*, p. 324.

70 See, for example, Ibn al-Qalānisī, *Ta'rīkh*, p. 474; idem, *Damascus Chronicle*, p. 294; idem, *Damas*, p. 307.

71 Ibn al-Qalānisī, *Ta'rīkh*, p. 511; idem, *Damascus Chronicle*, pp. 324–25.

pray God for speedy release from distress and to look upon His creatures with compassion and mercy, as He hath ever shown goodness and bounty to them in the past'.[72] Even here he does not make an explicit criticism of Nūr al-Dīn, though his comment can certainly be inferred as a prayer for God's aid against the Zengid ruler. Thus we see that on the whole Ibn al-Qalānisī is careful to present a largely favourable image of Nūr al-Dīn that would meet with the latter's approval, despite the troubles that he caused Ibn al-Qalānisī's home city.

Conclusion

The brevity of the above survey means it is not possible to do justice to the wealth of information that is to be found in Ibn al-Qalānisī's chronicle. However, it is possible to draw some initial conclusions. Firstly, the Damascene author's primary concern seems to have been, unsurprisingly, the welfare of his home city and its people. He periodically draws attention to examples of good and bad rulership, both from Damascus itself and elsewhere, in an attempt to encourage his readers to support the former and reject the latter. For Ibn al-Qalānisī, good rulers seek to govern their subjects justly and with the utmost concern for their welfare and security, which brings us to his second pre-occupation: the promotion of an adherence to orthodox Sunnī Islam, especially among the ruling classes of Damascus, who are expected to express it in both fair and responsible rule and military activity to protect their subjects. The last of these leads to the author's third major concern: the military jihad against the Franks. Ibn al-Qalānisī, who personally experienced the siege of Damascus during the Second Crusade, perceives the Franks as a serious threat and is therefore keen to encourage the rulers of both his own city and others to act in a unified fashion to rid the Levantine region of their presence. It may be that one of the reasons that he is so supportive of Nūr al-Dīn in his work is that he saw the latter as a figure who could indeed unite the Muslim Levant against the Frankish foe.

This exploration is intended to illustrate one of the many ways in which the *Dhayl* can be of use to modern historians of the Crusades. As indicated above, Ibn al-Qalānisī's work is vital for achieving a full understanding of the early crusading period, and it is hoped that this brief enquiry will encourage closer engagement with a source that gives an invaluable Damascene perspective on the Latin incursions into the Levant.

72 Ibn al-Qalānisī, *Ta'rīkh*, p. 502; idem, *Damascus Chronicle*, p. 317; idem, *Damas*, p. 339.

ʿImād al-Dīn al-Iṣfahānī*

Lutz Richter-Bernburg

ʿImād al-Dīn[1] al-Iṣfahānī[2] was born in the town of Isfahan in Persia on Monday 2nd Jumādā II 519/6th July 1125[3] and died in Damascus on 1st Ramaḍān 597/4th June 1201. 'The Secretary from Isfahan' (*al-Kātib al-Iṣfahānī*), as he was known,

---

* The following sketch is much indebted to the following studies: D.S. Richards, "Imād al-Dīn al-Iṣfahānī: Administrator, Littérateur and Historian', in M. Shatzmiller (ed.), *Crusaders and Muslims in Twelfth-Century Syria* (Leiden, 1993), 133–46, and idem, "Emād-al-Dīn Kāteb', in *EIr*, vol. VIII, 379–81 (also http://www.iranicaonline.org/articles/emad-al-din-kateb [revised XII 2011]). Durand-Guédy's continuing research in related areas has culminated in a monograph where references to his shorter works are to be found: D. Durand-Guédy, *Iranian Elites and Turkish Rulers—A History of Iṣfahān in the Saljūq Period* (Abingdon, 2010). Obviously, the present author has also drawn on his own *Der Syrische Blitz: Saladins Sekretär zwischen Selbstdarstellung und Geschichtsschreibung* (Stuttgart, 1998). Cf. also, critically, N. Elisséeff, *Nūr ad-Dīn—un grand prince musulman de Syrie au temps des Croisades (511–569 H./1118–1174)*, 3 vols (Damascus, 1967), esp. vol. I, pp. 27–31; N. Rabbat, 'My Life with Ṣalāḥ al-Dīn: The Memoirs of ʿImād al-Dīn al-Kātib al-Iṣfahānī', *Edebiyât* 7 (1997), 267–87; Y. Lev, *Saladin in Egypt* (Leiden, 1999), esp. pp. 26–33; R. Şeşen, 'Muqaddimat al-muḥaqqiq', in al-Bundārī, *Sanā 'l-Barq al-Shāmī* [solely preserved first volume, A.H. 562–83], ed. R. Şeşen (Istanbul, 2004), pp. *q–zz*. (For superficial, facile references to ʿImād al-Dīn and al-Qāḍī al-Fāḍil see M. El-Moctar, 'Saladin in Sunni and Shi'a [sic] Memories', in N. Paul & S. Yeager [eds.], *Remembering the Crusades: Myth, Image, and Identity* [Baltimore, 2012], 197–214). For his involvement in the Muslim side of the Crusades more generally, see Hillenbrand, *Crusades*, p. 641b (Index), *s.v.* ʿImād al-Dīn al-Iṣfahānī.

1 This honorific ('Support of Religion') had, most likely, been granted to ʿImād al-Dīn by the ʿAbbāsid caliph al-Muqtafī (r. 530–55/1136–60) in 554/1159 (cf. *Blitz*, p. 75). The fact that such honours which had once been the privilege of only the most meritorious or powerful individuals were now also bestowed on middle-ranking civil servants such as ʿImād al-Dīn al-Iṣfahānī illustrates their progressive devaluation.

2 His full name was Muḥammad ibn Muḥammad ibn Ḥāmid al-Kātib al-Iṣfahānī, ʿImād al-Dīn Abū ʿAbdallāh [or: Abū Ḥāmid] ibn Ṣafī al-Dīn Abī 'l-Faraj ibn Nafīs al-Dīn Abī 'l-Rajā'. His ancestry can be traced back to five generations before his grandfather (Ibn Muḥammad b. ʿAbdallāh b. ʿAlī b. Maḥmūd b. Hibatallāh, *known as* Āluh ['Eagle']), although these people survive as names alone; it is only the two generations immediately preceding our author who have left any trace in the sources. Foremost among these sources are ʿImād al-Dīn's own writings (discussed below); the at times only incidentally autobiographical information to be gleaned from them is amply supplemented by a succession of entries in biographical dictionaries, a well-developed genre in Arabic letters. For a list of these sources see *Blitz*, pp. 25, n. 1, and 102, n. 3.

3 Here, the date of his birth corresponds to what Ibn al-Sāʿī expressly transmitted on ʿImād al-Dīn's own authority (*Blitz*, p. 26, n. 1).

 | DOI 10.1163/9789004280687_004

hailed from a well-established family of civil servants in that town which was, at the time, the capital of the Turkish Seljūq sultans of the southwest of Persia. Yet internecine warfare amongst the Seljūqs and continual extortions by the Turkish military government against the better-off of Isfahan's families drove his into exile in 532/1138. Even before this, in 526/1132, when ʿImād al-Dīn was still a child, his paternal uncle ʿAzīz al-Dīn Abū Naṣr Aḥmad b. Ḥāmid (b. 472/1079–80), at that time the most prominent member of the family, had, after decades of distinguished service in the Seljūq sultanate's financial administration, lost his life to the murderous jealousy of a rival vizier, Abū ʾl-Qāsim al-Dargazīnī.[4] This experience, both of the casual killing and the unconcerned vacillation of the ruler, left a deep and indelible impression on ʿImād al-Dīn's father, who consequently retreated from the world into pious seclusion. Its effect on ʿImād al-Dīn himself was more complex; on the one hand it motivated him to erect literary monuments to his murdered relative, while on the other it did not permanently discourage him from seeking employment in the state administration. While his administrative career was not to be without critical and potentially fatal reversals of fortune, he eventually succeeded in finding two masters who did not just demand loyalty but were, exceptionally, prepared to reciprocate it: the Zengid ruler Nūr al-Dīn and, after his death, the Ayyūbid sultan Saladin.

In 534/1139–40, after two years spent by ʿImād al-Dīn and one of his brothers at school in Kāshān and a brief return to Isfahan, they settled with their father in Baghdad, the seat of the ʿAbbāsid caliphate and, despite a measure of decline, still one of, if not the, pre-eminent centres of learning in the Islamic world. Conditions must have appeared more favourable there than at strife-ridden Isfahan, although the source of the family's livelihood can only be guessed at. Possibly they derived income from inherited landholdings, but in his position as a madrasa student in the city ʿImād al-Dīn may have drawn on a stipend.

Given his family's administrative background ʿImād al-Dīn naturally received a full Islamic education. In Isfahan this had involved Persian language and literature, as this was the region's native and, since the mid-third/ninth century, literarily cultivated tongue, as well as the more demanding Arabic—the prestige, even compulsory language of religion and scholarship and still, in western Persia, of poetry. Thus the Quran, Arabic grammar and poetry were the core subjects of primary education. The so-called prophetic tradition (*ḥadīth*) were passed on in classes he attended and where, in contrast to other subjects

4 On him, see *Blitz*, pp. 30, 33f, 183f and 242f; cf. also C.E. Bosworth, 'Dargazīnī' in *EIr*, vol. VII, pp. 33–34 (see also http://www.iranicaonline.org/articles/dargazini [revised XI 2011]).

similarly taught, the fiction of an unbroken chain of orality and aurality—from the Prophet's or his immediate witnesses' mouths to the listener five centuries onward—established a quasi-sacramental communion. Even young children of pre-school age were taken to such lectures in order for them to receive a transmitter's licence, in the hope that they would be able to pass on their authoritative learning in their old age, which meant bridging centuries with a minimal number of 'links' in the chain.[5]

ʿImād al-Dīn studied poetry not merely by reading the 'classics', but through practical application as well, since the ability to produce verse was a craft in which any educated person was expected to have a measure of competence. There was a great need for incidental verse, especially in the numerous princely courts, but also in private social interaction.[6] As in previous centuries gifted poets enjoyed high reputations, although their precarious standing in society, dependent as they were on the favours of often unpredictably temperamental patrons and their arbitrary decisions, made their lives difficult.

Not long after his arrival in Baghdad ʿImād al-Dīn restarted his education in a madrasa.[7] This institution, which owed its diffusion throughout the Islamic world, although not its origin, to historic shifts and agents in the preceding (fifth/eleventh) century was not a 'university', but a place of learning geared towards the study of and instruction in religious law of the respective *madhhab* to which it was dedicated—in Sunnism, this meant one of the four established 'schools' of jurisprudence: the Ḥanafī, Mālikī, Shāfiʿī or Ḥanbalī.[8] In Persia, Iraq and the Jazīra, and particularly in Baghdad, the Ḥanafī and Shāfiʿī *madhhab*s were dominant—the former had been aggressively promoted by the Seljūq rulers, while the latter had been long established in urban centres, to an extent due to a large degree of public contrariness. It was to this Shāfiʿī *madhhab* that ʿImād al-Dīn's family adhered, as did that of Saladin.

---

5 See J. Robson, 'Ḥadīth', in *EI2*; I. Goldziher, *Muhammedanische Studien* II, (Halle, 1890), pp. 184–85 and 191 (= idem, *Muslim Studies* [*Muhammedanische Studien*], vol. II, ed. S.M. Stern, tr. C.R. Barber & S.M. Stern [Chicago, 1971], pp. 171–72 and 177–78); cf. Aḥmad b. ʿAlī b. Thābit, 'al-Khaṭīb al-Baghdādī', *Kitāb al-kifāya fī (maʿrifat) ʿilm al-riwāya* (Cairo, 1972), 103–18, esp. pp. 117–18.

6 Incidental verse had become *de rigueur* in polite society centuries earlier, but ʿImād al-Dīn's own correspondence with al-Qāḍī al-Fāḍil and other associates, as inserted into *al-Barq al-Shāmī*, illustrates this point as well; cf. M.M. Badawi, "Abbasid poetry and its antecedents', in J. Ashtiany et al (eds.), *ʿAbbasid belles-lettres* (Cambridge, 1990), 146–66, esp. pp. 162ff.

7 See notes 10–12, below, on the Niẓāmiyya and Thiqatiyya madrasas.

8 See, for example, C. Melchert, 'Education IV: The Medieval *Madrasa*', *EIr* vol. VIII, 182–84 (also http://www.iranicaonline.org/articles/education-iv-the-medieval-madrasa [revised XII 2011]); J. Petersen (G. Makdisi), 'Madrasa', in *EI2*.

In medieval Muslim education, studies were not declared complete by one comprehensive degree certificate, but piece by piece through the granting of licences of transmission for individual texts; thus, they could be a continuous process. Accordingly, ʿImād al-Dīn was able to pursue his legal studies even after ceasing his attendance at the Baghdad madrasa. In time, he gained such a high reputation as a legist that in the 560s/1170s he was offered a madrasa chair which had recently fallen vacant in Damascus. He accepted this and retained it until his death, managing to pass it on to his descendants. However, academic study was not, as shall be seen, his primary concern.[9]

If law was the queen discipline in a madrasa curriculum it was served by a number of ancillary fields: first those imparting a firm command of Arabic; then the study of the Quran and hadith as material sources of the law; and finally a grounding in arithmetic and geometry, due to their use in inheritance law. Other subjects, whether theology (*kalām*) proper or the 'ancient' disciplines of Greek or Indian derivation (the sciences, medicine, mathematics beyond its legal applications, philosophy etc.), were not formally part of the madrasa curriculum, although they might be taught privately by madrasa instructors.[10] Thus ʿImād al-Dīn pursued his interest in Ashʿarī theology on his own, as was common among Shāfiʿī jurists at the time, while he studied law at two madrasas of the same *madhhab* in Baghdad—up to 539/1144 at the famed Niẓāmiyya[11] and from mid-540/1145–46 until 543/1148 at the newly established Thiqatiyya.[12] By 541/1146 his career had advanced to the point where he was given a place in the delegation of Baghdad jurists who were dispatched to meet and welcome the Seljūq sultan Masʿūd b. Muḥammad b. Malikshāh upon his arrival.[13]

In the religious arena, a further prominent 'discipline'—in the dual sense of self-denying and self-mortifying practice as well as study—was the mystic

9 *Blitz*, esp. pp. 74, 88ff, and 132–35.

10 See 'Madrasa—6. Courses of instruction and personnel', in *EI2*, as in note 8 above.

11 Its eponym, the great Seljūq vizier Niẓām al-Mulk (408/1018 or 410/1019–20–485/1092), founded a string of such madrasas in order to strengthen Sunnī orthodoxy and to provide the empire with a cadre of competent and ideologically compliant administrators (cf. H. Bowen [C.E. Bosworth], 'Niẓām al-Mulk', in *EI2*).

12 This was named after its founder-donor Thiqat al-Dawla Abū 'l-Ḥasan ʿAlī b. Muḥammad al-Zuwīnī [?] al-Qazwīnī (d. 549/1155), who, from a modest background, rose in the world and, as the caliph al-Muqtafī's agent, apparently amassed a fortune (cf. Ibn al-Athīr, *al-Kāmil fī 'l-taʾrīkh*, ed. C.J. Tornberg as *Chronicon quod perfectissimum inscribitur*, 12 vols [Leiden 1851–71], vol. x, p. 200; partial tr. D.S. Richards as *The Chronicle of Ibn al-Athīr for the Crusading Period from* al-Kāmil fi'l-ta'rīkh *Part 2. The Years 541–589/1146–1193: The Age of Nur al-Din and Saladin* [Aldershot, 2007], p. 73).

13 *Blitz*, p. 39.

movement of 'Sufism' (*taṣawwuf*). By 'Imād al-Dīn's time this had fractured into diverse models and spread throughout all strata of society, and was frequently organised into brotherhoods or 'orders'. 'Imād al-Dīn was certainly in contact with individuals who followed Sufism but, until his own burial 'in the Sufis' cemetery' in Damascus, he does not seem to have exhibited mystical leanings.[14]

An additional part of public religious life on top of the prescribed mosque services were revivalist sermons given to mass audiences by speakers (*wuʿʿāẓ*; sg. *wāʿiẓ*) who depended solely on their own rhetorical talent and charisma.[15] Obviously at times they did not themselves practice what they preached and this caused scandals when made public.[16] 'Imād al-Dīn attended such meetings and apparently was more taken in by the stylistic flourish than any real substance.[17]

In addition to broadly religious subjects 'Imād al-Dīn spent an increasing amount of time devoted to literary studies and thereby acquired a certain fluency in poetic composition during his first decade in Baghdad, although he himself retrospectively judged his production of that time rather critically.[18] As mentioned above, poets were not highly regarded, yet it seems 'Imād al-Dīn did not rule out a position as court panegyrist in his search for employment in the early 540s/after 1145 and, throughout his life, his virtuoso poetical ability was to stand him in good stead.[19] Whether in view of a later publication or simply in order to gather poetic models for possible emulation—metric speech was, after all, a craft to be mastered—'Imād al-Dīn collected vast quantities of his teachers' verses during his first sojourn in Baghdad.

Despite his uncle al-'Azīz's violent end, which many may have considered a professional risk of court service, he had bequeathed a network of potentially useful contacts to his nephew 'Imād al-Dīn. However, this did not initially result in gainful employment. In 543/1148 'Imād al-Dīn's father returned with

---

14 On its location see below, note 60; it became a favourite burial place in the later Ayyūbid and, even more so, Mamlūk periods (see, for example, 'Imād al-Dīn 'Abd al-Qādir b. Muḥammad al-Nuʿaymī, *al-Dāris fī taʾrīkh al-madāris*, ed. J. al-Ḥasanī, 2 vols [Damascus, 1367/1948 and 1370/1951], esp. vol. II, p. 550 [Index], *s.v.* maqābir al-Ṣūfiyya). It should be noted that interment there should not automatically be taken to indicate a markedly 'Sufi' way of life.

15 See *Blitz*, p. 49, n. 1; cf. D. Talmon-Heller, *Islamic Piety in Medieval Syria: Mosques, Cemeteries, and Sermons under the Zangids and Ayyūbids (1146–1260)* (Leiden, 2007), esp. pp. 115–48.

16 *Blitz*, pp. 49ff.

17 *Ibid.*

18 *Blitz*, pp. 57 and 61.

19 *Blitz*, pp. 74–75, 77–78, 92–93, and 105–6.

his two sons to Isfahan, although the reasons for this are unknown.[20] Over the following five years ʿImād al-Dīn was predominantly engaged in the study of poetry, where his ability quickly developed alongside his knowledge of contemporary and near-contemporary poets.[21] If, as he claims, he had while still a youth thought of publishing a selection of panegyrics addressed to al-ʿAzīz, this had been thwarted by the loss of his uncle's papers in the pillaging of the latter's estate.[22] In its stead, ʿImād al-Dīn was to embark on the much larger project of a representative poetic and, to a far lesser extent, prose anthology of the sixth/twelfth century, which was to occupy him until the end of his life, though admittedly with long breaks in between. In ʿImād al-Dīn's own account, it was his chance discovery of al-Bākharzī's *Dumyat al-qaṣr wa-ʿuṣrat ahl al-ʿaṣr* ('The Treasured Idol of the Castle and the Refuge of the People of the Age') in an Isfahan library which triggered this decision.[23] Al-Bākharzī had followed in the footsteps of his own teacher, Abū Manṣūr ʿAbd al-Malik al-Thaʿālibī, whose *Yatīmat al-dahr fī maḥāsin ahl al-ʿaṣr* ('The Matchless Pearl of Time on the Beautiful Achievements of the People of the Age'), while not itself pioneering the format, set an example, through its title and content, for generations to come.[24] Al-Thaʿālibī himself treated it as a work in progress, as demonstrated by his own supplement to it, *Tatimmat* al-Yatīma ('The Completion of *The Matchless Pearl*'). Just like al-Bākharzī before him, ʿImād al-Dīn's choice of title—*Kharīdat al-qaṣr wa-jarīdat ahl al-ʿaṣr* ('The Pearl-like Virgin of the Castle and the Register of the People of the Age')—highlighted the affiliation of his work,[25] although he notably chose to omit mentioning the analogous undertaking *Zīnat al-dahr* ('The Ornament of the Age') of his Baghdad contemporary, the littérateur and book-dealer Abū 'l-Maʿālī al-Ḥaẓīrī,[26] while acknowledging his examination of his friend's other works.[27] While ʿImād

20 *Blitz*, pp. 61ff.

21 *Blitz*, pp. 63–69.

22 *Blitz*, p. 64.

23 *Blitz*, p. 64. On Abū 'l-Ḥasan/'l-Qāsim ʿAlī b. Ḥasan b. ʿAlī (who was born and died [was killed] in the district of Bākharz in 467/1075) see Z. Safa, 'Bāḵarzī, Abu'l-Qāsem ʿAlī', in *EIr*, vol. III, p. 534 (with errors; also http://www.iranicaonline.org/articles/bakarzi-abul-qasem-al- [rev. VIII 2011]); see also D.S. Margoliouth, 'al-Bākharzī', in *EI2*.

24 See E.K. Rowson, 'Al-T͟haʿālibī', in *EI2*.

25 For references to editions of this multi-volume work see Richards, "Emād-al-Dīn Kāteb', and ʿImād al-Dīn al-Iṣfahānī, *Kharīdat al-qaṣr* (sections on Iran), ed. ʿA.M. al-Ṭuʿma, 3 vols (Tehran, 1999).

26 On Saʿd b. ʿAlī al-Ḥaẓīrī see the introduction to his *Lumaḥ al-mulaḥ*, eds Y. ʿAbd al-ʿAẓīm & Ḥ. Naṣṣār, 2 vols (Cairo, 2007).

27 *Blitz*, esp. pp. 64–65.

al-Dīn substantially completed and published *al-Kharīda* in 573/1178, he continued collecting material for a supplement after this date; only in the last two years of his life did he finally release it under the title *Dhayl* al-Kharīda *wa-sayl* al-Jarīda ('The Train of the *Kharīda*['s Robe] and the Overflow of the *Jarīda*').[28] Apart from its value as a compilation of sixth/twelfth century poetry and prose as considered representative by an expert contemporary, the *Kharīda* offers a wealth of autobiographical information on its author. 'Imād al-Dīn's literary production was informed by, and may even have owed its existence to, a marked sense of his own and his family's worth, especially that of his 'martyred' uncle, which, through ignorance and envy, was often underappreciated in both worth and merit.

A certain insistence, at times plaintive, on his uncle al-'Azīz's and, later, his own indispensable role in the running of government, was a *leitmotif* of his historical writing. Thus, his 'Seljūq History', *Nuṣrat al-fatra wa-'uṣrat al-fiṭra* ('Help for Lassitude and Refuge for Creation') is focused on civilian administrators rather than the sultans themselves, or at least on those from among the former whom he credited with respect for the traditions of 'proper' royal rule.[29] To him, this entailed respect for this social stratum which could best provide the pervasive, makeshift military dictatorships with the required bureaucratic infrastructure for a functioning government. It may not be too far-fetched to say that 'Imād al-Dīn's historiographical agenda also represents a compensation for his and his peer's lack of any real power.[30]

Toward the end of the 540s/in the early 1150s 'Imād al-Dīn left his home-town of Isfahan for good, first in 548/1153–54 to perform the Hajj, and, after his return, to again go to Baghdad.[31] Even though he does not give his reasons for so doing, it is possible to hazard a few guesses. His contacts with some leading members of Isfahan's class of notables obviously did not offer him promising

---

28 *Blitz*, pp. 94 n. 1, 127, 134 and 338–39; 'Imād al-Dīn al-Iṣfahānī, *Dhayl Kharīdat al-qaṣr wa-Jarīdat ahl al-'aṣr*, ed. 'Ā.A. 'Abd al-Ghanī & M.Kh. al-Bādī (Damascus, 2010).

29 For more on the *Nuṣra*, see *Blitz*, pp. 126–27 and Index, *q.v.*; D. Durand-Guédy, 'Mémoires d'exilés: Lecture de la chronique des Saljūqides de 'Imād al-Dīn al-Iṣfahānī', *Studia Iranica* 35 (2006), 181–202; idem, *Iranian Elites and Turkish Rulers*, esp. pp. 13–14 (cf. also p. 430 [Index], s.v. 'Imād al-Dīn al-Iṣfahānī). It would appear that the bulk of 'Imād al-Dīn's work on it, which centers on his Arabic version of Anūshīrwān b. Khālid's memoir-chronicle, was undertaken in deference to his superior, mentor and friend the *qāḍī* al-Fāḍil in the years preceding publication in 579/1183; a supplement records events down to the death in battle of Ṭoghril b. Arslān in 590/1194. Yet 'Imād al-Dīn had been largely cut off from relevant information ever since 562/1167, when he left Baghdad for Syria.

30 See Durand-Guédy, as in previous note.

31 *Blitz*, pp. 69–73.

prospects of employment, and it may be that the situation of the Seljūq sultanate after the death of Masʿūd b. Muḥammad b. Malikshāh (d. 547/1152) did not appeal to him sufficiently to seek, in 549/1154, the favour of Malikshāh's successor, Muḥammad b. Maḥmūd b. Muḥammad.[32] Instead, he headed for the caliphal capital, via a rather leisurely detour, seeking out literary figures along the way in pursuit of his own studies and of material for the *Kharīda*.

After his arrival in Baghdad, no later than Shawwāl 550/December 1155, ʿImād al-Dīn again took up lodgings in the Niẓāmiyya madrasa. It seems that as he had by this time become an accomplished legal scholar some loosely 'academic' activity offered a convenient fall-back position from which to strike out for something more interesting and, not to be underestimated, more lucrative,[33] and from this time until his death ʿImād al-Dīn often drew on his juridical knowledge to earn his living. Just as important, though, was his predilection for poetry and, increasingly, for chancery work, and it was this which earned him his nickname *al-Kātib*. The duties of a 'scribe' or 'secretary' involved much more than the modern term suggests and included familiarity with financial and diplomatic affairs and, above all, the broad literary education and facility required for the drafting of chancery documents—decrees, diplomas, missives—in the customarily intricate and ornate style, as well as the composition of incidental poetry, which was just as rhetorically contrived.[34]

Yet the beginning of his administrative career, under the caliphal vizier Ibn Hubayra, is noted by ʿImād al-Dīn in a rather surly fashion, as if it were an unwanted favour which he felt he could not refuse. Yet it seems he soon adjusted to, and even came to enjoy, his new tasks, as his subsequent career demonstrates. Even the specific risk involved in government service of falling victim to persecution upon a sudden change of 'regime' and concomitant loss of patronage did not ultimately deter him from seeking administrative appointments again. From this point on the position of madrasa 'professor' served him only as a safe fallback position, one he was to require several times.

From 552/1157 until Ibn Hubayra's death in the spring of 560/1165 ʿImād al-Dīn was employed in Baghdad in the revenue service (as a *mushrif*) under the vizier's authority. This work apparently left him sufficient time to pursue his literary activities, both as an accomplished practising poet and as a student of literature, for whom the collection of material for *al-Kharīda* was an ongoing concern.

---

32 See Durand-Guédy, *Iranian Elites and Turkish Rulers*, pp. 264–65 (cf. [Index] pp. 424–25, *s.v.* Masʿūd b. Muḥammad and Muḥammad b. Maḥmūd, respectively).

33 *Blitz*, pp. 73–74.

34 *Blitz*, pp. 89–100.

The vizier's death meant the end of his family's and his clients' period of ascendancy. 'Imād al-Dīn was rather lucky to escape a few months of fairly lenient imprisonment unharmed, after which he retired to a teaching position in a madrasa.[35] But whether he missed the cachet of an administrative position or did not find the atmosphere in Baghdad under the new 'regime' safe, let alone congenial, he decided to travel to Syria in the spring of 562/1167, at first on a year's 'leave of absence'.[36] His own habitual reticence about his motives suggests that he was looking for administrative employment.[37] In the event, a long-standing relationship with the chief religious judge (*qāḍī*) of Damascus, whose son had been a fellow student with 'Imād al-Dīn at the Niẓāmiyya in Baghdad, provided him with his first academic foothold and, more importantly, helped pave his way to court.[38] From now (late 563/1167) until practically the end of his life, he held the position of *kātib*—chancery official and court poet—almost continuously, while also undertaking occasional diplomatic assignments.

'Imād al-Dīn's Syrian years, from early summer 562/1167 until his death in Damascus on the 1st of Ramaḍān 597/4th of June 1201, can be divided into two parts: his period of service to Nūr al-Dīn b. Zengī, and then his service to Saladin who was, essentially, Nūr al-Dīn's successor. These were augmented by some time spent outside the ruling circles during the critical transition of rule from Nūr al-Dīn to Saladin and by 'Imād al-Dīn's less than voluntary retirement from court service after Saladin's death when, despite the slight against him of his abandonment by the regime of Saladin's brother al-'Ādil in Damascus, he was able to fall back on his chair for life at the Shāfi'ī madrasa which Nūr al-Dīn had conferred on him in 567/1172.[39] Until Nūr al-Dīn's death in 569/1174 'Imād al-Dīn's career had progressed successfully, and from being a regular 'secretary' he rose to a position of near-vizierial authority.[40] Yet still he had some free time in which he could indulge his passion for literary pursuits. Cultivating a number of useful contacts, he continued collecting material for *al-Kharīda* while

35 *Blitz*, pp. 77–78 and 81–82.

36 *Blitz*, pp. 85–86.

37 *Blitz*, p. 86, n. 2.

38 *Blitz*, pp. 88ff.

39 Because of 'Imād al-Dīn presence there, this madrasa came to be known as al-'Imādiyya, and after his death his position was filled by one of his sons, and later again by his descendants; cf. *Blitz*, pp. 88 and 135. The madrasa, now vanished, was located close to ('inside from') Bāb al-Faraj, one of the northern gates of Damascus, and near the bath of al-Quṣayr; see D. Sack, *Damaskus: Entwicklung und Struktur einer orientalisch-islamischen Stadt* (Mainz, 1989), no. 1.23 (refs.; cf. map [Beilage] 4).

40 *Blitz*, pp. 93–100.

also applying his poetic talent to creating panegyrics to bolster his position in Damascene society.[41] It was particularly important to him in that city as he could not rely on the support of his family and the network that came with it.

Among his Damascus patrons the Kurdish officer brothers Ayyūb and Shīrkūh, the sons of Shādī, deserve special mention.[42] In their youth they had tried in vain to save ʿImād al-Dīn's uncle al-ʿAzīz, and they now provided a welcome for his nephew.[43] His acquaintance with Ayyūb's son Saladin[44] was to provide him with a springboard to advancement later in life, although it will be seen that strong personal relationships to those in authority were not in themselves sufficient to secure high office.[45] Possibly even more beneficial to ʿImād al-Dīn was his contact with the Egyptian 'secretary' al-Fāḍil, who was to rise to *de facto* vizierial position in Saladin's service, even though during this period such contact was still indirect.[46]

The precariousness of ʿImād al-Dīn's position as courtier, lacking his own power-base and owing his rank and influence solely to the ruler's favour, became apparent immediately after Nūr al-Dīn's death in 569/1174. Since Nūr al-Dīn left only an underage son as his successor the ensuing power vacuum led to a jockeying for position and influence among his most senior military commanders and civil administrators. Saladin's partisans, amongst them ʿImād al-Dīn, temporarily lost. Thus, in order to protect himself and his possessions in Syria, he joined the underage ruler's circle but, under a perceived threat to his life, slipped away to the Jazīra. En route to Baghdad he was delayed by illness in Mosul, where news reached him of Saladin's occupation of Damascus, making him decide to return.[47]

Yet ʿImād al-Dīn's long-standing friendly relations with Saladin and his relatives did not automatically provide him with a position similar to the one he

41 *Blitz*, pp. 109ff.

42 R.S. Humphreys, 'Ayyūbids', in *EIr*, vol. III, 164–67, (http://www.iranicaonline.org/articles/ayyubids [revised VIII 2011]); D.S. Richards, 'Shīrkūh', in *EI2*.

43 *Blitz*, pp. 86–87, n. 2, and 92–93.

44 Cf. M.C. Lyons & D.E.P. Jackson, *Saladin: The Politics of the Holy War* (Cambridge, 1982); A.-M. Eddé, *Saladin* (London, 2011).

45 *Blitz*, pp. 92–93.

46 As a self-styled defender of orthodox Islam against all manner of 'heretics', Nūr al-Dīn mounted several campaigns, with the Ayyūb clan in charge, against the Egyptian Fāṭimids, in the course of which Saladin rose to be a potentially threatening rival. It was Nūr al-Dīn's—in retrospect timely—death in 569/1174 which prevented a clash between him and Saladin (see Richards, 'Ṣalāḥ al-Dīn', in *EI2*). On the *qāḍī* al-Fāḍil see Lyons & Jackson, *Saladin*, p. 446 [Index], *s.v.* al-Fāḍil, and *Blitz*, p. 405 [Index], *s.v.* al-Fāḍil.

47 *Blitz*, pp. 101–5.

had held at Nūr al-Dīn's court. Intrigues had to be nullified, hesitation overcome. In 'Imād al-Dīn's own account al-Fāḍil's pragmatic argument during his own prolonged absence in Egypt—that Saladin would need a competent 'secretary', particularly one well-versed both in the protocol of 'Eastern' rulers and in Persian—prevailed.[48] Thus, in the summer of 570/1175 'Imād al-Dīn was formally appointed as 'secretary' and *de facto* deputy vizier;[49] thus, next to al-Fāḍil, 'Imād al-Dīn became Saladin's most influential civilian advisor, and apart from during short periods of illness he was in constant attendance. It is to Saladin's credit that he reciprocated these two servants' loyalty, keeping them in their respective positions until his own death in 589/1193.[50]

The balance of power between the competing members of the Ayyūbid dynasty which Saladin had barely succeeded in maintaining was upset soon after his death. Perhaps unsurprisingly, 'Imād al-Dīn found himself increasingly pushed aside after Saladin's brother al-'Ādil assumed power in Damascus in 592/1196, although he was left unmolested in his madrasa until his death five years later.[51]

During the final three decades of 'Imād al-Dīn's life the time he had for literary activity fluctuated significantly, depending on the demands of his position, although at all times he kept notes and documents for later use, as his 'chronicles' document.[52] From 570/1174–75 to 573/1177–78, in Damascus and Cairo, he was able to complete and publish *al-Kharīda*, incorporating the works of authors from Syria, Egypt, the Maghrib and al-Andalus that had only recently become accessible to him. Towards the end of the decade, he substantially finished work on *Nuṣrat al-fatra* (although this was updated during the early 590s/mid–1190s).[53] After an interval of several years spent on Saladin's campaigns against the Franks, he used the relative leisure which the drawn-out siege of Acre (586–87/1190–91) afforded him to compose his homage to Saladin as champion of correct Islam against internal and foreign enemies, *al-Fatḥ al-qussī fī 'l-fatḥ al-qudsī* ('The Inspiration of a Quss Regarding the Conquest of

48 *Blitz*, pp. 104–8.

49 *Blitz*, pp. 107–8.

50 In 584/1188, when unsafe traffic conditions between Egypt and Syria temporarily halted the transfer of funds and 'Imād al-Dīn found himself in financial straits, he seems to have toyed with the idea of leaving Saladin's service, but al-Fāḍil helped him regain his better judgement; cf. Lyons and Jackson, *Saladin*, pp. 293–94.

51 *Blitz*, pp. 130ff.

52 *Blitz*, pp. 93, 108–11, 126–27, 128–29, and 132ff.

53 *Blitz*, pp. 126ff.

al-Quds [Jerusalem]').[54] In part at least, this was presented and read to Saladin in Jerusalem in late 588/1192[55] after the signing of the peace treaty of Jaffa on the 22nd Shaʿbān/2nd September. About a year later, in the autumn of 589/1193, *al-Fatḥ* was completed and put into circulation.[56]

The initial peace between Saladin's successors, made up of a number of his sons and his brother al-ʿĀdil, did not last long. ʿImād al-Dīn clearly saw himself as the guardian of Saladin's legacy and so became an irritant to the new 'regime' in Damascus, and in the summer of 592/1196 he was unceremoniously ousted from his position.[57] Yet notwithstanding his complaints about the indignities he suffered, he could continue unmolested as a professor at his madrasa, while he kept assiduously working as a writer. The voluminous memoir-chronicle of his years with Nūr al-Dīn and Saladin, *al-Barq al-Shāmī* ('The Syrian Lightning'), was finished in early 595/Autumn 1198. In tune with the intended imagery of its title, which suggests instantaneously vanishing brilliance, this bolt of 'lightning' ended with Saladin's death.[58] But whatever his disaffection with the powers that be, ʿImād al-Dīn did not shirk what he may have considered his duty—in three consecutive, if separately named, 'appendices', he car-

54 This was admirably translated into French by H. Massé as *ʿImâd ad-Dîn al-Iṣfahânî (519–597/1125–1201): La conquête de la Syrie et de la Palestine par Saladin* (al-fatḥ al-qussî fî l-fatḥ al-qudsî), (Paris, 1972). Massé's cuts of sections available in *RHC Or.* and of over-ornate passages without 'historical' content are to be regretted for distorting the original. Unfortunately, the English edition of Francesco Gabrieli's anthology *Storici arabi delle crociate* (Milan, 1957) merely offers a secondary version from the Italian; F. Gabrieli, *Arab Historians of the Crusades*, tr. E.J. Costello (Los Angeles and Berkeley, 1969). In this work, a revision on the basis of direct translations from the Arabic would have been in order throughout, but especially for ʿImād al-Dīn's ornateness. For excerpts from *al-Fatḥ* in this volume see pp. 149–75, 234–37 and 238–40.

55 *Blitz*, p. 128; cf. Richards, 'Administrator', p. 141. Richards drew the obvious conclusion that Cahen's turn of phrase that *al-Fatḥ* was 'detached' from 'lightning' misrepresents the—chronologically and otherwise—unambiguous relationship of the two works. For Cahen's final assessment of ʿImād al-Dīn as historian see his 'History and Historians', in M.J.L. Young et al. (eds.), *Religion, Learning and Science in the ʿAbbasid Period* (Cambridge, 1990), 188–233, esp. pp. 207 and 222–23.

56 The oldest surviving copy, MS Istanbul—Esat Effendi 2333, dates to Damascus, 590/1194, as witnessed by an autograph note in it by ʿImād al-Dīn written on 26th Dhū 'l -Qaʿda/12th November, where he grants the manuscript's copyist a full transmission licence (*ijāza*) for all his own works and utterances (see J. Kraemer, *Der Sturz des Königreichs Jerusalem (583/1187) in der Darstellung des ʿImād ad-Dīn al-Kātib al-Iṣfahānī* [Wiesbaden, 1952], p. 23).

57 *Blitz*, p. 131.

58 See *Blitz*, pp. 133–34 and 194.

ried on his narrative until the very eve of his own death.[59] In these later years 'Imād al-Dīn also finished his long-term project of a supplement to *al-Kharīda* and put together collections of his own poetry and chancery prose (*inshā'*), neither of which survive.

As noted above, 'Imād al-Dīn died in 597/1201 and was interred in the Sufis' cemetery in the Damascus suburb al-Munaybi', which is not preserved; the entire area to the west of the ancient and medieval enceinte, fashionable in life and death during the later Ayyūbid and Mamlūk times, has fallen victim to modern urban expansion.[60]

Al-Fatḥ al-qussī fī 'l-fatḥ al-qudsī

Before entering upon a discussion of individual works by 'Imād al-Dīn, a few general remarks on the nature of his literary production will be useful. As was natural for a *kātib*, he had to be fluent in the highly ornate prose style which had been *de rigueur* for chancery documents since the fourth/tenth century. What earned our author the sobriquet of *al-kātib*—his professional position—may have been his single-minded determination to deploy his virtuoso chancery

59 See *Blitz*, pp. 133–34, and Richards, 'Administrator', pp. 141–42.

60 'The Gate of Victory' (Bāb al-Naṣr), which Ayyūbid and Mamlūk narrative sources name as a point of reference, was the city gate across the moat from the citadel's southwest tower (leading into the latter-day 'Rhomaeans' Market' [Sūq al-Arwām] which approximately corresponds to the western entrance of present-day Sūq al-Ḥamīdīya); its reported construction under Saladin tallies with Ibn Jubayr's list of the city's gates of 580/1184 (Ibn Jubayr, *The Travels of Ibn Jubayr*, tr. R.J.C. Broadhurst [London, 1952], p. 295). It was a double gate, possibly somewhat similar to Bāb al-Faraj (cf. Sack, *Damaskus*, nos. 1.5, 2.6, map [Beilage] 5) and was demolished in 1295/1878–79 (private communication by S. Weber, 11th Nov. 2012). See also A. von Kremer, 'Topographie von Damaskus [I]', *Denkschriften der Kaiserlichen Akademie der Wissenschaften—Philosophisch-Historische Classe* 5 [2] (1854), 1–51, esp. p. 14; J.L. Porter, *A Handbook for Travellers to Syria and Palestine* (rev. ed.), 2 vols (London, 1868), vol. I, esp. pp. 453–54. The Sufis' cemetery was located on the present grounds of Damascus University; see, for example, M.K. 'Alī, *Ghūṭat Dimashq* (Damascus, 1372/1952), pp. 171–73 (it was also mentioned by Porter in *Five Years in Damascus* vol. I, pp. 48–49). See also Sack, *Damaskus*, nos. 2.16, 2.33, 2.56 (also on map [Beilage] 5); M. Braune, 'Die Stadtmauer von Damaskus', *Damaszener Mitteilungen* 11 (1999), 67–86, esp. p. 71 (correct the date of the gate's demolition). The area of al-Munaybi', stretching westward, must have been verdant enough to allow pleasurable walks; 'Imād al-Dīn himself cited it in a long poem (*qaṣīda*) in praise of Damascus and its beauties (*apud* 'Izz al-Dīn Abū 'Abdallāh Muḥammad b. 'Alī b. Ibrāhīm Ibn Shaddād, *al-A'lāq al-khaṭīra, ta'rīkh Dimashq*, ed. S. Dahhān, 2 vols (Damascus, 1375/1956), vol. II, p. 347:2).

style to the fullest of his dazzling ability in all his historical works as well. However alien and even repellent the results may appear to modern readers—and it must be admitted that they left even his contemporaries unconvinced—'Imād al-Dīn did not merely give free rein to an idiosyncrasy or a caprice; rather he strove to do justice to his elevated subjects and their abilities by giving them a commensurate literary form. By 'Imād al-Dīn's time 'form', in its conventional sense, meant a rhetorical dressing-up of the style of the content to the fullest extent and the content itself was conceived of as autonomous and separable from form.

Clearly, given his cultural and social background, his attitude to his material was not that of a dispassionate chronicler of events and actions, but of an assayer of moral qualities, and it is here he fails. The intimate relationship with prime decision makers which his position as secretary and informal counsellor afforded him made him uniquely qualified to record 'history-in-the-making', and he acquitted himself well enough on that count. However, the very detail of his reporting at the same time reveals his failings; put bluntly, and perhaps anachronistically, he lacked the moral fibre to be a historian on a par with the Persian secretary-historian from the preceding century, Abū 'l-Fażl-e Bayhaqī,[61] as well as his own 'Frankish' contemporary William of Tyre.[62] Moreover, his failure is compounded by an inability to completely suppress self-awareness, which drives him to (over-)compensating. In much of his historical writing, overcompensation for lingering self-doubt manifests itself as breathless insistence, and at times strident rhetorical excess. The time-honored conceit of the pen being more powerful than the sword,[63] with the latter owing its memory and immortality to the former, takes on a particular urgency for 'Imād al-Dīn, and possibly reflects his realisation of the actual powerlessness of his class of civil administrators vis-à-vis autocratic military rule.

Yet there appears to be a deeper reason for his tendency towards over-identification, which is an inability to come to terms with imperfect, ambiguous reality.[64] The compromises he had to strike as a man of the world clearly

61 385–470/995–1077; see Ġ.-Ḥ. Yūsofī 'Bayhaqī, Abu'l-Fażl', in *EIr* vol. III, 889–94, (also http://www.iranicaonline.org/articles/bayhaqi-abul-fazl-mohammad-b); cf. *Blitz*, pp. 167–72 and 407 [Index], *s.v.* a. l-Fażl-e Baihaqī.

62 1130–c. 1185; see P. Edbury and J.G. Rowe, *William of Tyre: Historian of the Latin East* (Cambridge, 1988).

63 For earlier formulations in Arabic letters see Kraemer, *Der Sturz des Königreichs Jerusalem*, p. 62.

64 This and the following observations have primarily been derived from a study of the *'Lightning'*, situating it and its author in their own socio-cultural milieu; see *Blitz*, pp. 30ff, 82ff, 123–26, 189, 210–14, and 239ff. Contemporaneous authors, e.g. Ibn al-Jawzī, al-Fāḍil,

troubled him, as did his own shortcomings, and the trouble had to be silenced. Thus he himself and the people and causes he identified with, beginning with his uncle al-'Azīz, had to be perfect while their opponents were cast as villains, which tended to result in facile moral dualism. Sometimes, however, his intelligence and grasp of reality prevented him from going quite so far and in consequence he would obfuscate or pass over events in silence. He lacked the self-assurance of unquestioning belief as, for example, Bahā' al-Dīn displayed in his 'biography' of Saladin, as well as the robust sense of political expediency of the *qāḍī* al-Fāḍil. In any case, al-Fāḍil provides an interesting comparison. Unlike 'Imād al-Dīn, he had no problem admitting refractory reality[65] and his chancery prose, while ceding nothing to 'Imād al-Dīn in recherché ornateness, is happily free of the latter's panting insistence. As the number of extant manuscripts—in addition to indirect transmission—indicates, it won much greater favour with interested audiences too.[66] However, it has to be conceded that al-Fāḍil did not write chronicles like 'Imād al-Dīn, and not enough of his 'Notebooks', apparently a mine of information for social and economic history, survive to allow for the detailed comparison required.[67]

'Imād al-Dīn's historical works have two formal characteristics which to some extent balance his extremely ornate and verbose style: first, their division into relatively short chapters, and second, these chapters' clear separation by informative, detailed headings in an extra-large hand. In the absence of modern indices, these could provide an overview of the contents by rapidly leafing through the book, allowing specific passages to be located with relative ease.[68] The division of this material into fairly brief sections may also reflect the impact of a prominent and influential literary genre, the *maqāma* ('station'), a scene of oration or dialogue. By the time of 'Imād al-Dīn, the poet and littérateur al-Ḥarīrī (d. 516/1122) had come to be considered the master of the *maqāma* for his stupendous verbal acrobatics and it was he whom 'Imād al-Dīn set out to emulate.[69] Dividing up the narrative into self-contained units may also have resulted from and certainly facilitated a quasi-atomising perception

---

and Bahā' al-Dīn, provide ample material for comparison and contrast. Thus my assessment tends to be somewhat harsher than in Richards, 'Administrator'.

65 See, for example, *Blitz*, p. 212.

66 See Lyons & Jackson, *Saladin*, esp. pp. 435–36.

67 On the *qāḍī*'s 'journals' (*mājarayāt/mutajaddidāt/muyāwamāt*) see *Blitz*, pp. 168, 172–73, and 174, and Lev, *Saladin in Egypt*, pp. 25 and 213 [Index], *s.v.* Qadi al-Fadil (sic).

68 In modern print, these features may be obscured, but see *Blitz*, p. arab. 96, for a sample ms. page.

69 A.F.L. Beeston, 'Al-Hamadhānī, al-Ḥarīrī and the *maqāmāt* genre', in J. Ashtiany et al. (eds.), *'Abbasid Belles-Lettres* (Cambridge, 1990), 125–35 and 476–77 (for references).

of chains of events, actions and consequences, so serving as a narrative device to deflect blame from protagonists or other actors and so to further a preconceived panegyric intention.

Both 'Imād al-Dīn's contemporaries and later generations did not receive all his works favourably—the relative rejection his own collections of chancery prose and poetry met with has already been noted.[70] In contrast, two of his works stand out for solid transmission in multiple manuscripts: the anthology *al-Kharīda* and the two-volume encomium on Saladin as leader of the Counter-Crusade, *al-Fatḥ al-qussī*.[71] His other chronicles did not go unread, but they were excerpted or abridged by historians eager to glean factual information but impatient with his long-winded and stylistically demanding narrative.[72] Thus his enormous *al-Barq al-Shāmī*, running to seven hefty volumes,[73] and *Nuṣrat al-fatra* were abridged (in addition to being liberally quoted by later historians), which rendered the originals dispensable.[74] Of the seven parts of *al-Barq al-Shāmī* only two survive, each in a unique manuscript, and even the abridgement has not been preserved completely. *Nuṣrat al-fatra* has fared better; a single manuscript of the original has been preserved, but to date it remains notably understudied, whereas the shortened version, available in print for well over a century, has been duly recognized as an outstanding source.[75]

If in *al-Fatḥ al-qussī* 'Imād al-Dīn aspired to establish a new genre of 'historical prose epic', he may have overestimated his own powers to change the direction of Arabic literature. Yet it was not only his sympathetic superior and

70 His quatrains—a form introduced into Arabic letters from Persian—did not share this fate; see C. Pellat (ed.), *Dīwān Dawbait, Ḥawliyyāt al-Jāmi'a al-Tūnisīya* 12 (Tunis 1975), pp. 5–31.

71 For a review of mss and textual criticism see Kraemer, *Der Sturz des Königreichs Jerusalem*, pp. 8–9. The original division of *al-Fatḥ* into two volumes, pragmatically designed to avoid excessive bulk of a single heavy tome (*al-Kharīda*, in the same way, consisted of ten volumes), did not reflect a corresponding division of content.

72 See Richards, 'Administrator', p. 142.

73 It combines political history with personal memoirs and amply quotes from 'Imād al-Dīn's own and, to a greater extent, al-Fāḍil's official and private correspondence and poetry; see *Blitz*, esp. pp. 191–236.

74 Regarding the history of the Crusades, Ibn al-Athīr and Abū Shāma take precedence. The relevant sections of the former are now available in English in Richards, *Chronicle of Ibn al-Athīr*, and for Abū Shāma see *RHC Or.* vols IV–V.

75 To date, Durand-Guédy has been most forthright in giving 'Imād al-Dīn's original version of the 'Seljūq History' its due; see his *Iranian Elites and Turkish Rulers*, pp. 13–14 and 430 [Index], *s.v.* 'Imād al-Dīn al-Iṣfahānī, as well as p. 398 [bibliography], and his other studies (cf. *Blitz*, pp. 176–89 and 432 [Index], s.v. *Nuṣrat al-fatra*).

friend al-Fāḍil who admired his achievement. If ʿImād al-Dīn is to be believed, it was al-Fāḍil who suggested filling out the title with the rhyming reference to the proverbially eloquent semi-legendary pre-Islamic Arabian orator Quss ibn Sāʿida,[76] and the book's enduring success, as witnessed by the centuries-long sequence of transcripts, justified the compliment.

In contrast to the considerably more private and loosely organized *al-Barq al-Shāmī*, *al-Fatḥ* opens with a flourish: Saladin's victorious campaign against the crusaders in 583/1187 was chosen for its symbolic and propaganda value; the book fittingly ends with its heroic protagonist's death. The narrative varies in level of detail according to the importance of the events and deeds recorded, as can be seen by the differences across the six annual sections (discounting the seventh, with Saladin's death occurring barely two months into the year).[77] Furthermore, in contrast to *al-Barq al-Shāmī*, it is, within the conventional annalistic disposition, more tightly organized. The prose narrative, designed to carry the weight of heroic representation, is but rarely broken by the insertion of verse. Chancery documents, most often addressed to the caliphal government in Baghdad, drafted by ʿImād al-Dīn on behalf of Saladin or his son and successor al-Afḍal, are quoted regularly. Relations with the caliph were tense and on the caliph's part fraught with distrust of Saladin's ambitions in northern Mesopotamia, which were viewed as being threatening expansionism, and the inclusion of both diplomatic correspondence and narrative allows a useful comparison between the different modes of communication. ʿImād al-Dīn concludes a given year's account with obituaries of leading men deceased during it, thereby following a conventional pattern of annalistic historiography in medieval Islam, beginning in this case with the year 585/1189.[78]

As indicated above, ʿImād al-Dīn intended his work to be both celebratory and truthful, satisfying the demands of littérateurs and historian-scholars. In both, as a virtuoso stylist and as Saladin's secretary and close adviser, he was well-positioned to meet this challenge. It was only due to ill health that he ever left his post during the years covered by *al-Fatḥ*.[79] As for a potential tension,

76 Massé, *Conquête*, p. 11; for Quss, see Ch. Pellat, 'Ḳuss b. Sāʿida', in *EI2*.

77 Cf. the Table of Contents in Massé, *Conquête*, pp. 455–60; the adjustments necessitated by Massé's omission of certain sections would not change the overall picture.

78 Massé, *Conquête*, pp. 207, 280ff., 357–66, and 403ff.

79 After Saladin's conquest of Beirut in his victorious campaign of summer 583/1187 (on the 29th Jumādā I/6th August) ʿImād al-Dīn, gathering up his last strength, dictated a letter of safe-conduct before having himself taken, by litter, home to Damascus for rest and treatment. He only rejoined the camp after two months, exactly one day after the capitulation of Jerusalem (28th Rajab/3rd October); see Massé, *Conquête*, pp. 43 and 47.

or even conflict, in this dual purpose, he may half-subconsciously have suppressed the thought of it, as Saladin's achievements were too substantial to be denied or in need of embellishment, not to mention the constraints of ʿImād al-Dīn's personality and circumstances. It is these constraints which may explain a remarkable omission right at the beginning of *al-Fatḥ*, which it is hard to reconcile with ʿImād al-Dīn's expressly intended truthfulness. In *al-Barq al-Shāmī*, which he composed a few years after Saladin's death in disgruntled retirement, the author left it to al-Fāḍil to address an indirect admonition to Saladin. In 582/1186, there was a propitious moment for broaching touchy subjects to the sultan, as a severe illness had made him despondent and receptive to advice.[80] The *qāḍī* suggested that he win God's favour with the vow to kill, with his own hand, *al-ibrins* and *al-qūmiṣ*, Reynald of Châtillon[81] and Raymond III of Tripoli,[82] and also that he pledge to stop fighting other Muslims and to pursue with all his strength the jihad against the Franks. The intimation that Saladin needed such an admonition in the first place would not have been a fitting prelude to his presentation as an unwavering champion of holy war in *al-Fatḥ*, and it is hard not to see his reasons for thus ignoring this episode.

ʿImād al-Dīn's intentions notwithstanding, the years he chronicled in *al-Fatḥ* were not an unbroken chain of successes in the jihad against the infidel Franks. There were also reverses, and the longer the fighting went on, the greater the exhaustion of material and moral resources became. The ultimate triumph, the complete expulsion of the Franks from Syrian lands, proved elusive and a truce had to be concluded. ʿImād al-Dīn does not grossly falsify the record but, as mentioned above, at times he is clearly economical with the truth.[83] He does permit himself criticism of secondary actors, including, on the Muslim side, Saladin's men, accusing them of laggardness, selfishness or duplicity,[84] but never of Saladin himself, whose unwavering resolve he continually emphasizes. He also makes facile recourse to unfathomable, ineluctable divine decree, and superficial moralising sometimes takes the place of inquiry

80 *Apud* al-Bundārī, *Sanā ʾl-Barq al-Shāmī*, pp. 380–81, esp. 380: 11–15.

81 See A. Mallett, 'A Trip down the Red Sea with Reynald of Châtillon', *Journal of the Royal Asiatic Society*, Series 3, 18 (2008), pp. 141-53; B. Hamilton, 'The Elephant of Christ: Reynald of Châtillon', in *Studies in Church History* 15 (1978), 97–108.

82 See B. Hamilton, *The Leper King and his Heirs* (Cambridge, 2000), p. 286 [Index], *s.v.* Raymond III.

83 An illustrative example is provided by the all but deliberate vagueness with which he alludes to the unsuccessful siege of Tyre in the summer of 583/1187; see H. Möhring, *Saladin und der Dritte Kreuzzug* (Wiesbaden, 1980), pp. 36–63, esp. 37–38.

84 Indignantly so à propos of the embarrassment of the failed siege of Tyre in the winter of 583/1187–88; see Möhring, *Saladin*, p. 60, and Massé, *Conquête*, pp. 70–71.

into the remoter causes of tangible actions and effects. The Frankish adversaries, according to what could be described as ʿImād al-Dīn's Manichaeist dualism, are cast as villains, becoming more so the more effectively they functioned and the greater the danger they posed.

Following a time-honoured historiographical tradition, ʿImād al-Dīn enlivens his account by representing the *dramatis personae* through what are presented as their speeches, although these are more or less fictive utterances; a mark of their formal, if not material, fictiveness is their ornate rhyming style, which is obviously the author's. At momentous junctures, he even 'cites' speeches purportedly given by the enemy. These 'Frankish' statements stress what the author believes about them, while also expressing their pious zeal in terms which are a curious mixture of genuine, contemporaneous Christian beliefs and Quranic representations of Christianity.[85] Personal experience, as limited and twisted as it no doubt was, could not replace, in ʿImād al-Dīn's worldview, scriptural truths about Christian 'tritheists', but it did add to transmitted stereotypes. Like others in his generation, ʿImād al-Dīn understood the Christian belief in the holiness of Jerusalem and, above all, of the Holy Sepulchre.[86] Similarly, he shared an awareness of the Franks' veneration of the True Cross, which made it a valuable bargaining chip in negotiations which may have to be undertaken. Needless to say, for an orthodox Muslim like ʿImād al-Dīn, such Christian convictions did not amount to anything more than obdurate error, ignorance and idolatry.

In a cultural and, more specifically, academic environment in which the socio-cultural domain of sexualities and gender roles and relations is the subject of much research, ʿImād al-Dīn's fascination with Frankish women is not surprising. While, in general, foreigners', and particularly enemies', sexual mores are bound to elicit interest and frequently disdain, ʿImād al-Dīn's portrayal of Christian women displays a prurience which invites psychological speculation.[87] Witnessing, as he claims, fully armed women fighting in battle alongside men challenged his comprehension.[88] An even more egregious

85 See, for example, Gabrieli, *Arab Historians*, pp. 148–49.

86 Gabrieli, *Arab Historians*, p. 174; Massé, *Conquête*, p. 59.

87 Gabrieli, *Arab Historians*, pp. 204–7; Massé, *Conquête*, pp. 202–3 (truncated and bowdlerized); cf. S.B. Edgington & S. Lambert (eds.), *Gendering the Crusades* (Cardiff, 2001), p. 213 [Index], *s.v.* 'Imad ad-Din al-Isfahani [sic]; Hillenbrand, *Crusades*, pp. 278–80 and 347–51; C.T. Maier, 'The Roles of Women in the Crusade Movement', *Journal of Medieval History* 30 (2004), 61–82 (repr. in A. Jotischky [ed.], *The Crusades: Critical Concepts in Historical Studies*, 4 vols [London, 2008], vol. IV, 371–93).

88 Gabrieli, *Arab Historians*, p. 207.

violation of accepted norms is represented by those women who, as he reports, undertook to provide sexual relief to deprived warriors as a pious deed. Such modes of behaviour cannot but confirm his belief in the crusaders' fundamental depravity. Their sacred prostitution is couched in language which has appropriately been called pornographic.[89] A similar lasciviousness informs his strong evocation of the thousands of poor Jerusalemite women who, unable to ransom themselves, will be enslaved and subjected to their future masters' appetites.[90]

A linkage between libidinous and aggressive impulses similar to that which 'Imād al-Dīn felt towards Frankish women is manifested in his evocation of the corpse-strewn battlefield of Ḥaṭṭīn. The delight he takes in the scene of carnage can strike a modern reader as obscene, although to him the suffering and ignominious death met by the enemies of God and His final messenger are but their just desserts and merely heighten the triumph of the 'True Religion'.[91]

The hatred both underlying and fed by continuous warfare finds graphic expression in the treatment of the captured Templars and Hospitallers, as well as the notorious lord of Oultrejourdain, Reynald of Châtillon. Reynald's attack on a Muslim caravan in early 583/1187 provided the excuse for Saladin's campaigns later that year, and immediately after the battle of Ḥaṭṭīn Saladin proceeded to fulfill his vow to kill Reynald with his own hand. In contrast, he treated Guy of Lusignan to a refreshing cup of snow-chilled water, which was not only a relief in the burning mid-summer heat, but at the same time signified a guarantee of life.[92]

No such lenience was extended to the captured Templars and Hospitallers who were the backbone of the Frankish fighting force and expressly refused to be ransomed if taken prisoner. As early as nine years previously,[93] Saladin had had a group of captured Franks massacred; not merely killed but in a staged show butchered by whoever in his own entourage accepted the invitation. Then 'Imād al-Dīn had demurred, protesting that he was a man of the pen, not the sword, spreading news of victory rather than meting out death.[94] However, his deeper motive was *amour propre*; he was anxious about being ridiculed for poor swordsmanship, failing to dispatch the victim in one stroke. After Ḥaṭṭīn,

89 Gabrieli, *Arab Historians*, p. 204, n. 2.
90 Gabrieli, *Arab Historians*, p. 163; Massé, *Conquête*, p. 50.
91 Gabrieli, *Arab Historians*, p. 135; Massé, *Conquête*, pp. 28ff.
92 Gabrieli, *Arab Historians*, pp. 133–34; Massé, *Conquête*, pp. 27–28.
93 See *Blitz*, pp. 122–23; Lyons & Jackson, *Saladin*, pp. 131–32, 265–66, 406–7, and 421.
94 *Ibid.*

Saladin had the bloody spectacle repeated, and this time ʿImād al-Dīn, while not taking part, celebrates it unreservedly.[95]

Although continual warfare re-enforced the religio-political antagonism between the Franks and the Muslims and exacted its moral toll on people from both sides, including civilians such as ʿImād al-Dīn, the exigencies of diplomacy and *realpolitik* remained in force. Saladin's killing of Reynald with his own hand or his order for the captured rank and file of the Military Orders to be slaughtered did not, as we have seen, preclude his scrupulous observation of etiquette vis-à-vis his royal prisoner Guy of Lusignan or treating potentially useful captives like the Templar grand-master in a prudently humane way.[96] ʿImād al-Dīn gives a sober account of Saladin's diplomatic or otherwise non-belligerent dealings with the Franks, although a certain curt matter-of-factness is the extent of the restraint he musters on their account.[97] Chronicling the peace or 'truce' negotiations in 588/1192, he leaves it to Saladin's emirs to argue for peace, pointing out the devastation of the land and the inhabitants' and army's exhaustion, while he presents himself as his master's loyal follower in but grudgingly yielding to necessity.[98] In a different vein, though, he does spare the Frankish pilgrims who visit the holy sites in Jerusalem after the truce of 588/1192 his usual scorn and venom.[99] Previously, when confronted with Richard the Lionheart's massacre of the Muslim captives at Acre in 587/1191, ʿImād al-Dīn registered appropriate outrage at the accursed, treacherous perpetrators, but whether or not his professed belief in the victims' immediate assumption into paradise did mitigate their loss for him, he retained his composure—possibly

95 Gabrieli, *Arab Historians*, pp. 138–39; Massé, *Conquête*, pp. 30–31.

96 *Blitz*, pp. 122–23. Gerard of Ridefort (left unnamed by ʿImād al-Dīn) met his death on the battlefield before Acre two years later, in October 1189—Massé, *Conquête*, pp. 181ff; cf. M. Barber, 'The Reputation of Gerard of Ridefort', in J. Upton-Ward (ed.), *On Land and by Sea* (Aldershot, 2008), 111–19. Ibn al-Athīr's much later report of Gerard at Acre again falling into Saladin's hand and being killed by him would not seem to deserve credence over ʿImād al-Dīn's contrary testimony, considering the latter's aversion—to put it mildly—to the Templars: Barber, p. 118, n. 34; Ibn al-Athīr, *al-Kāmil*, vol. XII, p. 38; tr. Richards, *Chronicle of Ibn al-Athīr* 2, p. 368.

97 At some point Saladin decided to ransom, after a seven-year imprisonment, his wayward great-nephew Shāhanshāh b. Taqī al-Dīn ʿUmar, who had incautiously let himself be captured by the Templars. Saladin's agreement with them did not only involve a hefty payment, but also the release of captured Knights Templars—doubtless a mortifying situation for Saladin; *Blitz*, pp. 220ff.

98 Gabrieli, *Arab Historians*, pp. 234–37; Massé, *Conquête*, pp. 388–91.

99 *Ibid.*

even feeling vindicated in his conviction about the Franks' degradation.[100] In contrast to his fellow historian Bahā' al-Dīn Ibn Shaddād, 'Imād al-Dīn does not waste his own time in pondering the infidels' motives for the carnage, nor does he qualify his account by mentioning the few survivors, either persons of rank and substance who would be held for ransom or the able-bodied men to be put to work in construction.[101] Here as elsewhere, 'Imād al-Dīn would seem to content himself with reaffirming the Franks' fundamental depravity—a foregone conclusion anyway. The result is a reductionist, two-dimensional image of evil-doers; Bahā' al-Dīn on the other hand, no less devoted an adherent of Saladin's nor any less convinced of the justice and divine approbation of the Muslim cause, achieved a notably more rounded and life-like representation of the adversary. From among 'Imād al-Dīn's Muslim contemporaries arguably the most outstanding observer of the Muslim-Frankish Levant, whose intense hatred of the infidel invaders did not blind him to the complex, even ironic consequences of their presence on the ground, was the Andalusī traveller Ibn Jubayr; not only did he marvel at lively trade between Muslims and Franks continuing unabated even at times of acute conflict, but he went so far as to uphold the Franks' fair and lenient governance of their Muslim subjects as a model to arbitrary and extortionate Muslim rulers.[102] Notwithstanding 'Imād al-Dīn's inability, for subjective as well as objective reasons, to voice substantive criticism of Saladin, he might still have condescended to acknowledge—as Ibn Jubayr readily did—the sometime peaceable, mutually advantageous instances of Muslim-Frankish condominium.[103]

In conclusion, the question remains of the value of *al-Fatḥ* as a source in itself, considering that its 'factual' material was extracted and condensed in a clearer form by successive authors within a few decades of 'Imād al-Dīn's death. The answer is that regardless of his idiosyncracies, or possibly precisely because of them, 'Imād al-Dīn, confronted as he saw Islam, the Muslims and not least himself by Frankish aggression, unambiguously reflects and articulates

100 Massé, *Conquête*, p. 330; cf. J. Gillingham, *Richard the Lionheart*, 2nd ed. (London, 1989), esp. pp. 181–84.

101 Bahā' al-Din Ibn Shaddād, *al-Nawādir al-sulṭāniyya wa-'l-maḥāsin al-yūsufiyya*, tr. D.S. Richards as *The Rare and Excellent History of Saladin* (Aldershot, 2002), pp. 164–65; Gabrieli, *Arab Historians*, pp. 223–24.

102 Ibn Jubayr, tr. Broadhurst, pp. 313 and 315ff.

103 Ibn Jubayr, tr. Broadhurst, p. 317; for further examples of this see M. Köhler, *Alliances and Treaties between Frankish and Muslim Rulers in the Middle East*, tr. P.M. Holt, revised, edited, and with an introduction by K. Hirschler (Leiden, 2013).

many of the sentiments, values and beliefs that were shared by and shaped the image of 'self' (and 'other') of contemporaneous Muslim society. This is not to deny him individuality, as collectivities cannot articulate themselves except in individual refraction; and however self-centered and self-satisfied his authorial performance may at times appear, he still sought praise and recognition beyond the circle of his professional peers, as witnessed by the reading from *al-Fatḥ* to Saladin. Yet whatever the extent of the sultan's literary sensibility and appreciation, the argument must remain that 'Imād al-Dīn's intended audience, ideally represented by the *qāḍī* al-Fāḍil, was a narrow elite. Yet even if that is the case, it matters little, as 'Imād al-Dīn thought of this class as being rightfully privileged and entitled to have their voices heard and heeded.

Ibn al-Athīr

Françoise Micheau

Al-Kāmil fi'l-ta'rīkh, ('The Complete History'), which Ibn al-Athīr completed in Mosul in the late 620s/early 1230s, is almost unanimously considered to be 'one of the most impressive achievements of pre-modern historiography in any culture'[1] and 'the high point of Muslim annalistic historiography',[2] and its author to be 'l'un des plus grands historiens du Moyen Âge islamique'.[3] For the history of the crusading period this universal chronicle provides a clear, balanced and detailed account which makes it one of the principal Arabic sources for the sixth/twelfth and early-seventh/thirteenth centuries. Its importance for the history of the Crusades was first noted in the eighteenth century by Dom Berthereau and for this reason the first two volumes of the magisterial *Recueil des Historiens des Croisades: Documents Orientaux* combined an edition and translation of large extracts from *al-Kāmil fi'l-ta'rīkh*, under the wrongly transcribed title *Kamel-altevarykh*.[4] Later, Francesco Gabrieli made extensive use of Ibn al-Athīr's chronicle in his *Arab Historians of the Crusades*, using it for at least a third of the translations contained within his text.[5] Such a significant position accorded to Ibn al-Athīr's major chronicle is certainly justified, despite some scholars' criticisms surrounding his use of sources and his Zengid sympathies.

The Political Situation of Syria and the Jazīra and the Life of Ibn al-Athīr

Ibn al-Athīr (555/1160–630/1233) was born into a wealthy family of well-educated scholars, members of which rose to prominence in the service of the Zengid rulers of Mosul and who also had good relations with the Ayyūbids. Consequently, a brief survey of the political situation of the Jazīra and northern

1 R.S. Humphreys, 'Ta'rīkh', in *EI2*.

2 F. Rosenthal, 'Ibn al-Athīr', in *EI2*.

3 A.-M. Eddé, *La principauté ayyoubide d'Alep (579/1183–658/1260)* (Stuttgart, 1999), p. 20.

4 *RHC Or.*, vols. I–II.

5 This is the case at least for the period of time covered by Ibn al-Athīr's chronicle (from the First to the Fifth Crusade); F. Gabrieli, *Arab Historians of the Crusades* (Berkeley/Los Angeles, 1969).

 | DOI 10.1163/9789004280687_005

Syria in the sixth/twelfth and early seventh/thirteenth centuries will be useful in order to gain a better understanding of the context in which Ibn al-Athīr lived and worked, and how this may have influenced his writings.[6]

With the exception of the first few decades, the sixth/twelfth century had been marked by the emergence of a number of powerful Islamic rulers who, for the first time, were able to unite the Muslim forces and lead them to some success in the jihad against the Frankish crusaders. From 521/1127 to 541/1146, Zengī (or Zankī), who ruled Mosul and Aleppo in the name of the Seljūq sultan, held *de facto* independence over his territory, and his jihad credentials were suggested in 539/1144 by his capture of Edessa which, since the year 491/1098, had been the capital of a Latin county. After his death in 541/1146 Zengī's lands were divided among the members of his family. It was his son Nūr al-Dīn who succeeded him at Aleppo, ruling from 541/1146 until 569/1174, and during this period he made the fight against the Franks one of the main aspects of his wider policy of unifying and restoring Sunnī rule in Syrian territory, demonstrated in 549/1154 by his takeover of Damascus from the hands of a dynasty of Turkish emirs. Sayf al-Dīn Ghāzī I, Nūr al-Dīn's brother, received Mosul, the other centre of Zengid power, and henceforth the fortunes of the two cities diverged. After Sayf al-Dīn's death only three years later power passed to his brother Quṭb al-Dīn Mawdūd (r. 544–565/1149–1170), then to the latter's son Sayf al-Dīn Ghāzī II (r. 565–576/1170–1180), and finally to his second son ʿIzz al-Dīn Masʿūd I (r. 576–589/1176–1193). Other members of the Zengid family established themselves in Sinjār, to the west of Mosul, and in Jazīrat Ibn ʿUmar, on the upper Tigris, where they created their own petty principalities.[7]

However, the two main branches of the Zengid dynasty were threatened by the ambitions of Saladin, a Kurdish ruler who had hijacked the Zengid attempt to re-establish Sunnī authority in Egypt and made himself the champion of the fight against the Franks. Saladin had accompanied his uncle Shīrkūh in the expeditions by which the latter had captured Egypt in the name of Nūr al-Dīn in the 560s/1160s, and he was able to take advantage of the circumstances he encountered to further his own ambitions. Named as chief of the army and vizier in Cairo in 564/1169, Saladin became sole ruler of the country following the death of the last Fāṭimid caliph al-ʿĀḍid in 567/1171,[8] when he re-established Sunnism with the official, if only nominal, recognition of the

6 The bibliography for this is extremely rich. For an introduction, see J.-C. Garcin, 'Les Zankides et les Ayyūbides', in J.-C. Garcin et al. (eds), *États, sociétés et cultures dans le monde musulman médiéval xe–xve siècles*, 2 vols (Paris, 1995), vol. 1, pp. 233–55.

7 S. Heidemann, 'Zangids', in *EI2*.

8 See the analysis which Ibn al-Athīr gives of these events, below, p. 79.

caliph in Baghdad. On the death of Nūr al-Dīn in 569/1174 and with the latter's lands nominally split amongst his own sons, Saladin made every effort to re-unify Syria and Egypt under his authority alone. From his base in Egypt he quickly took possession of Damascus in 570/1174, but it took many campaigns against Aleppo before he was able to establish his power there, doing so only in 579/1183. On the other hand, by the terms agreed after a long siege of Mosul, Saladin had to content himself only with seeing his suzerainty recognised by 'Izz al-Dīn Mas'ūd I, the Zengid ruler of that city, in 581/1186. Only then did he turn his attention to the Franks, and on the 24th Rabī' II 583/4th July 1187 he won a crushing victory over them at the battle of Ḥaṭṭīn, destroying virtually the entire defensive capacity of the Latin Kingdom of Jerusalem. In the following months numerous Frankish towns and fortresses surrendered to him or were captured, before Jerusalem was taken on the 27th Rajab/2nd October after a two-week siege. This resounding triumph cemented Saladin's position as the great champion of the jihad, celebrated in the Muslim world ever since. However, these successes were soon followed by failures: he was forced to lift the siege of Frankish Tyre in 583/1188; he was unable to dislodge the troops of the Third Crusade who were besieging Acre; and he had to conclude the Treaty of Jaffa with Richard the Lionheart in 588/1192, which recognised Frankish rule over a coastal strip running from Tyre to Jaffa.

While still alive, Saladin had planned how his possesions would be partitioned amongst his sons, thereby continuing a practice of ensuring familial authority which had been put into practice before him by the Seljūqs and the Zengids. However, after his death in 589/1193 these plans were ignored and his lands split between other relatives. Each of the resulting states was organised around a single town and its hinterland, and was governed by an independent ruler who nonetheless recognised the overall suzerainty of the senior member of the Ayyūbid dynasty who ruled in Cairo—al-'Ādil from 596/1200 to 615/1218, then his son al-Kāmil. In this 'familial system' the principality of Aleppo became the possession of Saladin's son al-Malik al-Ẓāhir Ghāzī and his descendents, who ensured its prosperity.[9]

In the northern Jazīra, on the other hand, Zengid autonomy continued, as members of that dynasty remained as the rulers of Mosul: Nūr al-Dīn Arslān Shāh I (589–607/1193–1211), his son 'Izz al-Dīn Mas'ūd II (607–15/1211–18), and then the latter's sons Nūr al-Dīn Arslān Shāh II (615–16/1218–20) and Nāsir al-Dīn Maḥmūd (616–19/1219–22). But after the advent of Mas'ūd II, then a minor, real power was exercised by Badr al-Dīn Lu'lu', an aged freed slave who acted as regent and vizier for these last Zengid rulers. In 631/1233 he did

9 Eddé, *Principauté ayyoubide*.

away with all pretence and dispossessed the Zengids of their title of atabegs of Mosul, becoming the sole ruler of the principality until his death in 657/1259, just before the Mongol invasion of the region.[10] Yet despite this complex political history the Zengid period in Mosul was one of great cultural richness, attested, among other things, by the development of arts in metalwork and the copying of sumptious manuscripts,[11] and it was within this eventful and culturally rich political milieu that Ibn al-Athīr lived and worked. His life and those of his two brothers are known to us principally through the notices given in Ibn Khallikān's (608–81/1211–82) famous biographical dictionary, and by comments made by Ibn al-Athīr himself in his works.[12]

The three brothers were all born in Jazīrat Ibn ʿUmar, a town which their father, Muḥammad b. ʿAbd al-Karīm, administered in the name of Quṭb al-Dīn Mawdūd. This high official belonged to a wider family of some means which possessed significant landholdings in the region, and he himself also gained a substantial income through successful business activities.[13] His sojourn in Jazīrat Ibn ʿUmar ended in 579/1183 when he returned to Mosul with his sons, perhaps because the government of the former town had been taken by Muʿizz al-Dīn Sinjār Shāh, the son of Sayf al-Dīn Ghāzī II, upon the latter's death in 576/1180.

The eldest of the three brothers, Abu'l-Saʿādāt al-Mubārak Majd al-Dīn (544–606/1149–1210), was famous for the elegance of his writing, which gained him the position of chancellor, charged with drafting correspondence for ʿIzz al-Dīn Masʿūd and his successor Nūr al-Dīn Arslān-Shāh, the Zengid princes of Mosul, who held him in high esteem. But stricken by paralysis, he retired from public life and devoted himself to writing numerous works in the fields of religious science (Quranic commentary and hadith), Arabic grammar and *adab*. His collection of hadith, entitled *Jāmiʿ al-uṣūl* ('The Collection of Rules'), became an influential reference work which was frequently employed during the medieval period, as was a dictionary of uncommon words contained in the

10 For the dynastic history of the Zengids see C.E. Bosworth, *The New Islamic Dynasties* (Edinburgh, 1996), pp. 190–92.

11 See J. Raby (ed.), *The Art of Syria and the Jazīra. 1100–1250* (Oxford, 1985).

12 Ibn Khallikān, *Wafayāt al-aʿyān*, ed. I. ʿAbbās, 8 vols (Beirut, 1994), vol. III, pp. 348–50, vol. IV, pp. 141–43, and vol. V, pp. 389–97; tr. M. de Slane as *Ibn Khallikan's Biographical Dictionary*, 4 vols (Paris, 1843), vol. II, pp. 288–90 and 551–54, and vol. III, pp. 541–48. See also F. Rosenthal, 'Ibn al-Athīr', in *EI2*.

13 See Ibn al Athīr, *al-Taʾrīkh al-bāhir fi'l-dawlat al-atābakiyya*, ed. A.A. Ṭulaymāt (Cairo, 1963), pp. 147, 149 and 155.

hadith which he wrote, named *al-Nihāya fī gharb al-ḥadīth* ('The Last [Word] in the Uncommon Words in the Hadith').[14]

The youngest brother, Abu'l-Fatḥ Naṣr Allāh Ḍiyā' al-Dīn (558–637/1163–1239), had a brilliant but turbulent administrative career. He entered the service of Saladin in 587/1191 and worked with the *qāḍī* al-Fāḍil; after the death of Saladin he entered the service of al-Malik al-Afḍal, one of the sons of Saladin who, becoming ruler of Damascus upon the death of his father, chose him as his vizier. But Ḍiyā' al-Dīn was involved in so much enmity with his fellow-bureaucrats that he was obliged to seek refuge in Egypt (according to Ibn Khallikān) or, more likely, Mosul. He returned to the service of al-Afḍal in 595/1199, moved into the employment of al-Malik al-Ẓāhir Ghāzī, the Ayyūbid ruler of Aleppo, in 607/1211, and then returned to Mosul in 618/1221. He remained there until the end of his life in the service of Maḥmūd b. Mas'ūd b. Arslān Shāh and Badr al-Dīn Lu'lu', where he was employed to draft official letters. He also wrote many works in the field of *adab*, of which the best known are *al-Mathal al-sā'ir* and a collection of his letters discussing diverse literary subjects which he wrote to, or for, various notables of the time.[15]

As for the famous historian, Abu'l-Ḥasan 'Alī 'Izz al-Dīn was born on the 4th Jumādā I 555/12th May 1160, also at Jazīrat Ibn 'Umar, and it seems he spent most of his life in Mosul where he died in Sha'bān or Ramaḍān 630/May–June 1233, although most of his life is shrouded in obscurity. He most likely started his studies in his home town and continued them at Mosul and Baghdad, where he went several times, most notably during his return from the pilgrimage to Mecca in 573/1177.[16] Unlike his two brothers, he does not seem to have pursued an administrative career. Ibn Khallikān, who met him at Aleppo in 626/1229, described him as a famous but shy and retiring scholar who took pleasure in studying and writing. Nonetheless, according to Ibn al-Athīr's own comments in *al-Kāmil*, he was present in Syria in 584/1188–89 in the ranks of Saladin's armies,[17] and he was to be found at Damascus in 590/1193–94 during

14 Majd al-Dīn Ibn al-Athīr, *Jāmi' al-uṣūl fī aḥādīth al-rasūl*, ed. 'A.Q. al-Arnā'ūṭ, 2 vols (Beirut, 1983); idem, *al-Nihāya fī gharīb al-ḥadīth wa'l-athar*, s.n., 4 vols (Cairo, 1900–4).

15 Ḍiyā' al-Dīn Ibn al-Athīr, *al-Mathal al-sā'ir fī adab al-kātib wa'l-shā'ir*, ed. K.M.M. 'Uwayḍah, 2 vols (Beirut, 1998); idem, *Dīwān rasā'il Ḍiyā' al-Dīn Ibn al-Athīr*, ed. H. Nājī (Mosul, 1982).

16 *Al-Bāhir*, p. 180. Ṭulaymāt, in the introduction to his edition of this text, attempted to establish a list of teachers by whom Ibn al-Athīr could have been taught. See also M. ul-Hasan, *Ibn al-Athir: An Arab Historian. A Critical Analysis of his* Tarikh-al-Kamil *and* Tarikh-al-Atabeca (New Delhi, 2005), pp. 47ff.

17 He was at the siege of Kerak in Rabī' I 584/May 1188 and in the same year was present at the capture of Burzūya; *al-Kāmil fi'l-ta'rīkh*, ed. C.J. Tornberg, 13 vols (Beirut, 1965–67), vol. XII, pp. 6, 15, and 25; tr. D.S. Richards, *The Chronicle of Ibn al-Athīr for the Crusading*

the siege of the city by al-ʿAzīz.[18] He is known to have stayed at Aleppo for almost two years as the guest of the atabeg Ṭughril Shihāb al-Dīn and, from there, went to Damascus in 627/1229–30. Around this time he also resided in Baghdad for a period,[19] and in the introduction to *al-Bāhir* Ibn al-Athīr mentions the honours and gifts which had been lavished upon him by Nūr al-Dīn Arslān Shāh.[20] All this suggests that he led a richer life than Ibn Khallikān suggests and that he was, like his brothers, close to the corridors of power. This is clearly an important point as, on the one hand, it means he had access to good sources of information but, on the other, it does raise questions over his impartiality with regard to the rulers on which he and his family depended.

Ibn al-Athīr's historical works are formed of biographies and chronographies: he wrote *al-Lubāb fī tahdhīb al-ansāb*, an abridged version of al-Samʿānī's (d. 562/1166) voluminous biographical dictionary entitled *Ansāb*;[21] *Usd al-ghāba fī maʿrifat al-ṣaḥāba*, a history of the companions of Muḥammad;[22] *al-Taʾrīkh al-bāhir fīʾl-dawlat al-atābakiyya*, a history of the Zengid princes from 477/1084 to 607/1210; and *al-Kāmil fīʾl-taʾrīkh*, a universal chronicle which runs from the creation of the world until the year 628/1230–31. For the study of the crusading period, only the latter two texts are of significance.[23]

Period from al-Kāmil fi'l-ta'rīkh: *Part 2. The Years 541–589/1146–1193. The Age of Nūr al-Dīn and Saladin* (Aldershot, 2007), pp. 344, 350 and 357, although Ibn al-Athīr does not specify in what capacity he was present. He also writes that he could be found at Damascus when returning from a pilgrimage to Jerusalem after the capture of the town by the Muslims; *al-Bāhir*, p. 170.

18 *Al-Kāmil*, vol. XII, p. 109; tr. D.S. Richards, *The Chronicle of Ibn al-Athīr for the Crusading Period from* al-Kāmil fi'l-ta'rīkh: *Part 3. The Years 589–629/1193–1231. The Ayyūbids after Saladin and the Mongol Menace* (Aldershot, 2008), p. 16.

19 The vizier Ibn al-Qifṭī had given his huge library as a *waqf* to the al-Zubaydī mosque in Baghdad before his death and charged Ibn al-Athīr, a friend of his father, with transporting the books. Cf. Eddé, *Principauté ayyoubide*, p. 415.

20 *Al-Bāhir*, p. 1.

21 ʿIzz al-Dīn Ibn al-Athīr, *al-Lubāb fī tahdhīb al-ansāb*, s.n., 3 vols (Cairo, 1938–49).

22 ʿIzz al-Dīn Ibn al-Athīr, *Usd al-ghāba fī maʿrifat al-ṣaḥāba*, ed. M. Fāyid et al. (Cairo, 1964).

23 The ideas which follow were partially expounded in my study: F. Micheau, 'Le *Kitāb al-kāmil fī-l-tāʾrīkh* d'Ibn al-Athīr: entre chronique et histoire', *Studia Islamica* 104/105 (2007), 81–101. See also F. Micheau, 'Les croisades vues par les historiens arabes d'hier et d'aujourd'hui', in *Le Concile de Clermont de 1095 et l'appel à la Croisade. Actes du Colloque Universitaire International de Clermont-Ferrand (23–25 juin 1995)*, s.n. (Rome, 1997); reprinted in F. Micheau (ed.) *Les relations des pays d'Islam avec le monde latin du milieu du* X*e au milieu du* XIII*e siècle* (Paris, 2000), 52–71.

Al-Kāmil fi'l-ta'rīkh

Ibn al-Athīr's method of composition for *al-Kāmil* has proved challenging to unravel. It seems he composed an initial version of the text before he wrote *al-Bāhir*, giving it a different title, as there is every reason to believe that *al-Mustaqṣā fi'l-ta'rīkh*, to which references are made in *al-Bāhir*, is not a different work, but the original title of *al-Kāmil*. Ibn al-Athīr then devoted the years 609–15/1213–18 to writing *al-Bāhir*, after which he returned to composing his universal chronicle. Through a meticulous internal study of the text Donald Richards has shown that Ibn al-Athīr corrected it several times between 615/1218–19 and 628/1230–31 before completing it,[24] although the present ending has a less controlled feel than earlier sections, suggesting that the author did not have time to revise that part before he died. In the introduction, Ibn al-Athīr writes rather vaguely that he delayed the publication and the reason he did so, before stating that he decided to publish his work only after receiving an order to do so from Badr al-Dīn Lu'lu', the regent of the last Zengid rulers of Mosul. The book's dedication to Lu'lu', which the author made after completing the work, is a form of patronage where the powerful and generous prince would benefit from his association with the work, while the author would receive rewards and honour for the dedication.[25]

Al-Kāmil is preserved in half a dozen manuscripts and has been the object of numerous editions, firstly in the 19th century by the orientalist Tornberg, a version which has been re-published on numerous occasions in Cairo and Beirut.[26] Passages relating to the Muslim West were translated by Edmond Fagnan,[27] those concerned with the history of the Seljūqs by Donald Richards,[28] while the whole of the years 491/1097 to 628/1230–31, which had previously been edited and translated into French by Reinaud and Defrémery in the

---

24 D.S. Richards, 'Ibn al-Athīr and the Later Parts of the *Kāmil*: A Study of Aims and Methods', in D.O. Morgan (ed.), *Medieval Historical Writing in the Christian and Islamic Worlds* (London, 1982), 76–108.

25 See the study by H. Touati, 'La dédicace des livres en Islam médiéval', *Annales. Histoire, Sciences Sociales* (March–April 2000), 325–54.

26 Edited by C.J. Tornberg (Leiden, 1851–76) in 14 volumes including two indices; (Cairo, 1301–2/1884–85 and 1303/1886), in 12 volumes; (Beirut, 1965–67), based on the Tornberg edition, in 13 volumes including an index (all references to the text in this article refer to this edition); by 'U. Tadmurī (Beirut, 1417/1996), in 11 volumes of which the final is an index; and by 'A. al-Qāḍī (Beirut, 1418/1998), also in 11 volumes.

27 E. Fagnan, *Annales du Maghreb et de l'Espagne* (Algiers, 1898).

28 D.S. Richards, *The Annals of the Saljuq Turks. Selections from* al-Kāmil fi'l-Ta'rīkh *of 'Izz al-Dīn Ibn al-Athīr* (Aldershot, 2002).

Recueil des Historiens des Croisades, has recently been translated into English, also by Richards.[29]

The title of the work itself, *al-Kāmil fi'l-ta'rīkh*, 'The Complete History', reflects Ibn al-Athīr's aim, recorded in his introduction, to assemble all historical reports scattered across numerous other writings into one work. Such an encyclopaedic aim, and the pretension of offering all the important events of history within one historical text, is a well-known historiographical methodology in Arab culture. Yet in Ibn al-Athīr's case the result is remarkable, as unlike most other writers, he actually comes close to achieving his aim. He composed a universal history—which, to all medieval Islamic writers, meant a history beginning with the creation of the world rather than examining every people group within it[30]—which focusses on the lands of Islam from the time of Muḥammad's preaching and the Arab conquests. He thus follows the model of al-Ṭabarī (d. 310/923), the only historian he mentions in his introduction and on whom he largely relies for his account of pre-Islamic times and the first centuries of Islam.[31] Yet, in a departure from his predecessor, Ibn al-Athīr attempts to cover the whole history of *dār al-Islām*, East and West: 'the eastern [historians] neglect the reports (*akhbār*) about the West and the western [historians] neglect those concerning the East … seeing this, I decided to compose a work of history (*ta'rīkh*) which assembles the reports relevant to the rulers of the East and the West … I do not pretend to have been able to gather all historical facts, because that which has occurred in the East or the West may not have come to the notice of someone living in Mosul'.[32] The general organisation of the work shows an overall balance between the different regions of the Islamic world, although the history of Syria and the Jazīra is the main focus of the last two centuries: as Richards has shown, in volume XI (corresponding to the years 527–83/1132–87) the history of Syria, the Jazīra, and Iraq occupies 250 pages, that of the Islamic East 100 pages, and that of Egypt and the Muslim West 91 pages, while, in volume XII (the years 584–628/1188–1230) these areas

---

29 *RHC Or.* vols I and II; D.S. Richards, *The Chronicle of Ibn al-Athīr for the Crusading Period from* al-Kāmil fi'l-ta'rīkh. *Part 1: The Years 491–541/1097–1146. The Coming of the Franks and the Muslim Response* (Aldershot, 2006); *Part 2. The Years 541–589/1146–1193. The Age of Nūr al-Dīn and Saladin* (Aldershot, 2007); *Part 3: The Years 589–629/1193–1231. The Ayyūbids after Saladin and the Mongol Menace* (Aldershot, 2008).

30 On this idea of history, see B. Radtke, 'Das Wirklichkeitsverständnis islamischer Universalhistoriker', *Der Islam* 62 (1985), 59–70; idem, *Weltgeschichte und Weltbeschreibung im mittelalterlichen Islam* (Beirut/Stuttgart, 1992).

31 C. Brockelmann, *Das Verhältnis von Ibn-el-Aṯîrs Kâmil fit-ta'riḫ zu Ṭabaris Aḫbâr Errusul wal Mulûk* (Strasbourg, 1890); M. ul-Hasan, *Ibn al-A<u>th</u>ir*, pp. 93ff.

32 *Al-Kāmil*, vol. I, pp. 2–3.

have 205, 172 (due to substantial reports on India) and only 24 pages devoted to them respectively.[33]

As his aim was to write a history of all Islamic lands, the whole of the *umma*, significant space is devoted to all the great dynasties of Islam. Thus the Fāṭimids, even though they were Shīʿīs, are discussed at length. He writes 'this dynasty [which he calls *al-dawlat al-ʿalawiyya* ('The Alawite State')] extended to the limit of its power and existed for a long time. It seized power in this year [296/908-9] in Ifrīqiya and expired in Egypt in 567/1171'.[34] Over the course of his chronicle, he reports the deeds and the histories of the Fāṭimid caliphs in Cairo, and in so doing makes use of available Egyptian sources, including, for example, the writings of al-Quḍāʿī. When recounting the end of Fāṭimid rule, with the death of al-ʿĀḍid, he adopts a vocabulary marked with Sufi terms to express his perplexity at the fall of a great dynasty, but which contains no marked hostility against this Shīʿī power: 'The whole period of their rule from the time that al-Mahdī appeared at Sijilmāsa in Dhu'l-Ḥijja of the year 299/ July-August 912 until the death of al-ʿĀḍid was 272 [*sic*] years and one month approximately. This is the way of the world. It never gives without taking back, is never sweet without turning bitter and is never pure without becoming muddied ... We pray God Almighty to turn our hearts towards Him, to show us the world as it really is, to make us reject it and desire the Life-to-Come'.[35] How can this attitude be explained? Less, it seems, by claiming an exceptional type of impartiality on the part of this Sunnī scholar from Mosul than by seeing it as a manifestation of his desire to restore by the pen the unity of *dār al-Islām* which historical circumstances prevented. The fracturing of the caliphate from its original unity into a multitude of rival powers, the rupture between an East dominated by the Turks and a West dominated by the Berbers, and the successes of the Franks in the West and the Mongols in the East destroyed the dream of a unified *umma*. It was up to the historian to restore this ideal.

Ibn al-Athīr's famous description of the origin of the First Crusade must be read from this perspective.[36] His connection of the arrival of the crusaders in Syria with other Frankish conflicts against the lands of Islam—in al-Andalus

33 Richards, 'Ibn al-Athīr and the Later Parts of the *Kāmil*', p. 85.

34 *Al-Kāmil*, vol. VIII, pp. 24ff.

35 *Al-Kāmil*, vol. XI, pp. 370–71; tr. Richards, 2, p. 198. See also the brief comments on this passage in T. Khalidi, *Arabic Historical Thought in the Classical Period* (Cambridge, 1994), p. 215.

36 *Al-Kāmil*, vol. X, pp. 272–73; tr. Richards, 1, pp. 13–14. See also the translation and brief commentary in Gabrieli, *Arab Historians of the Crusades*, pp. 3–4.

with the fall of Toledo, in Sicily and on the coasts of Ifrīqiya—is primarily carried out to affirm the unity of *dār al-Islām*.

> The power of the Franks (*dawlat al-Franj*) and their increased importance were first manifested by their invasion of the lands of Islam (*bilād al-Islām*) and their conquest of part of them in the year 478/1085–6, for [that was when] they took the city of Toledo and other cities of Spain, as we have already mentioned.
>
> Then in the year 484/1091–2 they attacked and conquered the island of Sicily, as we have also mentioned. They descended on the coasts of Ifrīqiya and seized some part, which was then taken back from them. Later they took other parts, as you shall see.
>
> When it was the year 490/1096–7 they invaded Syria. The reason (*sabab*) for their invasion was that their ruler, Baldwin,[37] a relative of Roger the Frank who had conquered Sicily, gathered a great host of Franks and sent to Roger saying, 'I have gathered a great host and I am coming to you. I shall proceed to Ifrīqiya to take it and I shall be a neighbour of yours'. Roger assembled his men and consulted them about this. They said, 'By the truth of the Gospel, this is excellent for us and them. The lands will become Christian lands (*bilād al-naṣrānī*)'. Roger raised his leg and gave a loud fart. 'By the truth of my religion', he said, 'there is more use in that than in what you have to say!' 'How so?' they asked. 'If they come to me', he replied, 'I shall require vast expenditure and ships to convey them to Ifrīqiya and troops of mine also. If they take the territory it will be theirs and resources from Sicily will go to them. I shall be deprived of the money that comes in every year from agricultural revenues. If they do not succeed, they will return to my lands and I shall suffer from them. Tamīm[38] will say, "You have betrayed me and broken the agreement I have [with you]". Our mutual contacts and visits will be interrupted. The land of Ifrīqiya will be waiting for us. Whenever we find the strength we will take it.'
>
> He summoned Baldwin's envoy and said to him, 'If you are determined to wage holy war (*jihād*) on the Muslims, then the best way is to conquer Jerusalem. You will free it from their hands and have glory. Between me

37 The confusion between the leaders of the First Crusade and the first King of Jerusalem is obvious.

38 Tamīm ibn al-Mu'izz was the Zirid ruler of Ifrīqiya (454/1062–501/1108).

> and the people of Ifrīqiya, however, are oaths and treaties'. They therefore made their preparations and marched forth to Syria (*al-Shām*).[39]
>
> It has been said that the Alid rulers of Egypt became fearful when they saw the strength and power of the Saljuq state, that it had gained control of Syrian lands as far as Gaza, leaving no buffer state between the Saljuqs and Egypt to protect them, and that Aqsīs[40] had entered Egypt and blockaded it. They therefore sent to the Franks to invite them to invade Syria, to conquer it and separate them and the [other] Muslims, but God knows best.[41]

The lesson is clear: Syria—meaning all of Syria and not just the Holy Land and Jerusalem—was one of the directions taken by Franks filled with a spirit of conquest and an appetite for power.

Similarly, the capture of Damietta by the armies of the Fifth Crusade provokes a concerned rumination on the double menace now threatening Islam:

> Islam and all its people and its lands were on the point of foundering both in the east and the west. The Tatars[42] had come from the eastern lands and reached districts of Iraq, Azarbayjan, Arran and elsewhere, as we shall narrate, God willing. The Franks came from the west and had conquered a city the like of Damietta in Egypt, not to mention the fact that there were no fortresses to defend the territory from its enemies. Thus all the lands in Egypt and Syria were on the point of being overcome and all the people were fearful of them and had come to expect disaster at any time.[43]

It was external attacks, those of the Franks and the Mongols, as well as internal divisions, which threatened the integrity of the *umma*. As universal history is the history of an Islam which regards itself as being a unified polity the historian must reflect this unity in his writings, no matter how inaccurate the reality.

A cursory examination of *al-Kāmil* demonstrates its annalistic nature, with the material ordered strictly year by year from year 1 of the Hijra. Each year

39 For all medieval Arab writers, *Bilād al-Shām* referred to 'Greater Syria' and encompassed the modern states of Syria, Lebanon, Jordan, Israel and Palestine.

40 Or Atsiz, a Turkoman ruler who had seized Jerusalem in 463/1071, Damascus in 468/1076 and who attacked Egypt the following year.

41 This last notice is particularly interesting. It suggests that negotiations definitely took place between the Fāṭimids and the leaders of the First Crusade while the latter were besieging Antioch, as the Shīʿite ruler of Cairo saw in this alliance a way to resist the Seljūqs. Cf. C. Hillenbrand, *The Crusades. Islamic Perspectives* (Edinburgh, 1999), p. 46.

42 A term used by Arab writers at that time to refer to the Mongols.

43 *Al-Kāmil*, vol. XII, p. 327; tr. Richards, 3, p. 179.

commences with the phrase: *thumma dakhalat sanat...* ('then began the year...') and historical episodes are then reported one after the other, each preceded by a title indicating the general contents and introduced by the phrase *wa fī hadhihi'l-sana* ('and in this year'). Only sometimes does the listing of events reflect the internal chronology of the year when the precise month, or even day, is known; at other times it does not. At the end of each year there is one paragraph, introduced by *dhikr 'iddat ḥawādīth* ('Notice of a Number of Events'), which recount events regarded as of lesser importance, together with a list of those notables who died that year. Here, as an example taken at random, is the list of the notices in the year 543/1148–49:

- Account of the Franks' capture of al-Mahdiyya in Ifrīqiya
- How the Franks besieged Damascus and what Sayf al-Dīn Ghāzī ibn Zankī did
- How Nūr al-Dīn Maḥmūd ibn Zankī took the fortress of al-'Urayma
- The disagreement between Sultan Mas'ūd and several emirs, their coming to Baghdad and what they did in Iraq
- Account of the Franks' defeat at Yaghrā
- How the Ghūr took Ghazna and then withdrew
- How the Franks took some cities in Andalusia
- Miscellaneous events [the death of Abū Bakr al-Mubārak ibn al-Kāmil ibn Abī Ghālib al-Baghdādī; increase of food prices and a famine; others who died during this year].[44]

The advance of Christian troops in al-Andalūs, the siege of Damascus by the armies of the Second Crusade, and the defeat of the Franks at Yaghrā (to the north-east of Antioch) are listed in a factual framework in which they constitute just one aspect of a wide range of notices. The reports of battles and negotiations in which the Latins, as well as other actors, took part are mentioned in an analytical, fragmented, and complex narrative. This is typical of Arabic chronicles from this period: while there are large numbers of Arabic chronicles which cover the crusading period in some way, none of them are devoted to the history of the Crusades, their formation, their development, or the destruction of the Latin states, and none even to the jihad battles led by the rulers of Syria and Egypt against the Franks. There are no extant 'Arab chronicles of the Crusades'; instead the Crusades—which is, after all, a western construction and concept—are treated in a scattered manner in works which have their general framework devoted to something else. It is no different for *al-Kāmil*.

44 *Al-Kāmil*, vol. XI, pp. 125–37; tr. Richards, 2, pp. 18–26. The titles are those which Ibn al-Athīr gave to these different sections.

In the introduction, Ibn al-Athīr warns his reader that he will diverge from this annalistic framework if it is necessary to aid comprehension of the events described.[45] Such is the case with some reports relating to single, and very short, subjects, which do not benefit by being narrated across a number of years. Yet this occurs more frequently when the division of the account of one episode across several years would affect the reader's understanding of the chain of events. Thus, the narrative of the Fifth Crusade is placed wholly under the year 614/1217: 'The crisis from its beginning until its end [the arrival of the Franks in Syria, their capture of Damietta, the Ayyūbid victory at Manṣūra, and the reconquest of Damietta by the Muslims] lasted four years, less one month. We have mentioned it here because this was the year they made their appearance [in Syria] and we have made an unbroken narrative of it so that its various parts can follow one another'.[46]

Equally, it sometimes happens that Ibn al-Athīr fails to respect the chronological order within a year, again for the purpose of coherence. Thus, he places the report of a victory of Ṭughril over troops sent by al-Nāṣir, which had taken place on the 8th of Rabīʿ I/7th May 1188, at the end of the year 584/February 1189 in order to not interrupt the long narrative of the campaigns of Saladin during that year. He explains, 'by rights this account should have come earlier but we delayed it so that previous events could be recorded in succession, one after the other, because they are all interconnected'.[47]

This annalistic framework precludes the writing of history purely with the aim of reaching any real conclusions. Even a cataclysmic event such as the Mongol invasions—which Ibn al-Athīr describes under the year 617/1220 as 'the calamity whose sparks flew far and wide and whose damage was all-embracing'[48]—does not have any real eschatological overtones. Ibn al-Athīr's universal history finished in 628/1230–31, although certain manuscripts carry the title of the following year, 629/1231–32,[49] which leads to the possibility that the historian would have continued his work if he had been able. He sees time (*zamān*) as a linear process in which his own era (*waqt*) is only an instant, with no particular importance: 'I give [in this work] reports of events (*ḥawādith*) and of things which have occurred (*kāʾināt*) from the beginning of time (*awwal*

45 *Al-Kāmil*, vol. I, p. 4.
46 *Al-Kāmil*, vol. XII, p. 320; tr. Richards, 3, p. 174.
47 *Al-Kāmil*, vol. XII, p. 26; tr. Richards, 2, p. 358.
48 *Al-Kāmil*, vol. XII, p. 359; tr. Richards, 3, p. 202.
49 This addition is not in the Beirut (1965–67) edition, but is found in that of Tornberg, vol. XII, p. 330.

al-zamān), one after the other, up to our own time (*waqt*)'.[50] For Ibn al-Athīr, the historian's task is first and foremost to assign to the events their proper place in the course of time, as is illustrated by this notice, slipped in at the end of the year 560/1164-65: 'when he told me this story (*ḥikāya*), I did not ask him about the date (*ta'rīkh*). It was certainly in this period (*mudda*) in this area and so I have recorded (*athbat*) it under this year by plausible guesswork'.[51] This linear conception prevents all attempts at periodisation (for example by dynasty) as can be found in the works of Christian authors (Bar Hebraeus, for example), or Ibn Khaldūn. But this linear conception is used by Ibn al-Athīr for a specific purpose: in order to establish a chain of events.

Ibn al-Athīr often begins the report of an important event with a flashback which he introduces with the words *wa-sabab dhalika* 'the cause of which [was]'. One example among many is: 'In Shawwāl [593/August–September 1197] al-ʿĀdil Abū Bakr ibn Ayyūb conquered Jaffa on the Syrian coast, which was in the hands of the Franks—God curse them! This came about as follows (*wa-sabab dhalika*)'.[52] The historian then briefly recalls the treaty concluded by Saladin which left Jaffa to the Franks, the renewing of that treaty by al-Malik al-ʿAzīz, the actions of the emir of Beirut, the organisation of a new Crusade by the German Emperor Henry VI, the mobilisation by al-ʿĀdil of an army which retook and demolished Jaffa, and the late arrival of the Franks due to the announcement of the death of Henry. From this sequence it can be seen that Ibn al-Athīr means a cause less in the sense of a rational explanation, than as part of a chain of events leading up to the reported happening.[53] Etymologically *sabab* means a cord or a link, and this is what is meant by a sequence of history, with the events reported being considered as links in a chain.

Ibn al-Athīr aims to be concise in his writing: in the introduction he criticises authors whose numerous works of history he has read and found to be too verbose: they blacken their pages by relating things of no interest in his eyes, such as the delivery of a robe of honour to a *dhimmī*, the increase in the price of food, or the veneration or contempt in which someone was held.[54] Ibn al-Athīr here describes his predecessors by the term *mu'arrīkh*, and he seems to be, along with his contemporary Yāqūt, the first to use such a term. In the

50 *Al-Kāmil*, vol. I, p. 2.

51 *Al-Kāmil*, vol. XI, p. 320; tr. Richards, 2, p. 159 (this refers to a Nizārī raid on Qazwīn).

52 *Al-Kāmil*, vol. XII, p. 126; tr. Richards, 3, p. 28.

53 For this reason Richards usually translates the expression *wa-sabab dhalika* as 'this came about as follows'.

54 *Al-Kāmil*, vol. I, p. 2.

first centuries of Islam the authors of historical texts were designated by other terms, such as *akhbāriyyūn, nassābūn* and *aṣḥāb al-siyar wa'l-aḥdāth.*[55] It can be supposed that this use of the term *mu'arrīkh* reveals a break from the transmission of history in the mode of *akhbār*.

Thus, in effect, Ibn al-Athīr breaks with the mode of employing the historical methodology of the traditionist (hadith scholar) which had been that of al-Ṭabarī and which many of his contemporaries, Ibn 'Asākir and Ibn al-'Adīm among others, followed. Al-Ṭabarī—Ibn al-Athīr writes in his introduction—'mentioned for most of the events (*ḥawādith*) described many different versions (*riwāyāt*), each one being similar to the preceding, or more concise, sometimes adding or omitting some tiny thing. I aim to complete these versions, I have transcribed them and added what had been omitted, placing each thing in its place. Thus all [that which concerns] this event, despite the diversity of opinions [about it], has become one unique narrative'.[56] His purpose is thus to give just one single report. If he sometimes reports multiple versions of the same event, it is only because it has proved impossible for him to do so, meaning that in general the history he wrote is merely his personal synthesis of all the reports he received, and in this way differs from most previous Arabic historical texts. Examples of the juxtaposition of differing versions are very rare[57] and the narrative of *al-Kāmil* is thus very fluid. Ibn al-Athīr does not copy his sources word for word, but chooses them, summarises them, even rewrites them, and, exceptionally, critiques them.[58] Consequently, he judges it improper to give the *isnād*s of texts that he does not copy. This remarkable work of recomposition explains the fact, for which he has often been criticised, that he does not specify his sources, even if he does occasionally mention a name.

---

55 A. Cheddadi, *Les Arabes et l'appropriation de l'histoire* (Arles, 2004), pp. 70ff.

56 *Al-Kāmil*, vol. I, p. 3.

57 Some examples of this include the capture of Kurdish-held fortresses by Zengī (*al-Kāmil*, vol. XI, pp. 14–15; tr. Richards, 1, pp. 306–8), the defeat of the sultan Sanjar by the Qarā-Khiṭāy Turks in 536/1141-42 (*al-Kāmil*, vol. XI, pp. 81–86; tr. Richards, 1, pp. 359–63), and the eventful reign of the Khwārizmshāh Sultān-Shāh (*al-Kāmil*, vol. XI, pp. 377–85; tr. Richards, 2, pp. 203–9).

58 With regard to the size of Sayf al-Dīn Ghāzī's armies, Ibn al Athīr criticises 'Imād al-Dīn (on a rare occasion where he mentions his source) who, in *al-Barq al-Shāmī*, says that Saladin defeated the 20,000 horsemen of Sayf al-Dīn with only 6,000 riders. Ibn al Athīr judges this figure to be exaggerated, as he saw the list of troops who took part (which amounted to between 6,000 and 6,500, he says), and adds the important comments that the intention of 'Imād al-Dīn was clearly to magnify the success of his master (*al-Kāmil*, vol. XI, p. 429; tr. Richards, 2, p. 242).

Modern historians have nonetheless attempted to establish which works Ibn al-Athīr used.[59] For the history of Syria and the struggle led by the Muslim rulers of the region against the Franks during the first decades of the Crusades Ibn al-Athīr is primarily based on the chronicle of Ibn al-Qalānisī (d. 555/1160) and, for the time of Saladin, on *al-Barq al-Shāmī* by ʿImād al-Dīn al-Iṣfahānī (d. 597/1201). Hamilton Gibb, in his two studies, one of which compared Ibn al-Athīr and Ibn al-Qalānisī, the other Ibn al-Athīr and ʿImād al-Dīn, declared that *al-Kāmil* never brings anything new in relation to these sources and that he should only be used as secondary material for the history of the Crusades.[60] He reproached Ibn al-Athīr for changing earlier reports, for making mistakes, and even of inventing facts when he gives complementary information. For example, the historian of Mosul is the only one (along with Ibn al-Furāt) who mentions, at the time of the attack on Damascus by the Franks in 523/1129, secret negotiations between Baldwin II and the city's Ismāʿīlīs. For Gibb, 'the story, though not impossible, seems to be nothing more than romantic invention'.[61] Jean-Michel Mouton, in his study of Būrid Damascus, considers that 'ce marché [...] fut bien réel car après le massacre des ismaïliens de Damas la ville de Bāniyas fut livrée par des partisans de la secte aux Francs; ce qui témoigne pour le moins de rapports étroits'.[62]

This example suggests that far from simply using well-known written works, Ibn al-Athīr made use of other sources—both written and oral—and consequently he sometimes gives information which is absent both from the sources known to have been used by him and from other chronicles which have survived. As Claude Cahen wrote in his remarkable analysis of sources which opens his study of the Principality of Antioch: '[Il reste] bien d'autres passages dont il n'y a nulle part de parallèle et dont par conséquent l'origine est tout à fait obscure. C'est dire qu'il nous faut nous résoudre à utiliser Ibn al-Athīr

59 The most comprehensive investigation of this was conducted by ul-Hasan, *Ibn al-Athīr*. For the history of the Crusades, see also C. Cahen, *La Syrie du Nord à l'époque des croisades et la Principauté franque d'Antioche* (Paris, 1940), pp. 58–60; H.A.R. Gibb, 'Notes on the Arabic Materials for the History of the Early Crusades', *Bulletin of the School of Oriental and African Studies* 7 (1935), 739–54; idem, 'The Arabic Sources for the Life of Saladin', *Speculum* 25 (1950), 58–72.

60 See the above note. This position was also taken by F. Gabrieli, 'The Arab Historiography of the Crusades', in B. Lewis and P.M. Holt (eds), *Historians of the Middle East*, (London, 1962), 98–107, p. 103.

61 Gibb, 'Notes on the Arabic Materials', p. 752.

62 J.-M. Mouton, *Damas et sa principauté sous les Saljoukides et les Bourides (468–549/1076–1154). Vie politique et religieuse* (Cairo, 1994), p. 55 and n. 18.

comme une source originale'.[63] It can be added that this originality comes in part from oral information that the historian received from direct witnesses.[64]

One of the fundamental qualities of Ibn al-Athīr's text is his offering of a clear, ordered, coherent, concise, rich, and balanced summary of events. It is written in fine and lively prose which makes substantial use of dialogue, although this must be recognised as having been largely invented. On the other hand there is little room for poetry, anecdotes and literary flourishes, unlike in works of history which relate to *adab* literature, such as *Murūj al-dhahab* by al-Mas'ūdī or *al-Fatḥ al-qussī* by 'Imād al-Dīn al-Iṣfahānī. Because of its character—ample in content and concise in expression—this universal history was widely disseminated and utilised. Numerous later historians such as Sibṭ Ibn al-Jawzī, Ibn Wāsil, Ibn al-'Adīm, Bar Hebraeus, al-Yūnīnī and al-Nuwayrī all make references to *al-Kāmil*. And, in the ninth/fifteenth century, Ibn Ḥajar al-'Asqalānī affirmed: '[It] is the best of all histories in recording the happenings clearly and distinctly ... In addition, [the work] is well organized and [from the stylistic point of view] skilfully executed ... It therefore occured to me to write a supplement to it, from the year in which [Ibn al-Athīr] stopped, namely the year 628/1230-1'.[65] Interest in this universal history has never wavered, as the statement of a Dutch orientalist, who stayed in Mecca in 1884, demonstrates: 'the famous world history of Ibn al-Athīr was to be found in the libraries of some of the learned [of the city]'.[66]

Al-Ta'rīkh al-bāhir fi'l-dawlat al-atābakiyya, A History of the Zengids

Ibn al-Athīr wrote *al-Ta'rīkh al-bāhir fi'l-dawlat al-atābakiyya* ('The Dazzling History of the Atabeg State') for 'Izz al-Dīn Mas'ūd II, who ruled at Mosul from 607/1211 to 615/1218. While *al-Kāmil* is not addressed to any particular ruler—Ibn al-Athīr writes in the introduction that he wrote it due to his personal interest in history and only dedicated it to Badr al-Dīn Lu'lu' after he had completed

63 Cahen, *La Syrie du Nord*, p. 60.

64 For example, 'a Muslim dwelling in Ḥiṣn al-Akrād, one of the soldiers of its rulers who in former times surrendered it to the Franks, told me his tale' (*al-Kāmil*, vol. XII, p. 32; tr. Richards, 2, p. 364).

65 This is cited by al-Sakhāwī in *al-I'lān bi'l-tawbīkh li-man dhamma ahl al-ta'rīkh*, tr. F. Rosenthal, *A History of Muslim Historiography*, 2nd ed. (Leiden, 1968), p. 491. It should be noted that Ibn Ḥajar al-'Asqalānī (m. 852/1449) never carried out this project.

66 C.S. Hurgronje, *Mekka* (The Hague, 1888); English tr. as *Mekka in the Latter Part of the 19th Century*, 2 vols (Leiden-London, 1931; repr. Leiden, 1970), p. 164.

it—he wrote *al-Bāhir* for the Zengid ruler in order to highlight the merits of his forefathers to him and to urge him to imitate their conduct, and as a witness to his gratitude towards Masʿūd's father Nūr al-Dīn Arslān Shāh I, who had given him his benefits and rewarded him with various favours.[67] This work did not have the same popularity as *al-Kāmil*, as it is preserved in only one manuscript, of relatively late date, which is lacking a title and the name of the author, and is full of faults. However, Abū Shāma cites large extracts from it in his *Kitāb al-rawḍatayn fī akhbār al-dawlatayn*, which has allowed the text to be corrected. It has been reproduced and translated into French in the *Recueil des Historiens des Croisades*[68] and a good edition was published in Cairo[69] where the variations between the manuscript and the citations in other works are indicated in the footnotes.

In this work Ibn al-Athīr relates the history of the Zengid dynasty from its origins until the taking of power by ʿIzz al-Dīn Masʿūd II in 607/1211. The work is clearly organised, with short chapters of several pages in length, each of which carries a title, and each of which deals with important events in a chronological order, although this is not year by year as in *al-Kāmil*. The narrative focusses on the deeds of the Zengid rulers of Mosul and Aleppo, although he inserts reports on other events which had an impact on the history of the Zengids, such as the reigns of the ʿAbbāsid caliphs, the rivalries between the Seljūqs,[70] the siege of Damascus by the Second Crusade, and the fall of the Fāṭimids and the taking of power by Saladin. The Crusades and the Latin states appear solely among the rollcall of campaigns led by Zengī and Nūr al-Dīn, and Ibn al-Athīr explicitly asks the reader to refer to *al-Kāmil* for all the other events which took place. Thus, he writes, after having mentioned the rivalries between the sons of the Seljūq sultan Malik Shāh: 'It was during these battles that the Franks appeared in the Levant and captured Antioch, then other [towns] of the regions. We have written of this in great detail in *al-Mustaqṣā fi'l-ta'rīkh*'.[71]

67 *Al-Bāhir*, p. 1.

68 RHC *Or.* vol. II, pp. 5–375.

69 See above, note 13.

70 However, he explicitly states that he will not relate all the rivalries between the Seljūq princes, but only those in which Zengī participated, so as to not deviate from his main purpose in writing; *al-Bāhir*, p. 43.

71 *Al-Bāhir*, p. 12. It has been noted above that *al-Mustaqṣā fi'l-ta'rīkh* was the original title of *al-Kāmil*.

The pro-Zengid character[72] of *al-Bāhir* appears clearly in the long eulogising descriptions of Zengī (521–41/1127–46) and Nūr al-Dīn (541–69/1146–74). As these rulers engaged in the fight against the Latin states, Ibn al-Athīr exalts (and exaggerates) their role as champions of the jihad in these passages. Thus, after having described in shocking detail all the calamities inflicted by the Franks on the Muslims, he announces the arrival of Zengī, a providential man called to fight them:

> [God] took pity on Islam and his people. Outraged at seeing them oppressed, killed, or thrown into captivity, He resolved to do the same to the Franks and to send on these demons of the cross a fighter [lit. a projectile] who would destroy them and make them vanish. Having seen the small number of brave troops who had attached themselves to him and the band of cautious and decided men who were devoted to him, he saw only *al-mawlā al-shahīd* ʿImād al-Dīn Zengī as worthy and capable of this task.[73]

Throughout the many pages devoted to the great deeds of Zengī, Ibn al-Athīr consistently calls him a *shahīd*, 'martyr'; however, this revered title, given to those fighters who died in battle with the (usually non-Muslim) enemy, is usurped for his own ends by Ibn al-Athīr because in reality Zengī was killed in his tent by one of his own slaves while in a drunken stupor.[74]

After the death of Nūr al-Dīn it was by Saladin, who had become the ruler of Egypt and Syria, that the honour of leading the jihad was taken. The Zengid princes, withdrawing into the Jazīra and undermined by internal conflict, no longer played any role in the fight against the Franks. Ibn al-Athīr deliberately, and rather skilfully, left out all the deeds of Saladin after he had taken possession of Damascus in 570/1174. Saladin's expeditions into northern Syria and the Jazīra are recounted in just a few lines and his victories over the Franks passed over in silence. The years from 579/1183 to 607/1211, in which the Zengids had little reason to celebrate, are dealt with in a few pages and limited to references to the rulers of Mosul and some of their military endeavours; there is almost no reference either to Saladin or his Ayyūbid successors. However, in the eulogy

72 On the clearly pro-Zengid nature of *al-Bāhir*, see D.S. Richards, 'Some Consideration of Ibn al-Athīr's *al-Tāʾrīkh al-Bāhir* and its relationship to the *Kāmil*', in C.V. de Benito and M.A. Manzano Rodríguez (eds), *Actas XVI Congreso UEAI* (Salamanca, 1995), 443–46.

73 *Al-Bāhir*, p. 33.

74 It must be noted that in *al-Kāmil*, Ibn al-Athīr constantly refers to *al-atābak* Zengī rather than *al-shahīd* Zengī, as in *al-Bāhir*. The title *al-shahīd* only appears once in *al-Kāmil*, in the section referring to his assassination; *al-Kāmil*, vol. XI, p. 110; tr. Richards, I, p. 382.

for Nūr al-Dīn Arslān Shāh I on which the work ends, Ibn al-Athīr does not hesitate to highlight the merits of the Ayyūbid sultan al-Malik al-ʿĀdil,[75] writing that he was at that point 'master of Egypt, Syria, the Jazīra, Armenia and part of Diyār Bakr', and had considered the prince of Mosul to be his main rival, against whom he was often waging war. Ibn al-Athīr writes: 'If God had not come to our aid by frequently sending illnesses upon him, we would not have been able to resist him'. On learning of Nūr al-Dīn Arslān Shāh's death, Ibn al-Athīr suggests that the sultan would have cried: 'The one whom we feared is gone!'. Here the historian has become a courtier, altering the historical reality for his own ends, inventing a speech by the famous Ayyūbid sultan to embellish the standing of the subject of his panegyric.

Despite its less than impartial character, this history of the Zengids is highly important for the information it provides because Ibn al-Athīr relied heavily upon the recollections of his father—which he clearly states in the introduction and to which he explicitly refers on numerous occasions[76]—those of his brother Majd al-Dīn[77] and a large number of other eyewitnesses. When *al-Bāhir* and *al-Kāmil* relate the same events, for example the capture of Edessa by Zengī or the siege of Damascus by the armies of the Second Crusade, the reports are similar, but more detailed in *al-Bāhir* and much more inclined to underline the glory of the Zengids. In another significant difference, Ibn al-Athīr gladly exaggerates his narrative or adds anecdotes or poems, both of which were part of the propaganda deployed by Zengī and, much more so, by Nūr al-Dīn to legitimise their conquests in northern Syria and the Jazīra. As the editor writes, in *al-Kāmil* Ibn al-Athīr adopts 'the style of the historian who is more concerned with the historical material than with effective and artistic language […] whereas in the *Bāhir* he united the historian with the *adīb* (one who writes with a high literary style)'.[78]

Ibn al-Athīr's View of the Franks

When referring to those people whom Western historians commonly call 'Franks', 'Latins' or similar, Ibn al-Athīr, like all Arab chroniclers, consistently uses the term *al-Franj*. In Arabic geographical literature this word refers to the

75 *Al-Bāhir*, p. 200.

76 *Al-Bāhir*, p. 4.

77 On the other hand, he never cites his other brother, Ḍiyā al-Dīn, which leads to the question of whether there was some sort of rivalry between these two men.

78 *Al-Bāhir*, p. 4, cited and examined by Richards, 'Ibn al-Athīr and the Later Parts of the *Kāmil*', p. 91.

inhabitants of territories approximating the former Carolingian empire, the region of western Europe across the Mediterranean little known by the inhabitants of the Near East.[79] As a large number of the men of the First Crusade actually were Franks, the term was logically applied to them, and it naturally came to refer to all the crusaders regardless of geographic origin or language. Thus, when Ibn al-Athīr relates the siege of Damascus by the Second Crusade in *al-Kāmil* he calls the Emperor Conrad III 'the king of the Germans' and refers to the troops under his command as 'the Franks'.[80] Relating the same episode in *al-Bāhir*, he writes that 'the King of the Germans left the country of the Franks' and adds that these Germans are 'a sub-division (*naw'*)of the Franks who exceed the [other] Franks in number, size of their country and extent of possessions'.[81] The same term is also applied to the Latins permanently installed in the Middle East, which sometimes leads Ibn al-Athīr to refer to them as 'the Levantine Franks' (*al-Franj al-sāliḥiyya*) or 'the Franks of Syria' (*al-Franj bi'l-Shām*). There is also mention of 'Frankish territory' (*bilād al-Franj*) in Syria, meaning the crusader states. For example, he writes that Shirkūh left Syria for Egypt overland 'leaving Frankish territory on his right'.[82]

As for the Arabic term *naṣrānī* which is used to refer to Christians, it is reserved solely for Eastern Christians,[83] whose various churches existed before the Islamic conquests of the first/seventh century and whose members held *dhimmī* (protected) status in Islamic territory. Franks and Christians thus represent two distinct groups who did not have the same legal-religious status in *dār al-Islām*, and this is reflected in Ibn al-Athīr's writings. An example of this can be found during the siege of Jabala by Godfrey of Bouillon, when the *qāḍī* of the city 'agreed with the local[84] Christians that they should communicate with the Franks and promised them the surrender of one of the city's towers and the capture of the city'.[85] The Franks are also clearly distinguished from the Byzantines, who are called *al-Rūm*; this transposition of the word for 'Roman' into Arabic was a common way of referring to the inhabitants of the Eastern Roman Empire.

79 See the section referring to the Franks in A. Miquel, *La géographie humaine du monde musulman jusqu'au milieu de 11e siècle* (Paris-The Hague, 1973), pp. 354ff.
80 *Al-Kāmil*, vol. XI, p. 129; tr. Richards, 2, p. 21.
81 *Al-Bāhir*, p. 88.
82 *Al-Kāmil*, vol. XI, p. 324; tr. Richards, 2, p. 163.
83 Except rare exceptions in *al-Bāhir*.
84 For the sake of clarity, the translator added the 'local' adjective, which is not in the Arabic.
85 *Al-Kāmil*, vol. X, pp. 310–11; tr. Richards, 1, p. 39.

In very rare passages (a dozen at most in *al-Kāmil*), the term 'Franks' is followed by a formula such as 'God curse them!'[86] or 'May God Almighty forsake them!'.[87] Sometimes this also occurs when speaking of a Latin prince, for example '[Raymond of] St.-Gilles the Frank (God curse him!) had met Qilij Arslān . . .'.[88] Such curses are much more common in other Arabic chronicles, and in Ibn al-Athīr's writings they do not seem to be employed in any specific context; it may be that his sporadic use of such curses can be explained by his use of direct quotations from earlier authors.

Other appellations, such as 'infidels' (*al-kāfirūn*) and 'polytheists' (*al-mushriqūn*), are also rare in *al-Kāmil*.[89] On the other hand, in *al-Bāhir* the long panegyrics on the achievements of Zengī and Nūr al-Dīn are often accompanied by derogatory comments. The Franks are not only stigmatised as polytheists and infidels, but also labelled 'demon worshippers of the cross'[90] or 'the worshipers of idols and the cultists of the cross' over whom Zengī 'had determined that he would . . . make the people of Truth rule',[91] using vocabulary which is itself part of the jihad propaganda developed by the rulers of Syria.[92] It was thus internal Muslim politics surrounding the propagation of jihad propaganda and, even more, the exaltation of jihad fighters such as Zengī and Nūr al-Dīn, more than any real understanding on the part of the Arab author of the ideas and beliefs of the Franks, which led Ibn al-Athīr to present the Franks in terms of religious opposition using mechanisms of reciprocal exclusion.

For Ibn al-Athīr, the Franks were primarily invaders animated with warlike ambitions and desire for conquest, often showing great bravery.[93] Once permanently settled in Syria they were to remain enemies against whom Muslim rulers had a duty to fight in order to recover lost Muslim territories, although these new players who entered the Levant would come to participate fully in the local political manoeuvring in which the protagonists were many.

Of these fighters from across the seas, Ibn al-Athīr knows little and does not wish to better understand them. He knows that they come to the East to

---

86 See the passage about the conquest of Jaffa in 593/1197 above, note 52.

87 See below, the story of the great campaign by Saladin during the summer 583/1187, note 126.

88 *Al-Kāmil*, vol. x, p. 343; tr. Richards, 1, p. 59.

89 There is only one single example of each of these throughout *al-Kāmil*: *al-Kāmil*, vol. x, p. 663; tr. Richards, 1, p. 283; *al-Kāmil*, vol. xi, p. 455; tr. Richards, 2, p. 264.

90 *Al-Bāhir*, p. 33; see above, p. 70, for a translation of the whole the passage.

91 *Al-Bāhir*, p. 39.

92 See E. Sivan, *L'Islam et la croisade* (Paris, 1968).

93 For example, 'The Franks held firm, relying on their bravery': *al-Kāmil*, vol. x, p. 425; tr. Richards, 1, p. 114.

fight, to go on pilgrimage to Jerusalem and to trade.[94] On several occasions he alludes to the role of the Pope, who he says is the leader of the Franks: 'The Franks also received a letter from the pope (*bābā*), who is their leader, whose commands they follow and whose word is like the word of the prophets, not to be gainsaid'.[95] The reports of fighting and negotiations in which the Latins were often participants leads Ibn al-Athīr to give appraisals, although not always precise or accurate, on some of the Latin princes. For example,

> One of those killed [during Nūr al-Dīn's victory over the Antiochene Franks in 544/1149] was the Prince, lord of Antioch [Raymond of Poitiers, whom Ibn al-Athīr refers to as *al-brins*—the Prince—being ignorant of his name]. He was one of the most intransigent of the Franks and one of their great leaders. After his death his son, Bohemond, who was still a child, succeeded. His mother married a second prince [Reynald of Châtillon, whom Ibn al-Athīr does not name] to rule the land until her son grew up. He remained with her in Antioch.[96]
>
> It chanced that Amaury, king of the Franks (God curse him) had died at the beginning of this year [570/1174–75].[97] He was one of the bravest of their kings, the most outstanding for policy, cunning and intrigue. At his death he left a leper son, who was incapable of ruling. The Franks made him king in name with no substance to his position. The conduct of affairs was undertaken by Count Raymond with power of loosing and binding, whose command all followed.[98]

In a few passages Ibn al-Athīr reports the pious beliefs of the Franks which, in his eyes, have no credibility, and which are no more than superstition. The discovery of the Holy Lance during the siege of Antioch by Kerboghā is presented as a hoax orchestrated by a monk who had concealed the so-called relic in the city's main Church himself.[99] The importance to the Franks of the True Cross is highlighted when this relic was lost on the battlefield of Ḥaṭṭīn:

94 See, for example, *al-Kāmil*, vol. X, p. 479; tr. Richards, 1, p. 152; and vol. X, p. 657; tr. Richards, 1, p. 278.

95 *Al-Kāmil*, vol. XII, p. 53; tr. Richards, 2, p. 378. See also *al-Kāmil*, vol. XII, p. 465; tr. Richards, 3, p. 280, where the Pope is referred to as 'the leader of the Franks' (*malik al-Franj*).

96 *Al-Kāmil*, vol. XI, p. 144; tr. Richards, 2, p. 31.

97 Amaury died of typhus on July 11, 1174.

98 *Al-Kāmil*, vol. XI, p. 419; tr. Richards, 2, p. 234.

99 *Al-Kāmil*, vol. X, p. 277; tr. Richards, 1, p. 16.

> The Muslims captured their great cross which they call the True Cross (*ṣalib al-ṣalbūt*, literally 'the cross of the crucifixion'), claiming that it contains a part of the wooden structure on which the Messiah (on him be peace) was crucified, as they assert. The seizure of it was one of their greatest misfortunes, after which they were sure they were doomed to death and destruction.[100]

In the long narrative of the reconquest of Jerusalem by Saladin, Ibn al-Athīr reported a detail which shows the Franks' particular devotion to these holy places:

> The Franks had laid a marble pavement above the Rock and covered it over. This he [Saladin] ordered to be uncovered. The reason why it had been paved over was that the priests sold much of it to the Franks who came to them from overseas on pilgrimage (*li-ziyārat*). They would buy it for its weight in gold, hoping to benefit from its sanctity. When one of them returned to his homeland with a little piece of it he would build a church for it and place it on its altar. One of their kings feared that it would be all lost, so he ordered it to be paved over to preserve it.[101]

Later, Ibn al-Athīr describes the propaganda deployed following the reconquest of Jerusalem by Saladin:

> The monks, priests and a large number of their noble and knights donned black and declared their grief at the loss of Jerusalem. The patriarch, who had been in Jerusalem, brought them together and took them into the Frankish lands to travel around with them as they sought the people's aid and succour and urged them to take vengeance for Jerusalem. They portrayed the Messiah (peace be upon Him) along with an Arab, depicted as beating him. They put blood on the portrait of the Messiah and said to people, "This is the Messiah with Muḥammad, the prophet of the Muslims, beating him. He has wounded and slain Him".
>
> The Franks were much distressed …
>
> A certain Frankish captive told me that he was his mother's only son. They possessed no wordly goods other than a house which she sold and

100 *Al-Kāmil*, vol. XI, p. 536; tr. Richards, 2, pp. 322–23.
101 *Al-Kāmil*, vol. XI, p. 552; tr. Richards, 2, p. 334.

> used the purchase money to equip him and send him to free [Jerusalem] and that he was taken prisoner. This is an extreme example of the religious and spiritual motivation that the Franks had.[102]

Yet apart from these few passages, which are designed primarily to enrich the story and provide additional explanation, Ibn al-Athīr does not show any particular interest in the culture and religion of the Franks. This finding is not surprising; he was writing a chronicle which, above all, aims to report the achievements of the Muslim rulers from a political perspective. When the Franks arrived from the West and took up residence in Syria, they became first and foremost aggressors who threatened *dār al-Islām*, enemies encountered almost exclusively, to him at least, in the course of conflict, either on battlefields or during sieges.

A Political Writing of History

At the end of his introduction to *al-Kāmil* Ibn al-Athīr enumerates the merits of historical writing, and thereby also responds to detractors who consider the discipline frivolous. Its central argument is the usefulness of history for rulers:

> Furthermore, kings and persons in authority may find the biographies of oppressors and tyrants treated in books which circulate among the people and which are transmitted from generation to generation. They look at the ill fame and disgrace that were the consequence of oppression and tyranny, the resulting destruction of countries and human lives, the financial loss and the general corruption. Thus, they come to disapprove of and avoid practices of oppression and injustice. Likewise, they may see the biographies of just governors. They read about the good reputation that survived them after their death, and the development and financial prosperity of their countries and realms. Thus, they come to approve of their example and to desire to practice permanently what they did as well to omit all that works to the contrary. Kings and persons in authority derive an additional advantage from the study of history.[103]

102 *Al-Kāmil*, vol. XII, pp. 32–33; tr. Richards, 2, pp. 363–64.

103 *Al-Kāmil*, vol. I, p. 7. The translation cited here is from Rosenthal, *A History of Muslim Historiography*, p. 298 (which is itself taken from the citation of the introduction of *al-Kāmil* by al-Sakhāwī in *al-Iʿlān bi'l-tawbīkh li-man dhamma ahl al-taʾrīkh*).

In history's role as a means of guidance for rulers one significant anecdote provides a useful example. Majd al-Dawla, the governor of Rayy, had been taken prisoner by Maḥmūd of Ghazna. The latter called for him and asked him: '"Have you read the *Shāh-nāma*, which is the history (*ta'rīkh*) of the Persians?" "Yes". "And the *Ta'rīkh* of al-Ṭabarī, which is the history (*ta'rīkh*) of the Muslims?" "Yes". Maḥmūd then retorted: "Yet your conduct is not that of a man who has read these [books]" '.[104] History as a source of examplars for rulers is not a new idea; it had already been formulated in some detail by Miskawayh (d. 421/1030).[105] Ibn al-Athīr follows this ideal by giving *al-Kāmil* a function which can be described as ethico-political, and which is related to the long tradition of 'Mirrors for Princes' works.[106] These belong to the genres of moral works (enumeration of virtues), history (biographies of kings as models for behaviour), and political science (the portrait of the just king and of his good government), and so writing works of history as 'Mirrors for Princes' is part of the duty of *naṣīḥa*, counsel, which a subject can give the ruler.[107] Al-Harawī, whom Ibn al-Athīr may have known—as this Sufi of Shīʿī orientation, who led an ascetic existence which ended with his death in Aleppo in 611/1215, was originally from Mosul—wrote two small tracts on goverment for al-Ẓāhir Ghāzī.[108] His recommendations on how to administer with justice and to lead the war with effectiveness were suffused with political realism: 'Treating your subjects well is better than assembling troops'.[109]

Thus, far from just being a rhetorical argument suggested at the beginning of *al-Kāmil*, the principle of offering a ruler examples to follow guided Ibn al-Athīr in his writing. In this spirit, he introduces the image of Nūr al-Dīn

---

104 *Al-Kāmil*, vol. IX, pp. 371–72.

105 See M. Arkoun, 'Éthique et histoire d'après les Tajārib al-umam', in his *Essais sur la pensée islamique* (Paris, 1973), 51–86.

106 This term has been used in the modern age (it first appeared in 1902 as the German phrase 'Fürstenspiegel') to denote treatises whose objective was to describe the ideal ruler, particularly his role and conduct. Numerous texts, both in Arabic and Persian, are part of this literary genre; Cf. L. Marlow, 'Advice and Advice Literature', in *EI3*.

107 See C.E. Bosworth, 'Naṣīḥat al-Mulūk', in *EI2*.

108 Al-Harawī, *al-Tadhkira al-Harawiyya fi'l-ḥiyal al-ḥarbiyya*, ed. and tr. J. Sourdel-Thomine in 'Les conseils du šayḫ al-Harawī à un prince ayyoubide', *Bulletin d'Études Orientales* 17 (1961–1962), 205–66; idem, *al-Wasiyya al-Harawiyya*, ed. and tr. in J. Sourdel-Thomine, 'Le testament politique du shaikh 'Alī al-Harawī', in G. Makdisi (ed.), *Arabic and Islamic Studies in Honour of Hamilton A.R. Gibb*, (Leiden, 1965), 609–18. Al-Harawī's best-known work is his pilgrimage guide, *Kitāb al-ishārāt ilā maʿrifat al-ziyārāt*, ed. J. Sourdel-Thomine as *Guide des lieux de pèlerinage* (Damascus, 1953–57).

109 Sourdel-Thomine, 'Les conseils du šayḫ al-Harawī', p. 219.

Maḥmūd in 'the hope that those who wield authority will peruse it and take him as their model'.[110] History is a source of examplars for princes to ruminate on, and they are exhorted to follow rules of behaviour which assure prosperity, justice and victory. Because the historian considers caliphs, sultans, kings, princes, governors and emirs as actors on the stage of history, accounting for their military and political successes, he gives a central place to their actions and deeds to the point that the narrative, as in the majority of medieval chronicles, essentially becomes limited to the political and military. The images with which he often accompanies the announcement of their death reveal as much a code of thought as a precise picture of their character. The eulogies underline the moral and religious virtues of the deceased and, moreover, the qualities of good government which they displayed: justice, simplicity, courage, magnanimousness, discernment, and evergetism. These values are themselves those which are highlighted in 'pure' Mirrors for Princes works, such as the *Treatise on Government* by the late 11th-century Seljūq vizier Niẓām al-Mulk,[111] and as such represent a 'royal model'. The religious aspect, through the ruler's own piety, is not absent, but is of only secondary concern; the writers never tried to sketch a sacred or divine, still less a theocratic, character to the figures.[112] Taking this political dimension into consideration can provide insights into one of the most debated questions surrounding the writings of Ibn al-Athīr: his attitude towards Saladin.

It has often been claimed that Ibn al-Athīr was markedly biased in favour of the Zengids and, consequently, was unduly harsh on Saladin. Thus, for Gibb, Ibn al-Athīr's position in a family of scholars in the service of the Zengids made the historian of Mosul 'the devil's advocate', with his works reflecting the hostility of the milieux of northern Syria and the Jazīra towards Saladin, whose ambitions ran counter to those of the Zengids.[113] This theory, which has been often repeated by, among others, Gabrieli, must be revised. Certainly, one cannot find within Ibn al-Athīr's writings any very intense pro-Saladin propa-

110 *Al-Kāmil*, vol. XI, p. 403; tr. Richards, 2, p. 222.

111 Niẓām al-Mulk, *Siyāsat-nāma*, tr. H. Darke as *The Book of Government or Rules for Kings* (New Haven CT, 1960).

112 On the purely political tradition of power in the Muslim context, see J. Dakhlia, *Le divan des rois. Le politique et le religieux dans l'islam* (Paris, 1998).

113 Gibb believed that Ibn al-Athīr did not hesitate to change his information and misquote his sources because of his hostility to Saladin: 'Playing the useful, if rarely attractive, part of devil's advocate, he portrays for us the hostility and party-spirit with which Saladin had to contend in building up his political and military force'; Gibb, 'The Arabic Sources for the Life of Saladin', p. 71.

ganda of the kind which was put forward by the sultan and his own entourage;[114] instead, as Anne-Marie Eddé has written in the introduction to her excellent biography of Saladin, 'le récit d'Ibn al-Athîr, synthétique et clair, vient très utilement compléter et parfois contrebalancer les témoignages de ses devanciers'.[115] Here, as elsewhere, the Mosul historian composed a clear and coherent account reflecting his overriding desire to understand what allowed the sultan of Egypt to triumph and what caused the fall of the Zengids. In his account, the image of Saladin is not one written by a close servant and admirer as is the case with Saladin's biographers but, instead, he writes of a sovereign whose fortune and fate he wished to understand and analyse, without indulgence or hostility. Because it is just such a reflection on power—the ways of getting it, methods of exercising it, and conditions for success and failure—which interested the historian of Mosul. For example, Saladin's taking of power in Egypt, written identically in *al-Kāmil* and *al-Bāhir*, is related as a happy coincidence of circumstances, as, he writes, Saladin had had no ambition to leave Syria; the two books instead recount the tradition that Saladin had accompanied his uncle Shirkuh to Egypt against his will and with no desire to carve out a principality.[116]

When Nūr al-Dīn threatened to intervene to re-establish his authority a meeting set the emirs, who were ready to take up arms, against Najm al-Dīn Ayyūb, Saladin's father, who advised feigning submission by sending a messenger to Nūr al-Dīn in order to stop his march to Egypt. Ibn al-Athīr concludes: 'Saladin did what he advised and Nūr al-Dīn gave up his purpose and busied himself with other matters. It turned out as Ayyūb expected. Nūr al-Dīn died without having made a move against him and Saladin ruled the land. This was an example of really good and excellent advice'.[117] By these words, Ibn al-Athīr

114 Letters from the sultan's chancellory, poems, sermons, and official biographies suggested simple yet powerful ideals: the necessity of the unity of the Muslim world in the face of the Franks, the centrality of Jerusalem in Islamic thought, and the obligation of jihad to recover the lost lands. See Sivan, *L'Islam et la croisade*.

115 A.-M. Eddé, *Saladin* (Paris, 2008), p. 16.

116 The story is the same in both of Ibn al-Athīr's histories: *al-Kāmil*, vol. XI, pp. 338 and 342–43; tr. Richards, 2, pp. 174 and 177; and *al-Bāhir*, pp. 139 and 141. In the first passage of *al-Kāmil*, it is said that Saladin accompanied his uncle against his wishes using an explicit reference to a Quranic verse (Q. 2:216): 'It may be that you dislike something, though it is best for you, and it may be that you want something, although it is worst thing for you'. The second passage reports the account of the expedition to Egypt as Saladin himself had related to an associate of Ibn al-Athīr in which he explained that he did not want to leave (Syria) but that he had to obey the order given by Nūr al-Dīn.

117 *Al-Kāmil*, vol. XI, p. 373; tr. Richards, 2, p. 200; *al-Bāhir*, p. 159.

underlines the political ability of Saladin's father which he admired for its effectiveness, although perhaps not for its moral values.

Similarly, Ibn al-Athīr explains the taking of Damascus by Saladin as occurring because the town's emirs were preoccupied by their own interests,[118] and his conquest of Aleppo as caused by the divisions amongst the Zengids and, especially, by the error of ʿIzz al-Dīn Mawdūd, who had given the town to his brother ʿImād al-Dīn.[119] The latter proved incapable of defending the town and so sold it 'for the most paltry of prices; he gave up a fortress like Aleppo and received in exchange some villages and fields! ... With this gain Saladin's power became established, although it had been shaky; through the surrender of this place his foot became firmly fixed, although it had been on the brink of an overhanging precipice. When God wills a matter, there is no turning it away'.[120]

The campaign against the Franks in the summer of 583/1187 is the subject of a long report in *al-Kāmil*[121] which Ibn al-Athīr concluded soberly but clearly with this eulogising statement: 'This blessed deed, the conquering of Jerusalem, is something achieved by none but Saladin—God have mercy on him—since the time of ʿUmar ibn al-Khaṭṭāb—God be pleased with him. This is his sufficient glory and honour'.[122] On the other hand, Saladin's lifting of the siege of Tyre raises no moral disapproval on the part of the author but an attempt at an explanation. For Ibn al-Athīr, Saladin's error was to have promised safety (*aman*) to the inhabitants of the towns he conquered from the Franks, which allowed them to leave and take refuge in great numbers in Tyre and to create there a base for resistance: 'God willing, we shall mention what the sequel of these events was to make it known that a ruler ought not to give up resoluteness, even if fates are aiding him. That he should fail while being resolute is better than that he should succeed while being remiss and losing his resolve and is more likely to justify him in the eyes of men'.[123]

118 *Al-Kāmil*, vol. XI, p. 415; tr. Richards, 2, p. 231.

119 In 577/1181, at the death of al-Malik al-Ṣāliḥ Ismāʿīl (the son of Nūr al-Dīn), the town of Aleppo had returned to the ruler of Mosul, ʿIzz al-Dīn Masʿūd I, but he was forced to hand it over the following year to his brother ʿImād al-Dīn, ruler of Sinjār.

120 *Al-Kāmil*, vol. XI, p. 497; tr. Richards, 2, p. 294. The expression 'his foot became firmly fixed' (*fa-thabbata qadamahu*) is a direct references to Q. 47:7. The same explanation is put forward in *al-Bāhir*, p. 183.

121 As has been stated above, the fight led by Saladin against the Latin states and the Third Crusade is not covered in *al-Bāhir*.

122 *Al-Kāmil*, vol. XI, p. 552; tr. Richards, 2, p. 335.

123 *Al-Kāmil*, vol. XI, p. 556; tr. Richards, 2, p. 337. See also the translation of this passage in Gabrieli, *Arab Historians of the Crusades*, p. 180, who adds this comment: 'This is only one of the passages in which an ill-disguised hostility to Saladin can be seen in the

Ibn al-Athīr makes no mention of the criticisms which are sometimes levelled against Saladin, such as that he was an usurper who turned against his master Nūr al-Dīn and his descendants.[124] The question that Ibn al-Athīr poses is not one of the legitimacy of the sultan's taking of power, but that of his comportment in directing his political and miitary affairs. The access to and maintainance of power depended on the ability of a ruler to govern according to the principles of justice and benevolence, skill and discernment, firmness and foresight.[125] On the contrary, an inability to administer and defend his territory would lead to his—and its—decline. And it is just such carelessness by the early rulers of the crusading period whom Ibn al-Athīr denounces which explains the great successes of the Franks, writing: 'when the Franks—may God Almighty forsake them—vaunted their conquests of Islamic territory and, luckily for them, the armies and princes of Islam were distracted by fighting one another, then the Muslims were divided in their opinions, their aspirations were at variance and their wealth dissipated'.[126] Al-Sulamī, the Damascene jurist who tried to call a jihad against the Franks in 1105, wrote similarly while attempting to mobilise the rulers of his day.[127] This accusation is surely an acceptable historical explanation, often highlighted in the histories of the Crusades, but in writing it Ibn al-Athīr aims above all to awaken the conscience of the princes of Islam to their obligation. Such negligence by the rulers is also demonstrated and criticised in the face of the Mongols, who were terrorising the Muslim world while Ibn al-Athīr was writing: 'for now we do not see among the princes of Islam one who has a desire to wage the Jihad or to aid the religion. On the contrary, each of them looks to his pleasures, his sport and the oppression of his subjects. For me this is more frightening than the enemy'.[128]

Mesopotamian historian's writings, caused by his preference for the Zangid dynasty supplanted by Saladin'. I suggest these criticisms on the conduct of war should be read less as an expression of hostility than as an element of the author's political analysis.

124 At Mosul, Saladin was accused of treason and treated as a 'chien qui aboie contre son maître' (Michael the Syrian, cited in Eddé, *Saladin*, p. 89).

125 The need to ensure troops are properly remunerated is often mentioned by Ibn al-Athīr. See G. Hoffmann, 'Militärhistorisches bei Ibn al-Aṯīr', in *Gedenkschrift Wolfgang Reuschel. Akten des III. Arabischen Kolloquiums. Leipzig 21–22 november 1991*, s.n., (Stuttgart, 1994), 157–64.

126 *Al-Kāmil*, vol. X, p. 373; tr. Richards, 1, p. 79.

127 E. Sivan, 'La genèse de la contre-croisade : Un traité damasquin du début du XIIe siècle', *Journal Asiatique* 254 (1966), 197–224, pp. 207 (Arabic text) and 215–216 (French trans.).

128 *Al-Kāmil*, vol. XII, p. 497; tr. Richards, 3, pp. 304–5.

Ibn al-Athīr's writing of history thus focusses on *siyāsa*, in terms of political ideology or, more precisely, as the art of good government, which allows for a certain realism, and indeed a certain cynicism. There is a need to consider further the tension between *siyāsa* and *sharīʿa*, between *realpolitik* and religious law, a tension which, from the fifth/eleventh century onwards, is seen in religious, cultural and political discourses.[129] In the historical judgement of Ibn al-Athīr, *siyāsa*, the abilities required to govern, is parallel to, but not identical with, the ethico-prophetic principles of the *sharīʿa*. Above all, Ibn al-Athīr, concerned to posit a temporal and political explanation—that of the individual responsibility of the ruler—concludes nonetheless, from time to time, with expressions which affirm that the events which he is going to relate come from the unstoppable will of God. For example, he writes about the unexpected surrender of the fortress of al-ʿImādiyya to Badr al-Dīn in 622/1225–26: 'When God wills a matter, there is no avoiding it'.[130]

A systematic analysis carried out on *al-Kāmil* for the years 451/1059 to 583/1187 allows for a greater understanding of Ibn al-Athīr's use of the divine will, and there are essentially two types of situation which leads him to appeal to it. The first of these is an improbable and surprising resolution, which stirred and completely destroyed the pre-visible succession of facts. Thus in 519/1125–26 when Ṭughril, allied to the Mazyadid ruler Dubays b. Ṣadaqa, marched against Baghdad with every chance of success, it was because 'God Almighty decreed that [he] was stricken by a severe fever' that the caliph and the sultan were saved.[131] Or, in another example, when the caliph al-Mustanjid unexpectedly escaped from a plot hatched against him, it was because 'God protected him'.[132] Noting that the Ismāʿīlīs could have been definitively eliminated from Khurāsān if troops had not, at that time, been occupied fighting the Oghuz, he wrote: 'However, God has a purpose which He will achieve'.[133] However, comments of this kind are rare, with only a dozen in total for the years studied.

Occurring more frequently are references to divine intervention in a second set of circumstances—that of victories over the enemies of Sunnī Islam: Bāṭinīs, Armenians, Byzantines and, particularly, Franks. The account of the massacre of thousands of Bāṭinīs in Damascus in 523/1129 has this conclusion: 'Thus God saved the Muslims from their wickedness and turned their plotting

129 On these passages see the comments in Khalidi, *Arabic Historical Thought*, pp. 193ff.
130 *Al-Kāmil*, vol. XII, p. 446; tr. Richards, 3, p. 266.
131 *Al-Kāmil*, vol. X, p. 627; tr. Richards, 1, p. 256.
132 *Al-Kāmil*, vol. XI, p. 257 (*wa-dafaʿa Allāh ʿanhu*); tr. Richards, 2, p. 114.
133 *Al-Kāmil*, vol. XI, p. 199; tr. Richards, 2, p. 72, with an allusion to Q. 65:3.

back upon the infidels'.[134] When Ibn al-Athīr reports the defeat inflicted on Baldwin I in 495/1102 by the troops of Egypt, he adds 'God gave victory to the Muslims'.[135] The report of operations led by the Muslims against the Sicilian fleet which besieged Alexandria in 570/1174 is punctuated by phrases such as: 'God sent down His aid to them and His signs became manifest' and 'Thus God delivered the Muslims from their wickedness'.[136] The occurrence of such phrases increase with the successes of Saladin, Ibn al-Athīr resuming his account with the idea which accompanied the deeds of Saladin, that of jihad against the Franks. It is the same in *al-Bāhir* where Zengī and Nūr al-Dīn appear as the conduits of the divine will. Thus he concludes the report of the fall of the fortress Baʿrīn with these words: 'God put an end, thanks to the *shahīd*—God bless him—to this great calamity [which was the pillaging of the lands of Hama and Aleppo by the garrison of Baʿrīn]'.[137]

In conclusion, Ibn al-Athīr was very much a Muslim of his time for whom the victories of the Muslims over the infidels are a manifestation of God's will: to make truth triumph over error, to reconquer lost territories, and to ensure the unity of *dār al-Islām*.[138] The theological question, fundamental in the monotheist context, of the contradiction between divine decree and individual responsibility of people in the conduct of events does not affect his work. Respectful of a superior will which exceeds him, anxious about the fate of the lands of Islam in the face of external threats and internal division, concerned to propose an explanation for the course of events, and desirous to exhort the rulers to follow good examples, Ibn al-Athīr remains above all a chronicler for whom the aim, first and foremost, is to record the facts.

(Translated by Olivier Berrou)

134 *Al-Kāmil*, vol. X, p. 657; tr. Richards, 1, p. 278.

135 *Al-Kāmil*, vol. X, p. 346; tr. Richards, 1, p. 61.

136 *Al-Kāmil*, vol. XI, pp. 413 and 414; tr. Richards, 2, pp. 229 and 230.

137 *Al-Bāhir*, p. 61.

138 It must be remembered that Ibn al-Athīr was principally trained in the fields of *fiqh* and hadith studies, and that he had written a work on the Companions of the Prophet.

Sibṭ Ibn al-Jawzī

Alex Mallett

Sibṭ Ibn al-Jawzī was a hugely influential figure in Syria, and particularly Damascus, in the first half of the seventh/thirteenth century. His fame in his lifetime and in the later medieval period was based primarily on his oratorical skills as a teacher and preacher in the mosques and madrasas of Damascus, and in his *majālis al-waʿẓ* ('assemblies of exhortation'), which were extremely popular. His renown in these fields echoed down the ages across the Islamic world, and centuries later writers were still holding him up as a model preacher. His ability as a speaker also seems to have had an impact on the ruling elites of Damascus, as he developed close relationships with a number of them over the course of his life. In addition to these main activities Sibṭ Ibn al-Jawzī was also known in his capacity as a writer, although in this regard he was not as prolific as others, as he seems to have written a maximum of only thirty known works, just five of which are extant. As was typical for someone with his position in the ranks of the *ʿulamāʾ*—the religious classes—his writings focussed on religious issues, and so included Quranic commentaries, books on hadith, a biography of Muḥammad, and assessments of various aspects of *fiqh* (Islamic law). Yet for modern historians of the crusading period and Islamic history more widely, as well as for many of his contemporaries, Sibṭ Ibn al-Jawzī's most important text was his historical work *Mirʾāt al-zamān fī taʾrīkh al-aʿyān* ('The Mirror of the Age in the History of the Famous'), a universal chronicle running from the Creation until the year 654/1256.[1] This provides much unique, inside knowledge of the Ayyūbid states, and particularly Damascus, during the first half of the seventh/thirteenth century, and consequently is a basic text for studying events surrounding the crusader states and their Muslim opponents during this time.

The Life of Sibṭ Ibn al-Jawzī

Despite spending the majority of his life in Damascus and achieving his fame there the family background of Shams al-Dīn Abu'l-Muẓaffar Yūsuf b.

1 In the Islamic historiographical sense from this period, a 'universal history' was a historical account of the Islamic world which detailed events from all eras, rather than referring to every part of the world, Muslim and non-Muslim; cf. C.F. Robinson, *Islamic Historiography* (Cambridge, 2003), pp. 134–38.

 | DOI 10.1163/9789004280687_006

Qizoghlu, Sibṭ Ibn al-Jawzī was the city of Baghdad, which was the seat of the ʿAbbāsid caliphate and hence the centre of the Sunnī world, with all the political, cultural and religious activity that went with it, where he was born around the year 582/1186.[2] His father, Qizoghlū b. ʿAbdallāh, was originally a Turkish slave whose own father had also been a slave to the vizier Ibn Hubayra in the 550s/1150s.[3] Sibṭ Ibn al-Jawzī's father had been freed by Ibn Hubayra when he was still a fairly young age,[4] and the latter then arranged for him to be married to Rābiʿa, the daughter of the hugely important Baghdad scholar and preacher Ibn al-Jawzī (d. 597/1200).[5] It was this union which produced Sibṭ Ibn al-Jawzī, meaning that he was, as his name demonstrates (*Sibṭ* meaning 'grandson' in Arabic), the grandson of Ibn al-Jawzī. This union also meant that Sibṭ Ibn al-Jawzī was half Arab and half Turkish, which led to him occasionally being referred to as 'al-Turkī', although he seems to have been generally accepted as an Arab, at least partially, one suspects, on account of the importance of his Arab grandfather.[6]

The family into which he was born was an extremely influential one. Ibn al-Jawzī had been a famous preacher and scholar whose writings concerned history, hadith, Quranic commentaries, Islamic law and many other fields of enquiry. He wrote hundreds of works on these and many other subjects which

2 References to Sibṭ Ibn al-Jawzī's life can be found in, amongst others: Sibṭ Ibn al-Jawzī, *Mirʾāt al-zamān fī taʾrīkh al-aʿyān*, s.n., 2 vols numbered VIII/1 and VIII/2 (Hyderabad, 1951–52), vol. VIII/2, *passim*; al-Yūnīnī, *Dhayl mirʾāt al-zamān*, s.n., 2 vols in 4 (Hyderabad, 1954–61), vol. I, pp. 39–45; Ibn Wāṣil, *Mufarrij al-kurūb fī akhbār Banī Ayyūb*, ed. J. al-Shayyāl et al., 6 vols (Cairo, Beirut and Wiesbaden, 1953–2004), *passim*; al-Ṣafadī, *Kitāb al-wāfī bi'l-wafayāt*, ed. H. Ritter et al., 29 vols (Leipzig and Beirut, 1931–2008), vol. XXIX, pp. 276–77; Ibn Taghrībirdī, *al-Nujūm al-zāhira fī mulūk Miṣr wa'l-Qāhira*, ed. M. Ḥusayn, 16 vols (Beirut, 1992), vol. VII, p. 35; al-Dhahabī, *Taʾrīkh al-Islām wa wafayāt al-mashāhīr wa'l-aʿlām*, ed. ʿU. Tadmurī, 55 vols (Beirut, 1999), vol. LI (years 651–660), pp. 183–85; Ibn Kathīr, *al-Bidāya wa'l-nihāya fi'l-taʾrīkh*, s.n., 14 vols in 7 (Beirut, 1932–39), vol. XIII, pp. 194–95; Ibn Shākir al-Kutubī, *Fawāt al-wafayāt wa'l-dhayl ʿalayhā*, ed. ʿI. ʿAbbās, 4 vols (Beirut, 1973–74), vol. IV, pp. 356–57; Ibn al-ʿImād, *Shadharāt al-dhahab fī akhbār man dhahab*, s.n., 8 vols (Cairo, 1931–32), vol. V, p. 226. These are primarily his obituaries, and other references to his life are scattered throughout these and some other texts.

3 Ibn Kathīr, *al-Bidāya wa'l-nihāya*, vol. XII, p. 250; Ibn al-ʿImād, *Shadharāt al-dhahab*, vol. V, p. 226.

4 Al-Yūnīnī, *Dhayl*, vol. I, p. 40. Ibn Hubayra was the caliphal vizier in Baghdad in the 550s/1150s–60s. During this time he also employed ʿImād al-Dīn al-Iṣfahānī in the administrative service, raising the possibility that the latter was known by Sibṭ Ibn al-Jawzī's father; see above, p. 36.

5 Ibn al-Jawzī, *Al-Muntaẓam fī taʾrīkh al-mulūk wa'l-umam*, s.n., 6 vols numbered 5–10 (Hyderabad, 1938–40), vol. X, p. 257.

6 See, for example, al-Ṣafadī, *al-Wāfī bi'l-wafayāt*, p. 276, who refers to him as 'al-Turkī'.

have been employed by Muslim writers ever since. He had originally been the 'resident' preacher in Ibn Hubayra's house and was then employed by the caliph to give sermons in the palace mosque before becoming, in 556/1161, the head of the Ma'mūniyya and Bāb al-Azaj madrasas in Baghdad. He composed a sermon celebrating Saladin's conquest of Egypt in 556/1171, as well as numerous others which were so popular that the caliph built a special dais just for him in the palace mosque. By 574/1179 he had become the head of five of the most important learning establishments in Baghdad and was thus one of, if not the, most important religious figures in the city after the caliph. Although he was dispossessed of his positions by a new vizier for political reasons in 590/1194 he remained highly influential for the rest of his life.[7]

Thus, Sibṭ Ibn al-Jawzī was born into one of the most important families in the main city of the 'Abbāsid caliphate, and as family background was the most important aspect in determining future career advancement in the medieval Islamic world, he found doors relatively easy to open. The importance of having Ibn al-Jawzī as a relative can be seen in the lives of all three of his sons, particularly his middle son Muḥyī al-Dīn, who became a famous preacher in Baghdad and was chosen by the caliph to deliver robes of honour to various Muslim rulers and to act as a peace envoy to the warring Ayyūbid rulers—for example, in 635/1237–38, he brokered peace between al-Kāmil and al-Ṣāliḥ Ayyūb following a war between them.[8] Thus, Sibṭ Ibn al-Jawzī had good relations with people close to the centre of power in the 'Abbāsid caliphate and a family background which ensured he would have influence.[9]

Sibṭ Ibn al-Jawzī's father died when he was still young, and he was henceforth looked after by his mother and her father Ibn al-Jawzī until the death of the latter in 597/1200. During this period Ibn al-Jawzī took his grandson to the classes and preaching sessions he gave in Baghdad, where Sibṭ Ibn al-Jawzī learned hadith and other aspects of the religious sciences, while he also went to the classes of many other famous scholars of the city, who were among the most respected and influential within the Islamic world. In this aspect of his

---

7 H. Laoust, 'Ibn al-Djawzī', in *EI2*; A. Mallett, 'Ibn al-Jawzī', in *Christian-Muslim Relations: A Bibliographical History. Volume 3: 1050–1200*, ed. D. Thomas and A. Mallett (Leiden, 2010), 731–35, pp. 731–32.

8 Ibn Wāṣil, *Mufarrij al-kurūb*, vol. V, p. 152; Ibn Kathīr, *al-Bidāya wa'l-nihāya*, vol. XIII, p. 164; al-Maqrīzī, *Kitāb al-sulūk li-ma'rifat duwal al-mulūk*, ed. M.M. Ziyāda and S.'A. 'Āshūr, 4 vols (Cairo, 1956–72), vol. I, pt 2, p. 258.

9 Talmon-Heller has suggested that his background in Baghdad was useful for his later life in Syria as it 'may have provided him with the perspective and somewhat protected status of an outsider from the rundown but still prestigious caliphal city, together with the intimate

life his grandfather clearly had a significant impact on Sibṭ Ibn al-Jawzī, as his life's work followed closely that of his relative and he was, from an early age, deeply immersed in Islamic learning.

It was in the year 600/1203–4, a little after the death of his grandfather, that Sibṭ Ibn al-Jawzī, by now grown-up and apparently a good-looking man,[10] left the place of his birth and went on an academic pilgrimage around the main centres of learning in the Near East. His aim in so doing was to be taught by other learned scholars of the age in order to further increase his knowledge, and during this journey he would be taught subjects including hadith, poetry, Quranic commentary, Arabic philology and history. His first stop was Aleppo, where he stayed until 606/1209–10,[11] while making numerous trips to other towns in order to preach and learn, including Damascus, Hebron, Mosul and Jerusalem. After this initial residence in northern Syria he moved permanently to Damascus, where he was to spend the majority of the rest of his life.[12]

Over the course of his time in Damascus Sibṭ Ibn al-Jawzī became known, like his grandfather, as a famous preacher. He was to hold teaching positions in a number of madrasas within the city, including the Ḥanafiyya, Shibliyya, and Badriyya madrasas, as well as a number of other establishments over the course of his life.[13] Ibn Kathīr suggests that his official teaching positions—and the significant stipends that went with them—were at least partly granted to him because of the good relations he managed to cultivate with the Ayyūbid rulers of Syria, and especially those of Damascus.[14]

knowledge of the insider'; D. Talmon-Heller, *Islamic Piety in Medieval Syria: Mosques, Sermons and Cemeteries under the Zangids and Ayyūbids (1146–1260)* (Leiden, 2007), p. 128.

10 Ibn Kathir, *al-Bidāya wa'l-nihāya*, vol. XIII, p. 194.

11 Sibṭ Ibn al-Jawzī, *Mir'āt al-zamān* (Hyderabad), vol. VIII/2, p. 685.

12 He records his travels to and arrival in Damascus in Sibṭ Ibn al-Jawzī, *Mir'āt al-zamān* (Hyderabad), vol. VIII/2, p. 517; see also al-Kutubī, *Fawāt al-wafayāt*, vol. IV, p. 356; and Ibn Kathīr, *al-Bidāya wa'l-nihāya*, vol. XIII, pp. 193–95. At this time Damascus was an important centre of learning and attracted scholars from all over the Islamic world; see M. Chamberlain, *Knowledge and Social Practice in Medieval Damascus* (Cambridge, 1994), and J.E. Gilbert, 'The Institutionalization of Muslim Scholarship and Professionalization of the *'Ulamā'* in Medieval Damascus', *Studia Islamica* 52 (1980), 105–34. Despite his relatively permanent settlement in Damascus, he also spent some time elsewhere after his arrival, particularly the years 626/1229 to 633/1235–36, which were spent in Kerak, and a period after 638/1240–41 spent in exile.

13 Al-Kutubī, *Fawāt al-wafayāt*, vol. IV, p. 356; Ibn Kathīr, *al-Bidāya wa'l-nihāya*, vol. XIII, pp. 193–95.

14 Ibn Kathīr, *al-Bidāya wa'l-nihāya*, vol. XIII, p. 194.

However he came by his positions, his preaching was certainly popular and powerful, as demonstrated by his fame as a preacher in more 'unofficial' gatherings known as *majālis al-waʿẓ*. These were a staple part of religious instruction in the medieval Islamic world, and were for a large proportion of society the main method by which religious knowledge and ideas were imbibed.[15] It is reported that Sibṭ Ibn al-Jawzī was one of the most important and influential preachers in this kind of session, and his renown in this capacity was such that he was given the title of *wāʿiẓ al-Shām* ('the [best] preacher of Syria') or *raʾīs al-wuʿʿāẓ* ('the head of the preachers'), seemingly able to hold audiences spellbound with his eloquence and to create a remarkable emotional response in those listening.[16] These gatherings were given every Saturday at either the Umayyad mosque or the mosque on Mt. Qāsiyūn until, in his old age, they were restricted to Saturdays in the sacred months. They were attended by rulers, fellow-members of the *ʿulamāʾ*, members of the bureaucracy, merchants and slaves, among others, and were so large that the audience would spill out into the surrounding area. He was consequently extremely popular across all sections of society, and this gave him significant political power through his ability to influence large numbers of people.[17]

One of the most famous of his preaching sessions occurred in Damascus in 607/1210–11, when he was just over 25 years of age and only one year after he had arrived in the city. In this, he recounted the third/ninth century story of Abū Qudāma, in which a woman wished for her long hair to be cut off to make reins for the horses of the jihad warrior who is the hero of the story. This was done, and the hero subsequently found himself fighting alongside a

15 For the *majālis al-wāʿẓ* in general see J. Berkey, *Popular Preaching and Religious Authority in the Medieval Islamic Near East* (Seattle, 2001). For a study more focussed on the crusading period, see Talmon-Heller, *Islamic Piety*, pp. 115–48.

16 D. Talmon-Heller, 'Islamic Preaching in Syria during the Counter-Crusade (Twelfth and Thirteenth Centuries)', in I. Shagrir, R. Ellenblum and J. Riley-Smith (eds), *In Laudem Hierosolymitani. Studies in Crusades and Medieval Culture in Honour of Benjamin Z. Kedar* (Aldershot, 2007), 61–75, p. 70. For example, al-Yūnīnī writes that many *ahl al-dhimma* ('People of the Book', i.e. Jews and Christians) became Muslims on the strength of his preaching; al-Yūnīnī, *Dhayl*, vol. I, p. 40.

17 Al-Yūnīnī, *Dhayl*, vol. I, p. 40; Ibn Kathīr, *al-Bidāya*, vol. XIII, p. 58; Tāj al-Dīn Subkī, *Ṭabaqāt al-Shāfiʿiyya*, ed. ʿA.M. al-Ḥulū' and M. al-Tanāḥī, 10 vols (Cairo, 1964–76), vol. VIII, p. 239; cf. Talmon-Heller, *Islamic Piety*, pp. 128–30. How much of his popularity was due to his own persuasive powers is debatable; it is well known that the audience at these events was as much a driving force for what was said as the speakers themselves, and it may be that Sibṭ Ibn al-Jawzī was simply much more attuned to the concerns of his listeners than others; see Berkey, *Popular Preaching*, pp. 54–55.

courageous boy who was killed in the battle. Abū Qudāma went back to the boy's home in Medina to inform his family, and found that the boy's mother was the woman who had given her hair for Abū Qudāma's own horse. The woman then gave thanks that her son became a martyr as she and he had both desired. In response to this story, the crowd listening to Sibṭ Ibn al-Jawzī marched out of Damascus to Nablus where the story was given again and, joined by people from the surrounding countryside, went on a (seemingly impromptu) raid against Frankish-held territory around Nablus.[18]

While this sermon is presented as having been a success, other attempts at provoking action against the Franks were not so fruitful; those that failed included a session given in response to a letter written to Sibṭ Ibn al-Jawzī by al-Muʿaẓẓam, telling him to exhort the people of Damascus to go on a raid against Frankish Syria at the time of the Fifth Crusade in 616/1219–20.[19] Perhaps the most famous of his sermons, in which he again attempted to play a direct part in the struggle with the Franks, was that pronounced in the Great Umayyad mosque in Damascus following the handover of Jerusalem to the Franks by the sultan of Egypt, al-Kāmil, in 626/1229. As al-Kāmil was his rival, Damascus' ruler al-Nāṣir Daʿūd directed Sibṭ Ibn al-Jawzī to preach a sermon deploring the loss of Jerusalem, a sermon in which the city's merits were expounded and its loss bewailed and which, if the preacher himself is to be believed, reduced his listeners to tears, although again there was little real reaction to it.[20] Despite this disinterest from the people of Damascus, his preaching at sessions such as these demonstrates he had a direct personal interest in the struggle with the Franks, and it seems unlikely that Talmon-Heller is correct in her belief that he only preached jihad against the Franks in response to requests from the rulers, particularly since he personally took part in both the attack around Nablus in

18 Sibṭ Ibn al-Jawzī, *Mirʾāt al-zamān* (Hyderabad), vol. VIII/2, pp. 544–45; cf. Talmon-Heller, *Islamic Piety*, pp. 131–33.

19 Sibṭ Ibn al-Jawzī, *Mirʾāt al-zamān* (Hyderabad), vol. VIII/2, p. 604; cf. Talmon-Heller, *Islamic Piety*, p. 134.

20 Sibṭ Ibn al-Jawzī, *Mirʾāt al-zamān* (Hyderabad), vol. VIII/2, p. 654; Gabrieli, *Arab Historians*, pp. 273–74. There were, however, almost certainly different motivations at work in the two men—Sibṭ Ibn al-Jawzī seems to have been truly concerned with the religious significance of the handover, while the ruler of Damascus was trying to whip up and exploit the religious outrage of the populace to make political capital against his relative; see below, p. 159. See also S.A. Mourad & J.E. Lindsay, *The Intensification and Reorientation of Sunni Jihad Ideology in the Crusader Period* (Leiden, 2013), pp. 95–99.

607/1210 and another one from Homs into the lands of the County of Tripoli in 618/1221.[21]

Sibṭ Ibn al-Jawzī had close relations with the Ayyūbid rulers of Damascus and other notables on the Syrian political scene, probably because of both his broad appeal and his fame and contacts in Baghdad. For example, he was entrusted with bearing a secret message to the ruler of Aleppo by al-Malik al-Ashraf of Damascus in 612/1215–16. He was friendly with members of the Ayyūbid establishment such as the *nāʾib* al-Ṣāliḥ Ismāʿīl[22] and al-Amjad, ruler of Baalbek,[23] and clearly admired at least some of the rulers of Damascus, such as al-ʿĀdil who, he approvingly states in his obituary of the Ayyūbid ruler, enforced Islamic law, banning such inappropriate behaviour as alcoholic drinks, homosexual acts and non-canonical taxes.[24] He seems to have been particularly close to al-Muʿaẓẓam ʿĪsā as, in the words of Humphreys, they 'became such close friends that much of Sibṭ's information about this prince is probably a personal memoir'.[25] Similarly, he seems to have had a good relationship with al-Malik al-Ashraf, as al-Muʿaẓẓam ʿĪsā attempted to enlist Sibṭ Ibn al-Jawzī's help in persuading al-Ashraf to join him in his war against the Franks of the Fifth Crusade in 618/1221.[26] Because of the generally good relations he had with the Ayyūbid rulers he was also called on by various members of Damascene society to plead their case with the rulers; one example of this is the occasion he was visited by Ibn al-Ṣalāḥ, another member of the *ʿulamāʾ*, who asked him to intervene on his behalf.[27] Through these close relations with the rulers he was able to have detailed knowledge of the events which occurred

21 Talmon-Heller, *Islamic Piety*, p. 134. This is unlikely because although he preached every week for decades both in Damascus and elsewhere we know very little of what he actually said with the exception of those sermons which he mentions he was told to preach by the rulers, which he presumably highlights because he wanted to demonstrate the importance of the *ʿulamāʾ* to the functioning of society. As preachers such as him would very often give sermons on things which were important to the general population of the region he must have preached on a number of occasions against the Franks; cf. A. Mallett, *Popular Muslim Reactions to the Franks in the Levant* (Farnham, 2014), pp. 63–66. For the attack around Homs see Sibṭ Ibn al-Jawzī, *Mirʾāt al-zamān* (Hyderabad), vol. VIII/2, p. 619.

22 Sibṭ Ibn al-Jawzī, *Mirʾāt al-zamān* (Hyderabad), vol. VIII/2, pp. 665–66.

23 Sibṭ Ibn al-Jawzī, *Mirʾāt al-zamān* (Hyderabad), vol. VIII/2, pp. 667–68.

24 Sibṭ Ibn al-Jawzī, *Mirʾāt al-zamān* (Hyderabad), vol. VIII/2, pp. 594–95.

25 R.S. Humphreys, *From Saladin to the Mongols* (Albany NY, 1977) pp. 436–37, n. 18.

26 For the whole episode see Sibṭ Ibn al-Jawzī, *Mirʾāt al-zamān* (Hyderabad), vol. VIII/2, pp. 618–21; cf. Humphreys, *From Saladin to the Mongols*, p. 169.

27 Sibṭ Ibn al-Jawzī, *Mirʾāt al-zamān* (Hyderabad), vol. VIII/2, p. 758; cf. Chamberlain, *Knowledge and Social Practice*, p. 120.

and the political circumstances which surrounded them, which partly explains his significance as a historian.

Yet relations between Sibṭ Ibn al-Jawzī and the Ayyūbids were not always good, and either side could move to alter this dynamic if they believed the other had erred in some way. For example, Sibṭ Ibn al-Jawzī narrates how, in 638/1240–41, following a conversation with one of the other teachers at the Shibliyya madrasa, he was reported to the vizier ʿAmīn al-Dawla, falsely (he says) accused of having helped secure the release of the ruler of Egypt from his imprisonment in Kerak to the disadvantage of the Damascene hierarchy. As punishment for his perceived betrayal Sibṭ Ibn al-Jawzī was immediately banished from the city for several years, although he was later able to return and carry on his activities.[28] On the other hand, relations could also go the other way, as Sibṭ Ibn al-Jawzī on occasion criticised the Ayyūbid rulers for what he saw as their betrayal of the Islamic values he held dear. For example, the Ayyūbid ruler of Damascus al-ʿĀdil had abolished non-canonical taxes (*mukūs*) in the city, but they were quickly reinstated in 615/1218 by his successor al-Muʿaẓẓam ʿĪsā, causing Sibṭ Ibn al-Jawzī to complain bitterly about them, despite the fact that he was informed by the ruler they were required to pay for the struggle against the Franks.[29]

One of the more notable and controversial acts in his career was his 'conversion' from the Ḥanbalī school of Islamic law to the Ḥanafī, which occurred during the reign of al-Muʿaẓẓam ʿĪsā (r. 615/1218–624/1227).[30] Ḥanbalism had been the juridical school of his grandfather Ibn al-Jawzī, while Ḥanafism was that of the Ayyūbid ruler of Damascus at the time of his conversion and also the traditional school of the Turks, thus possibly making a link to his deceased father. Sibṭ Ibn al-Jawzī himself attempted to justify his conversion by writing that Ḥanafism was the best path by which to follow Islam.[31] He certainly benefitted in worldly terms from his conversion as it was around this time, in 623/1226, that he gained the position as head of the (Ḥanafī) Shibliyya madrasa, and there were people at the time who accused him of having converted for materialistic reasons.[32] It must have been more than a coincidence that he moved to the *madhhab* of the Ayyūbid rulers of Damascus and this, more than anything,

---

28 Sibṭ Ibn al-Jawzī, *Mirʾāt al-zamān* (Hyderabad), vol. VIII/2, pp. 734–35. For the circumstances surrounding this episode, see Humphreys, *From Saladin to the Mongols*, p. 279.

29 Sibṭ Ibn al-Jawzī, *Mirʾāt al-zamān* (Hyderabad), vol. VIII/2, pp. 597 and 634–35; cf. Humphreys, *From Saladin to the Mongols*, p. 188.

30 This conversion is discussed in al-Yūnīnī, *Dhayl*, vol. I, p. 41.

31 Sibṭ Ibn al-Jawzī, *al-Intisar wa'l-tarjih*, s.n., (Cairo, 1941).

32 For example, see al-Kutubī, *Fawāt al-wafayāt*, vol. IV, p. 356.

suggests that he was very much concerned with his own place in society and that he wished to be close to and to influence those at the centre of political power. Whether this was due to high religious reasons or simply because he was keen on power is impossible to know, but it seems that he wished to influence the course of events and government policy and he saw converting as an effective way of achieving this.

During the course of his time in Damascus he made numerous journeys outside the city. In addition to diplomatic missions, such as the journey to Aleppo in 612/1215–16, he undertook others for scholarly reasons. In 603/1207 he went to Aleppo, Jerusalem and Hebron, and he went on pilgrimage to Mecca three times, in 604/1208, 613/1217, and 619/1223, where he not only performed the necessary rituals but also took the opportunity to engage with some of the most important Islamic thinkers and teachers in the city.[33] Likewise, he also spent time in Mosul.[34] Such trips were performed as pilgrimages of sorts to other scholars, and a way in which knowledge could be gained and ideas exchanged,[35] and his travel must have broadened his horizons and meant that he was not only the possessor of deep knowledge of the theoretical side of Islamic studies, but also that he was attuned to the wider political situation across Islamic territory.

Sibṭ Ibn al-Jawzī died on the 21st Dhu'l-Ḥijja 654/9th January 1257 in the Badriyya madrasa and he was buried in the cemetery on Mount Qāsiyūn, the same place where the Ayyūbids were traditionally buried, and was greatly mourned.[36]

Sibṭ Ibn al-Jawzī's Written Works

From the modern perspective *Mi'rāt al-zamān* is Sibṭ Ibn al-Jawzī's most famous work, being an important source for any study of the history of Syria in the first half of the seventh/thirteenth century and, as will be seen, the history of the wider Islamic world in the fifth/tenth century. However, he also wrote a number of other works for which he found fame in his lifetime, although if surviving numbers of manuscripts are to be regarded as reliable (and whether or not they can is debatable, particularly in the context of source material for the medieval Islamic world) these were not as popular as *Mi'rāt al-zamān*. One

33 Sibṭ Ibn al-Jawzī, *Mir'āt al-zamān* (Hyderabad) vol. VIII/2, pp. 533, 574–75 and 624.
34 Al-Kutubī, *Fawāt al-wafayāt*, vol. IV, p. 356.
35 Chamberlain, *Knowledge and Social Practice*, p. 120.
36 Al-Yūnīnī, *Dhayl*, vol. I, p. 42; Ibn Kathīr, *al-Bidāya wa'l-nihāya*, vol. XIII, p. 195.

of these is *Kitāb al-jalīs al-ṣāliḥ wa'l-anīs al-nāṣiḥ*, an exhortation to the art of good government written in 613/1216 in honour of the Ayyūbid sultan al-Malik al-Ashraf whose aims were to encourage spiritual exhortation, admonish the sultan to do right, and inform the ruler 'of the allegiance and affection of the writer', and was written partly in praise of the ruler and partly as an exposition of his good qualities.[37] Another text he wrote was entitled *al-Intiṣār wa'l-tarjīḥ li'l-madhhab al-ṣaḥīḥ*, a book praising Abū Ḥanīfa, the founder of the Ḥanafī school of Sunnī Islamic jurisprudence, which was written for the Ayyūbid ruler al-Muʿaẓẓam ʿĪsā, himself a Ḥanafī, and probably also as a justification of sorts for Sibṭ Ibn al-Jawzī's own 'conversion' to that law school. It focusses on Abū Ḥanīfa's good qualities, his links to Muḥammad through the latter's Companions, the positive aspects of the Ḥanafī legal school, and its basis in the Quran and Sunna.[38] He also wrote a historical piece entitled *Tadhkirat al-khawāṣṣ*—which is a biographical study of the caliph ʿAlī, his family, and the twelve Shīʿī Imams who followed him[39]—while the final extant work is *Kanz al-mulūk fī kaifiyyat al-sulūk* ('The Treasure of Princes in the Fashion of Behaviour'), the contents of which are a summary of the longer, now lost text *Jawharat al-zamān fī tadhkirat al-sulṭān*. This is a collection of writings on various topics, and includes short works of history, *adab* literature and others, and the overall aim of the book was, like *Kitāb al-jalīs al-ṣāliḥ*, to urge the rulers of society to good behaviour.[40] Sibṭ Ibn al-Jawzī seems to have written a large number of other works now lost, which would itself be unsurprising; these seem to have included a commentary on the Quran, a book on hadith, other historical works, writings on *fiqh*, and a biography of Muḥammad.[41]

Mirʾāt al-zamān fī taʾrīkh al-aʿyān

Despite his wide-ranging interests and significant written output Sibṭ Ibn al-Jawzī's modern fame, and the primary reason for his importance to crusader studies, comes from just one of his works, *Mirʾāt al-zamān fī taʾrīkh al-aʿyān*.

37 Sibṭ Ibn al-Jawzī, *Kitāb al-jalīs al-ṣāliḥ wa'l-anīs al-nāṣiḥ*, ed. F.Ṣ. Fawwāz (London, 1989); cf. T. Kronholm, 'The Introduction to the *Kitāb al-Jalīs aṣ-Ṣāliḥ wa-l-anīs an-nāṣiḥ*, ascribed to Sibṭ Ibn al-Jauzī (d. 654/1257)', *Orientalia Suecana* 38–39 (1989–1990), 81–91.

38 Sibṭ Ibn al-Jawzī, *al-Intiṣār wa'l-tarjīḥ li'l-madhhab al-ṣaḥīḥ*, s.n. (Cairo, 1941).

39 Sibṭ Ibn al-Jawzī, *Tadhkirat al-khawāṣṣ*, ed. M.Ṣ.B. al-ʿUlūm (Najaf, 1964).

40 Sibṭ Ibn al-Jawzī, *Kanz al-mulūk fī kaifiyyat al-sulūk*, ed. C.W.K. Gleekrup (Lund, 1970).

41 A summary of these lost works can be found in F.Ṣ. Fawwāz, *The Life and Works of Sibṭ Ibn al-Jawzī* (Manchester, 1984: Diss. University of Manchester), pp. 38–57.

This is ostensibly a universal history and, as such, it begins with the Creation and continues up to the year 654/1256, the (Islamic) year of the author's death. It is not clear when he commenced his project, although he must have started it and brought it up to his own time before continuing to update it until his own death, as it finished in the year that he died.

His reason for writing this historical work is expounded in the introduction, which is preserved in the ninth/fifteenth century historical work *al-Iʿlān bi'l-tawbīkh li-man dhamma al-ta'rīkh* of al-Sakhāwī. Sibṭ Ibn al-Jawzī writes:

> (People of) a sound disposition and straightforward mind strive eagerly to obtain a knowledge of the origins and the causes of growth. By pondering the currents of destiny and the origins of night and day, they come to be like persons who themselves lived in the times and experienced the events (which they had been studying). God, through Muḥammad, referred to (history) in the Qur'an and said, and what He says is the truth: "In fact, we shall tell you ... for the believers". He further said: "This belongs to the news of the villages. We shall tell it to you. Some of them stand still and (others) are mown down" ... It was a favour of God to give Muḥammad (historical) information ... People follow different purposes in their occupation with history ... The purpose of some is to become acquainted with the biographies of either prudent or incompetent persons, respectively, in order to learn the good management of affairs or to learn thoroughly how to avoid incompetence. Herein lies the real significance of biography for those who know and understand what it is about.[42]

Thus, Sibṭ Ibn al-Jawzī saw history primarily as a method of instruction for people as to how best to live, and that it is a God-given gift; this attitude is clearly reflected in the structure and contents of the book. Additionally however, his history also seems to have been aimed at being entertainment for the reader, as Sibṭ Ibn al-Jawzī brings his subjects to life much as he must have done as a preacher, where stories or amusing asides would keep the audience enraptured. For example, his description of the German Emperor Frederick II (discussed below) seems to have been as much for the entertainment of his audience than anything else.

Although running from the Creation to Sibṭ Ibn al-Jawzī's own lifetime, *Mi'rat al-zamān* is not wholly useful for scholars of all periods. As with most other historical texts from this period, much of the account focussing on the

42 This translation from F. Rosenthal, *A History of Muslim Historiography*, 2nd ed. (Leiden, 1968), pp. 301–2.

time prior to the life of the author is rather derivative. Like the modern historian, the medieval writer could only write what his sources told him, and for most of the text up to his own life the originals are well-known, as will be seen below. However, the work was extremely influential in its day, and was used extensively by later historians such as Ibn Taghrībirdī, Ibn Kathīr, Ibn al-Furāt, al-Maqrīzī and Ibn al-Dawadarī, as well as being regarded as the template for much of later medieval Syrian historical writing.[43] It was so popular that al-Yūnīnī wrote both an abridged version of it, known as *Mukhtaṣar mi'rāt al-zamān*, and then wrote a continuation called simply *Dhayl mi'rāt al-zamān fī ta'rīkh al-a'yān* ('The Continuation of *Mi'rāt al-zamān* …').[44] Al-Yūnīnī's work with Sibṭ Ibn al-Jawzī's original chronicle reflects a deep appreciation of and admiration for the latter's text, made clear in al-Yūnīnī's writing where the reason he decided to produce both an abridgement and a continuation is expounded: 'I saw it to be the most comprehensive in its plan, the most reliable in its sources, the best in presentation and the most accurate in its narratives as if its stories were eye-witnessed'.[45]

Yet there were criticisms of *Mi'rāt al-zamān* even during Sibṭ Ibn al-Jawzī's lifetime, with some complaining it had an unreliable version of early Islamic history and that it regularly used unsound hadiths. Some later writers, such as the 14th-century historians al-Ṣafadī and al-Dhahabī, made vituperative attacks on the text, although it seems that these were more out of jealously than anything else, as their points were rarely given credence by most other scholars of the time.[46] However, the work has also been criticised by modern scholars, particularly for 'its poor planning, confusing presentation and less-than-perfect writing'.[47] Despite these criticisms, *Mi'rāt al-zamān* remains a vital source of information for medieval Syria in the seventh/thirteenth century and, in general, a significant achievement of medieval Islamic historiography.

---

43 Li Guo, *Early Mamluk Syrian Historiography: Al-Yūnīnī's* Dhayl mir'āt al-zamān, 2 vols (Leiden, 1998), vol. 1, p. 18; H.R. Krauss-Sánchez, 'Sibṭ Ibn al-Jawzī', in *EMC*, vol. II, pp. 1356–57.

44 For a partial edition, translation and study of this work, see Li Guo, *Early Mamluk Syrian Historiography*. Cf. also al-Yūnīnī, *Dhayl*.

45 Al-Yūnīnī, *Dhayl*, vol. 1, p. 2; this translation is from Li Guo, *Early Mamluk Syrian Historiography*, vol. 1, p. 16.

46 'A. al-'Azzāwī, 'Sibṭ Ibn al-Jawzī—al-Quṭb al-Yūnīnī—aw *Mir'āt al-zamān* wa-dhayluhu: jawāban li-mā ṭalabhu al-ustādh Salīm al-Krankū', *Majallat al-majma' al-'Ilmī al-'Arabī bi-Dimashq* 22 (1947), 374–77; Li Guo, *Early Mamluk Syrian Historiography*, p. 17.

47 Li Guo, *Early Mamluk Syrian Historiography*, p. 17; cf. Humphreys, *From Saladin to the Mongols*, p. 395; and C. Cahen, 'Ibn al-Djawzī, Shams al-Dīn Abu'l-Muẓaffar Yusūf b. Ḳizoghlu, known as Sibṭ', in *EI2*.

From the perspective of modern scholarship one of the most difficult areas of dealing with the text is that the manuscript tradition for *Mir'āt al-zamān* is rather tricky to unravel due to uncertainty about what actually constitutes the text itself. The most detailed investigation into Sibṭ Ibn al-Jawzī's writing was performed by Cahen, who suggested there are two different versions of the text retained within the extant manuscripts. The first is an incomplete version, written by Sibṭ Ibn al-Jawzī himself, which exists only as a draft, as his death intervened before he could complete the fair copy.[48] The second version appears to be al-Yūnīnī's *Mukhtaṣar mir'āt al-zamān*, an abridged version altered through deletions and occasional additions by al-Yūnīnī where he believed it was necessary.[49] The main problem with these texts is that there are dozens of manuscripts across the world entitled either *Mir'āt al-zamān* or *Mukhtaṣar mir'āt al-zamān*, and without proper investigation it is impossible to know whether those entitled *Mir'āt al-zamān* contain Sibṭ Ibn al-Jawzī's original draft or al-Yūnīnī's abridgement. Until the mammoth task of a detailed study of all the extant manuscripts is performed, hopefully as a precursor to a critical edition, the precise, complicated relations between the various manuscripts will remain unclear.[50]

For the period of the Crusades there have been three versions of the text published. However, none of these are satisfactory, and not only because of their failure to address the issues relating to the manuscript tradition which have been mentioned above. The first edition was published in the third volume of the series *Receuil des Historiens des Croisades: Documents Orientaux*. This consisted of an edition of selected extracts of varying length from the years 490/1097–532/1138, together with a French translation which, as is usual for the *Recueil*, needs to be treated with caution. A number of manuscripts were used in order to produce this edition, although it is not a full critical edition. It is also, in modern terms, sub-standard, with inconsistencies, mistakes, and unclear sections, while the decision to use only selected extracts means that it is impossible for the reader to understand the historian's overall agenda

48 In terms of size of the original draft version, Ibn Khallikān says that when he saw it in Damascus it consisted of 40 volumes; Ibn Khallikān, *Wafayāt al-a'yān*, vol. III, p. 239.

49 Cahen, 'Ibn al-Djawzī … known as Sibṭ', in *EI2*. Despite the changes made, it has been suggested that al-Yūnīnī's *Mukhtaṣar* should form the basis of any future edition of *Mir'āt al-zamān*; Li Guo, *Early Mamluk Syrian Historiography*, vol. I, p. 18, n. 92.

50 Li Guo, *Early Mamluk Syrian Historiography*, p. 208; a list of manuscripts known to definitely contain the *Mukhtaṣar* is given on pp. 208–11. The list given in Brockelmann, *GAL* vol. I, p. 347 and S., vol. I, p. 589, by contrast, is little more than a random sample of the extant manuscripts, and does not differentiate between the two versions of the text.

or to place the events described into the wider context of events within the Islamic world at the time.[51] The next edition or, strictly speaking, publication of the text was produced in 1907. This was a lithographic reproduction of one manuscript of the text, found in Yale University library.[52] This manuscript was not included in the *Recueil* edition, and has been heavily criticised, particularly since the manuscript used was a poor one—its pages are disordered, it is missing significant information found in other manuscripts, lacks any critical apparatus whatsoever, and requires the reader to have excellent Arabic palaeographical skills given the difficulty of the script.[53] These problems were partially rectified by the final edition of the text, produced in two volumes in Hyderabad in 1951–52, which used the Jewett facsimile as its basis, producing a proper typescript and some critical apparatus. However, it still contains disordered pages, is marred by serious deficiencies in the editing process, and Cahen has commented that the Hyderabad edition is 'a misleading one in that it suggests to the reader that this text is the genuine text of Sibṭ Ibn al-Jawzī, which is by no means the case'.[54] This means that despite the text's central importance for understanding the events of the Ayyūbid period there is still no decent edition for that era, still less a critical one.

One result of this is that there is also no full translation of the text, although there have been a number of partial translations. In addition to the French translations in the *Recueil* running alongside the edited sections cited above, Gabrieli included sections relevant to the failure of the siege of Damascus during the Second Crusade and the aftermath of the handover of Jerusalem to the German Emperor Frederick II by the Egyptian leader al-Kāmil in 626/1229 in his oft-used text.[55] However, these suffer from similar problems to the text in the *Recueil*: that it is a random sample with no attempt at contextualisation, while the translations are from Arabic into Italian and then into English rather than straight from Arabic to English. Finally, Jackson has translated sections

51 *RHC Or.*, Vol. III, pp. 517–70.

52 MS New Haven CT—Yale, Landberg 136; Sibṭ ibn al-Jawzī, *Mir'ât az-zamân (A.H. 495–654) / by Sams ad-Dīn Abū al-Muẓaffar Yūsuf ben Qizughlū ben 'Abdallah, commonly known by the surname of Sibṭ ibn al-Jauzī; a facsimile reproduction of manuscript no. 136 of the Landberg collection of Arabic manuscripts belonging to Yale university, edited with introduction by James Richard Jewett* (Chicago, 1907).

53 C. Cahen, 'Editing Arabic Chronicles: A Few Suggestions', *Islamic Studies* 1 (1962), 1–25, p. 2.

54 Cahen, 'Editing Arabic Chronicles', p. 2. Despite this, for most of the period in question this edition remains the best 'full' version, and so has been employed throughout this article.

55 Gabrieli, *Arab Historians*, pp. 62–63 and 273–75.

relevant for the events of the Crusade of Louis IX of France which provide some welcome political context to the machinations of the Ayyūbids and a superior translation to that found in Gabrieli, although taken in isolation these still do not allow the reader to fully make sense of Sibṭ Ibn al-Jawzī's overall aims and methods.[56]

If a scholar's only exposure to *Mir'āt al-zamān* is through these translations, it may naturally be assumed that the text's main focus is the events of the years described. However, Sibṭ Ibn al-Jawzī did not follow the majority of medieval Muslim historians preceding him by writing an almost purely chronographical text, but instead copied his grandfather's methodological lead. In his universal chronicle *al-Muntaẓam fī ta'rīkh al-mulūk wa'l-umam* ('The Methodical Arrangement in the History of Kings and Nations') Ibn al-Jawzī had essentially combined two of the main sub-genres of medieval Arabic historical writing—chronography and biographical dictionary—in one work, presenting the text in an annalistic framework throughout, but under each year devoting space first to the historical events of that year, and then to a section given over to biographies of famous people—and particularly members of the *'ulamā'*—who had died in that year. In *Mir'āt al-zamān* Sibṭ Ibn al-Jawzī does likewise, combining the same two historiographical forms while keeping to a strict annalistic format.[57]

Sibṭ Ibn al-Jawzī's employment of this approach was more than the simple copying of a relative. Instead, it marked a fusion of the historiographically-based chronography and the Muslim traditionist-based prosopographical approach at a period in time when madrasas were employing traditionist historians and when there seems to have been a rapprochement between historiography and traditionism. Sibṭ Ibn al-Jawzī, coming firmly from a traditionist background but also having an interest in history, seems to have been an ideal exponent of this 'combined' historiographical approach.[58]

The result of this methodology was that Sibṭ Ibn al-Jawzī focussed a significant part of his chronicle on the death notices of prominent members of society who had died in the year in question. The majority of the notices given are for members of his fellow religious scholars while the full title of the piece, *Mir'āt al-zamān fī ta'rīkh al-a'yān* ('The Mirror of the Age in the History of the Famous'), demonstrates his primary concern was to relate the lives of people

56 P. Jackson, *The Seventh Crusade, 1244–1254. Sources and Documents* (Farnham, 2009), pp. 154–62 and 223–25.

57 While it had its origin in Iraq, this form became very popular and was to be the template for Syrian historical writing throughout the rest of the medieval period; Li Guo, *Early Mamluk Syrian Historiography*, vol. I, p. 18.

58 See Robinson, *Islamic Historiography*, p. 169.

he considered worthy of being remembered. The examples he gives come from a variety of backgrounds, although the common thread between them is that they were almost all involved in some way in the life of his city of residence, Damascus, and although the amount of biographical material varies depending on the relative level of importance the author assigns to the year's events and the deceased, in any given year it can make up to 70% of the information.[59] For modern scholars of the medieval Islamic world these biographies allow for a better understanding of the political, social and cultural conditions of the time and place in which Sibṭ Ibn al-Jawzī was writing.[60] However, the subjects of these obituaries did not, in general, make much impact on the history of relations between the Muslim states and the Franks, which is why these sections were removed from the translations of the text related to the Crusades. Yet they form a fundamental aspect of the text as a whole, and Sibṭ Ibn al-Jawzī's historiographical agenda cannot be understood without knowing that he included these obituaries and why they constitute such a significant part of the overall text. The principle reason Sibṭ Ibn al-Jawzī chose to lay out the text in this manner was to highlight the importance of the *ʿulamāʾ*—including himself—to the correct functioning of Islamic society, and how its members produced examples which the rest of that society, including its leaders, should seek to emulate. More widely, he also wished to include examples of other famous people whose conduct could be held up as a model for how—or how not—to live.

One well-known example of this in Crusade scholarship is his death notice of the aged *faqīh* al-Findalāwī, who met his death fighting against the armies of the Second Crusade as they besieged Damascus in 543/1148. Although this episode is related in most of the Arabic historical works which recount the siege, Sibṭ Ibn al-Jawzī's description is much longer and more detailed than others—for example, Ibn al-Athīr in *al-Kāmil* gives the episode five

59 For example, see the year 613/1216–17, which is made up of around 70% obituaries. Rather unusually, Sibṭ Ibn al-Jawzī's death notices could include women, such as Niʿma bt. al-Ṭarāḥ (d. 604/1207–8), who, he reports, was a teacher of hadith in Damascus; *Mirʾāt al-zamān* (Hyderabad), vol. VIII/2, p. 539 (though, in an example of the poor quality of this text, it is written as p. 339).

60 Although the information in *Mirʾāt al-zamān* has not been fully utilised by modern historians, the potential for its use in understanding the social makeup of Damascus during the early seventh/thirteenth century can be seen through comparison with one of the best modern examples of how such data can be exploited for historical research: R. Bulliet, *The Patricians of Nishapur: A Study in Medieval Islamic Social History* (Cambridge MA, 1972). A similar approach was also taken in D.W. Morray, *An Ayyubid Notable and his World. Ibn al-ʿAdīm and Aleppo as Portrayed in His Biographical Dictionary of People Associated with the City* (Leiden, 1994).

lines while Ibn al-Qalānisī, the town chronicler of Damascus who was present at the siege, relates it in less than two.[61] Yet in *Mir'āt al-zamān* the obituary takes up almost a page and a half of text, a full page of which is an account of his heroic death and martyrdom: how he was excused combat by Unur, the ruler of Damascus, and his determination to fight anyway because it was the correct thing to do by Islam, followed by an example of the poetry written in celebration of his martyrdom.[62] Sibṭ Ibn al-Jawzī concentrates on al-Findalāwī in particular because of his background as a member of the *'ulamā'* and his martyrdom, as he was an almost perfect symbol of what the author was trying to say in his text; that this was an example of correct Islamic behaviour which should be emulated by others. Such a message was different to that which other writers, who only briefly mentioned the *faqīh*'s death, wished to impart, thus explaining their relative ignoring of the event. Such a perspective is evident throughout the majority of the obituaries and provides, as stated in his introduction to the text, examples for his readers—primarily the *'ulamā'* and members of the ruling classes—to seek to emulate.

Moving to the chronographical part of the text, the original material contained in *Mir'āt al-zamān* is limited. For pre-Islamic history and the first centuries of Islam it relies heavily on already well-known chronicles, particularly the voluminous and extremely important *Ta'rīkh al-rusul wa'l-mulūk* by al-Ṭabarī (d. 310/923), which formed the basis of many historical accounts about the first centuries of Islam written before, during and after the crusading period.[63] In the two centuries immediately preceding his lifetime, the fifth/eleventh and sixth/twelfth, he relied on a wider range of sources and, particularly for Iraq and Persia, on the chronicle written by his grandfather, *al-Muntaẓam fī ta'rīkh al-mulūk wa'l-umam*. For Syria and Egypt in the latter part of the fifth/eleventh century and the first half of sixth/twelfth he employed earlier and now well-known chronicles such as those of Ibn al-Qalānisī, Ibn al-Athīr and Ibn al-Azraq,[64] while for the latter half of that century he added 'Imād al-Dīn's *al-Barq al-Shāmī* to his corpus of source material. Ibn al-Qalānisī, Ibn al-Athīr

61 Ibn al-Athīr, *al-Kāmil fi'l-ta'rīkh*, ed. 'U. Tadmurī, 11 vols (Beirut, 2006), vol. IX, p. 159; Ibn al-Qalānisī, *Dhayl ta'rīkh Dimashq*, ed. H.F. Amedroz (Leiden, 1908), p. 298.

62 Sibṭ Ibn al-Jawzī, *Mir'āt al-zamān* (Hyderabad), vol. VIII/1, pp. 200–1.

63 Al-Ṭabarī, *Ta'rīkh al-rusul wa'l-mulūk*, ed. M. de Goeje, 15 vols (Leiden, 1879–1901).

64 Ibn al-Athīr, *al-Kāmil fi'l-ta'rīkh*; Ibn al-Qalānisī, *Dhayl ta'rīkh Dimashq*; Ibn al-Azraq, *Ta'rīkh Mayyāfāriqīn*, partial ed. and tr. C. Hillenbrand as *A Muslim Principality in Crusader Times* (Istanbul, 1990). For an analysis of how Sibṭ Ibn al-Jawzī employed source material from the latter, see C. Hillenbrand, 'Some Medieval Islamic Approaches to Source Material: The Evidence of a 12th Century Chronicle', *Oriens* 27/28 (1981), 197–225, pp. 199–205.

and Ibn al-Jawzī have all been published, while ʿImād al-Dīn's text, though mostly now lost, is extensively quoted by Abū Shāma and was abridged by al-Bundarī, and both of these have been edited by modern scholars, meaning the information contained within them is now well known.[65]

As Sibṭ Ibn al-Jawzī based his accounts of events from the first half of the crusading period on now-familiar chronicles, the overwhelming majority of information contained within it for this period contains little which is new, particularly when dealing with the arrival of the Franks. The account of the capture of Jerusalem in 492/1099 by the First Crusade, for example, is essentially lifted straight from Ibn al-Qalānisī's *Dhayl taʾrīkh Dimashq*.[66] His account of the Muslim victory at Balāṭ/the Field of Blood in 513/1119 also seems to be based on Ibn al-Qalānisī's version, albeit in a very cut-down form,[67] as is the case for most other events in southern Syria.[68] Other events in the first half of the sixth/twelfth century are based on the account of Ibn al-Athīr and are little altered. For example, the account of the diplomacy between Baldwin I of Jerusalem and Shams al-Khilāfa, ruler of Ascalon, which upset the Egyptians in the year 504/1110–11 is almost identical in both works,[69] as is also the case for Fulk of Jerusalem's march north to the region around Aleppo and raids against the surrounding region in the year 527/1132–33.[70] Thus, for events in the eastern part of the Islamic world during the first half of the sixth/twelfth century Sibṭ Ibn al-Jawzī is mostly dependent upon Ibn al-Jawzī, while for the lands of *al-Shām*

65 Abū Shāma's *Kitāb al-Rawḍatayn*, along with a French translation, is to be found in RHC *Or.*, vols IV–V; al-Bundarī, *Sanā al-barq al-Shāmī*, ed. F. al-Nabarawī (Cairo, 1979).

66 Sibṭ Ibn al-Jawzī, *Mirʾāt al-zamān* in RHC *Or*, vol. III, p. 520; Ibn al-Qalānisī, *Dhayl taʾrīkh Dimashq*, p. 135; partial tr. H.A.R. Gibb as *The Damascus Chronicle of the Crusades* (London, 1932), pp. 47–48. Other events where Sibṭ Ibn al-Jawzī copied Ibn al-Qalānisī include the Frankish siege of Aleppo in 518/1124, where he states that he is quoting directly from the earlier Damascene writer: Sibṭ Ibn al-Jawzī, *Mirʾāt al-zamān* (Hyderabad), vol. VIII/1, pp. 113–14; Ibn al-Qalānisī, *Dhayl taʾrīkh Dimashq*, pp. 211–12; Gibb, *Damascus Chronicle*, pp. 172–73.

67 Sibṭ Ibn al-Jawzī, *Mirʾāt al-zamān* (Hyderabad), vol. VIII/1, pp. 80–81; Ibn al-Qalānisī, *Dhayl taʾrīkh Dimashq*, pp. 200–1; Gibb, *Damascus Chronicle*, pp. 159–61.

68 For example, the siege of Tyre by the Franks in 505/1111–12 (Sibṭ Ibn al-Jawzī, *Mirʾāt al-zamān* [Hyderabad], vol. VIII/1, pp. 38–39; Ibn al-Qalānisī, *Dhayl taʾrīkh Dimashq*, pp. 178–81; Gibb, *Damascus Chronicle*, pp. 119–25).

69 Sibṭ Ibn al-Jawzī, *Mirʾāt al-zamān* (Hyderabad) vol. VIII/1, p. 35; Ibn al-Athīr, *al-Kāmil*, vol. VIII, p. 583; tr. D.S. Richards as *The Chronicle of Ibn al-Athir for the Crusading Period from* al-Kāmil fi'l-Taʾrīkh, 3 vols (Aldershot, 2006–8), 1, pp. 152–53.

70 Sibṭ Ibn al-Jawzī, *Mirʾāt al-zamān* (Hyderabad), vol. VIII/1, p. 146; Ibn al-Athīr, *al-Kāmil*, vol. IX, p. 43; tr. Richards, 1, pp. 299–300.

(Greater Syria) he, unsurprisingly, primarily employs his predecessor as historian of Damascus and Ibn al-Athīr.

However, and particularly with information concerning events in his city of residence, Damascus, Sibṭ Ibn al-Jawzī does add small snippets of information which are not to be found elsewhere regarding this period, and which must have come either from lost historical works or oral testimony. For example, during his account of the siege of Damascus by the armies of the Second Crusade, he adds details not found elsewhere, such as his relation that the Franks who were besieging the city gathered the harvest of Damascus' crops, which was at that time ripe, and ate it. This, he writes, gave them dysentery, a disease which killed a significant number of them and incapacitated many more which was a factor in causing them to lift the siege.[71]

Despite this relative paucity of new material overall, in two parts *Mir'āt al-zamān* is extremely important in terms of the originality of information. The first of these is from the period preceding the Crusades, in the fifth/eleventh century, as it contains significant and unique information from now lost chronicles such as that of Hilāl al-Ṣābi', essential for reconstructing events from this time such as the Seljūq takeover of Syria and the battle of Manzikert.[72] The second is the period in which Sibṭ Ibn al-Jawzī lived in Damascus—the first half of the seventh/thirteenth century. During this time he was an eyewitness to and, if he is to be believed, regular actor in many of the events he describes, and so his text becomes extremely important because of its originality, the proximity of the author to the main actors of the time, and his access to oral sources, to letters and to other documents. While its focus is generally restricted geographically to Damascus and Syria and socially to the religious and political elites of the city for the information it provides it is, alongside Ibn Wāṣil's chronicle *Mufarrij al-kurūb*, the main Muslim source for reconstructing events from the first half of the seventh/thirteenth century.

Despite this, for the history of the Frankish presence in the Levant the amount of directly related information it contains is limited, and even this is usually restricted to the 'main' Crusades of the first half of the seventh/thirteenth centuries: the Fifth Crusade, the Crusade of Frederick II, and the Crusade of Louis IX of France. Even here, however, little is generally reported, as can be seen in his recounting of the Fifth Crusade. Current scholarship for

71 Sibṭ Ibn al-Jawzī, *Mir'āt al-zamān* (Hyderabad), vol. VIII/1, p. 198; Gabrieli, *Arab Historians*, p. 62.

72 See, for example, J. Rassi, *Mir'āt al-zamān fī tārīḫ al-a'yān (Le miroir du temps) de Sibṭ ibn al-Ǧawzī* (Damascus, 2005); C. Hillenbrand, *The Battle of Manzikert: Turkish Myth and Muslim Symbol* (Edinburgh, 2007), pp. 67–74; Cahen, 'Editing Arabic Chronicles', p. 3.

this event generally and sensibly uses Ibn al-Athīr's account as the basis for Muslim perspectives on the events during this episode, as Sibṭ Ibn al-Jawzī contains little information on the Franks themselves, which explains why his contemporary report on the subject has not been translated into a western language.[73]

Perhaps the most well-known description of the Franks and of Muslim relations with them in *Mir'āt al-zamān* is that surrounding the handover of Jerusalem to the German Emperor Frederick II by the Egyptian sultan al-Kāmil in 626/1229. This passage's fame rests both on the fact that it is one of the few passages from *Mir'āt al-zamān* to have been translated by Gabrieli, but it is also one of the most dramatic in tone, especially through Hillenbrand's excellent rendering of perhaps the most vivid part: 'al-Kamil gave Jerusalem to the emperor... The news of the handing over of Jerusalem to the Franks arrived and all hell broke loose in the lands of Islam'.[74] His perspective on this episode, reinforced by the sermon he gave in the mosque of Damascus in response to it, highlights how he regarded himself, and the rest of the *'ulamā'*, as being protectors and champions of true Islamic ideals—although he is careful not to directly criticise the Ayyūbid leadership in his speech as reported. Not only does he give an impassioned speech against the handover, but the opposition of the *'ulamā'* in general to the decision is underlined by his report that the *qāḍī* of Jerusalem 'forgot' to give the city's muezzin al-Kāmil's order to not give the call to prayer while Frederick was in the city, meaning the German Emperor was assailed with Quranic verses about Christians, such as 'God has no son'.[75] Such blatant disregard for the ruling authorities by his fellow-members of the *'ulamā'* doubtless pleased Sibṭ Ibn al-Jawzī, as they were placing the demands of the *sharī'a* ahead of the orders of their earthly rulers which, in his opinion, went against the divine law, and thus the former were demonstrating what he believed to be correct behaviour. This passage about the handover of Jerusalem to Frederick gives modern scholars the perspective of Damascus' religious classes to these events, and so forms a counter-weight to the account of Ibn Wāṣil, which more reflects the Ayyūbids' 'official' perspective on events. This was not the only oration that he gave in response to and against the Frankish presence. His sermons in 607/1210 and 616/1219, which had

---

73 Ibn al-Athīr, *al-Kāmil*, vol. X, pp. 302–11; Gabrieli, *Arab Historians*, pp. 255–64; Richards, 3, pp. 174–82.

74 Sibṭ Ibn al-Jawzī, *Mi'rāt al-zamān* (Hyderabad), vol. VIII/2, p. 654; Hillenbrand, *Crusades*, p. 221.

75 Q. 23:93; Sibṭ Ibn al-Jawzī, *Mi'rāt al-zamān* (Hyderabad), vol. VIII/2, p. 656; Gabrieli, *Arab Historians*, p. 275.

mixed results, have been noted above and, despite not always being successful, the author still includes them in his book, partly in order to demonstrate his own devotion to the idea of jihad, partly to demonstrate to his readership that he, as a member of the *ʿulamāʾ*, still had some political relevance—as he was asked by the Ayyūbid rulers to give these speeches—but mostly to demonstrate to his readership what correct conduct was.

As with his other accounts of the major Crusades, his report of Louis IX's Crusade and the Frankish capture of Damietta in 647/1249–50 is rather brief. The capture of the town is related in the simple phrase 'in this year the Franks forced their way into Damietta in Rabīʿ I (14th June–13th July 1249)'. After this short summary the writer then moves swiftly on to comment on his main concern—the behaviour of the Ayyūbid sultan al-Ṣāliḥ. When the sultan was told that the people had abandoned Damietta he demanded that some of the city's leading men be hanged. Their response, which must be seen as articulating the author's opinion, was to ask why they should be hanged as the army had fled first and destroyed all the city's weapons. The sultan, however, ignored their pleas and, to underscore his cruelty, forced a father to watch his son be hanged before suffering the same fate. Ibn Wāṣil, writing of the same episode, omits this distressing detail and, while not seeking to blame the people who were hanged, does not openly criticise the Ayyūbid ruler for this course of action, which reflects the latter's own, generally more favourable perspective on the dynasty.[76]

Following this, the Franks do not appear as much more than a shadowy force for the rest of the period of Louis IX's Crusade. They are mentioned only when they do something which is of significance for the Muslims, such as when a group of Templars fell upon Fakhr al-Dīn, one of the leading Muslim emirs involved in Ayyūbid power politics,[77] or at the defeat of the Franks at Manṣūra which brought glory to Islam,[78] although both of these are recounted in no more than a few lines. The extent to which his focus is elsewhere can be seen from the fact that the few passages on Louis IX's Crusade (compared to the length given over to it by Ibn Wāṣil) written by Sibṭ Ibn al-Jawzī are all

76 Sibṭ Ibn al-Jawzī, *Mirʾāt al-zamān* (Hyderabad), vol. VIII/2, p. 773; Ibn Wāṣil, *Mufarrij al-kurūb*, vol. VI, p. 74; Gabrieli, *Arab Historians*, pp. 285–86; Jackson, *Seventh Crusade*, pp. 131 and 155. For Ibn Wāṣil's attitudes to and relations with the Ayyūbids, see below, pp. 136–60.

77 Sibṭ Ibn al-Jawzī, *Miʾrāt al-zamān* (Hyderabad), vol. VIII/2, pp. 776–77; Jackson, *Seventh Crusade*, p. 158.

78 Sibṭ Ibn al-Jawzī, *Miʾrāt al-zamān* (Hyderabad), vol. VIII/2, pp. 778–79; Jackson, *Seventh Crusade*, p. 159.

those which were translated by Jackson. Yet such a perspective on the part of the author is not surprising, as the Frankish invasion of Egypt paled into insignificance alongside the momentous political changes which were occurring concurrently with Louis IX's expedition and which it may have helped to cause—the overthrow of the Ayyūbid rulers of Egypt and their replacement by the Mamlūks. Compared to these events, and especially as he knew that the Frankish attack on Egypt would prove to be an abject failure, it is unsurprising that Sibṭ Ibn al-Jawzī pays little heed to them. Furthermore, the lack of a direct threat to his town of residence, Damascus, and to Jerusalem over the course of this Crusade meant there was little to pique Sibṭ Ibn al-Jawzī's concern directly.

In terms of his views of the Franks themselves, the author again gives little information, only occasionally providing any description of them. One of the few instances of this again comes from the passage surrounding the handover of Jerusalem to Frederick II. Unlike the description of him by Ibn Wāṣil, which has a rather sympathetic view of the German Emperor, Sibṭ Ibn al-Jawzī describes him in a distinctly unflattering way: 'The emperor... had red skin, was bald and short sighted', and would not have been worth two hundred dirhams had he been a slave. He read, the historian says, Aristotle's book of logic—which, to Sibṭ Ibn al-Jawzī, was to be engaging in the at best pointless and at worst downright sinful activity of philosophical reflection—and his Christianity was merely a game, meaning that he was not even devoted to his religion.[79] Such an image would have appealed to the sensibility of the majority of his audience by highlighting the laughable nature of the Muslims' opponent while also pandering to the pre-existing prejudices this audience had, an approach that had by this time become a *topos* for Muslim writers describing 'the other'.[80] This lack of much meaningful description suggests that, as for the information concerning Frankish activity, he did not care enough about them to produce any detailed presentation of them. This may also help to explain why he rarely employs curses in his writings against the Franks. Even when they took Jerusalem there is nothing said against the Franks in terms such as these, and so it almost seems that the Franks are so irrelevant to him, and such an insignificant threat to Islam by that time, that he sees no reason to employ such terms.

Thus, there is little overall original 'factual' material regarding the Franks within his report of the first half of the seventh/thirteenth century, and years

---

79 Sibṭ Ibn al-Jawzī, *Mi'rāt al-zamān* (Hyderabad), vol. VIII/2, p. 656; Gabrieli, *Arab Historians*, p. 275.

80 Cf. A. Al-Azmeh, 'Barbarians in Arab Eyes', *Past and Present* 134 (1992), 3–18.

can pass in his text without any mention of them.[81] Instead, *Mi'rāt al-zamān* primarily contains, like the almost contemporaneous chronicle of Ibn Wāṣil, vital information on inter- and intra-Ayyūbid relations during this period, particularly from the viewpoint of Damascus. This is particularly the case with his account of the Fifth Crusade as, immediately after the report that the Franks had arrived at Damietta, the author devotes considerable space to recounting the frantic diplomatic manoeuvres amongst the various Ayyūbid rulers in response to this.[82] There is less information given on the Franks than in *al-Kāmil*, but as he was well placed, close to the Ayyūbid government, Sibṭ Ibn al-Jawzī had better information than Ibn al-Athīr who was based in Zengid Mosul and so did not have the same level of access that Sibṭ Ibn al-Jawzī did. Similarly, in the case of events in the Ayyūbid world during the course of Louis IX's Crusade Sibṭ Ibn al-Jawzī reports the death of the sultan Tūrān Shāh in some depth, while there is also detailed information about events in Syria during the period 648/1250–651/1254, some of which has been translated by Jackson, and which should be utilised by historians to understand the background to Ayyūbid responses to Louis IX's presence in the region.[83] While only rarely focussed on events actually involving the Franks, Sibṭ Ibn al-Jawzī's chronicle allows for a better understanding of the Ayyūbid politics which dictated how the various Muslim polities interacted with the Franks in this period. The good use to which this chronicle can be put has been amply demonstrated by Humphreys, who used it extensively in his study of the Ayyūbids of Damascus in the years 1193–1260 to highlight the circumstances surrounding Ayyūbid rule in this period, which were then used to explain why the Ayyūbids related to the Franks as they did.[84] It is, therefore, unfortunate for historians of the crusading period that there is neither a critical edition of *Mi'rāt al-zamān* nor a full translation of this text into a western language. It would not be going too far to say that without this, and also a translation of Ibn Wāṣil's *Mufarrij al-kurūb*, it is impossible to fully understand the history of the crusading period in the Levant in the seventh/thirteenth century, particularly after Ibn al-Athīr's *al-Kāmil* ends. It is therefore of prime importance that a critical edition and translation of this chronicle is produced.

---

81 For example, there is no reference to the Franks between the years 608/1211 and 611/1214 inclusive.

82 Sibṭ Ibn al-Jawzī, *Mir'āt al-zamān* (Hyderabad), vol. VIII/2, pp. 592–94; 601–6; 608–10; and 619–21.

83 Sibṭ Ibn al-Jawzī, *Mir'āt al-zamān* (Hyderabad), vol. VIII/2, pp. 779–89; Jackson, *Seventh Crusade*, pp. 223–25.

84 Humphreys, *From Saladin to the Mongols*.

Conclusion

Sibṭ Ibn al-Jawzī's chronicle is, along with Ibn Wāṣil's *Mufarrij al-kurūb*, one of the most important historical works for information concerning the Levant in the first half of the seventh/thirteenth century and for relations between the Franks and the Ayyūbid states in this period. However, it is not a chronicle of the Crusades or of Muslim reactions to them; rather it is a combination of a universal history and a biographical dictionary focussed on the most important members of Sibṭ Ibn al-Jawzī's own professional circle of the *ʿulamāʾ* and the Ayyūbid leaders, particularly those of Damascus. Within this basic historiographical approach Sibṭ Ibn al-Jawzī had a number of aims. Foremost amongst these is a desire to articulate the importance which—in his eyes—the Sunnī *ʿulamāʾ*, best personified by his own self through his numerous and almost heroic appearances in the chronicle, should hold within the Islamic political system. This finds its expression in a number of ways, the most obvious of which is the significant space devoted to members of the *ʿulamāʾ* in the obituaries which follow each year, but also in the important role he presents them—and himself—as holding within society. He wishes to present himself as being almost the ideal example of a member of his social group, demonstrated through his attempts to whip up the Damascenes into a religious frenzy over the Frankish presence, such as during the raid of 607/1210 around Nablus or his sermon after Frederick II had been given Jerusalem, and on the numerous occasions he apparently helped 'encourage' the Ayyūbid leadership to do what he believed was the right thing. The fact that members of the *ʿulamāʾ* were not always held in such high regard—either by the rulers or the general population—and that their good example was often not followed was a source of frustration to him.

Linked to this, and also somewhat caused by it, is the fact that he wrote during a period when there was a debate between two different schools of thought in Islam over the best basis for political rule—*siyāsa* (that which is actually required to preserve and uphold the state) or *sharīʿa* (Islamic law). Like many other Muslim historians from this period, Sibṭ Ibn al-Jawzī had his own idea of what good Islamic government should look like, best demonstrated by his composition of a 'Mirrors for Princes' text which spells this out exactly and, for him, this was the *sharīʿa*, as he believed the *sharīʿa* to be the perfection of *siyāsa*, as a number of anecdotes within his text demonstrate.[85] His history

85 For example, in 613/1216 a woman was brought before the ruler al-Ẓāhir Ghāzī of Aleppo, accused of lying in her testimony against another, to which she had confessed. When the ruler asked what the punishment for this should be Bahāʾ al-Dīn Ibn Shaddād (the famous

overall was a call for a return to the *sharīʿa*, and his highlighting of the *ʿulamāʾ* was his attempt to underline their importance, for it is only they who could bring about its application by highlighting its main aspects and being a living example of its rules. The examples of good behaviour which he stated in his introduction he wished to highlight are, therefore, examples of how the *sharīʿa* looked in action.

Consequently, he is also concerned to highlight and criticise behaviour which runs contrary to the *sharīʿa*. An example of this can be seen in his description of Muslim soldiers fighting under Frankish crosses at the battle of Ḥarbiyya/La Forbie in 632/1244 and his comment that 'such had not happened at the beginning of Islam or in the time of Nūr al-Dīn and Saladin'.[86] He uses the almost mythical perfection of the early Islamic rulers and the two famous leaders of the Counter-Crusade to highlight his attitude not only to the specific incident, but also to the wider idea of fighting alongside the Franks; it must have been particularly galling to him that it was troops from his own city of Damascus who fought alongside the Franks.

These ideas run right through *Mirʾāt al-zamān*, and when using the text to write the history of the crusading period—or any other area of historical research—they need to be appreciated. His account of the handover of Jerusalem to Frederick, of the heroism of al-Findalāwī at Damascus and the events surrounding the Crusade of Louis IX, as well as everything else he describes, are all based on and influenced by these aims.

---

biographer of Saladin who was at the time *qāḍī* of Aleppo) said that according to the *sharīʿa* it was to be whipped, and according to the *siyāsa* it was to have her tongue cut off, and that she should have both as an exemplary punishment. Sibṭ Ibn al-Jawzī claims that he then intervened to point out that the *sharīʿa* is the perfection of *siyāsa*, so she should not have her tongue cut off. The ruler agreed, and the woman was only whipped. Sibṭ Ibn al-Jawzī, *Mirʾāt al-zamān* (Hyderabad), vol. VIII/2, p. 580; cf. T. Khalidi, *Arabic Historical Thought in the Classical Age* (Cambridge, 1994), pp. 193–200, esp. 195–96.

86 Sibṭ Ibn al-Jawzī, *Mirʾāt al-zamān* (Hyderabad), vol. VIII/2, p. 746.

Kamāl al-Dīn ʿUmar Ibn al-ʿAdīm

Anne-Marie Eddé

Kamāl al-Dīn ʿUmar b. Aḥmad Ibn al-ʿAdīm, the jurist and historian, was born in Aleppo in 588/1192 into the Banu'l-Abī Jarāda, a well-established family of Ḥanafī Sunnīs of Iraqi origin who had settled in Aleppo in the third/ninth century.[1] In the following century members of this family became famous in the fields of *belles-lettres*, poetry and Islamic law. In the fifth/eleventh and sixth/twelfth centuries members of the Banu'l-Abī Jarāda, more commonly known as the Banu'l-ʿAdīm,[2] almost continuously held the position of grand *qāḍī* of Aleppo, a role most often associated with that of preacher either in the Great Umayyad mosque or in the mosque of the citadel. When Saladin

1 On Kamāl al-Dīn Ibn al-ʿAdīm and his family, see Ibn al-ʿAdīm, *Bughyat al-ṭalab fī taʾrīkh Ḥalab*, ed. S. Zakkār, 11 vols (Damascus, 1988), vol. III, pp. 1210–14 (for the biography of his father Aḥmad Abu'l-Ḥasan); Yāqūt, *Irshād al-arīb ilā maʿrifat al-adīb* (or *Muʿjam al-udabāʾ*), ed. D.S. Margoliouth, 20 vols in 10, 3rd edition (Cairo, 1980), vol. XVI, pp. 5–57 (a detailed biography of Ibn al-ʿAdīm); Ibn al-Ṣuqāʿī, *Tālī kitāb wafayāt al-aʿyān*, ed. and tr. J. Sublet (Damascus, 1974), no. 143, p. 122; Abu'l-Fidāʾ, *Kitāb al-mukhtaṣar fī akhbār al-bashar*, ed. M.ʿA.L. al-Khaṭīb, 4 vols in 2 (Cairo, 1325/1907), vol. III, pp. 215–16; al-Dhahabī, *Taʾrīkh al-Islām wa wafayāt al-mashāhīr wa'l-aʿlām*, ed. ʿU. Tadmurī, 55 vols (Beirut, 1988–2008), vol. LI (years 651–660), pp. 421–24; al-Yūnīnī, *Dhayl mirʾāt al-zamān*, s.n., 4 vols (Hyderabad, 1951–61), vol. I, pp. 510–12; Ibn Shākir al-Kutubī, *Fawāt al-wafayāt*, ed. I. ʿAbbās, 4 vols (Beirut, 1973–74), vol. III, pp. 126–29; al-Ṣafadī, *al-Wāfī bi'l-wafayāt*, 30 vols, ed. H. Ritter et al. (Wiesbaden, 1931–2009), vol. XXII, pp. 421–26; Ibn Kathīr, *al-Bidāya wa'l-nihāya*, ed. Ṣ. al-ʿAṭṭār et al., 11 vols (Beirut, 1998–2001), vol. IX, pp. 119–20; Ibn Taghrībirdī, *al-Nujūm al-zāhira fī mulūk Miṣr wa'l-Qāhira*, s.n., 16 vols (Cairo, 1963–71), vol. VII, pp. 208–10 and *al-Manhal al-ṣāfī wa'l-mustawfī baʿd al-wāfī*, ed M.M. Amīn et al., 8 vols (Cairo, 1956–99), vol. VIII, pp. 270–73; Ibn al-ʿImād, *Shadharāt al-dhahab fī akhbār man dhahab*, ed. ʿA. and M. al-Arnaʾūṭ, 11 vols (Damascus and Beirut, 1986–95), vol. VII, pp. 525–26; R. Ṭabbākh, *Iʿlām al-nubalāʾ bi-taʾrīkh Ḥalab al-shahbāʾ*, ed. M. Kamāl, 7 vols (Aleppo, 1923–26), vol. IV, pp. 491–99; C. Brockelmann, *Geschichte der Arabischen Literatur*, 2 vols (Weimar-Berlin, 1898–1902; repr. Leiden, 1943–1949) with 3 supplements (Leiden, 1937–42), vol. I, p. 332 and S., vol. I, p. 568. See also the introduction by S. Dahhān in his edition of Ibn al-ʿAdīm, *Zubdat al-ḥalab min taʾrīkh Ḥalab*, 3 vols (Damascus, 1951–68), vol. I, pp. 13–79; D. Morray, *An Ayyubid Notable and his World. Ibn al-ʿAdīm and Aleppo as Portrayed in his Biographical Dictionary of People Associated with the City* (Leiden, 1994), pp. 40–44; A.-M. Eddé, *La principauté ayyoubide d'Alep (579/1183–658/1260)* (Stuttgart, 1999), pp. 366–67.

2 Ibn al-ʿAdīm comments that he did not know the exact origin of this family name, and suggests that it may have been because one of his ancestors evoked poverty, destitution (*ʿudm*), and the difficulties of his time in his poetry; Yāqūt, *Irshād*, vol. XVI, p. 6.

 | DOI 10.1163/9789004280687_007

(r. 569–89/1174–93) seized Aleppo in 579/1183, he removed these prestigious positions from the Banu'l-ʿAdīm and handed them over to Shāfiʿīs,[3] but the family continued to play a very important role in the religious and cultural life of northern Syria.

During his youth, Kamāl al-Dīn came under the dual influence of his father Najm al-Dīn Aḥmad and his uncle Jamāl al-Dīn Muḥammad, a noted ascetic. Under their direction he started at a young age to devote himself to the religious sciences (Quran and hadith studies), grammar, *fiqh* and *belles-lettres*, as well as calligraphy, for which he showed an early gift which gained him the admiration of his family and friends. His father, who had ardently awaited the birth of this only son, was constantly by his side, encouraging him in his studies and, from the age of nine we are told, the young Kamāl al-Dīn could already recite the Quran by heart. Between the ages of 15 and 18 he twice accompanied his father to Damascus and Jerusalem where he completed his training with a number of famous teachers.[4]

Around the year 611/1214–15 he married a young girl from a notable family of Aleppan Shāfiʿīs, the Banu'l-ʿAjamī, with whom he had a son the following year. Kamāl al-Dīn named him Najm al-Dīn after his own father, who just had time to see his grandson before he died. Najm al-Dīn (the younger) would later, like Kamāl al-Dīn, be a teacher in a madrasa in Aleppo, before he died in 638/1240–41 aged just 26. Najm al-Dīn's younger brother, Majd al-Dīn ʿAbd al-Raḥmān, lived longer, and was a teacher in several madrasas in Aleppo, a preacher in Cairo and, from 673/1274 until his death in 677/1278, the chief Ḥanafī *qāḍī* in Damascus, thus continuing the family tradition. A third son of Kamāl al-Dīn, named Jamāl al-Dīn Muḥammad, who was born in 635/1237–38 and who died in 694/1295, was also a teacher in a madrasa and held the position of *qāḍī* of Ḥamā. Additionally, Kamāl al-Dīn also had a daughter named Shuhda (d. 709/1309–10) who received a strict religious education, especially in the field of hadith studies, which she transmitted to a number of students

3 Eddé, *Principauté ayyoubide*, pp. 36 and 350.

4 He took, among others, lessons given by the head of the Ḥanafīs, Iftikhār al-Dīn al-Hāshimī (d. 616/1219), the Baghdadi traditionist Ibn Ṭabarzadh (d. 607/1210), the traditionist ʿAbd al-Raḥmān ibn ʿAlwān (known as Ibn al-Ustādh) (d. 623/1226) and his son-in-law, the chief Shāfiʿī *qāḍī* Bahāʾ al-Dīn Ibn Shaddād (d. 632/1234) at Aleppo; at Damascus, he attended the classes of the grammarian and linguist Tāj al-Dīn al-Kindī (d. 613/1217) and the chief Shāfiʿī *qāḍī* ʿAbd al-Ṣamad Ibn al-Ḥarastānī (d. 614/1218). The names of his numerous other teachers, as well as those of his students (one of whom was the famous Egyptian traditionist ʿAbd al-Muʾmin al-Dimyāṭī, d. 705/1306), are in al-Dhahabī, *Taʾrīkh al-Islām*, pp. 422–23.

before retiring from the world to lead an ascetic existence for the last thirty years of her life.[5]

Almost all Kamāl al-Dīn's professional career was based in Aleppo. From 616/1220 he was a professor of *fiqh* in the Ḥanafī madrasa named al-Shādhbakhtiyya, situated to the west of the citadel.[6] In 623/1226, he made the pilgrimage to Mecca,[7] and ten years later he held one of the most prestigious chairs in Aleppo, being made head of the Ḥanafī madrasa named al-Ḥallāwiyya, situated to the west of the Grand Mosque.[8]

Contrary to what some modern historians have suggested, Kamāl al-Dīn never held the role of *qāḍī* in Aleppo, unlike his father and grandfather before him. In this respect he followed the advice of his father who had told him:

> By God my son, I will never advise you to be a *qāḍī*, and if you are ever asked do not accept the proposal. From the moment this position was given to me until the moment I left it I knew no rest. Instead, I advise you to be a teacher and to take over al-Ḥallāwiyya madrasa.[9]

---

5 Cf. Eddé, *Principauté ayyoubide*, p. 367.

6 On this madrasa, see *Répertoire chronologique d'Épigraphie Arabe*, directed by Et. Combe et al., 17 vols (Cairo, 1937–82), vol. IX, nos. 3467–68, pp. 189–90; 'Izz al-Dīn Ibn Shaddād, *al-Aʿlāq al-khaṭīra fī dhikr umarāʾ al-Shām waʾl-Jazīra*, ed. D. Sourdel (Damascus, 1953), pp. 113–14; D. Sourdel, 'Les professeurs de madrasas à Alep aux XIIe et XIIIe siècles d'après Ibn Šaddād', *Bulletin d'Études Orientales* 13 (1949–51), pp. 92–94; H. Gaube and E. Wirth, *Aleppo. Historische und geographische Beiträge zur baulichen Gestaltung, zur sozialen Organisation und zur wirtschaftlichen Dynamik einer vorderasiatischen Fernhandelsmetropole*, 2 vols (Wiesbaden, 1984), no. 167, p. 364; Y. Tabbaa, *Constructions of Power and Piety in Medieval Aleppo* (University Park PA, 1997), pp. 134–35.

7 Morray, *Ayyubid Notable*, p. 151, says that he performed the Hajj three times, in 603–4/1207, 608–9/1212, and 623–24/1226–27. However I have only found mention in the sources of a pilgrimage to Mecca in the year 623/1226. Ibn al-ʿAdīm himself states that he returned to Aleppo from this journey in the month of Ṣafar 624/January–February 1227 (Ibn al-ʿAdīm, *Bughya*, vol. IV, p. 1643, and *Zubda*, vol. III, p. 200). On his stay in Sinjār, cf. Ibn al-ʿAdīm, *Bughya*, vol. VII, p. 3453.

8 This mosque had been founded by Nūr al-Dīn in 544/1149–50 on the site of a former Byzantine cathedral which had been transformed into a mosque in 518/1124. Cf. Ibn Shaddād, *al-Aʿlāq al-khaṭīra*, pp. 110–13; Gaube and Wirth, *Aleppo*, no. 73, p. 353; and Sourdel, 'Professeurs de madrasas', pp. 94–95.

9 Ibn al-ʿAdīm, *Bughya*, vol. III, p. 1211. It is, however, not impossible that Kamāl al-Dīn invented this recommendation from his father in order to justify the fact that he never held the position of *qāḍī*.

Kamāl al-Dīn was never vizier either. Ibn Kathīr, who attributes this title to him, also describes him as an 'emir', a position he certainly never held. These titles must be seen as essentially honorific, and Ibn al-Ṣuqāʿī should probably be believed when he writes: 'He occupied an important position in Damascus during the reign of al-Nāṣir Yūsuf, the ruler of Syria, but he refused the vizierate'.[10]

In the diplomatic arena, on the other hand, Kamāl al-Dīn played a leading role in the service of the Ayyūbid rulers, first of Aleppo and then of Damascus. During the reign of al-ʿAzīz (613–34/1216–36), and especially that of his son al-Nāṣir Yūsuf II (634–58/1236–60), he was charged with many missions and ambassadorial roles which gave him plenty of opportunity to travel. During these travels he visited many scholars where he gained much of the information he would later use in his writings. In 634/1236 al-ʿAzīz, who was on the verge of death, despatched Ibn al-ʿAdīm to his brother al-Ṣāliḥ Aḥmad, who was living in ʿAyntāb, north of Aleppo, to demand that the latter recognise as the next ruler al-ʿAzīz's son al-Nāṣir Yūsuf, who was then aged seven. A few months later the grandmother and regent for the young prince, Ḍayfa Khātūn, sent Ibn al-ʿAdīm as an ambassador to the Seljūq sultan of Rūm Kayqubād (r. 618–34/1221–37) to gain his support against al-Kāmil, the Ayyūbid ruler of Egypt, although when the ambassador arrived at Qayṣariyya the sultan had already died. Ibn al-ʿAdīm therefore gave his condolences to the new sultan Kaykhusraw II (r. 634–43/1237–46) instead and renewed with him an agreement which Kayqubād had concluded with Aleppo. The following year, when the Aleppans had concluded a double matrimonial alliance with the Seljūqs of Rūm through both the marriage of the sister of al-Nāṣir Yūsuf to the sultan Kaykhusraw II and al-Nāṣir Yūsuf's nuptials with the sultan's sister, it was Ibn al-ʿAdīm who was charged with concluding the agreement in the name of the young Ayyūbid princess, who was still a minor, according to the Ḥanafī rite which was both his own and that of the Seljūqs of Rūm. A few weeks after this he set out for the Seljūq capital, this time to sign the marriage contract with the Seljūq princess in the name of al-Nāṣir Yūsuf.[11]

He was also sent on numerous occasions as ambassador to other Ayyūbid princes: to the Jazīra, where he was very well received by al-Ashraf, a great admirer of his calligraphy; to Syria and Egypt in 638/1240, where he was charged with congratulating the sultan al-ʿĀdil II (r. 635–37/1238–40) for his recent vic-

10 Ibn Kathīr, *al-Bidāya*, vol. IX, p. 120, copied by al-ʿAynī, *ʿIqd al-jumān fī taʾrīkh ahl al-zamān*, ed. M.M. Amīn, 4 vols (Cairo, 1987–92), vol. I, p. 339; al-Yūnīnī, *Dhayl*, vol. I, p. 150, who also gives him the title of *sayyid al-wuzarāʾ* ('head of the viziers'); Ibn al-Ṣuqāʿī, *Tālī*, no. 143, p. 122; Morray, *Ayyubid Notable*, p. 187, n. 81; Eddé, *Principauté ayyoubide*, p. 364.

11 Ibn al-ʿAdīm, *Zubda*, vol. III, pp. 232 and 237–40.

tory over the Franks and with bringing back to Syria Ḍayfa Khātūn's sisters. However, rather ironically, al-ʿĀdil II was deposed in favour of his brother al-Ṣāliḥ Ayyūb (r. 637–47/1240–49) while the embassy was still in Cairo. In 648/1250 Ibn al-ʿAdīm was sent to the caliph in Baghdad with the rather delicate task of announcing to him the capture of Damascus by al-Nāṣir Yūsuf II.[12] The capture of this city was to change the course of his life, as he left Aleppo and followed al-Nāṣir Yūsuf II to Damascus, having handed over al-Ḥallāwiyya madrasa to his son Majd al-Dīn. During the final years of Ayyūbid rule in Syria he was to make two further trips to Baghdad as an ambassador.

Materially speaking, Kamāl al-Dīn always had a comfortable existence. His family held a number of important possessions in Aleppo and landed estates to the south-west of the city, in the regions around Maʿarrat Miṣrīn and Jabal Samʿān, where they possessed several villages. Kamāl al-Dīn himself received a village called al-Hūta, in the region of Aleppo, as an *iqṭāʿ*, and Yāqūt writes that his fortune was made up of land-holdings, slaves, horses and luxury clothes. In the capital, the comfortable means by which he lived allowed him to buy back a house which had once belonged to his ancestors, to restore the *miḥrāb* of al-Ḥallāwiyya madrasa where he taught, and to found, in 639/1241, his own madrasa outside the eastern wall of Aleppo. However, that building was only completed in 649/1251 and Kamāl al-Dīn, then in the service of al-Nāṣir Yūsuf II in Damascus, did not have time to appoint a teacher there before the arrival of the Mongols in 658/1260.[13]

The Mongol invasions were the cause of his last ambassadorial mission to Cairo at the end of the year 657/1259. Sent by an Ayyūbid ruler who was in desperate trouble to ask for help from the Mamlūks of Egypt, he was received by the emir and future sultan Quṭuz (657–58/1259–60) in the presence of the principal *ʿulamāʾ* of the capital. The embassy arrived at an opportune moment for Quṭuz as it enabled him to impose his power under the pretext that he was the only military man capable of defending Islamic territory against the terrible

12 See the description of this embassy and the text of the *khuṭba* pronounced on this occasion by Ibn al-ʿAdīm in al-Nuwayrī, *Nihāyat al-arab fī funūn al-adab*, ed. M.Ḍ.D. al-Rayyis et al., 33 vols (Cairo, 1923–98), vol. XXIX, pp. 370–76 (based on the eyewitness description by the historian Ibn al-Sāʿī). On the diplomatic activity of Ibn al-ʿAdīm see Morray, *Ayyubid Notable*, pp. 151–54.

13 This madrasa, which is still standing and is known currently as Jāmiʿ al-Ṭurunṭāʾiyya, was originally called al-Kamāliyya al-ʿAdīmiyya; cf. Yāqūt, *Irshād*, vol. XVI, pp. 53–54; Ibn Shaddād, *al-Aʿlāq al-khaṭīra*, p. 121; J. Sauvaget, *Alep: essai sur le développement d'une grand ville syrienne des origines au milieu du XIXe siècle* (Paris, 1941), pl. XXXIV and LVII; Gaube and Wirth, *Aleppo*, no. 657, p. 411; Tabbaa, *Constructions of Power*, pp. 137–38; Eddé, *Principauté ayyoubide*, pp. 367 and 648.

invaders.[14] Ibn al-ʿAdīm returned to Syria where he watched helplessly as the Mongols captured Aleppo in a bloodbath in Ṣafar 658/January 1260 and then entered Damascus, encountering no resistance, on 17th Rabīʿ I 658/2nd March 1260.[15] In contrast to what Dahhān once wrote, the Mongols never suggested to Kamāl al-Dīn that he be named *qāḍī* of Syria and the Jazīra.[16] This allegation which, to the best of my knowledge, is based only on the report of the historian al-Yūnīnī, is doubtless the result of a copyist having confused Kamāl al-Dīn ʿUmar Ibn al-ʿAdīm with Kamāl al-Dīn ʿUmar al-Tiflīsī (d. 672/1273), another Damascene jurist, who replaced the previous Shāfiʿī chief *qāḍī* of Damascus. Most other Arab writers, among them al-Yūnīnī himself in his obituary of al-Tiflīsī, confirm that it was to the latter that the Mongols made their offer.[17]

In the aftermath of these tragic events, Kamāl al-Dīn Ibn al-ʿAdīm fled, like many of his Syrian contemporaries, to Egypt. He returned to Aleppo only when the Mongols definitively left in Jumāda I 659/April 1261. The destruction he encountered there inspired him to write a poem in which he expressed, for the final time, his attachment to his hometown and his sadness when faced with its desolation.[18] He returned to Cairo, dying shortly after, on the 20th Jumāda I 660/12th April 1262, and was buried at the foot of the Muqaṭṭam.

---

14 R.S. Humphreys, *From Saladin to the Mongols. The Ayyubids of Damascus, 1193–1260* (Albany NY, 1977), p. 345; Eddé, *Principauté ayyoubide*, p. 173.

15 Humphreys, *From Saladin to the Mongols*, p. 353.

16 Dahhān, *Zubda*, vol. I, p. XXVII.

17 Al-Tiflīsī accepted the Mongols' offer; this led him to be praised by some for having avoided further bloodshed, and condemned by others for having collaborated with the enemy. After the Mamlūk re-capture of Damascus in September 1260 he was exiled to Cairo where, until his death, he spent his time as a teacher of theology (*uṣūl al-dīn*) and of *fiqh* theory (*uṣūl al-fiqh*). Cf. al-Yūnīnī, *Dhayl*, vol. I, p. 350 (copied by Ibn Taghrībirdī, *al-Nujūm al-zāhira*, vol. VII, p. 76 and n. 4) and vol. III, p. 64; Abū Shāma, *Tarājim rijāl al-qarnayn al-sādis wa'l-sābiʿ*, ed. M. al-Kawtharī (Cairo, 1947), p. 204; al-Dhahabī, *al-ʿIbar fī khabar man ʿabar*, ed. Ṣ.D. al-Munajjid, 5 vols (Kuwait, 1960–66), vol. V, pp. 298–99; Ibn al-ʿImād, *Shadharāt*, vol. VII, p. 589; al-Subkī, *Ṭabaqāt al-shāfiʿiyya al-kubrā*, ed. ʿA.F.M. al-Ḥilū and M.M. al-Ṭanāḥī, 10 vols (Cairo, 1964–70), vol. VIII, pp. 309–10; L. Pouzet, *Damas au VIIe/XIIIe siècle. Vie et structures religieuses dans une métropole islamique* (Beirut, 1988), pp. 119 and 293.

18 Cf. al-ʿAynī, *ʿIqd al-jumān*, vol. I, pp. 339–42 (following al-Nuwayrī but these verses are absent in the edition of the *Nihāya*); Abu'l-Fidā', *al-Mukhtaṣar*, pp. 215–16, reproduces some of the verses. See also Dahhān, *Zubda*, vol. I, p. XXXVIII.

Ibn al-ʿAdīm's Written Works

From the age of 22, while carrying out his numerous responsibilities, Ibn al-ʿAdīm was constantly writing. 'When he travelled', writes al-Kutubī, 'he used to ride in a litter that had been rigged up for him between two mules, and he would sit in it, writing'.[19]

His writings, some of which are now lost, reflect his main interests: education, calligraphy, history and poetry. Although a jurist, he never wrote a book on Islamic law, but his knowledge of and interest in hadith is perceptible in much of his work.[20] His first book was a small treatise on the education of children, dedicated to the son of Saladin, al-Malik al-Ẓāhir Ghāzī (r. 589–613/1193–1216), on the occasion of the birth of the latter's son and heir al-ʿAzīz in 610/1214;[21] a little later, he seems to have written a treatise of consolation for parents who had lost a child, entitled *Kitāb tabrīd ḥarārat al-akbād fi'l-ṣabr ʿalā faqd al-awlād*, one of the very first works in this genre which developed considerably in Syria and Egypt from the end of the seventh/thirteenth century.[22] He dedicated a work with the evocative title *Kitāb ḍaw' al-ṣabāḥ fi'l-ḥathth ʿala'l-samāḥ* ('The Morning Light in the Encouragement of Forgiveness') to the Ayyūbid prince al-Ashraf.[23] Like his uncle, Ibn al-ʿAdīm was well known for his talents in calligraphy, and he wrote a now-lost treatise on calligraphy and calligraphic tools entitled *Kitāb fi'l-khaṭṭ wa ʿulūmihi wa waṣf adābihi wa aqlāmihi wa ṭurūsihi* and, at the request of his friend, the geographer and biographer Yāqūt al-Rūmī (d. 626/1229), wrote a history of his own family called *al-Akhbār al-mustafāda fī dhikr Banī Abī Jarāda* which provides the majority of the information we have on him and his ancestors.[24]

---

19 Al-Kutubī, *Fawāt*, vol. III, p. 127; cf. Morray, *Ayyubid Notable*, p. 154.

20 See the detailed list of his works by Dahhān: *Zubda*, vol. I, pp. XLI–LVIII.

21 Ibn al-ʿAdīm, *Kitāb al-darārī fī dhikr al-dharārī*, in *Thalāth Rasā'il*, s.n., (Istanbul, 1298/1880–81), pp. 21–50.

22 Cf. A. Giladi, 'Concepts of Childhood and Attitudes towards Children in Medieval Islam', *Journal of the Economic and Social History of the Orient* 32 (1989), 121–52. This work is only mentioned by two authors: al-Kutubī, *Fawāt*, vol. III, p. 127, and Ḥajjī Khalīfa, *Kashf al-ẓunūn*, 2 vols in 4 (Istanbul, 1941–47), vol. I, p. 337.

23 A copy of this currently lost work was reported to exist in the libraries of Aleppo at the end of the seventh/thirteenth centuries; cf. P. Sbath, *Choix de livres qui se trouvaient dans les bibliothèques d'Alep (au XIIIe siècle)* (Cairo, 1946), p. 33, no. 599.

24 This small work, in which the author traces his family's genealogy back almost ten generations, is lost, but the essentials are known to us thanks to Yāqūt, *Irshād*, vol. XVI, pp. 5–57.

His taste for literature and poetry led him to write, around the year 640/1242–43, a piece in praise of the Syrian poet al-Maʿarrī (d. 449/1058), entitled *Kitāb al-inṣāf wa'l-taḥarrī fī dafʿ al-ẓulm wa'l-tajarrī ʿan Abi'l-ʿAlāʾ al-Maʿarrī*, which is today one of our principle sources for the life of that poet.[25] In another work, the *Tadhkira*, he gives us an anthology of poems and rhyming prose written by numerous men of letters.[26] More curiously, another work attributed to him is that of recipes of both perfume and food called *al-Wuṣlat ila'l-ḥabīb fī waṣf al-ṭayyibāt wa'l-ṭīb*,[27] which was one of the most important culinary works of the Middle Ages, in the words of Maxime Rodinson, who studied the text in his important article.[28] However, no medieval author mentions this work amongst those of Kamāl al-Dīn, and this attribution is based solely on the title page of a relatively late Berlin manuscript of which there remains only four folios.[29] Ten of the extant manuscripts of this work do not name the author of the work in the text, while the manuscript preserved in Cairo, which seems to be part of an independent recension, contains a phrase which indicates that at least part of the text was, in fact, written by a nephew of the Ayyūbid prince al-Ashraf.[30] After an in-depth analysis of the text and the extant manuscripts, Rodinson sensibly put forward the hypothesis that this work had been written during the Ayyūbid period by someone who was familiar with the Ayyūbid court, and that it was then the object of a number of later revisions. He suggested that among the authors of the original text (or of the revisions), besides an Ayyūbid prince, was Kamāl al-Dīn Ibn al-ʿAdīm.[31] While the first part, that it was a text written by an author who had been at the heart of Ayyūbid government, is credible, the arguments in favour of attributing it to Ibn al-ʿAdīm remain unconvincing. The recipes, so accurately described, can only have been

---

A copy was still held in one of the libraries of Aleppo at the end of the seventh/thirteenth century; cf. Sbath, *Choix de livres*, p. 3, no. 38.

25 Ed. ʿA.ʿA. Ḥarfūsh (Damascus, 2007). See also *Taʿrīf al-qudamāʾ bi-Abi'l-ʿAlāʾ*, ed. Ṭ.Ḥ. Bek (Cairo, 1944), p. 483.

26 A manuscript of this work is preserved in Cairo; cf. Brockelmann, GAL, S. I, p. 569.

27 Ibn al-ʿAdīm, *al-Wuṣla ila'l-ḥabīb fī waṣf al-ṭayyibāt wa'l-ṭīb*, ed. S. Maḥjūb and D. al-Khaṭīb, 2 vols (Aleppo, 1986–88).

28 M. Rodinson, 'Recherches sur les documents arabes relatifs à la cuisine', *Revue des Études Islamiques* 17 (1949), pp. 95–165.

29 MS Berlin—Staatsbibliothek 5463; W. Ahlwardt, *Verzeichniss arabischer Handschriften der Königlichen Bibliothek zu Berlin*, 10 vols (Berlin, 1887–89), vol. V, pp. 39–40.

30 MS Cairo—Dār al-kutub, Ṣināʿa 74.

31 This was based on his name being found on the Berlin manuscript and because he had been a regular at the Ayyūbid court. This was followed word for word by the editor of the *Wuṣla*.

written by someone with enormous culinary experience. Moreover, in the preface, the author specifies 'that he has not put anything in this book that he did not prepare or make himself on numerous occasions, or which he did not order for himself, or which he did not touch and taste'. Furthermore, the differences between the preface of the culinary treatise, which contains numerous Quranic verses, and the three prefaces written with certainty by Ibn al-ʿAdīm, in which the traditional religious invocations are much shorter, must be taken into consideration.[32] Finally, what is known about Ibn al-ʿAdīm's life and interests does not suggest that the authorship of this work should be attributed to him; in contrast to some of his contemporaries, Ibn al-ʿAdīm was not one of the prolific littérateurs who wrote on any subject whatsoever.

Yet despite these other writings, Ibn al-ʿAdīm's fame rests primarily on his historiographical works, one of which was his history of Aleppo entitled *Zubdat al-ḥalab min taʾrīkh Ḥalab*, and the other his voluminous biographical dictionary of people who had some link with that city, entitled *Bughyat al-ṭalab fī taʾrīkh Ḥalab*.[33]

Bughyat al-ṭalab fī taʾrīkh Ḥalab

This work, which was generally known under the shortened title of *Taʾrīkh Ḥalab* ('The History of Aleppo') by medieval writers, was originally composed of forty volumes, of which only ten survive (containing some 2081 notices on around 2500 folios). In his conception of this dictionary, Ibn al-ʿAdīm was doubtless inspired by the work of al-Khaṭīb al-Baghdādī (d. 463/1071), the author of *Taʾrīkh Baghdād* ('The History of Baghdad'), and by Ibn ʿAsākir (d. 571/1176), who wrote *Taʾrīkh madīnat Dimashq* ('The History of the City of Damascus'). It is important to note that during this period the term *taʾrīkh* ('history') did not necessarily imply a chronological narrative of events, but could also be applied to works written in the form of biographical dictionaries of people who were deemed important enough by the author to merit inclusion. Consequently, this kind of historical work was similar to the biographical dictionaries which had been widespread in the Islamic world as early as the third/ninth century and which had originally been aimed at establishing the infallibility of the transmitters of hadith (the sayings of Muḥammad). Providing for each of the scholars the chains of transmission (*isnād*-s) of which they were a link by quoting

32 In the *Zubda*, *Kitāb al-darāri* and the *Kitāb al-inṣāf waʾl-taḥarrī*.

33 Ibn al-ʿAdīm, *Zubdat al-ḥalab min taʾrīkh Ḥalab*, ed. S. Dahhān, 3 vols (Damascus, 1951–68), and *Bughyat al-ṭalab fī taʾrīkh Ḥalab*, ed. S. Zakkār, 11 vols (Damascus, 1988).

the names of their teachers and students and by giving examples of hadiths they had transmitted, the authors of these dictionaries were aiming to authenticate hadiths. These dictionaries could be general works, or could be classified according to the profession of the people listed, their juridical school, the time when they lived, or their place of origin.[34]

In the case of biographical dictionaries focussed on specific towns, a topographical description usually precedes the list of biographies. The first volume of the *Bughya* follows this trend, but does so using a particularly broad perspective, as all of northern Syria is described, rather than just Aleppo. Like his predecessors, Ibn al-ʿAdīm gives much space to hadith scholars, to the *ʿulamāʾ* in general, and to their *isnād*-s, but more than these he is interested in various other people who had an impact on the cultural, social, and political history of his home town, such as poets or military leaders.

Each notice follows more or less the same pattern: the person's name, training and career. When the notice describes a scholar it states the names of his teachers from whom he learned the hadiths, his students to whom he transmitted them, and which hadiths he transmitted; when a poet is described there are usually some examples of the verses he composed; and for a military leader various examples of his battles are recounted. Each notice is often enlivened with anecdotes, and concludes with the circumstances and date of the subject's death when they are known.

In the majority of the entries Ibn al-ʿAdīm cites his sources of information, and the number of works he consulted is testimony to his erudition and to the size of his library: more than 500 books, not counting those with unknown titles. To this must be added the large number of contemporary oral testimonies he used. An analysis of Ibn al-ʿAdīm's sources allows for a better understanding firstly of his working method, secondly of how this scholar benefitted from his many travels—in the course of which he consulted large numbers of manuscripts—and thirdly of the reliability of his sources. It also highlights the abundant literary and historical production of various times and places allowing us, at least in part, to have access to sources which are today lost.

In writing the *Bughya* Ibn al-ʿAdīm used a vast range of sources, including chronicles and works of genealogy and dynastic history, as well as biographical dictionaries, anthologies, hadith collections, travel narratives and literary works. All these were written by scholars originating from different places (Iran, Iraq, Syria, Egypt) and from varying religious sensibilities (Sunnī for the most part but also Shīʿī in some cases). Ibn al-ʿAdīm used his sources with great

34 For the relationship between hadith studies and Islamic historical writing, see C.F. Robinson, *Islamic Historiography* (Cambridge, 2003).

care, comparing and sometimes criticizing them, referring, if necessary—as with hadiths—to a chain of transmission which could guarantee their authenticity, concerned as he was to prove the veracity of his information.

A work of such scope must have taken many years to complete. The preface of the work, in which the reasons and circumstances of writing were no doubt expounded, is unfortunately lost, but various indications suggest that it was probably at the instigation of the Ayyūbid prince of Aleppo, al-Malik al-Ẓāhir Ghāzī, that Ibn al-ʿAdīm commenced writing his 'History of Aleppo' which is, as noted previously, the title usually assigned to the *Bughya* by medieval writers.[35] In his notice on Ibn al-ʿAdīm, Yāqūt mentions it[36] but the work, originally written in draft form, was only completed later on in Egypt,[37] even if its author had no time to complete a fair copy before his own death.[38] Today, besides the first volume which is devoted to the description of Aleppo and northern Syria, the extant notices concern people whose names start with letters from the first part of the Arabic alphabet, from Aḥmad to Saʿīd (with lacunae), and people known by their *kunyā* (Abū), *nasab* (Ibn), *laqab* (surname, honorific title), or *nisba* (which indicates their relation to a tribe, a place, a profession, or a physical characteristic). Additionally, later sources preserve excerpts of some other notices.[39]

35 For example, see al-Dhahabī, *Taʾrīkh Islām*, p. 424; cf. Morray, *Ayyubid Notable*, p. 145.

36 Yāqūt, *Irshād*, vol. XVI, p. 45.

37 This is clearly shown by the notices of persons who died in 656/1258 after the fall of Baghdad to the Mongols; cf. Ibn al-ʿAdīm, *Bughya*, vol. VII, pp. 3453–65; Morray, *Ayyubid Notable*, pp. 166–75.

38 The volumes preserved in Istanbul (see note 42) are probably the autograph draft of the author as witnessed by the corrections and additions in the margins and, above all, by the commentary made by his son Jamāl al-Dīn in the margin of one folio, which reads: 'My father—God have mercy on him—left this blank space to indicate the death of the person concerned. But the latter died after my father. I myself filled it in'. Cf. Morray, *Ayyubid Notable*, p. 168.

39 Cf. al-Dhahabī, *Taʾrīkh al-Islām*, ed. B.ʿA. Maʿrūf, S. al-Arnaʾūṭ and Ṣ.M. ʿAbbās, 4 vols (Beirut, 1988), section 61, p. 358 and section 62, pp. 310–12: the biographies of ʿAbdallāh al-Yūnīnī (d. 617/1220) and Ibrāhīm b. Khalaf al-Sanhūrī (d. 610/1213–14); Ibn Abiʾl-Wafāʾ al-Qurashī, *al-Jawāhir al-muḍiyya fī ṭabaqāt al-Ḥanafiyya*, s.n., 2 vols (Hyderabad, 1332/1913), vol. I, no. 890, p. 329: the biography of ʿAbd al-Muṭṭalib al-Hāshimī Iftikhār al-Dīn (d. 616/1219); B. Lewis, 'Kamāl al-Dīn's biography of Rashīd al-Dīn Sinān', *Arabica* 13 (1966), 225–67 (taken from al-Yūnīnī, al-Dhahabī, and al-Ṣafadī); al-Kutubī, *Fawāt*, vol. IV, p. 363: the biography of al-Malik al-Nāṣir Yūsuf II; al-ʿAynī, *ʿIqd al-jumān*, vol. I, p. 97: the biography of Bakbars Najm al-Dīn al-Turkī (d. 652/1254); Ibn al-ʿImād, *Shadharāt*, vol. VI, p. 555: the biography of ʿAbd al-Wahhāb Ibn al-Naḥḥās (d. 599/1202–3); Taqī al-Dīn b. ʿAbd al-Qādir al-Ghazzī al-Tamīmī, *al-Ṭabaqāt al-saniyya fī tarājim al-sādat al-ḥanafiyya*,

The dispersal of the various volumes of the *Bughya* was not a recent occurrence. Although the libraries of Aleppo retained one copy of the work at the end of the seventh/thirteenth century[40] despite the Mongol destruction of the city in 658/1260, Ibn al-Shiḥna (d. 890/1485) noted that the majority of the work had been lost even before the invasion of Tamerlane in 803/1400. He himself possessed only one volume of the work, containing the names beginning with the letter *mīm*. It was in Egypt that the autograph volumes which have come down to us were preserved. The Egyptian historian al-Sakhāwī (d. 902/1497) cites them one by one adding one more volume now lost (which lists persons from Musharriq b. ʿAbdallāh to al-Walīd b. ʿAbd al-ʿAzīz).[41]

The limited number of extant manuscripts may suggest that the work had only a limited circulation.[42] Yet it is cited, most often under its abridged title of 'The History of Aleppo', by many later historians who reproduce extracts of it: Ibn Khallikān (d. 681/1282), ʿIzz al-Dīn Ibn Shaddād (d. 684/1285), al-Yūnīnī (d. 726/1326), al-Dhahabī (d. 748/1348), Ibn Shākir al-Kutubī (d. 764/1363), al-Ṣafadī (d. 764/1363), Ibn Abi'l-Wafā' al-Qurashī (d. 773/1373), Ibn Taghrībirdī (d. 815/1412), Sibṭ Ibn al-ʿAjamī (d. 818/1415), al-ʿAynī (d. 855/1451), al-Suyūṭī (d. 911/1505), and Ibn al-ʿImād (d. 1089/1679). The *Bughya* also inspired other writers to continue the work by writing about the lives of Aleppans who lived

ed. ʿA.F.M. al-Ḥulw (Cairo, 1970), p. 199: the biography of Ibrāhīm b. Aḥmad al-Mawṣilī (d. 560/1165); Murtaḍā al-Zabīdī, *Tāj al-ʿarūs min jawāhir al-qāmūs*, 10 vols (Cairo, 1306/1888–89), vol. VII, p. 109: the biography of Barmak al-Aṣghar (the eponymous ancestor of the Barmakids).

40 However, we cannot tell if this copy was complete. Sbath, *Choix des livres*, p. 12, no. 210.

41 Cf. al-Sakhāwī, *al-Iʿlān bi'l-tawbīkh li-man dhamma ahl al-taʾrīkh*, tr. in F. Rosenthal, *A History of Muslim Historiography*, 2nd rev. ed. (Leiden, 1968), pp. 263–529 (especially pp. 443–44). Al-Sakhāwī saw 11 volumes of this work, including the volume which deals with geographical material.

42 One volume is preserved in London (vol. X; MS London—British Library Add. 23354), another in Paris (vol. IV; MS Paris—BNF arabe 2183), and a third in Mosul (MS Mosul—Madrasa al-Ḥasaniyya 8/9). But it is in Istanbul where the greater part of the work's ten extant volumes are to be found, in manuscripts which are probably autograph: MS Istanbul—Süleymaniye, Aya Sofia 3036 (vol. I); Top Kapı, Ahmet III, 2925/I–VIII (vols. II–IV and VII–X); Feyzullah 1404 (vol. V). Cf. C. Cahen, 'Les chroniques arabes concernant la Syrie, l'Égypte et la Mésopotamie, de la conquête arabe à la conquête ottomane dans les bibliothèques d'Istanbul', *Revue des Études Islamiques* 10 (1936), p. 359. It was not until the late 1980s that there was a complete facsimile publication (ed. F. Sezgin, *Everything Desirable about the History of Aleppo*, 11 vols [Frankfurt, 1986–1990]), and a critical edition was then produced by S. Zakkār: 11 vols (Damascus, 1988). Cf. Morray, *Ayyubid Notable*, pp. 199–201.

after the death of Ibn al-ʿAdīm, as was the case with Ibn al-Khaṭīb al-Nāṣiriyya (d. 843/1451) and Ibn al-Ḥanbalī (d. 971/1563).[43]

In comparison to the *Zubda* the *Bughya* has been exploited less by crusade historians, for two main reasons. Firstly, reported episodes from the Crusades are present less in the *Bughya* than in the *Zubda*, and secondly, unlike the *Zubda*, the *Bughya* has never been fully translated into a European language.[44] However, the information the *Bughya* provides in relation to the Crusades is far from negligible and Claude Cahen was the first to point out its importance as a source for the history of northern Syria.[45]

Some very useful information relating to the Crusades is to be found within the introductory topographical chapter of the *Bughya*. For example, the Frankish conquest of northern Syrian towns (Antioch, Maʿarrat al-Nuʿmān, Maʿarrat Miṣrīn, Kafarṭāb) are reported without significant details, but at times the author alludes to the flight of their inhabitants towards towns remaining in Muslim hands (Aleppo, Ḥamā, Damascus). Elsewhere, it is reported that caves in the region surrounding Maʿarrat Miṣrīn allowed the population to escape the ravages of the Franks.[46]

However, it is in the biographies of the princes and emirs of northern Syria, in the first half of the sixth/twelfth century, that Ibn al-ʿAdīm gives the most original information about relations between Franks and Muslims. His report on the Seljūq ruler Riḍwān cites, for example, his defeats at the hand of the Franks and his reaction to the arrival of the sultan's army sent to bring help to Syria in 505/1111.[47] The detailed biographies of the Arab emir Dubays b. Ṣadaqa

43 Ibn al-Khaṭīb al-Nāṣiriyya, *al-Durr al-muntakhab bi-takmilat taʾrīkh Ḥalab*. Cf. Brockelmann, *GAL* S. vol. I, p. 568; MS Damascus—al-Asad Library 14501–2 (formerly MS Aleppo—Madrasa al-Aḥmadiyya 1214); B. Martel-Thoumian, *Catalogue des manuscrits historiques de la Bibliothèque de Damas. Période Mamlouke (648–922H./1250–1517)* (Damascus, 2003), pp. 121–23. See also Ibn al-Ḥanbalī, *Durr al-ḥabab fī taʾrīkh aʿyān Ḥalab*, ed. M. al-Fākhūrī and Y. ʿAbbāra, 2 vols in 4 (Damascus, 1972–74).

44 Parts of MS Paris—BNF arabe 2183, concerning the following Aleppan rulers, were translated into French in *RHC Or.* vol. III, pp. 695–732: Shams al-Mulūk Ismāʿīl b. Būrī; al-Ṣāliḥ Ismāʿīl b. Nūr al-Dīn; Qasīm al-Dawla Aq Sunqur; Aq Sunqur al-Bursuqī; and Alp Arslān b. Riḍwān. See also J. Sauvaget, 'Extraits du *Buġyat aṭ-ṭalab* d'Ibn al-ʿAdīm', *Revue des Études Islamiques* 7 (1933), 393–409 (translation of short extracts); and Lewis, 'Kamāl al-Dīn's Biography of Rāšid al-Dīn Sīnān'.

45 C. Cahen, *La Syrie du Nord à l'époque des Croisades et la principauté franque d'Antioche* (Paris, 1940), p. 37.

46 Ibn al-ʿAdīm, *Bughya*, vol. I, pp. 87 and 135.

47 Ibn al-ʿAdīm, *Bughya*, vol. VIII, pp. 3659–67. Elsewhere, Ibn al-ʿAdīm also recounts the reaction of Riḍwān after a revolt by Frankish prisoners in the fortress of al-Rāwandān, to the north of Aleppo; *Bughya*, vol. I, p. 324.

(d. 529/1135) and the Turkish ruler Aq Sunqur al-Bursuqī (d. 520/1126) also provide a significant amount of original material regarding the clashes between the Franks and the Muslims around Aleppo in 518/1124: the captivity and subsequent ransoming of king Baldwin II (r. 1118–31); his violation of the promises he had made at that time; his alliance with Dubays and the harsh siege he inflicted on Aleppo; and the Aleppan embassy (in which the great-grandfather of the historian took part) sent first to Mardin where Timurtāsh, on whom Aleppo's defence in principle depended, remained deaf to its request for help, and then to Mosul where the ambassadors managed to persuade its ruler Aq Sunqur al-Bursuqī to come to their aid.[48]

In his biography of Zengī (the ruler of Aleppo from 522/1128 to 541/1146) Ibn al-ʿAdīm gives an unusual version of the conquest of Edessa in 539/1144. Reporting the remarks of the *qāḍī* Bahāʾ al-Dīn Ibn Shaddād, who claimed to have heard them from the principal protagonist of the tale, he reports that the muezzin of Mosul, who was blond and 'of Armenian appearance', entered Edessa during the siege. While the town was still being defended by a garrison of Franks perched on the ramparts, he gave the call to prayer from the minaret of the town's mosque, which led the town's population to believe that it had fallen into the hands of the Muslims. The Franks fled and Zengī rewarded the muezzin by offering him as reward a nearby village.[49]

Other passages in the *Bughya* deal with various aspects of everyday relations between Franks and Muslims. Particularly interesting is the biography of the historian Ḥamdān al-Athāribī (d. 542/1147–48), the author of a now-lost history of Aleppo and of the Frankish conquest which began in the year 490/1096–97 and finished sometime after 520/1126,[50] which traces the life of this man of letters who had detailed knowledge of history, astronomy and medicine, and who was at some times employed by the Franks while at others in the service of the Muslim leaders of Aleppo. The latter sent him many times as a member of embassies to Damascus, Cairo, Baghdad and the Frankish states. Alan, the lord of al-Athārib, whose illness he had treated and cured, gave him a village in the region of Maʿarrat Miṣrīn in 521/1127, which he was allowed to keep after the Muslim re-conquest of the place.[51]

48 Ibn al-ʿAdīm, *Bughya*, vol. IV, pp. 1963–70, and vol. VII, pp. 3478–93.

49 Ibn al-ʿAdīm, *Bughya*, vol. VIII, pp. 3845–57.

50 Ibn al-ʿAdīm, *Bughya*, vol. VI, pp. 2926–32. This is the only known Arabic work from this period which is devoted to the Crusades.

51 Ibn al-ʿAdīm calls this Frankish lord Manuel and says that he was the nephew (the son of the sister) of the prince of Antioch; Cahen, *Syrie du Nord*, p. 540.

There is also the biography of a Sufi ascetic named Abu'l-Ḥusayn who, we are told, one day profited from the deep sleep of a group of drunken Frankish knights by stealing their horses which he then gave to the Muslim inhabitants of a nearby village. Nūr al-Dīn offered this same ascetic a Frankish prisoner to whom the latter gave the freedom to come and go as he pleased and who, in the end, converted to Islam.[52] Ibn al-ʿAdīm also relates safe-conducts the Franks gave to Muslims who wished to traverse their lands and the permission they gave to those who wished to visit the holy places of Jerusalem.[53] Such is the case of an ascetic named Rabīʿ (d. 602/1205), a native of Mardin, who worked in Frankish Jerusalem for some monks who allowed him to practise his religion. Those Muslims wishing to pray in the Dome of the Rock were normally charged for the right to enter, but he was exempted from this one day as he had no money.[54] During his description of Antioch, the author also tells us that he himself went to Frankish territory, to Antioch, in 613 or 614 (1216–18) and that he visited the church of al-Qusyān (Cathedral of Saint Peter), which was decorated with marble and mosaics, and where the princes and patriarchs of Antioch were buried.[55] Such examples show that a careful reading of the *Bughya* provides a great deal more information on relations between Franks and Muslims during the Crusades than may be initially assumed.

Zubdat al-ḥalab min taʾrīkh Ḥalab

The historical work of Ibn al-ʿAdīm which provides the richest source of evidence for the Crusades is, unquestionably, *Zubdat al-ḥalab min taʾrīkh Ḥalab* ('The Cream of the Milk from the History of Aleppo'). In his preface to the work, Ibn al-ʿAdīm explains his reasons for writing, his aims and the conception of the work:

> He whose orders I have to carry out, the assistance and kindness of whom I have to obey, asked me to comment on the information that I could find concerning the emirs of Aleppo, its governors, its princes and its people. I rushed to satisfy his request and to serve him I undertook what he prescribed. In the pages that follow I have evoked those who have ruled and

52 Ibn al-ʿAdīm, *Bughya*, vol. x, pp. 4411–19.

53 Ibn al-ʿAdīm, *Bughya*, vol. ix, pp. 4304 and 4310, and vol. x, p. 4356.

54 Ibn al-ʿAdīm, *Bughya*, vol. viii, p. 3593.

55 Ibn al-ʿAdīm, *Bughya*, vol. i, p. 87; on the Cathedral of Saint Peter during the Frankish period, see Cahen, *Syrie du Nord*, p. 130.

> whatever I have learned about its viziers and *qāḍīs*. I have also mentioned those who founded it in ancient times together with the meaning of the name which characterizes it among all other cities. I entitled this book *Zubdat al-ḥalab min taʾrīkh Ḥalab* because I extracted it from my greater *History of Aleppo al-Shahbāʾ* (the White) in which [people's] names are arranged in alphabetical order.[56]

In giving his work this title Ibn al-ʿAdīm was making use of a pun (*ḥalab* in Arabic being the name for both Aleppo and 'milk'), and he expresses equally clearly that he wanted to extract the 'cream' (*zubda*), i.e. the best part or the essence, of the *Bughya* in order to satisfy the wish of his sponsor. Strangely, Ibn al-ʿAdīm does not mention who this was, even though this clearly refers to the ruler of Aleppo. Dahhān, arguing from the fact that Ibn al-ʿAdīm had already offered a small treatise on children to al-Ẓāhir Ghāzī on the occasion of the birth of al-ʿAzīz (r. 613–34/1216–36) and from the good relations which united him to these two rulers, once thought that the sponsor of the *Zubda* was none other than al-ʿAzīz or perhaps his atabeg and regent Ṭughril (d. 631/1233). He also believed that Ibn al-ʿAdīm failed to name him because he only completed his work after al-ʿAzīz's death. Yet from Ibn al-ʿAdīm's own comments this hypothesis is difficult to sustain. We have seen, in effect, that the *Bughya* was composed over several decades and that it was probably not completed before the Mongol invasion of Syria in 658/1260 and the settlement of Ibn al-ʿAdīm in Egypt. The *Zubda* was, according to the author's own words, an 'extract' of the *Bughya*, so it is improbable that the former had been completed before 1236, when al-ʿAzīz died. It is, instead, much more likely that it was written for his son and successor, al-Nāṣir Yūsuf II (634–58/1236–60) who, as we have seen, made Ibn al-ʿAdīm one of his most trusted ambassadors. It is possible that al-Nāṣir is not mentioned in the preface because at the time of the work's final redaction he was a prisoner of the Mongols—and probably already executed—and that in Egypt, during the initial period of Mamlūk rule, he was not a popular figure. In any case, Ibn al-ʿAdīm did not have time to finish the *Zubda*, which ends abruptly at the beginning of the year 641/June–July 1243.

Even though the historian made abundant use in his *Zubda* of the source material he had assembled for the *Bughya*, the form and contents of the two books differ considerably. It is of course possible to find in the *Zubda* information on the people listed in the *Bughya*, but while the introduction to the *Bughya* lists the merits (*faḍāʾil*) of Aleppo—its appearance in hadith and its

56 Ibn al-ʿAdīm, *Zubda*, vol. 1, pp. 5–6. *Al-Shahbāʾ* ('The White') was a name given to Aleppo because of the white colour of the stones used in its construction.

importance for the first Muslims, together with a description of its buildings and its people—the first chapters of the *Zubda* highlight the origin of the town's name and its pre-Islamic history. There then follows the chronological record of events affecting the town which occurred during the reigns of the different princes and governors of the town from the Muslim conquest until 641/1243.

One other important difference between the two works is that in the *Zubda* Ibn al-ʿAdīm never cites his sources, whereas he systematically specifies them in his biographical dictionary. It is possible to count in the *Bughya*, for example, for the reign of the Ḥamdānid prince Sayf al-Dawla (r. 333–56/944–67) alone, some 90 oral and written sources of which 67 come from works of various literary genres (histories, biographies, geographical works, literature, and poetry).[57] For the sixth/twelfth and seventh/thirteenth centuries, Ibn al-ʿAdīm used more than fifty works.[58] Through careful study of the sources of the *Bughya* it is therefore possible to indirectly ascertain those of the *Zubda*, which is clearly important when attempting to judge the reliability of the latter work.

The space accorded to each historical period by Ibn al-ʿAdīm significantly varies according to his available source material, although this is not always the case: we know, for example, that he wrote the biographies of persons of the Umayyad era using a huge number of written and oral sources, all of which are cited in the *Bughya*,[59] although devoting only nine pages out of the *Zubda*'s total of 885 (in the Dahhān edition) to the history of that dynasty at Aleppo. On the other hand, his work became much fuller from the reign of Sayf al-Dawla, the time at which Aleppo began to play an extremely important role in the politics of the region. The largest sections are those concerning the fifth/eleventh, sixth/twelfth and seventh/thirteenth centuries, with a particular focus on the Ayyūbid period in which the author himself lived.[60] These choices

57 A.-M. Eddé, 'Les sources d'Ibn al-ʿAdīm sur le règne de Sayf al-Dawla en Syrie du Nord (333–356/944–967)', in C.F. Robinson (ed.), *Texts, Documents and Artefacts. Islamic Studies in Honour of D.S. Richards* (Leiden, 2003), 121–56.

58 A.-M. Eddé, 'Sources arabes des XIIe et XIIIe siècles d'après le dictionnaire biographique d'Ibn al-ʿAdīm (*Buġyat al-ṭalab fī taʾrīḫ Ḥalab*)', in *Itinéraires d'Orient. Hommages à Claude Cahen: Res Orientales* 6 (1994), 293–307.

59 A.-M. Eddé, 'Les sources de l'histoire omeyyade dans l'oeuvre d'Ibn al-ʿAdīm', in A. Borrut and P.M. Cobb (eds), *Umayyad Legacies. Medieval Memories from Syria to Spain* (Leiden, 2010), 131–66.

60 112 pages of the Dahhān edition are devoted to the Ḥamdānid dynasty, for a period of slightly less than 70 years. The expansion of Ibn al-ʿAdīm's account is even more pronounced for the following periods: Mirdāsid (157 pages for around 70 years), Seljūq and Artuqid (162 pages for 48 years), Zengid (151 pages for 56 years) and finally Ayyūbid (207 pages for 63 years).

reflect, on the one hand, Ibn al-ʿAdīm's wish to highlight the periods during which his home city grew in importance and, on the other, his desire to please his sponsor.

The *Zubda* is not technically a chronicle because, even though the historical accounts occur chronologically, the events are not reported year by year but rather in the form of a continuous narrative.[61] Its contents were employed from the earliest times by western historians of the Crusades. At the end of the eighteenth century Dom Berthereau (1732–94), a Benedictine scholar from the congregation of Saint-Maur, drew the attention of the orientalist Antoine-Isaac Silvestre de Sacy (1758–1838) to the importance of this text amongst all the Arab manuscripts concerning the history of the Crusades that he had gathered and was starting to translate into Latin. His work was interrupted first by the events of the French Revolution and then by his death, but Silvestre de Sacy continued it, translating extracts from the *Zubda* covering the period of the First Crusade to the death of Nūr al-Dīn (488–569/1095–1174) into French. Around 1810, he gave this inedited translation to the German historian F. Wilken (1777–1840) who used it to write his 'History of the Crusades', before giving it to the royal library of Berlin.[62] It was here that G.R. Röhricht examined it before publishing it in 1874, under the name of Silvestre de Sacy, in the first volume of his *Beiträge zur Geschichte der Kreuzzüge*.[63]

Between 1819 and 1830, G.W. Freitag and J.J. Müller edited and translated, in turn, into Latin or German, numerous other portions of the *Zubda* relating to the history of Aleppo from the beginnings of Islam until the fifth/eleventh

61 It must be underlined that the titles of the chapters and sub-chapters, and how they are numbered, such as appear in Dahhān's edition, are the additions of the editor and do not appear in the manuscripts.

62 J.T. Reinaud (*Bibliothèque des croisades*, 2nd ed., 4 vols [Paris, 1829], vol. IV, pp. VIII–IX) says that Silvestre de Sacy began his translation at the request and during the lifetime of Dom Berthereau. He also reports that Silvestre de Sacy gave his translation to F. Wilken around 1810. In his article on the manuscripts of Dom Berthereau published in 1801, Silvestre de Sacy, while noting the interest of editing the text of Ibn al-ʿAdīm, did not mention his French translation, which leads to the conclusion that he only finished it after this date; A.I. Silvestre de Sacy, *Notice des manuscrits laissés par Dom Berthereau, religieux bénédictin de la congrégation de Saint-Maur, mort en 1794* (Paris, 1801), p. 13; see also F. Wilken, *Geschichte der Kreuzzüge nach morgenländischen und abendländischen Berichten*, 7 vols (Leipzig, 1807–33), vol. II, pp. VIII–IX.

63 The manuscript is preserved in the Staatsbibliothek in Berlin under the shelfmark MS Gall. Quart 78. Cf. R. Röhricht, *Beiträge zur Geschichte der Kreuzzüge*, 2 vols (Berlin, 1874–78), vol. I, pp. VIII–X and 209–346.

century.[64] In 1829, J.T. Reinaud made a somewhat imprecise and summarized translation of extracts from the *Zubda* concerning the Crusades,[65] but it was only in 1854 that C. Défrémery published the first translation, more or less faithful to the Arabic original, which covered the first fifteen years of the Crusades.[66] His translation seems to be independent from that of Silvestre de Sacy, of which he probably was not aware, as there are some errors to be found in it which are absent from Silvestre de Sacy's text and omissions which the latter did not make. Défrémery's translation was then taken, significantly improved and, more importantly, extended until the year 541/1146–47, by Barbier de Meynard in the third volume of *Recueil des Historiens des Croisades: Documents Orientaux*, published in 1884.[67] More than ten years later, E. Blochet translated the rest of the work running from 541 to 641/1147 to 1243, albeit with lacunae and rather poorly.[68] It was only in the mid-twentieth century that a good edition of the *Zubda* finally became available, but a full modern translation of the work is still awaited.[69]

In the *Zubda* the Crusades are not treated as a separate topic from other events; the Franks are simply considered to be one military force amongst many,[70] and the numerous clashes between Franks and Muslims during the first decades of the crusading period are described soberly. The author does not ignore the pillages of the Franks nor the weaknesses and divisions of

---

64 G.W. Freitag, *Selecta ex Historia Halebi* (Paris, 1819) (Arabic edition and annotated Latin translation of snippets from the Muslim conquest to the year 336/947–48); idem, *Regierung des Saahd Aldaula zu Aleppo* (Bonn, 1820) (Arab edition and German translation of the reign of Saʿd al-Dawla [356/967–381/991]); idem, *Locmani fabulae et plura loca ex codicibus maximam partem historicis selecta in usum scholarum arabicarum* (Bonn, 1823), pp. 41–71 (Arabic edition); J.J. Müller, *Historia Merdasidarum ex Halebensibus Cemaleddini Annalibus excerpta* (Bonn, 1830) (Latin translation of the years 392/1001–472/1080).

65 J.T. Reinaud said he knew of the Latin translations of the text by Dom Berthereau. His French translation is in general a résumé and does not literally translate the Arabic (names of places and people are removed, while explanatory sentences are added); Reinaud, *Bibliothèque des Croisades*, vol. I, pp. VIII–IX and 4–31.

66 C. Défrémery, *Mélanges d'histoire orientale*, 1 volume in 2 parts (Paris, 1854), part I, pp. 35–65 (this translation runs from 490/1096–97 until the death of Tancred in 506/1112, with some omissions).

67 *RHC Or.*, vol. III, pp. 578–690.

68 E. Blochet, 'L'Histoire d'Alep de Kamal al-Dîn, version française d'après le texte arabe', *Revue de l'Orient Latin* 3 (1895), 509–65; 4 (1896), 145–225; 5 (1897), 37–107; and 6 (1898), 1–49; these cover the years 541–641/1147–1243, with lacunae.

69 Ed. Dahhān.

70 Ibn al-ʿAdīm addresses the subject of the Franks from the year of their arrival in Syria, 490/1097; Ibn al-ʿAdīm, *Zubda*, vol. II, p. 129.

the Muslims, while the alliances between Muslims and Franks against other Muslims and Franks do not raise any particular comment. The Franks, however, are not viewed equally, and Ibn al-ʿAdīm is particularly indignant about the conduct of those who betrayed their oaths, blasphemed against Islam or devastated the region around Aleppo. Such was the case with Joscelin I of Courtenay, who was first the lord of Tell Bāshir (the Franks' Turbessel) and then the count of Edessa (r. 1119–31), who attacked Aleppan territory almost uninterruptedly for a period of approximately thirty years. This is also the case with King Baldwin II of Jerusalem (r. 1118–31), the former count of Edessa, whom Ibn al-ʿAdīm criticises for, among other things, breaking the promise he had made to the Muslims which had earned him his freedom. But, more than this, Ibn al-ʿAdīm does not forgive these two Frankish leaders for the excessively inflammatory acts perpetrated by their troops during the siege of Aleppo in 518/1124: desecrating Muslim graves, profaning the Quran and the nearby sanctuaries, and insulting Muḥammad. Ibn al-ʿAdīm is the only writer—along with Ibn Abī Ṭayyiʾ[71]—who describes, in great detail, these acts, the consequence of which was the conversion of a number of the city's churches into mosques. It is for this reason that, of all the Franks, only Baldwin II and Joscelin are the objects of Ibn al-ʿAdīm's opprobrium; his comments on them are otherwise not generally hostile.[72] As is well known, the Muslims held a very low opinion of Reynald of Châtillon, and when writing of him Ibn al-ʿAdīm is no different, although this is because he merely follows the hostile account of Bahāʾ al-Dīn Ibn Shaddād. About Bohemond III of Antioch, on the other hand, his point of view is quite different to that of other writers and he is keen to relate the good relations between 'the Prince' and the Ayyūbid ruler of Aleppo.

The first question which historians of the Crusades must ask is that of the historical value of this work as far as the Franks and the Latin states are concerned in the period between 1097 and 1243. While there is no doubt that the author was a witness—and sometimes an actor—in the events he reports for the end of the sixth/twelfth and the beginning of the seventh/thirteenth

71 A Shīʿī historian whose chronicle is partially preserved in later works. On these events, see his account preserved in Ibn al-Furāt, *Taʾrīkh al-duwal waʾl-mulūk* vol. I, MS Vienna—Österreichische Nationalbibliothek A.F. 117 (formerly 814), vol. I, f. 179v.

72 Throughout the *Zubda*, Ibn al-ʿAdīm only rarely employs the expressions 'God curse them!' or 'the accursed'. When he does, it is always about people whose behaviour seems to him to be excessively wicked, such as the Qarmaṭī leader in 290/903, the Byzantine generals who ravaged Aleppo and its hinterland in the mid-fourth/tenth century, a Christian vizier from the fifth/eleventh century to whom the *qāḍīs* and Muslim governor were forced to pay homage, or the armourer who delivered Antioch over to the Franks; *Zubda*, vol. I, pp. 88, 140, 171, and 232, and vol. II, pp, 134, 196, and 222.

century, his originality for the first half of the sixth/twelfth century can be understood only through a study of his sources. It is well known that contemporary Arabic sources from the first decades of the crusading period are very few. The oldest ones to have survived, other than some works of poetry and the jihad treatise of the Damascene jurist al-Sulamī (d. 500/1106), are the chronicles of al-ʿAẓīmī (d. after 556/1161) and Ibn al-Qalānisī (d. 555/1160), two Syrian writers who wrote towards the middle of the sixth/twelfth century. The text of al-ʿAẓīmī survives only in an abridged version, and one interesting aspect of the *Bughya* is that it gives us unknown extracts of al-ʿAẓīmī's chronicle, and even if Ibn al-ʿAdīm cites this chronicle in the *Zubda* only to contradict it,[73] it is clear that he used it as one of his sources for the history of northern Syria in the first half of the twelfth century.

It has previously been noted that Ibn al-ʿAdīm was familiar with the now-lost history of Aleppo and of the Frankish conquest by Ḥamdān al-Athāribī (d. 542/1147–48), who was an eyewitness to many of the events that he reported. In the *Bughya*, Ibn al-ʿAdīm specifies that he had in his possession a number of autograph pages of this work, which leads to the assumption that he was not, however, familiar with the entire work.[74] Nevertheless, it is not impossible that he drew some of his information on the Frankish conquest of northern Syria, and of Antioch in particular, from this work.

Other historical writings cited in the *Bughya* could also be the origin of some of the information reported in the *Zubda*: ʿAbd al-Munʿim Ibn al-Luʿayba al-Ḥalabī (d. 555/1160) was an Aleppan man of letters about whom not a great deal is known, but Ibn al-ʿAdīm draws much of his information on the expedition of Aq Sunqur al-Bursuqī against the Franks in 518/1124 from one of his works, which contains details not recorded in other sources.[75] Two of Ibn al-ʿAdīm's distant cousins, Muḥammad b. ʿAbd al-Malik Ibn Abī Jarāda (d. 565/1169–70 or 566/1170–71) and particularly ʿAlī b. ʿAbdallāh Ibn Abī Jarāda (d. 548/1153–54), were the authors of important works, the former of a biographical dictionary of Aleppan notables and the latter of a history of the rulers of Aleppo. These works were known by Ibn al-ʿAdīm, but it is not certain whether he used the information on the events which occurred in northern Syria in the first half of the sixth/twelfth century found within them. Similarly, even though it is known that he used the works of several members of the Banū Munqidh family, among them Usāma (d. 584/1188)—the author of the famous 'Book of Learning by Example' (*Kitāb al-iʿtibār*)—for his redaction of

73 For example, Ibn al-ʿAdīm, *Zubda*, vol. II, p. 254.
74 Ibn al-ʿAdīm, *Bughya*, vol. IX, p. 4238.
75 Ibn al-ʿAdīm, *Bughya*, vol. IV, p. 1967.

the *Bughya*, we cannot be sure that he took material from these books for his account of the first decades of the crusading period.[76]

However, it is certain that he made abundant use of the oral testimony of his father and uncle for this period, who themselves received it from their father and grandfather, both of whom were eyewitnesses to and directly involved in the events reported. Ibn al-ʿAdīm also profited from the testimony transmitted to him by other notables and scholars, such as ʿAbdallāh b. ʿAbd al-Raḥmān Ibn al-ʿAjamī, to whom he was related by marriage, and the great historian Ibn al-Athīr (d. 630/1233), from whom he collected both oral and written accounts of the events described.[77]

The originality of all these sources is in no doubt and is the reason the account of Ibn al-ʿAdīm is so interesting and important for the whole first half of the sixth/twelfth century, even if he himself was not a witness to the events described. Thus, while his report for the fall of Antioch to the Franks in 491/1098 seems fairly similar to those of Ibn al-Qalānisī and Ibn al-Athīr, the two other main Arab sources for these events, it remains an independent account:[78] he is, for example, the only source which reports the arrival of 22 boats from Cyprus (at that time under Byzantine control) at Lattakia on the 8th of Ramaḍān 490/19th August 1097 and of the pillage of both the port and the town by the Armenians.[79] He is the only historian to recount the Armenian revolt at Ḥārim at the beginning of Rabīʿ I 491/February 1098 and the alliance of the Armenians of the region with the Franks. These clashes, he states, left many dead on both sides, while 1,500 Armenian prisoners were taken to Aleppo where the majority of them were executed.[80] He is also the only writer to highlight the fate of the governor of the Antiochene citadel, Aḥmad ibn Marwān, who surrendered

76 On all these texts, cf. Eddé, 'Sources arabes des XIIe et XIIIe siècles', pp. 294–97.

77 Some examples of this are in Ibn al-ʿAdīm, *Bughya*, vol. IV, pp. 1878, 1960 and 1967.

78 Ibn al-ʿAdīm was well acquainted with the works of these two historians whom he cites several times in the *Bughya*, but his account of events in northern Syria is much more detailed than that of his predecessors whose work principally concerns the region of Damascus in the case of Ibn al-Qalānisī, *Dhayl taʾrīkh Dimashq*, ed. H.F. Amedroz (Leiden, 1908), partial tr. H.A.R. Gibb as *The Damascus Chronicle of the Crusades* (London, 1932) and R. Le Tourneau as *Damas de 1075 à 1154* (Damascus, 1952), and the wider Muslim world in the case of Ibn al-Athīr, *al-Kāmil fiʾl-taʾrīkh*, ed. C.J. Tornberg, 13 vols (Beirut, 1965–67), partial tr. D.S. Richards, *The Chronicle of Ibn al-Athīr for the Crusading Period from* al-Kāmil fiʾl-taʾrīkh, 3 vols (Aldershot, 2006–8).

79 Ibn al-ʿAdīm, *Zubda*, vol. II, p. 130; Cahen, *Syrie du Nord*, p. 222 and n. 46.

80 Ibn al-ʿAdīm, *Zubda*, vol. II, p. 132. A number of these prisoners were freed during negotiations between Riḍwān and Tancred after the fall of al-Athārib to the Franks in Jumāda II 504/December 1110–January 1111.

to the Franks, along with the garrison there, after the defeat of the army of the ruler of Mosul, Kerboghā. Freed by the Franks, the governor and his men were attacked by Armenians while on their way to Aleppo.[81] Likewise, Ibn al-ʿAdīm tells us that these same Armenians participated in the pillaging of Kerboghā's defeated army and later, in November 1098, in the pillage of Maʿarrat al-Nuʿmān by the Franks, together with other Christians. His account of the revolt by the governor of ʿAzāz against Riḍwān in the autumn of 491/1098 is also unique. The Franks, who were called in by this rebellious governor, looted and pillaged the surrounding lands before returning to Antioch, taking the son of the governor as a hostage. Soon afterwards Riḍwān regained control of ʿAzāz, arrested the governor and executed him.[82]

The originality of Ibn al-ʿAdīm's material for events in northern Syria involving the Franks is demonstrated throughout the *Zubda*. He recounts unique details of the consequences of the fall of al-Athārib in 504/1110 on the economy of the region;[83] the reign of Il-Ghāzī at Aleppo (512–16/1118–22);[84] the battle of Balāṭ (the Field of Blood, *Ager Sanguinis*) in 513/1119, in the course of which Roger of Antioch was killed, and the fate of the prisoners taken;[85] and the siege of Aleppo by Franks allied with the ruler Dubays b. Sadaqa in 518/1124, together with the embassy sent from Aleppo to secure help from the Muslims of the Jazīra, in which his great-grandfather participated.[86]

Aspects of his account of the reign of Zengī are, as has been stated previously, unique, and give a clear indication of the historian's working method.[87] A comparison between the *Zubda, Bughya*, and the other available Arabic sources shows that while for martial affairs related to the fall of Edessa Ibn al-ʿAdīm summarises, in the *Zubda*, the account of Ibn al-Qalānisī,[88] he draws on lengthy extracts from the *Bughya* for other aspects of Zengī's reign. This is most notably the case for passages concerning his marriage to the daughter of Riḍwān and their subsequent divorce,[89] verses to the glory of Zengī inscribed on the *miḥrāb* of the mosque of Edessa and the alleviation of a property tax

81 Ibn al-ʿAdīm, *Zubda*, vol. II, p. 137.
82 Ibn al-ʿAdīm, *Zubda*, vol. II, p. 141.
83 Ibn al-ʿAdīm, *Zubda*, vol. II, p. 157.
84 Ibn al-ʿAdīm, *Zubda*, vol. II, pp. 180–81 and 185–86.
85 Ibn al-ʿAdīm, *Zubda*, vol. II, pp. 187–93.
86 Ibn al-ʿAdīm, *Zubda*, vol. II, pp. 222–27.
87 Ibn al-ʿAdīm, *Zubda*, vol. II, pp. 241–86.
88 Ibn al-Qalānisī, *Dhayl taʾrīkh Dimashq*, ed. p. 279; tr. Le Tourneau, p. 266; tr. Gibb, pp. 266–68.
89 Ibn al-ʿAdīm, *Zubda*, vol. II, p. 244.

which had been placed on the people of the town,[90] and the circumstances surrounding Zengī's death.[91] Most of these events reported by Ibn al-ʿAdīm are based on the eyewitness accounts of his father and uncle and on the works of two contemporaneous historians: Bahāʾ al-Dīn Ibn al-Khashshāb (d. 648/1250), a Shīʿī *qāḍī* and historian from Aleppo whose history, covering the years 500–648/1106–1250, has not survived,[92] and Abu'l-Maḥāsin b. Salāma Ibn al-Ḥarrānī (d. after 624/1226), the author of a 'History of Ḥarrān', also now lost.[93]

For the second half of the sixth/twelfth century, and the reign of Saladin in particular, Ibn al-ʿAdīm was familiar with the work of the *qāḍī* al-Fāḍil (d. 596/1200) entitled *Mutajaddidāt*, a type of official journal in which this faithful administrator and counsellor of Saladin recorded the main events of which he was a witness. From ʿImād al-Dīn al-Iṣfahānī (d. 597/1201), the secretary and biographer of the sultan, and Ibn Abī Ṭayyiʾ, one of the few Shīʿī Syrian historians from this era, Ibn al-ʿAdīm mainly used, it seems, works of poetry as well as, from the former, his 'History of the Seljūqs'. Yet it is the *qāḍī* Bahāʾ al-Dīn Ibn Shaddād (d. 632/1234), the biographer of Saladin who lived in Aleppo in the last forty years of his life, who provided Ibn al-ʿAdīm with the majority of his information.[94] Ibn al-ʿAdīm was close to the *qāḍī* and often cites him as an oral source in the *Bughya* using phrases such as 'the *qāḍī* Bahāʾ al-Dīn informed me … (*akhbaranī*)' or 'I heard (*samiʿtu*) the *qāḍī* say', etc. A comparison between these extracts and the corresponding passages in the *Zubda* on the one hand, and the original of Bahāʾ al-Dīn on the other, shows that in reality Ibn al-ʿAdīm must have heard the *qāḍī* read chapters from his work *Kitāb al-nawādir al-sulṭāniyya wa'l-maḥāsin al-Yūsufiyya*. The notice on the conquest of the fortresses of Shughr and Bakās, as well as that of Burzey, by Saladin from the Franks in 584/1188 is, for example, identical in the *Bughya* and Bahāʾ al-Dīn's biography of Saladin. In the *Zubda*, Ibn al-ʿAdīm relates a summary, removing one or more sentences here and there, but in broad terms preserving the narrative. It is also clear that all the passages in the *Zubda* relating to Saladin's conquests in northern Syria have been copied from the work of Bahāʾ

90 Ibn al-ʿAdīm, *Zubda*, vol. II, pp. 279–80.

91 Ibn al-ʿAdīm, *Zubda*, vol. II, pp. 281–83.

92 It is from this source that Ibn al-ʿAdīm reports that Zengī was encouraged to besiege Edessa by the *raʾīs* of Ḥarrān, Jamāl al-Dīn Faḍl Allāh Ibn Māhān, who notified him of Joscelin's absence: Ibn al-ʿAdīm, *Zubda*, vol. II, p. 279 and *Bughya*, vol. VIII, pp. 3850–51; Eddé, 'Sources arabes des XIIe et XIIIe siècles', p. 304.

93 Ibn al-ʿAdīm, *Bughya*, vol. VIII, pp. 3850–51; Eddé, 'Sources arabes des XIIe et XIIIe siècles', pp. 300–1 and 304.

94 Eddé, 'Sources arabes des XIIe et XIIIe siècles', pp. 299–301.

al-Dīn, who himself participated in the majority of the events described: the conquests of Anṭarṭūs, Jabala, Lattakia, Sarmāniyya, Darbasāk and Baghrās, the welcome given to Saladin by his son at Aleppo, and the fall of Ṣafad and Kawkab. It must, however, be noted that the further away from Northern Syria events occurred, the less detailed they are in his descriptions.[95]

While Ibn al-ʿAdīm simply summarised the work of Bahā' al-Dīn Ibn Shaddād for aspects of the reign of Saladin, for the following decades he provides much original material on the political and military history of northern Syria, among which he describes the clashes between Turks and Franks in the region of Antioch[96] and operations conducted against the Cilician Armenians.[97] Particularly important is his information on the alliance between al-Ẓāhir Ghāzī and Bohemond III of Antioch, which lasted until the death of the Ayyūbid ruler.[98] For example, importantly, his account permits the refutation of the idea that in 1197 Bohemond III had planned to attack Jabala and Lattakia, the two ports in northern Syria still retained by the Muslims.[99] Similarly, for the first half of the seventh/thirteenth century information provided on the conflicts between the Aleppan army and the Frankish Military Orders in 628/1231 and 634/1237, around Jabala, Marqab, Bāniyās and the region of ʿAmq, is of great interest.[100]

Conclusion

The life, and consequently the written works, of Ibn al-ʿAdīm share the general characteristics of Arab historians of his time: men who rarely confined themselves to a single discipline, often studying law, religious sciences, philology, *belles-lettres* and poetry. They belonged to important scholarly local families within a society in which the main religious and cultural positions

95 Cf. Bahā' al-Dīn Ibn Shaddād, *Kitāb al-nawādir al-sulṭāniyya wa'l-maḥāsin al-Yūsufiyya*, ed. J. al-Shayyāl (Cairo, 1967), pp. 87–96, tr. D.S. Richards as *The Rare and Excellent History of Saladin* (Aldershot, 2001), pp. 82–89; Ibn al-ʿAdīm, *Bughya*, vol. I, pp. 327–28, and *Zubda*, vol. III, pp. 104–7.

96 Ibn al-ʿAdīm, *Zubda*, vol. III, pp. 142–43.

97 Ibn al-ʿAdīm, *Zubda*, vol. III, pp. 91 and 156–57; Eddé, *Principauté ayyoubide*, p. 81.

98 Ibn al-ʿAdīm, *Zubda*, vol. III, pp. 140–41 and 166–67.

99 This idea was formulated using Latin sources by R. Grousset in *Histoire des croisades et du royaume franc de Jérusalem*, 3 vols (Paris, 1934–36), vol. III, p. 158; Cahen, *Syrie du Nord*, p. 590; Eddé, *Principauté ayyoubide*, pp. 68 and 82.

100 Ibn al-ʿAdīm, *Zubda*, vol. III, pp. 209–10 and 230–32; Eddé, *Principauté ayyoubide*, pp. 101 and 112.

were often hereditary but which also readily integrated scholars who came from other regions of the Muslim world, particularly Iran and Iraq. The profession of 'historian' did not exist, and these historians were for the most part jurists, teachers in madrasas, preachers or administrators who moved more or less in the ruling circles. Their attachment to a region, town, dynasty or sovereign inspired them to write a work destined to enhance the place of one of these in history. While some authors wrote panegyrics and tended to give the focus of their narrative an exemplary image, this was not the case with Ibn al-ʿAdīm. Even though he was among the most influential men of his age and mixed with the Ayyūbid rulers of Syria, for whom he wrote a large part of his work, he showed, in his own way, a definite rigour in the presentation of facts, in research and in the verification of his sources, and only rarely made errors of chronology.[101] As the good Aleppan Ḥanafī that he was, he never conceals his sympathy for the Zengid rulers, nor the tensions between Saladin and Nūr al-Dīn at the end of the latter's life, although this did not prevent him from eulogising Saladin nor from entering the service of his descendants himself.[102] Likewise, his proximity to the Ayyūbid rulers and his wish to please them did not prevent him from further highlighting the numerous familial divisions which weakened the dynasty on the eve of the Mongols invasions.

For relations with the Franks, paradoxically the richest information provided by Ibn al-ʿAdīm covers more the first two-thirds of the sixth/twelfth century than the period for which he was an eyewitness. The reason for this can be found in the fact that the first decades of the Frankish presence in the region were particularly difficult and oppressive for the town of Aleppo, and it is natural that the historian would have taken such an interest in it. For the reign of Saladin his account is essentially inspired by that of Bahāʾ al-Dīn Ibn Shaddād, and adds only a few new pieces of information. Over the course of the following fifty years (until 641/1243, the date at which the *Zubda* ends), the more or less peaceful relations which were established between the rulers of Aleppo and the Franks of northern Syria provided less material for the historian. With the exception of some localised clashes (usually involving the Military Orders), the territorial *status quo* was, in general, respected, and commercial relations developed. The foci of strategic issues between Franks and Muslims during the crusading period were, at this time, centred on Egypt (the Fifth Crusade) and Jerusalem (regained by Frederick II in 626/1229 and by the Muslims in 637/1239, before again being under Frankish rule from 638/1240 until 642/1244). It is important to note, for example, that the agreement

101 Eddé, *Principauté ayyoubide*, pp. 80–81, no. 327.

102 Ibn al-ʿAdīm, *Zubda*, vol. III, pp. 124–25.

between Frederick II and the Ayyūbid sultan al-Kāmil, sealed by the treaty of Jaffa (626/1229), which caused such outrage in Damascus, is related in barely four lines by Ibn al-ʿAdīm. The final chapters of the *Zubda*, in which the main issues are the divisions between the Ayyūbid princes, the links with the Seljūqs and the Khwārazmian and Mongol attacks, clearly show that Ibn al-ʿAdīm was aware—undoubtedly *a posteriori* after he had found refuge in Egypt—that the new dangers from the East were much more serious for the future of Muslim Syria than the Frankish presence in the region.[103]

103 Ibn al-ʿAdīm, *Zubda*, vol. III, p. 205.

Ibn Wāṣil: An Ayyūbid Perspective on Frankish Lordships and Crusades

Konrad Hirschler

Ibn Wāṣil (604/1208–697/1298) was a relatively prominent scholar and administrator who had close links with the political and military elites of Ayyūbid- and early Mamlūk-period Egypt and Syria throughout his career.[1] Partly due to these relations he held a variety of posts, ranging from teaching appointments in Ayyūbid Jerusalem and early Mamlūk Cairo, via positions as *qāḍī* in Egypt and Ḥamā, to his role as Mamlūk ambassador to the court of the Hohenstaufen ruler Manfred (d. 1266) in southern Italy. In addition, he served as Ayyūbid ambassador to Baghdad and (probably as *kātib* [secretary]) at the provincial Ayyūbid courts of Ḥamā and Kerak.

Ibn Wāṣil was born into a middle-ranking family of scholars and administrators in the northern Syrian town of Ḥamā. Although his family was not the kind that was able to monopolise posts in the town over long periods in the same way that the Banu'l-Bārizī did at the turn of the seventh/thirteenth and eighth/fourteenth centuries,[2] Ibn Wāṣil's father held various teaching posts in Ḥamā and its surrounding towns, as well as the position of chief *qāḍī* there. Ibn Wāṣil's maternal uncle Burhān al-Dīn Ismāʿīl Ibn Abi'l-Damm was one of the notables of the town and, together with his cousin Shihāb al-Dīn Ibrāhīm Ibn Abi'l-Damm (d. 642/1244), was involved in the deposition of the town's ruler

1 On Ibn Wāṣil and the relevant primary and secondary sources see: K. Hirschler, *Medieval Arabic Historiography: Authors as Actors* (London, 2006), pp. 18–28; D.S. Richards, 'Ibn Wasil, Historian of the Ayyubids', in R. Hillenbrand and S. Auld (eds), *Ayyubid Jerusalem* (London, 2009), 456–59; K. Hirschler, 'Social Contexts of Medieval Arabic Historical Writing: Court Scholars Versus Ideal/Withdrawn Scholars—Ibn Wāṣil and Abū Šāma', in U. Vermeulen and J. Van Steenbergen (eds), *Egypt and Syria in the Fatimid, Ayyubid and Mamluk Eras IV* (Leuven, 2005), 311–31; K. Hirschler, 'Ibn Wasil', in *EMC*, vol. I, p. 842.

2 Three members of the Bārizī family held the position of chief *qāḍī* in Ḥamā for some sixty years in the period after 652/1254–55: Ibrāhīm b. al-Musallam b. Hibat Allāh (652/1254–55 to 669/1270–71; cf. al-Dhahabī, *Ta'rīkh al-Islām wa-wafayāt al-mashāhīr wa'l-aʿlām*, ed. ʿU. Tadmurī, 55 vols [Beirut, 1987–2000], vol. LII, p. 276), ʿAbd al-Raḥīm b. Ibrāhīm b. Hibat Allāh (669/1270–71 to 670/1271–72; cf. al-Ṣafadī, *al-Wāfī bi'l-wafayāt*, ed. H. Ritter et al., 27 vols [Istanbul, 1931–97], vol. XVIII, pp. 317–19), and Hibat Allāh b. ʿAbd al-Raḥīm b. Ibrāhīm b. Hibat Allāh (699/1271–72 to mid-730s/1330s; cf. Abu'l-Fidā', *al-Mukhtaṣar fī akhbār al-bashar*, s.n., 4 vols [Cairo, 1907], vol. IV, p. 124).

 | DOI 10.1163/9789004280687_008

al-Malik al-Nāṣir in 626/1229. Shihāb al-Dīn was also the chief *qāḍī* of Ḥamā for twenty years from 622/1225.[3] To cite a final example, a paternal cousin of Ibn Wāṣil, Sa'd Allāh b. Wāṣil (d. 673/1275), served as a physician at the court of Ḥamā.[4]

Although Ibn Wāṣil was trained in the religious sciences and held positions as *mudarris* and *qāḍī*, his scholarly fame rested on his learning in fields such as logic, in which 'he rose like the sun'.[5] In contrast, his biographers scarcely noted his activities in religious disciplines. An isolated reference to *fiqh*,[6] some references to hadith, and his activities as a *Mufti* pale in comparison with the constant references to logic. Ibn Wāṣil pursued his interest in the rational sciences mainly in Kerak and Ḥamā, the two places renowned for these disciplines in Syria and Egypt during his lifetime. For instance, Ibn Wāṣil spent several years in Kerak during the late 620s-early 630s/first half of 1230s, during which time he studied the 'theoretical sciences' with scholars such as 'Abd al-Ḥamīd b. 'Alī al-Khusrūshāhī (d. 652/1254).[7] When Ibn Wāṣil subsequently moved back to his home town he continued these studies and in 641/1243–44 he assisted the astronomer and mathematician 'Alam al-Dīn Qayṣar (d. 649/1251) to construct an astrolabe for the ruler of Ḥamā.[8]

Owing to his interest in the rational sciences, Ibn Wāṣil composed a total of four works on logic—a number only equalled by his historical works. Two of these were commentaries on treatises by his teacher al-Khūnajī (d. 646/1248), who was the most outstanding scholar of the rational sciences in Egypt during his lifetime.[9] His commentary on al-Khūnajī's *al-Jumal fi'l-manṭiq* ('The Sum of Logic') seems to have been Ibn Wāṣil's most popular work in the field, with four copies surviving—of which three were produced either during his lifetime or

3 On Shihāb al-Dīn Ibn Abi'l-Damm, see Abu'l-Fidā', *Mukhtaṣar*, vol. III, p. 173; al-Dhahabī, *Ta'rīkh*, vol. L, p. 112; al-Ṣafadī, *Wāfī*, vol. VI, pp. 33–34; R.S. Humphreys, *From Saladin to the Mongols. The Ayyubids of Damascus, 1193–1260* (Albany NY, 1977), p. 262.

4 Ibn Wāṣil, *Mufarrij al-kurūb fī akhbār Banī Ayyūb*, eds J. al-Shayyāl, Ḥ. al-Rabī' and S. 'Āshūr, vols 1–5 (Cairo 1953–77); ed. M. Rahim, vol. 6, as *Die Chronik des ibn Wasil. Kritische Edition des letzten Teils (646/1248–659/1261) mit Kommentar. Untergang der Ayyubiden und Beginn der Mamlukenherrschaft* (Wiesbaden, 2010) (the edition of the 6th part by 'U. Tadmurī [Sidon, 2004] is inferior), vol. V, p. 227; al-Dhahabī, *Ta'rīkh*, vol. LIII, p. 130.

5 Al-Ṣafadī, *A'yān al-'aṣr wa-a'wān al-naṣr*, ed. F. Bakkūr, 4 vols (Beirut, 1998), vol. IV, p. 1660: *'bara'a fi'l-'ulūm al-shar'iyya wa-ṭala'a ka'l-shams fi'l-'ulūm al-'aqliyya'*.

6 Abu'l-Fidā', *Mukhtaṣar*, vol. IV, p. 38.

7 Ibn Wāṣil, *Mufarrij*, vol. V, p. 35: *'al-'ulūm al-naẓariyya'*.

8 Ibn Wāṣil, *Mufarrij*, vol. V, pp. 342–44.

9 Ibn Qāḍī Shuhba, *Ṭabaqāt al-shāfi'iyya*, ed. 'A. Khān, 4 vols (Beirut, 1987), vol. II, p. 125: *'bālagha fī 'ulūm al-awā'il ḥattā tafarrada bi-ri'āsat dhālika fī zamānihi'*.

in the following fifty years.[10] Ibn Wāṣil's only other surviving work on logic is the treatise *al-Risāla al-anbrūriyya* ('The Imperial Treatise'), which he originally wrote for Manfred, ruler of southern Italy, and which he later reworked under the title *Nukhbat al-fikar fi'l-manṭiq* ('The Pick of Reflection on Logic').[11]

Although Ibn Wāṣil's contributions to the field were not particularly significant,[12] they earned him the hostility of later writers; Ibn Taymiyya, for example, described him in his treatise against logic as a 'leading philosopher'.[13] Ibn Wāṣil stood in the tradition of the Western school of logic, as it had developed in the preceding century.[14] The leading figure in the development of this school had been Fakhr al-Dīn al-Rāzī (d. 606/1209), who had himself taught several of Ibn Wāṣil's teachers, most importantly al-Khūnajī, al-Khusrūshāhī and the Egyptian chief physician Ibn al-Nafīs (d. 687/1288). The indirect influence of al-Rāzī on Ibn Wāṣil was not limited to the field of logic. Ibn Wāṣil's only work close to the field of the religious sciences was a summary of a theological work by al-Rāzī: *Mukhtaṣar al-arbaʿīn fī uṣūl al-dīn* ('The Summary of [the] Forty [Questions] on the Bases of Religion').[15] The summary was not widely popular, and no manuscript of it has apparently survived. However, it is significant that Ibn Wāṣil's only work dealing with problems related to religious questions in a narrow sense dealt with issues of speculative theology (*kalām*).

Finally, Ibn Wāṣil held a degree of fame for his work in the field of poetry. He summarized the fourth/tenth-century work *Kitāb al-aghānī*, which contained songs performed at various rulers' courts. In the preface to his summary, entitled *Tajrīd al-Aghānī*, he stated that he had undertaken the work at the request of the ruler of Ḥamā, al-Malik al-Manṣūr, and it enjoyed limited local success.[16] His second study on poetry was a commentary on a work on

---

10 Cf. Hirschler, *Medieval Arabic Historiography*, p. 60. The three dated manuscripts were copied around 680/1281, in 738/1337–38 and in 746/1345.

11 The only manuscript is in the Reinecke Rare Book and Manuscript Library, Yale University, no. 1406 with the title *Nukhbat al-fikar fī tathqīf al-naẓar*; copied in 680/1281 by one Yūsuf b. Ghanā'im al-Sāmirī in Ḥamā from an autograph draft manuscript (f. 133r/v).

12 N. Rescher, *The Development of Arabic Logic* (Pittsburgh, 1964), p. 199.

13 Ibn Taymiyya, *Jahd al-qāhira fī tajrīd al-naṣīḥa* (translation of al-Suyūṭī's abridgement: W.B. Hallaq, *Ibn Taymīya against the Greek Logicians* [Oxford, 1993], p. 59).

14 Cf. Rescher, *Development*, pp. 64–67, on the development of the Western and Eastern schools.

15 Ibn Wāṣil's student Ibn al-Akfānī (d. 749/1348) cited it as *Lubāb al-arbaʿīn* (*Gist of the Forty*); see Ibn al-Akfānī, *Kitāb irshād al-qāṣid ilā asnā al-maqāṣid*, ed. J.J. Witkam (Leiden, 1989), pp. 43–44.

16 Three manuscripts of this work have been preserved (cf. C. Brockelmann, *Geschichte der arabischen Litteratur*, supplement vols I–III [Leiden, 1937–42], rev. ed. vols I and II

metrics by his teacher Ibn al-Ḥājib: it was the first of a series of commentaries and summaries which were produced in the following century.[17] Ibn Wāṣil's remaining writings on astronomy and medicine were also not very popular, and no extant manuscripts of them are known.[18]

Building on his education and family network Ibn Wāṣil succeeded in forging a remarkable transregional career, moving with ease between positions in the administration, judiciary and education posts in Cairo and Syrian cities. His father and, especially, Shihāb al-Dīn, who had lived in Cairo, Damascus and Aleppo, were key figures in introducing Ibn Wāṣil to important members of the scholarly, political and military elite of the Ayyūbid period. Ibn Wāṣil secured his first full teaching position, for instance, in a madrasa in Jerusalem in 624/1227 at the age of 20 (lunar years) by standing in as a replacement for his father who had left to go on the Hajj and for an extended stay in Mecca.[19] In the following decades Ibn Wāṣil established himself as a prominent member of the section of the scholarly elite, the *ʿulamāʾ*, that maintained close ties with courts and who also often served in administrative positions, in a similar manner to his contemporary Ibn al-ʿAdīm.[20]

Of particular importance in his network, and also as a source for his chronicle, was the *amīr* Ḥusām al-Dīn al-Hadhabānī (d. 658/1260), with whom Ibn Wāṣil had a particularly close friendship and client-patron relationship. Ḥusām al-Dīn had begun his career as an officer in Ibn Wāṣil's home town of Ḥamā, where the Hadhabānī family belonged to the military elite. Ḥusām al-Dīn later entered the service of the Egyptian Ayyūbid sultan al-Malik al-Ṣāliḥ Ayyūb (d. 647/1249), first becoming one of his advisors, after which he was tutor (*atābeg*) to his young son al-Malik al-Muʿaẓẓam Tūrānshāh (d. 648/1250) in Ḥiṣn Kayfa, then al-Malik al-Ṣāliḥ's mayor of the palace (major-domo, *ustādh al-dār*), and finally viceroy of Egypt.[21] On account of this close relationship

[Leiden, 1943–49], S. vol. I, p. 226). MS London—BL. Add. 7339 was copied in early twelfth/late seventeenth-century Ḥamā by the Shaykh of the ʿUlwān Mosque.

17 Ḥajjī Khalīfa (Kātib Çelebī), *Kashf al-ẓunūn fī asāmī al-kutub wa'l-funūn*, ed. Ş. Yaltkaya and K.R. Bilge, 2 vols (Istanbul, 1941–43), vol. I, p. 1134. Ibn Wāṣil's commentary has survived in two manuscripts: MS Paris—BNF arabe 4451 and MS Princeton—Garrett Collection, no. 503.

18 Medicine: Summary of *al-Mufrada* by his teacher Ibn Bayṭār; astronomy: *Nukhbat al-amlāk fī hayʾat al-aflāk*.

19 This was in the Shāfiʿī Nāṣiriyya Madrasa, also called al-Madrasa al-Ṣalāḥiyya. On this madrasa see al-Nuʿaymī, *al-Dāris fī taʾrīkh al-madāris*, ed. J. al-Ḥasanī, 2 vols (Damascus, 1948–51), vol. I, pp. 331–33; Ibn Wāṣil, *Mufarrij*, vol. IV, p. 208.

20 For this historian, see above, pp. 109–35.

21 Humphreys, *From Saladin to the Mongols*, pp. 251 and 290.

with Ḥusām al-Dīn, Ibn Wāṣil stayed at the officer's house after he had moved from Syria to Egypt in 643/1245 and they performed the Hajj to Mecca together in 649/1252.[22] However, Ibn Wāṣil had not put all his eggs into one basket and after Ḥusām al-Dīn's fall from power in the Ayyūbid-Mamlūk transition period in the early 650s/1250s he was able to use his close relationships with other leading commanders and administrators to retain a prominent position within the newly emerging early Mamlūk elites.

For example, when Ibn Wāṣil went on the pilgrimage with Ḥusām al-Dīn they were accompanied by a third individual, 'Izz al-Dīn al-Afram (d. 695/1295), who was a rising star in the emerging Mamlūk sultanate. He became governor (*wālī*) of the upper-Egyptian town of Qūṣ in the early 650s/1250s and received the command of the royal household guard (*amīr jāndār*) under al-Malik al-Ẓāhir Baybars; with only short interruptions, he kept this post until his death.[23] Another military commander who was instrumental for Ibn Wāṣil in the transition period was Jamāl al-Dīn Aydughdī (d. 664/1265).[24] This *amīr* played a very important role in the Mamlūk government, especially under Baybars, who made him one of his trusted men and gave him a considerable *iqṭā'*. The ruler relied on his advice, particularly with regard to religious affairs and the appointment of judges. He was, for example, seen to have been influential in the introduction of a chief judge to each legal school (*madhhab*) in the Mamlūk realms in 663/1265.[25] Ibn Wāṣil was linked to Jamāl al-Dīn Aydughdī by ties of friendship and was present when Aydughdī was briefly arrested in his camp in 653/1255–56 because of his presumed involvement in a conspiracy against the then ruler Aybak (r. 648/1250–655/1257).[26]

In his various appointments Ibn Wāṣil was a close observer of, and sometimes participant in, the political events of his lifetime. During the Ayyūbid period and the first decade of Mamlūk rule he was often at the centre of events, which makes this the most valuable part of his chronicle in terms of factual information. His chronicle ends at the point when his political career ceased in Syrian and Egyptian lands, in the 660s/1260s, and he returned to his home town

22 Ibn Wāṣil, *Mufarrij*, vol. V, p. 334, and vol. VI, p. 128.

23 Ibn Wāṣil, *Mufarrij*, vol. VI, p. 128. On al-Afram see al-Ṣafadī, *Wāfī*, vol. IX, p. 478; Ibn Taghrībirdī, *al-Nujūm al-zāhira fī mulūk Miṣr wa'l-Qāhira*, ed. F.M. Shaltūt et al., 16 vols (Cairo, 1929–72), vol. VIII, pp. 80–81; J.-C. Garcin, 'Le Caire et la province: Constructions au Caire et à Qûs sous les Mameluks Bahrides', *Annales Islamologiques* 8 (1969), 47–62, pp. 48–51.

24 Al-Dhahabī, *Ta'rīkh*, vol. LII, pp. 172–73.

25 J.H. Escovitz, *The Office of Qāḍī al-Quḍāt in Cairo under the Baḥrī Mamlūks* (Berlin, 1984), pp. 20–28.

26 Ibn Wāṣil, *Mufarrij*, vol. VI, p. 133.

of Ḥamā and became the Shāfiʿī *qāḍī* there.[27] He remained in the town until his death in 697/1298 and there are no indications that he ever left it again.

On account of his close involvement with the political and military elites during his transregional years we repeatedly find him in army camps or observing military campaigns. For example, in 626/1229 he was in Damascus where he witnessed the intra-Ayyūbid conflict over the city and its siege by Egyptian troops;[28] some ten years later he accompanied the troops of al-Malik al-Ṣāliḥ Ayyūb when the latter was in the process of establishing his authority in Syrian;[29] in 641/1244 Ibn Wāṣil passed through the army camp of the same ruler just before the battle of Ḥarbiyya/La Forbie in which the Ayyūbid-Frankish coalition of Syrian lords was defeated;[30] in 647/1250, during the Crusade of Louis IX, Ibn Wāṣil again spent several days in the Ayyūbid army camp in the Nile Delta;[31] and, as discussed above, in 653/1255–56, during one of the early intra-Mamlūk conflicts, Ibn Wāṣil was in the Mamlūk army camp with the high-ranking officer Jamāl al-Dīn Aydughdī when the latter was arrested.[32]

In the same vein, Ibn Wāṣil maintained good relationships with crucial players within the Ayyūbid family such as his patron al-Malik al-Nāṣir Dāʾūd (d. 656/1258), at whose court in Kerak he served. After his subsequent patron al-Malik al-Ṣāliḥ Ayyūb, the last grand Ayyūbid sultan of Egypt, died in 647/1249, Ibn Wāṣil was amongst those who greeted the late sultan's son and successor al-Malik al-Muʿaẓẓam Tūrānshāh upon his arrival in Egypt. Taking advantage of his link with Ḥusām al-Dīn, then viceroy of Egypt, Ibn Wāṣil immediately secured a place in the new ruler's entourage.[33] When the Mongols invaded northern Syria and refugees were arriving in Cairo, Ibn Wāṣil also grasped the opportunity, in 658/1260, to build up a close relationship with his future patron al-Malik al-Manṣūr (d. 683/1284), the ruler of Ḥamā.[34]

Due to his involvement in Syrian-Egyptian politics Ibn Wāṣil also closely witnessed events linked to the Frankish presence in Syria and newly arriving Crusades. His reports are of particular importance when they are based on his

27 Al-Dhahabī, *Taʾrīkh*, vol. LV, p. 337.

28 Ibn Wāṣil, *Mufarrij*, vol. IV, pp. 253–57.

29 Ibn Wāṣil, *Mufarrij*, vol. V, pp. 210 and 231.

30 Ibn Wāṣil, *Mufarrij*, vol. V, pp. 333–34.

31 Ibn Wāṣil, *Mufarrij*, vol. VI, p. 59; P. Jackson, *The Seventh Crusade, 1244–1254: Sources and Documents* (Aldershot, 2007), p. 145.

32 Ibn Wāṣil, *Mufarrij*, vol. VI, p. 133.

33 Ibn Wāṣil, *Mufarrij*, vol. VI, pp. 59 and 64; cf. also vol. V, p. 296; Jackson, *Seventh Crusade*, p. 145.

34 Ibn Wāṣil, *Mufarrij*, vol. VI, p. 213.

direct observations of developments on the Ayyūbid side during the major Crusades of the first half of the seventh/thirteenth century. Ibn Wāṣil was a very well-placed observer for such reports, in contrast to two other important chroniclers of the period, Sibṭ Ibn al-Jawzī and Abū Shāma, who were both much less involved in the political scene of their time and who both tended to have a purely Damascene outlook. In addition to his reports on Muslim reactions to newly arriving Crusades, the main value of his chronicle is his detailed reports on Ayyūbid/Mamlūk-Frankish diplomatic relationships in which, again, he was personally involved.

His most famous diplomatic endeavour, his mission in 659/1261 as Mamlūk envoy to the court of Manfred, son of Frederick II, meant Ibn Wāṣil was also relatively well acquainted with Latin European politics. We do not know exactly how long he remained in southern Italy, but it was for a prolonged period in Apulia, near Lucera, where he met the ruler.[35] Ibn Wāṣil was arguably chosen for this task because he had previous experience undertaking diplomatic missions. Some two decades earlier, in 641/1243, he had accompanied his relative Shihāb al-Dīn on a mission from the ruler of Ḥamā to Baghdad, where they stayed for two months.[36] On their way they also held talks with the rulers of Aleppo, Mardin and Mosul. Furthermore, they also held talks—with the help of a translator—with the leader of a new outside force that had started to play a role in Syrian politics at this time, the Khwārazmians, who had recently arrived from the East. From the various positions he held at a number of courts, Ibn Wāṣil was also well acquainted with diplomatic ritual and negotiation; some two years after his mission to Baghdad, for instance, he was among the courtiers of al-Malik al-Ṣāliḥ Ayyūb who welcomed the envoy from Baghdad bringing with him the caliphal insignia for the Egyptian ruler.[37]

Ibn Wāṣil may also have been appointed to the diplomatic mission to southern Italy because he had been such a close observer of diplomatic contacts between the Ayyūbids and Mamlūks on the one hand and the Franks and Latin Europeans on the other. This stance is reflected throughout his chronicle, which displays much less of a 'jihadist' outlook towards the Franks of Syria

35 Ibn Wāṣil, *Mufarrij*, vol. IV, pp. 234 and 248–51 (F. Gabrieli, *Arab Historians of the Crusades*, tr. E.J. Costello [Berkeley/Los Angeles, 1969], pp. 268 and 277); Abu'l-Fidā', *Mukhtaṣar*, vol. IV, pp. 38–39 (tr. P.M. Holt as *The Memoirs of a Syrian Prince* [Wiesbaden, 1983], pp. 31–32). Ibn Wāṣil does not comment on the purpose of this mission, but it was arguably aimed at building up an anti-Īlkhānate coalition in the framework of the increasing Mamlūk-Īlkhānate conflicts from 1260 onwards.

36 Ibn Wāṣil, *Mufarrij*, vol. V, pp. 323–26.

37 Ibn Wāṣil, *Mufarrij*, vol. V, p. 352.

and the Hohenstaufen rulers of southern Italy than other scholars and chroniclers of his period, such as Abū Shāma. This non-jihadist outlook goes back to two main factors in Ibn Wāṣil's background. First of all, he was not only interested in exclusively Islamic fields of knowledge such as Islamic law, but he also pursued other disciplines such as logic and philosophy that facilitated communication across religious borders. It was certainly not by chance that his most important teacher, ʿAlam al-Dīn, had been asked by the Egyptian sultan al-Malik al-Kāmil (d. 635/1238) to respond to Frederick II's questions on mathematics and natural sciences.[38] In the same vein Ibn Wāṣil dedicated his treatise on logic, *al-Risāla al-anbrūriyya* ('The Imperial Treatise'), to Manfred. Had Ibn Wāṣil focused more narrowly on the religious disciplines it is unlikely that he would have enjoyed the intellectual atmosphere of his stay in southern Italy so much.

The second main reason for Ibn Wāṣil's relatively neutral description of anything related to Latin Europeans and the Franks was that his years of active political involvement occurred during the period of Ayyūbid rule. In these years the idea of military jihad against the Franks took a back seat compared with the previous eras (under the Zengids and Saladin) and the following Mamlūk period. The Frankish lordships of Syria were to a large extent integrated into the highly pluralistic political landscape of the region and the conclusion of truces between Frankish and Muslim rulers was standard practice.[39] Ibn Wāṣil was consequently deeply influenced by the regionalised character of political rule that resulted from the division of Syria into a multitude of lordships ranging from Damascus and Aleppo through medium-sized entities such as Homs, Acre/Jerusalem, Ḥamā and Antioch, to minor lordships such as Baalbek, Tripoli, Boṣrā and Kerak.

Ibn Wāṣil had a particularly strong degree of understanding about such diplomatic relationships, as he had spent his formative years at the small courts of Ḥamā and Kerak.[40] Unlike the large cities, these lordships had to engage in a wider variety of diplomatic strategies to secure their survival in the ever-

38 For ʿAlam al-Dīn Qayṣar b. Abiʾl-Qāsim (d. 649/1251), see Ibn Khallikān, *Wafayāt al-aʿyān wa-abnāʾ al-zamān*, ed. I. ʿAbbās, 8 vols (Beirut, 1968–72), vol. V, pp. 315–16; al-Dhahabī, *Taʾrīkh*, vol. L, pp. 429–30; al-Ṣafadī, *Wāfī*, vol. XXIV, p. 304.

39 M.A. Köhler, *Alliances and Treaties between Frankish and Muslim Rulers in the Middle East: Cross-Cultural Diplomacy in the Period of the Crusades*, tr. P.M. Holt; rev., ed., introduced K. Hirschler (Leiden, 2013), pp. 267–75, and L. Atrache, *Die Politik der Ayyūbiden. Die fränkisch-islamischen Beziehungen in der ersten Hälfte des 7./13. Jahrhunderts unter besonderer Berücksichtigung des Feindbildes* (Münster, 1996).

40 Hirschler, *Medieval Arabic Historiography*, pp. 99–100.

shifting political landscape of Syria and northern Mesopotamia, and due to his close relationships with members of the military elite Ibn Wāṣil was an attentive observer of these strategies. For instance, in the late 630s/1240s Ḥamā found itself increasingly in conflict with its Ayyūbid neighbours, especially Homs, on account of its pro-Damascene policy. When troops from Ḥamā were required in Damascus in the year 637/1240 they had to be securely moved through the hostile territories of Homs. In an attempt to secure safe passage the rulers of Ḥamā set up an elaborate, but ultimately doomed, ruse: the leading commander of Ḥamā, a cousin of Ibn Wāṣil's friend and patron Ḥusām al-Dīn, feigned falling out with Ḥamā's ruler and left the town with his troops, among them Ḥusām al-Dīn's father, and many members of the civilian elite, including Ibn Wāṣil's cousin Sa'd Allāh. Troops from the County of Tripoli were closely involved in the build up of the ruse. In order to enhance the credibility of the friction within the town's elite, rumours were spread that the Ayyūbid ruler was to hand over the town to the ruler of Tripoli and a group of Latin knights was indeed garrisoned in the town's citadel.[41]

Just as Ibn Wāṣil was used to diplomatic relations with the Franks, the Nizārī ('Assassin') lords of Syrian castles appear in the same capacity. For instance, the Ḥamā ruse of 637/1240 ultimately failed as the ruler of Homs arrested the entire party of Ḥamāwī troops and incarcerated its members without hesitation. The better part of the Ḥamāwī elite, among them Ibn Wāṣil's cousin, had to be ransomed, but many perished in gaol. In the protracted negotiations for ransoming the prisoners, the Nizārī lord of the nearby castle of Maṣyāf was one of the third parties that played an important intermediary role.[42] Ibn Wāṣil was able to include such detailed information because he was a friend of the spiritual leader of the Nizārīs in Syria during this period.[43]

In many ways Ibn Wāṣil thus personifies the decentralized and pluralistic political landscape of Syria during the Ayyūbid period. Yet, shortly after the rise of the Mamlūk dynasty he ended his involvement in trans-regional politics and upon his return from his mission to Apulia withdrew to his hometown of Ḥamā. This move is highly significant as Ḥamā was the only Ayyūbid principality that survived the imposition of Mamlūk authority on Syria in the aftermath of the Battle of 'Ayn Jālūt in 658/1260. Although Ḥamā became part of the Mamlūk Empire it retained at least nominal independence under its Ayyūbid rulers. As the town's chief judge Ibn Wāṣil was closely involved in local politics, yet he was never again able or willing to take up a formal or informal position

41 Ibn Wāṣil, *Mufarrij*, vol. v, pp. 222–27.

42 Ibn Wāṣil, *Mufarrij*, vol. v, p. 227.

43 Ibn Wāṣil, *Mufarrij*, vol. v, p. 251: '*wa-kānat baynanī wa-baynahu mawaddatun*'.

anywhere else in Syria or Egypt. Just as he started his career in an Ayyūbid landscape, he chose to end it in the last Ayyūbid enclave.

Mufarrij al-kurūb: Ayyūbid Politics and Frankish-Ayyūbid Diplomacy

Ibn Wāṣil not only wrote a number of works in the fields of logic and literature, but also in history. For the study of the Crusades the most interesting and useful work is his *Mufarrij al-kurūb fī akhbār Banī Ayyūb* ('The Dissipater of Anxieties on the Reports of the Ayyūbids'), an annalistic chronicle that covers most of the sixth/twelfth and the first half of the seventh/thirteenth century.[44] His second chronicle, *al-Taʾrīkh al-Ṣāliḥī* ('The Ṣāliḥī History') is a universal history from the creation of the world down to the year 636/1239 which he attempted to dedicate first to al-Malik al-Ṣāliḥ and, after the latter's death, to al-Malik al-Muʿaẓẓam Tūrānshāh. This chronicle ends in the year in which Ibn Wāṣil's future patron al-Malik al-Ṣāliḥ arrived in Damascus and briefly took power. Much like the *Mufarrij*, it was a work in the tradition of earlier chronicles in that it contained hardly any obituary notices and focused on political events.[45] This chronicle is of some interest for the early crusading period, as it contains material not found in the *Mufarrij*. For instance, it is here that we find Ibn Wāṣil's report on the 1099 conquest of Jerusalem.[46] This report is of interest as it is one of the last texts that still emphasises the Frankish massacre of the town's Jewish inhabitants—an event that had featured prominently in early accounts, but was increasingly sidelined in subsequent Arabic historiography.[47] However, up to the point when he starts to draw on information unique to him, i.e. from the mid-620s/1220s onwards, Ibn Wāṣil relied as much on earlier sources as he did for the *Mufarrij* and there are few additional factual details. As the *Taʾrīkh Ṣāliḥī* ends as early as 636/1239 its relevant parts thus only cover some ten years.

The *Taʾrīkh Ṣāliḥī* is much more concise than the *Mufarrij* and excludes important features that make the latter such an interesting work. Most importantly, in the *Taʾrīkh Ṣāliḥī* Ibn Wāṣil hardly makes any personal observations based on direct involvement in the politics of the day. For instance, while his

44 For editions of this, see above, n. 4.

45 Ibn Wāṣil, *Kitāb al-taʾrīkh al-Ṣāliḥī*, ed. ʿU. Tadmurī, 2 vols (Sidon/Beirut, 2010).

46 Ibn Wāṣil, *Ṣāliḥī*, vol. II, pp. 154–55.

47 K. Hirschler, 'The Jerusalem Conquest of 492/1099 in the Medieval Arabic Historiography of the Crusades: From Regional Plurality to Islamic Narrative', *Crusades* 13 (2014), pp. 37–76.

reports in the *Mufarrij* on the intra-Ayyūbid conflict around Damascus in 626/1229 are those of an eyewitness, the parallel report in the *Taʾrīkh Ṣāliḥī* excludes such observations.[48] The importance of this chronicle is further curtailed by the fact that the author repeatedly leaves out entire years. Particularly in the early seventh/thirteenth century, there are a cluster of years that are not covered, such as the years 601/1204–5, 602/1205–6, 605/1208–9, 608/1211–12, 609/1212–13, 611/1214–15, 612/1215–16 and 614/1217–18. These omissions are particularly regrettable as this is one of the most interesting periods in the *Mufarrij* for Frankish-Muslim relations. As will be seen, Ibn Wāṣil has considerable detail on this period's northern Syrian alliance system between Aleppo, Antioch and the Rūm Seljūqs of Anatolia against the Ayyūbid Sultan of Egypt and the Armenian Kingdom. In the *Taʾrīkh Ṣāliḥī*, however, one gets little sense of the political dynamics in northern Syria in the early seventh/thirteenth century. Ibn Wāṣil wrote a third chronicle which he refers to in the *Mufarrij* as *al-Taʾrīkh al-kabīr* ('The Great History') in the course of the text.[49] Yet aside from this indirect evidence of its existence no manuscript has survived. To judge from references in the *Taʾrīkh Ṣāliḥī* it was probably also a universal history focusing on political and military events.[50]

Ibn Wāṣil wrote his main chronicle, the *Mufarrij*, after he had returned to Ḥamā in the 660s/1260s. The chronicle starts in the 520s/1120s during the Zengid period, with reports on the Ayyūbid dynasty's founder Najm al-Dīn Ayyūb, and ends in 659/1261.[51] His main aim in writing this chronicle was to celebrate the Ayyūbid dynasty that was about to disappear; tellingly, the chronicle stops at the point when the Mamlūk dynasty established its authority in Syria. However, Ibn Wāṣil's narrative went further than just being a panegyric of the Ayyūbids, and he was also concerned to show that ideal rule was a constant reality irrespective of a specific dynasty, and though his work focused on the Ayyūbids it hardly ascribed an outstanding place to them in the longer course of Islamic history. This dynasty merely provided a further example that ideal rule had existed in the past, existed in the present and would exist in the

48 Ibn Wāṣil, *Mufarrij*, vol. IV, pp. 253–57; Ibn Wāṣil, *Ṣāliḥī*, vol. II, pp. 294–95.

49 Ibn Wāṣil, *Mufarrij*, vol. I, pp. 204 and 236.

50 Such large universal histories were typical for the period. To take just early seventh/thirteenth-century Ḥamā, we find two authors writing similar works: Ibn Wāṣil's maternal relative Shihāb al-Dīn Ibn Abi'l-Damm and the court official Muḥammad b. ʿAlī b. al-Naẓīf (d. after 634/1236–37). Their grand universal histories have also been lost but, as with Ibn Wāṣil's *Taʾrīkh Ṣāliḥī*, their shorter universal histories, which were dedicated to rulers, have survived.

51 Ibn Wāṣil, *Mufarrij*, vol. VI, pp. XL–XLIII (intro. M. Rahim).

future. It is the ongoing existence of ideal rule—with slight variations—under a wide variety of different dynasties which forms the underlying message of his chronicle.[52]

The major difference with works of other writers from the crusading period, such as Bahā' al-Dīn Ibn Shaddād, 'Imād al-Dīn al-Iṣfahānī and Abū Shāma, was that Ibn Wāṣil—like Ibn al-ʿAdīm—did not consider anti-Frankish military jihad to be a crucial element of ideal rule. Abū Shāma's concern, for instance, was to present the two reigns of Nūr al-Dīn and Saladin, including their jihad activities, in a revivalist light, as a brief re-enactment of the early Islamic period. With the end of Saladin's reign political life, according to Abū Shāma, reverted to the same *jāhilī*-like period of darkness that had also existed up until the rule of Nūr al-Dīn. For this author the period before Nūr al-Dīn, as well as the post-Saladin period (i.e. Abū Shāma's present), were eras of deviation scarcely worthy of mention in his *Rawḍatayn*.[53] This difference in the role ascribed to the Franks also influenced how the chronicles presented the Latin East and the Crusades: while for some chroniclers the anti-Frankish jihad was key to ideal rule, for Ibn Wāṣil the Franks were to a large extent just another group of political actors among many in the pluralistic landscape of the period. An example of how this difference is evident in his text is the fact that he only very rarely used curses, such as 'May God forsake them' and 'May God curse them', after mentioning the Franks.[54] In this regard his chronicle clearly differs from Abū Shāma's work and other chronicles where the use of such curses regularly occur.

Since Ibn Wāṣil's work was first and foremost a chronicle of the Ayyūbids the Latin lordships do not play a central role in the narrative. At the start of each year, for instance, the author generally gives a summary of the main events. This consists mostly of an overview of the state of affairs within the Ayyūbid family confederation, in particular the name of the sultan in Egypt and of those who ruled the major Syrian and Mesopotamian cities, such as Aleppo and Damascus. The Franks only enter these summaries when major Crusades arrived in Syria or Egypt and threatened to destabilize the political status quo.

From the point of view of the history of the Crusades and the Latin East the *Mufarrij* must be divided into two parts. Up until the mid-620s/1220s the author

52 Hirschler, *Medieval Arabic Historiography*.

53 Hirschler, *Medieval Arabic Historiography*, pp. 63–114.

54 On the use of curses cf. N. Christie, 'The Origins of Suffixed Invocations of God's Curse on the Franks in Muslim Sources for the Crusades', *Arabica* 48 (2001), 254–66; idem, ' "Curses, Foiled Again!" Further Research on Early Use of the "Ḫaḏalahum Allah" Invocation during the Crusading Period', *Arabica* 58 (2011), 561–70.

relied on the works of his predecessors and contemporaries, such as Bahāʾ al-Dīn Ibn Shaddād, ʿImād al-Dīn al-Iṣfahānī, Ibn al-Athīr and Abū Shāma. It is only in the following years that his chronicle becomes a truly independent work from a factual point of view; in its metanarrative on the continuity of ideal rule, by contrast, it is an original work right from the start. In the first part of his chronicle Ibn Wāṣil relied to a large extent on authors who had written their works in a more 'jihadist' mode. Consequently, we also see that his outlook on the Crusades and Frankish rulers of Syria is slightly different in this section. Though Ibn Wāṣil tones down the focus on anti-Frankish endeavours it is here that we find, for instance, curses brought against the Franks,[55] and it is evident that these are citations from previous works, especially quotes from epistles to Baghdad.[56] In the second part of his work, when Ibn Wāṣil increasingly relies on his own observations and hardly uses any other chronicles, the curses virtually disappear, except in reports of Louis IX's Crusade.[57] In the same vein, the characterisation of the Franks as unbelievers (*kuffār*) and thus as the perennial enemies of Islam is restricted to the first part of his chronicle.[58] In the second part the term, if used at all, refers to the Mongols rather than to the Franks.[59] It only appears with reference to the Franks in a poem referring

55 Ibn Wāṣil, *Mufarrij*, vol. I, p. 93 (the Fall of Edessa); vol. I, p. 136 (the defeat of Nūr al-Dīn in 558/1163); vol. I, p. 160 (the Franks in Egypt fighting Shīrkūh); vol. II, p. 16 (the Frankish attack on Alexandria); vol. II, p. 101 (Reynald of Châtillon); vol. II, p. 188 (the battle of Ḥaṭṭīn); vol. II, p. 243 (quoting ʿImād al-Dīn on Saladin's post-Ḥaṭṭīn campaign); vol. II, pp. 284 and 302 (Saladin's post-Ḥaṭṭīn campaign).

56 Ibn Wāṣil, *Mufarrij*, vol. II, p. 2 (epistle written by ʿImād al-Dīn on behalf of Saladin); vol. II, p. 65 (epistle by al-Fāḍil on behalf of Saladin); vol. II, p. 353 (epistle by al-Fāḍil on behalf of Saladin).

57 Jackson, *Seventh Crusade*, p. 141; Ibn Wāṣil, *Mufarrij*, vol. VI, p. 48 (quoting an epistle calling for jihad); vol. VI, p. 83 (Louis IX).

58 Ibn Wāṣil, *Mufarrij*, vol. I, p. 150 (Shīrkūh in Egypt fighting Franks and Fāṭimids); vol. I, p. 175 (Saladin facing Fāṭimid rebels who had contacted the Franks); vol. I, p. 199 (the Frankish castle on Île de Graye); vol. I, p. 225 (Saladin writing to Nūr al-Dīn); vol. II, p. 18 (Saladin justifying his conquest of Damascus); vol. II, p. 102 (Reynald of Châtillon); vol. II, p. 111 (epistle written by ʿImād al-Dīn on behalf of Saladin); vol. II, p. 127 (Reynald of Châtillon); vol. II, p. 148 (Saladin fighting the Franks); vol. II, p. 207 (quoting ʿImād al-Dīn on Saladin's post-Ḥaṭṭīn campaign); vol. II, p. 208 (on Saladin's post-Ḥaṭṭīn campaign); vol. II, p. 254 (reference to the battle of Ḥaṭṭīn); vol. II, p. 329 (on Saladin's post-Ḥaṭṭīn campaign).

59 Ibn Wāṣil, *Mufarrij*, vol. IV, pp. 46 and 216; vol. V, p. 285 (also referring to Khwārazmian troops).

back to Saladin's conquest of Jerusalem and in a verbal quote from the ruler of Ḥamā after the battle of Ḥarbiyya/La Forbie.[60]

A further consequence of the work's profile is that in the second part we see not only that curses against Franks and their association with unbelief take a backseat, but also that Latin European rulers can be presented in a quite sympathetic manner. During his mission to southern Italy, Ibn Wāṣil was certainly impressed by Manfred, whom he describes as 'distinguished, inclined to the rational sciences and knows by heart ten chapters of Euclid's work on geometry'.[61] At the ruler's request, Ibn Wāṣil composed his *Imperial Treatise* on logic during his stay at the court, upon which the ruler supposedly praised him with the words: 'O my judge! We did not ask you about the allowed and forbidden in your religion of which you are a judge. Rather we asked you about things which were only known to the ancient philosophers. You answered them although you had no books or other material with you which you could consult'.[62] Furthermore, Ibn Wāṣil praised the ruler for his 'sympathy for the Muslims, for he dwelled, was born and raised in the Sicilian lands. He himself, his father and his grandfather had been kings there and the majority of the population of this island is Muslim'.[63] That the Muslims could openly practise their religion and that the majority of the ruler's close entourage was supposedly Muslim impressed him as much as the fact that the call for prayer (*adhān*) and the ritual prayer (*ṣalāt*) were performed in the army.[64]

Ibn Wāṣil not only took a rather sympathetic approach towards Latin European rulers, but he was one of the few Arab chroniclers of his period who had an interest in Latin European politics. For instance, he gave in his chronicle the Arabic translation of the term emperor,[65] and described the office of the Pope as follows: 'According to them, the Pope in Rome is the successor [*khalīfa*] of the Messiah and the one acting in his place. He has the right to ban and to permit … He crowns the kings and nominates them. Nothing is done in their Holy Law [*sharīʿa*] except with his consent. He has to be a priest'.[66] Due to his acquaintance with Latin Europe he was also aware that the category 'Frankish' was not entirely satisfactory and stressed that Frederick II had been 'from among the Germans and this is one of the Frankish groups

60 Ibn Wāṣil, *Mufarrij*, vol. v, pp. 247 and 339.
61 Ibn Wāṣil, *Mufarrij*, vol. iv, p. 248.
62 Al-Ṣafadī, *Aʿyān*, vol. iv, p. 1661.
63 Ibn Wāṣil, *Mufarrij*, vol. iv, p. 234.
64 Ibn Wāṣil, *Mufarrij*, vol. iv, p. 248.
65 Ibn Wāṣil, *Mufarrij*, vol. iv, p. 234.
66 Ibn Wāṣil, *Mufarrij*, vol. iv, p. 149.

(*ajnās*)'.[67] In the same vein, he stated when discussing the Crusade of Louis IX that 'Afrans is one of the most important Frankish communities (*umma*), and the meaning of Raydafrans is King of Afrans. In their language, *rayd* means "king" '.[68] In the field of European politics, the conflict between the Papacy and the Hohenstaufen dynasty was of particular interest to him. One of the few instances in his texts where he reported an event that actually took place after the year in which his chronicle ended is a report on the Battle of Benevento between Charles of Anjou and Manfred in 1266 (which is misdated by one year to 663/1264–65).[69] Ibn Wāṣil was also the only medieval Arabic author who contributed his own anecdote on disputed elections in the Holy Roman Empire to the rich material that originated in Normandy, Byzantium, France and Germany.[70] The close interest in European politics is further evidenced by Ibn Wāṣil's reference to an unknown Latin knight when reporting on the alleged correspondence between Frederick II and al-Malik al-Ṣāliḥ Ayyūb during Louis IX's Crusade[71]—a source that we would certainly not find in the works of authors such as 'Imād al-Dīn al-Iṣfahānī, Bahā' al-Dīn Ibn Shaddād or Abū Shāma.

The main interest of the *Mufarrij* in terms of factual information lies in its coverage of the Ayyūbid period and the Crusades of the first half of the thirteenth century, those of the Fifth Crusade to Egypt, the Crusade of Frederick II, and the Crusade of Louis IX to Egypt. Within this second part of his chronicle Ibn Wāṣil alternated how he depicted the Franks and the crusaders. In reports on Crusades arriving from Latin Europe his text could take a jihadist tone, although this disappears in his descriptions of Ayyūbid-Frankish relations within Syria. Though his depiction of the crusaders is not as hostile as that of other chroniclers, the Crusade led by Louis IX clearly discomforted him and he ended its description with the words: 'The sultan's standard entered Damietta … and was hoisted on the walls, and Islam was proclaimed there. … God cleansed Egypt of them … The good news of his [victory] was transmitted to the rest of the Islamic world, where there were displays of gladness and rejoicing'.[72]

67 Ibn Wāṣil, *Mufarrij*, vol. IV, p. 250.

68 Jackson, *Seventh Crusade*, p. 129; Ibn Wāṣil, *Mufarrij*, vol. VI, p. 9.

69 Ibn Wāṣil, *Mufarrij*, vol. IV, p. 251.

70 Ibn Wāṣil, *Mufarrij*, vol. IV, pp. 249–50. On this issue cf. B. Weiler 'Tales of Trickery and Deceit: The Election of Frederick Barbarossa (1152), Historical Memory and the Culture of Kingship in later Staufen Germany', *Journal of Medieval History* 38 (2012), 295–317.

71 Ibn Wāṣil, *Mufarrij*, vol. III, pp. 247–48; Jackson, *Seventh Crusade*, p. 47.

72 Ibn Wāṣil, *Mufarrij*, vol. VI, pp. 82–83; Jackson, *Seventh Crusade*, p. 154.

By contrast, when it came to daily diplomatic life in Syria he used a decidedly different tone. Ibn Wāṣil did not deem truces between Ayyūbid and Frankish rulers to be scandalous or even problematic. For instance, he reported on al-Malik al-ʿĀdil's (d. 615/1218) policy towards the Latin lordships, which veered between defensive and complaisant, without passing any judgement. Throughout his rule al-Malik al-ʿĀdil struggled to impose his authority on the Syrian Ayyūbid lordships and showed little inclination to open up new theatres of conflict or change the status quo with the Frankish lordships. Agreements such as the three-year truce of 594/1198 with Amalric II of Jerusalem and that of 604/1207 with the County of Tripoli are described as matter-of-factly as that of 601/1204, which involved the surrender of Jaffa and the condominia (*munāṣafāt*) in Palestine around Ramla and Lydda to Amalric II.[73] After the 604/1207 truce had expired in 607/1210 there was some conflict between Damascus and forces from the Kingdom of Jerusalem, which Sibṭ Ibn al-Jawzī describes with his typical jihad fervour as having been driven on the Damascene side by popular will. According to this author, a sermon he delivered in the Umayyad Mosque, which praised the virtue of fighting the Franks, led to spontaneous armed action by the Damascene populace. Al-Malik al-ʿĀdil, in contrast to the principled stance by the Damascenes and the city's governor al-Malik al-Muʿaẓẓam ʿĪsā, appears here in a rather dubious light as he quickly entered into a truce.[74] Ibn Wāṣil, by contrast, has nothing on popular military action and principled rulers, but focuses again rather on the diplomatic side: 'Al-Malik al-ʿĀdil moved out of Damascus [against the Franks]. Envoys went back and forth between them until a truce was concluded for a limited period'.[75]

Ibn Wāṣil has a particular penchant for reporting the multitude of truces between Frankish lordships and the less important Muslim lords, especially those in central and northern Syria. His chronicle is of particular importance in understanding interactions between his hometown of Ḥamā, on the one hand, and the Hospitallers of Ḥiṣn al-Akrād/Crac des Chevaliers and the County of Tripoli on the other.[76] Again, such diplomatic relationships were only soberly

73 Ibn Wāṣil, *Mufarrij*, vol. III, pp. 78 (594/1198), 173 and 175 (604/1207), and 162 (601/1204). On the use of condominia in Frankish-Muslim diplomacy cf. Köhler, *Alliances and Treaties*, pp. 312–19.

74 Sibṭ Ibn al-Jawzī, *Mirʾāt al-zamān (A.H. 495–654)*, facs. ed. J.R. Jewett (Chicago, 1907), pp. 355–56.

75 Ibn Wāṣil, *Mufarrij*, vol. III, p. 201.

76 On the information in the *Mufarrij* regarding the Hospitallers of Ḥiṣn al-Akrād/Crac des Chevaliers cf. Balázs Major, 'Al-Malik al-Mujahid, Ruler of Homs, and the Hospitallers (The Evidence in the Chronicle of Ibn Wasil)', in Z. Hunyadi and J. Laszlovsky (eds), *The*

registered. When Ḥamā entered into a truce with the Hospitallers in 601/1204 after a series of attacks on the town Ibn Wāṣil wrote, using a similar refrain, 'The envoys of al-Malik al-Manṣūr and the Franks travelled back and forth until the truce was confirmed between them for a limited period'.[77] Authors who did not share Ibn Wāṣil's typically Ayyūbid perspective on the pluralistic Syrian political landscape, such as Ibn al-Athīr and Abū Shāma, reported the Hospitallers' attacks on Ḥamā, but omitted the conclusion of the truce.[78]

The relationship between the Hospitallers and Ḥamā is also a prime example of the level of detail that the *Mufarrij* includes on diplomatic matters. Two years before the 601/1204 truce, Ibn Wāṣil gives a long account of an aborted attempt by an envoy from the Templars to mediate a truce between the Hospitallers and Ḥamā at the Ḥamāwī court.[79] The details on diplomacy in the *Mufarrij* also allow us to establish that in the following year Ḥamā entered into a truce with the Hospitallers after troops from the town besieged the castle of Baʿrīn/Montferrand between Ḥiṣn al-Akrād/Crac des Chevaliers and Ḥamā: 'Letters were exchanged between him [al-Malik al-Manṣūr] and the Franks concerning the truce. The end of the matter was that he concluded a truce with them'.[80] Particularly valuable is the information he offers when he digs even deeper into the politics of central Syria and discusses minuscule Ayyūbid proto-lordships. These lordships usually remain below the radar of the period's chronicles, yet they often conducted their own diplomatic policy. For instance, al-Malik al-Muẓaffar of Ḥamā (r. 626/1229–642/1244) had granted the castle of Baʿrīn/Montferrand to his deposed brother al-Malik al-Nāṣir (r. 617/1221–626/1229) in the year 626/1229. According to Ibn Wāṣil, Baʿrīn/Montferrand had, by 630/1232–33, become a tributary of the Hospitallers of Ḥiṣn al-Akrād/Crac des Chevaliers and the Templars of Ṣāfītā/Chastel Blanc. In addition, al-Malik al-Nāṣir had entered into condominia-agreements over several villages with the neighbouring 'Franks'.[81]

Crusades and the Military Orders: Expanding the Frontiers of Medieval Latin Christianity (Budapest, 2001), 61–75.

77 Ibn Wāṣil, *Mufarrij*, vol. III, p. 164.

78 Abū Shāma, *al-Dhayl ʿala'l al-Rawḍatayn*, ed. M. al-Kawtharī as *Tarājim rijāl al-qarnayn al-sādis wa'l-sābiʿ*, (Beirut, 1974), p. 51; Ibn al-Athīr, *al-Kāmil fi'l-ta'rīkh*, ed. C.J. Tornberg, 13 vols (Beirut, 1965–67), vol. XII, p. 195; tr. D.S. Richards, *The Chronicle of Ibn al-Athir for the Crusading Period from* al-Kāmil fi'l-ta'rīkh. *Part 3: The Years 589–629/1193–1231: The Ayyubids after Saladin and the Mongol Menace* (Aldershot, 2008), p. 79.

79 Ibn Wāṣil, *Mufarrij*, vol. III, pp. 145–47.

80 Ibn Wāṣil, *Mufarrij*, vol. III, p. 154.

81 Ibn Wāṣil, *Mufarrij*, vol. V, p. 67.

The example of the conflict between Ḥamā on the one hand and the Hospitallers and the County of Tripoli on the other hand at the beginning of the seventh/thirteenth century also shows the *Mufarrij*'s worth for understanding the intra-Ayyūbid dynamics in conflicts with the Frankish lordships. The conflict had started to gain in intensity with al-Malik al-Manṣūr's 599/1203 attack on Baʿrīn/Montferrand. In preparation for this attack he tried to build up a larger coalition that would involve, most crucially, the Egyptian sultan al-Malik al-ʿĀdil. While al-Malik al-ʿĀdil verbally supported al-Malik al-Manṣūr's jihad he refrained from getting his troops or those of Damascus involved. For al-Malik al-ʿĀdil this was a local conflict in central Syria that did not require his attention or resources. Instead, he urged the local Ayyūbid rulers of the area, in particular Baalbek and Homs, and to a lesser degree Aleppo, to support Ḥamā. Despite the verbal grandeur of al-Malik al-ʿĀdil's messages the *Mufarrij* clearly shows that anti-Frankish warfare was too low on his agenda to form a large-scale Ayyūbid coalition including the two most significant contingents from Egypt and Damascus.[82]

Beyond the conclusion of truces, Ibn Wāṣil is also the main Arabic source that we have for longer-lasting Frankish-Ayyūbid alliances. Though these occurred less frequently than during the early sixth/twelfth-century *lā maqām*-period,[83] the *Mufarrij* discusses in detail, for instance, the northern Syrian alliance between Aleppo and Antioch in the early seventh/thirteenth century. Aleppo under al-Malik al-Ẓāhir (d. 613/1216) was one of the centres of Syrian Ayyūbid resistance to the attempts of his uncle al-Malik al-ʿĀdil in Egypt to impose his hegemony on the Syrian lands. The neighbouring lordships in northern Syria and Anatolia were drawn into this interminable conflict, and Aleppo thus entered into an increasingly close alliance with the Rūm Seljūqs of Anatolia and with Frankish Antioch which, for its part, was increasingly unable to rely on support from the Kingdom of Jerusalem. In addition, this alliance not only developed due to a shared enmity towards al-Malik al-ʿĀdil, but also because a strengthened Armenian Kingdom in the north was seeking to gain a foothold in the region. The Armenian Kingdom in turn entered into an alliance with al-Malik al-ʿĀdil to bolster its position against this north Syrian Frankish-Ayyūbid-Seljūq alliance. For details on the northern Syrian alliance

---

82 Ibn Wāṣil, *Mufarrij*, vol. III, pp. 141–45.

83 Köhler, *Alliances and Treaties*, pp. 59–174. '*Lā maqām*' is the doctrine shared among the various Frankish and Muslim lords of Syria that they would form a coalition against any outside intruder (such as the Great Seljūqs from the East). The underlying rationale was the fear that there would be 'no place' (*lā maqām*) left for any of these small lordships within a more centralised political landscape.

between Aleppo and Antioch (much less so for the Armenian-Egyptian and Seljūq sides of the story) Ibn Wāṣil is—in addition to Ibn al-ʿAdīm's *Zubda*—consistently the principle Arabic source.

It is the *Mufarrij* that best informs us of one of the earliest manifestations of this alliance. When the Armenian King Leon II besieged Antioch in 600/1203 the ruler of Aleppo, al-Malik al-Ẓāhir, immediately moved with his army to support Bohemond IV in Antioch and thus forced Leon to retreat. However, in a surprise move some three weeks later Leon was able to bring Antioch under his control. Bohemond's situation was so desperate that he declared his full submission to Aleppo and his men sent urgent calls for help by carrier pigeon. Al-Malik al-Ẓāhir again promptly moved towards Antioch to reinstall the balance of power in northern Syria and Leon was again obliged to withdraw.[84] The following year Leon raided Aleppan territory and al-Ẓāhir requested support from Antioch, in the framework of an increasingly tight alliance, for the counter raid. Antioch duly fulfilled its part and sent, according to Ibn Wāṣil, 10,000 men.[85] The importance of Ibn Wāṣil's report is evident through a comparison with other Arabic accounts. Ibn al-Athīr, for instance, deliberately silenced the Antiochene contribution in this counter raid and merely stated: '[al-Malik al-Ẓāhir] asked for assistance from other rulers'. Towards the end of the report Ibn al-Athīr even turned the northern Syrian conflict into a simple Muslim-Armenian clash where seemingly 'Muslims' and 'Armenians' fought.[86] Abū Shāma adopted the same strategy, writing Antioch out of the conflict and simplifying it as a binary Muslim-Armenian affair.[87]

The *Mufarrij* is also an important source that supports Cahen's argument that the large Ayyūbid coalition army of 603/1207 under al-Malik al-ʿĀdil must be seen in the context of this northern Syrian alliance system.[88] In this year al-ʿĀdil succeeded in uniting virtually all Syrian Ayyūbid rulers to fight the Hospitallers and the County of Tripoli who were increasingly undertaking raids in central Syria. What seems at first glance to be a classical jihad endeavour appears to have been more problematic in Ibn Wāṣil's report. Al-Malik al-Ẓāhir of Aleppo only sent a detachment, but did not participate in person.

84 Ibn Wāṣil, *Mufarrij*, vol. III, pp. 154–55. Ibn al-ʿAdīm, *Zubdat al-ḥalab min taʾrīkh Ḥalab*, ed. S. Dahhān, 3 vols (Damascus, 1951–68), vol. III, pp. 140–41, mentions an earlier correspondence between Bohemond III and al-Ẓāhir in 594/1197.

85 Ibn Wāṣil, *Mufarrij*, vol. III, pp. 170–71.

86 Ibn al-Athīr, *al-Kāmil*, vol. XII, pp. 238–39; tr. Richards, 3, p. 111.

87 Abū Shāma, *Dhayl*, p. 53.

88 C. Cahen, *La Syrie du nord à l'époque des Croisades* (Paris, 1940), p. 614; Humphreys, *From Saladin to the Mongols*, p. 135.

Furthermore, Ibn Wāṣil reports that throughout the campaigns al-Malik al-ʿĀdil sent messages to al-Malik al-Ẓāhir scolding him for his absence and thus prompting the latter to fear an attack and to reinforce the defences of Aleppo. For Ibn Wāṣil, al-Malik al-ʿĀdil's move was thus not only in retaliation for Frankish raiding but also an attempt to embarrass al-Malik al-Ẓāhir who faced the dilemma of whether to enter into conflict with Antioch or stay out of the largest anti-Frankish campaign since the era of his father Saladin. In this light al-ʿĀdil's campaign was aimed as much at weakening Aleppo's ally Antioch, at this point in control of Tripoli, as at supporting al-Malik al-ʿĀdil's principal ally in the region, the Armenian Kingdom. The intra-Ayyūbid dynamics underlying this anti-Frankish jihad are conveniently glossed over by other chroniclers such as Ibn al-Athīr, who has nothing on al-Malik al-Ẓāhir's reluctance to participate nor the subsequent exchange of messages. In addition, according to Ibn Wāṣil, al-Malik al-ʿĀdil ended this campaign with yet another truce, while Ibn al-Athīr explicitly states that a truce was not concluded. As there were no military conflicts with Tripoli in the subsequent years and as Ibn Wāṣil is in general better informed of Ayyūbid diplomacy, his account is more probable.[89]

A final reason why the *Mufarrij* is essential when tracing the development of this northern Syrian alliance system is that it also provides in detail the developments that led to its breakdown. The political landscape started to change in 611/1214 when a Frankish coalition of troops from Cyprus, Tripoli, Acre and Antioch was joined by Leon. The presence of these forces close to Ḥiṣn al-Akrād/Crac des Chevaliers quite understandably worried the north Syrian rulers of nearby Ḥamā and Homs as well as the Nizārīs. Al-Malik al-Ẓāhir's role as protector of Ḥamā in the early stages of this conflict did not constitute a break of the established patterns of cooperation between Aleppo and Antioch. Yet his subsequent protection and assistance for the Nizārīs arguably was a considerable shift because the Frankish attack on the Nizārī castle of al-Khawābī was meant as retaliation for the murder of Bohemond's son Raymond the previous year.[90]

---

89 Ibn Wāṣil, *Mufarrij*, vol III, pp. 172–74; Ibn al-Athīr, *al-Kāmil*, vol. XII, p. 274; tr. Richards, 3, p. 13; F.-J. Dahlmann, *al-Malik al-ʿĀdil: Ägypten und der Vordere Orient in den Jahren 589/1193 bis 615/1218, ein Beitrag zur Ayyūbidischen Geschichte* (Giessen: Diss. University of Giessen, 1975), pp. 126–28.

90 Ibn Wāṣil, *Mufarrij*, vol. III, pp. 223–24. Cf. A.-M. Eddé, *La principauté ayyoubide d'Alep: (579/1183–658/1260)* (Stuttgart, 1999), p. 82, who argues that al-Ẓāhir's capacity to intervene shows that this event is rather a sign of the continuing relationship between Aleppo and Antioch.

It is also the *Mufarrij*, to cite a final example on the alliance system, that describes in great detail the final stage of the breakdown from the perspective of Aleppo. While Aleppan assistance to the Nizārīs had arguably weakened the relationship between Aleppo and Antioch, Aleppo effectively exited the northern Syrian-Anatolian entente only when it broke with the Rūm Seljūqs in 613/1216. In that year the Rūm Seljūq Sultan ʿIzz al-Dīn Kay Kāwūs I (r. 608/1211–616/1220) requested Aleppo's support for a pincer attack on the Armenian Kingdom. After a prolonged advance and retreat, al-Malik al-Ẓāhir refused to participate because his relationship with al-Malik al-ʿĀdil in Egypt was improving and Aleppo was losing interest in its former Rūm Seljūq allies. According to Ibn Wāṣil, al-Malik al-Ẓāhir also focused on the issue of diplomatic relations with the Frankish lordships in the ensuing negotiations with al-Malik al-ʿĀdil. He demanded that Aleppo and Egypt would no longer enter into separate truces with them, but act in unison.[91] This must be seen against the background of Bohemond IV's deposition in Antioch in the previous year 612/1216 when Leon was finally able to take control of the city, thus rendering the entire alliance system fundamentally altered.

How deeply the *Mufarrij* was embedded in Ayyūbid politics is also evident from reports on the intra-Ayyūbid conflict between the Egyptian sultan al-Malik al-Ṣāliḥ Ayyūb and the Damascene ruler al-Malik al-Ṣāliḥ Ismāʿīl. Ismāʿīl had come under increasing pressure from his Egypt-based nephew and desperately tried to build an anti-Egyptian Syrian coalition. When he failed in this Ismāʿīl turned in 638/1240 to the Kingdom of Jerusalem, which had a significant military force at its disposal due to the recent arrival of the Crusade led by Theobald of Champagne. In exchange for Frankish support against Ayyūb, Ismāʿīl surrendered his possessions in Galilee (it is unclear whether Jerusalem was surrendered as well) and further to the north.[92] This in turn led to such sharp criticism in Damascus that Ismāʿīl decided to exile two vocal scholars, including the *khaṭīb* of the Umayyad Mosque ʿIzz al-Dīn al-Sulamī. Ibn Wāṣil was clearly not at ease with Ismāʿīl's wide-ranging territorial concessions, probably because the resulting Frankish-Damascene coalition was directed against his patron Ayyūb: 'These two castles [that had been surrendered to the Franks] became painful coals and the affliction of the Muslims strongly increased'.[93] However, he is also at pains to explain Ismāʿīl's motives for his alliance with the Franks. He underlined Ayyūb's previous dubious behaviour towards Ismāʿīl, including the incarceration of the latter's son. In addition, he

91 Ibn Wāṣil, *Mufarrij*, vol. III, pp. 234–37.

92 Humphreys, *From Saladin to the Mongols*, p. 266.

93 Ibn Wāṣil, *Mufarrij*, vol. V, p. 302.

put al-Sulamī's criticisms into perspective somewhat by depicting him as a zealot who was also deposed as *khaṭīb* in Cairo shortly after his arrival because he again ran into trouble with the military elite.[94] Finally, Ibn Wāṣil excluded details of the surrender that might have set it into a too negative light, such as the execution of the Muslim commander of one of the castles who refused to hand it over to the Franks.[95]

The *Mufarrij* is also the text that expresses most clearly one of the rationales of the Ayyūbid rulers for their non-aggressive conduct towards the Frankish rulers of Syria. The painful and costly experience of the Third Crusade was a constant reminder for the Ayyūbids that a more aggressive stance towards the relatively weak Frankish lordships would lead to renewed crusading activity and thus the arrival of a more serious enemy. The fiscal and budgetary problems under Saladin had been a consequence of his campaigns of expansion and were something the later Ayyūbid rulers wanted to avoid. In addition, they were well aware that the long periods of military conflict had strained Saladin's relationship with his leading officers, who became increasingly reluctant to support him in his belligerent policies. These issues also arose towards the end of the Fifth Crusade when the Egyptian sultan al-Malik al-Kāmil faced the decision of whether to annihilate the remaining crusading troops or to settle for a negotiated withdrawal. The *Mufarrij* quotes his reasoning for opting for the latter solution as: 'These who are here are not all the Franks. If we eliminate them, we could only take ... Damietta after a fairly long time. The kings of the Franks overseas and the Pope will hear what has happened to the Franks and then they will send further reinforcements to Egypt'.[96]

Finally, the *Mufarrij* is unique in presenting the developments on the Ayyūbid side during the major Crusade campaigns. For the Fifth Crusade his text is of limited value; from the arrival of the main crusading troops in 614/1217 to the end of the Crusade in 618/1221 Ibn Wāṣil was not yet directly involved in the political life of the Ayyūbid lordships, and although his account certainly adds some valuable detail, such as the above-quoted statement by al-Malik al-Kāmil on the danger of new crusades, it does not fundamentally change the picture of earlier sources, most importantly the report by Ibn al-Athīr.[97]

For the Crusade of Frederick II, however, Ibn Wāṣil's reports do become an important source for understanding intra-Ayyūbid dynamics in response to its arrival. A crucial point for understanding these dynamics is the occasion of

94 Ibn Wāṣil, *Mufarrij*, vol. v, p. 304.

95 Sibṭ Ibn al-Jawzī, *Mir'āt al-zamān*, ed. Jewett, p. 493.

96 Ibn Wāṣil, *Mufarrij*, vol. iv, p. 97.

97 Ibn al-Athīr, *al-Kāmil*, vol. xii, pp. 320–31; tr. Richards, 3, pp. 174–82.

the Egyptian sultan al-Malik al-Kāmil's move to Syria in 625/1228, ostensibly to confront Frederick II. The ruler of Damascus, al-Malik al-Nāṣir, had little faith in al-Malik al-Kāmil and, fearing for his lordship, called for help from al-Malik al-Ashraf (d. 635/1237), the only Ayyūbid ruler who could match al-Malik al-Kāmil's forces. Ibn al-Athīr gives a broad outline of the ensuing conflicts among the Ayyūbid rulers, but he clearly lacked deep insight into the developments.[98] Ibn Wāṣil, in contrast, goes into much more detail and lists, for instance, the names of two Ayyūbid princes who were in al-Malik al-Kāmil's company. These princes were not only fiercely loyal to him but they both had territorial ambitions in Syria—crucial information to understand the concerns of al-Malik al-Nāṣir and other Syrian rulers vis-à-vis the Egyptian 'support'.[99] Similarly, Ibn Wāṣil digs deep into Syrian local politics to explain why al-Malik al-ʿAzīz, al-Malik al-Kāmil's brother, performed a *volte-face* upon his brother's arrival and joined forces with him.[100] The originality of the account given by Ibn Wāṣil—who was in Damascus during this period—is also evident from the increasing number of cases where he explicitly uses his authorial voice in the long passages that he devoted to intra-Ayyūbid dynamics.[101]

The *Mufarrij*—like Ibn al-ʿAdīm's *Zubda*—describes the Crusade of Frederick II, which evidently did not endanger the Ayyūbid Syrian political landscape in any serious way, as a rather curious endeavour.[102] Even the surrender of Jerusalem to Frederick II by the Egyptian sultan al-Malik al-Kāmil in 626/1229 could for him be easily justified. He first quotes his own father who was in Jerusalem at this point: 'When it was proclaimed that the Muslims were to leave Jerusalem as it had been handed over to the Franks, the population of Jerusalem started to wail and cry'.[103] However, Ibn Wāṣil immediately made sure that the handover was given a more positive spin underlining that al-Malik al-Kāmil knew that 'the Franks will not be able to defend Jerusalem as its wall has been destroyed. So whenever he wishes and the circumstances allow he will be able to purify it from the Franks and drive them away'.[104] It comes as little surprise that the *Mufarrij* is the best Arabic source for the negotiations that led to the handover of Jerusalem. It is his summary of the final treaty, for

98 Ibn al-Athīr *al-Kāmil*, vol. XII, pp. 479–80; tr. Richards, 3, pp. 292–93.
99 Ibn Wāṣil, *Mufarrij*, vol. IV, pp. 226–27.
100 Ibn Wāṣil, *Mufarrij*, vol. IV, pp. 226–27.
101 Ibn Wāṣil, *Mufarrij*, vol. IV, pp. 225–31 and 236–40.
102 Ibn al-ʿAdīm, *Zubda*, vol. III, p. 305.
103 Ibn Wāṣil, *Mufarrij*, vol. IV, p. 243.
104 Ibn Wāṣil, *Mufarrij*, vol. IV, pp. 243–45.

instance, that has the most detailed account of this document in all contemporary Arabic sources.[105]

In contrast, Ibn Wāṣil's contemporary Sibṭ Ibn al-Jawzī reported the handover of Jerusalem not as a political manoeuvre within the Syrian/Egyptian political landscape, but rather as part of a major Frankish-Muslim confrontation: 'The news of the handover of Jerusalem to the Franks arrived and all hell broke loose in the lands of Islam'.[106] The difference between these two crucial chroniclers of the Ayyūbid period is also evident from Ibn Wāṣil's report on Sibṭ Ibn al-Jawzī's preaching activities in Damascus in the aftermath of the agreement between al-Malik al-Kāmil and Frederick. While Ibn Wāṣil was evidently impressed by Sibṭ Ibn al-Jawzī's oratory skills, he could not help but set the religious uproar against the handover within the *realpolitik* of his day. After describing how al-Malik al-Nāṣir of Damascus approached Sibṭ Ibn al-Jawzī and asked him to preach on 'this humiliation of the Muslims and the shame', Ibn Wāṣil continues '[Al-Malik al-Nāṣir's] aim with this was to arouse the people's aversion to his uncle [al-Malik al-Kāmil]'.[107]

In what is another rather unusual move for the Arabic sources Ibn Wāṣil devoted a lengthy passage to Frederick's visit to Jerusalem. In his detailed account Ibn Wāṣil could rely directly on the Muslim judge whom al-Malik al-Kāmil had appointed to accompany the emperor. Though he reserved his most positive comments for Frederick's son Manfred he clearly liked Frederick as well. He focussed in his report again on the issue of the emperor's supposedly pro-Muslim tendencies, demonstrated by Frederick banning a priest from entering the Aqṣā Mosque with a testament in his hand, and longing to hear the Muslim call to prayer.[108] Sibṭ Ibn al-Jawzī was obviously of a different opinion and it is he who gave the famous description of the emperor as having 'red skin' and being 'bald and short-sighted'. In terms of religiosity he described him rather as a 'materialist' whose 'Christianity was simply a game to him'.[109]

105 Ibn Wāṣil, *Mufarrij*, vol. IV, pp. 243–44. The other main contemporary chronicle is Sibṭ Ibn al-Jawzī (see above, pp. 84–108). Further contemporary chronicles have only very brief comments that add no substantial information such as Abū Shāma, *Dhayl*, p. 154 and Ibn al-Athīr, *al-Kāmil*, vol. XII, pp. 482–83; tr. Richards, 3, pp. 293–94.

106 Sibṭ Ibn al-Jawzī, *Mir'āt al-zamān*, s.n., 2 vols numbered VIII/1 and VIII/2 (Hyderabad, 1951–52), vol. VIII/2, p. 653; tr. C. Hillenbrand, *The Crusades. Islamic Perspectives* (Edinburgh, 1999), p. 221.

107 Ibn Wāṣil, *Mufarrij*, vol. IV, p. 245; cf. S.A. Mourad & J.E. Lindsay, *The Intensification and Reorientation of Sunni Jihad Ideology in the Crusader Period* (Leiden, 2013), pp. 95–99.

108 Ibn Wāṣil, *Mufarrij*, vol. IV, pp. 244–45.

109 Sibṭ Ibn al-Jawzī, *Mir'āt al-zamān*, ed. Jewett, p. 433.

Ibn Wāṣil's chronicle is thus, for the first half of the seventh/thirteenth century, of central importance for understanding Frankish-Ayyūbid diplomatic relationships and the ways in which Ayyūbid rulers reacted to the arrival and presence of the Franks. This was understood by subsequent medieval chroniclers such as Abu'l-Fidā' (d. 732/1332), Ibn al-Furāt (d. 807/1405) and Ibn Khaldūn (d. 808/1406), who drew from him extensively for this period. Despite the outstanding importance of this chronicle it has so far not played a prominent role in modern European and American historiographies of the Crusades as it remains virtually untranslated.[110] The only exceptions are the passages relating to the Crusade of Louis IX which Peter Jackson skilfully translated.[111] The importance of his translation lies in the fact that he not only translated those passages dealing directly with events involving the Franks, but also those that deal with the much more important issue of intra-Ayyūbid dynamics. In contrast, the second work that has substantial passages of Ibn Wāṣil in translation fails for a related reason; while Gabrieli took the right decision to rely mostly on Ibn Wāṣil for the Crusade of Frederick II, his choice of passages gives an entirely erroneous impression of the text's focus. He only translated those passages that directly deal with the Crusade and Frederick II, but the much more interesting sections on the Ayyūbid dynamics are left out.[112] From the perspective of the history of the Latin East and the Crusades a full translation of the *Mufarrij* thus remains an urgent desideratum.

---

110 Except for earlier translations such as those by J. Michaud, *Bibliothèque des croisades vol. 4* (Paris, 1829), s.v. 'Gemal-Eddin'.

111 Jackson, *Seventh Crusade*, pp. 128–54.

112 Gabrieli, *Arab Historians*, pp. 264–73, 276–80, 284–300 (Louis IX's Crusade); these sections are also included in J. Bird, E. Peters and J.M. Powell (eds), *Crusade and Christendom. Annotated Documents in Translation from Innocent III to the Fall of Acre, 1187–1291* (Philadelphia, 2013).

Taqī al-Dīn Aḥmad ibn ʿAlī al-Maqrīzī

Frédéric Bauden

Taqī al-Dīn Aḥmad b. ʿAlī b. ʿAbd al-Qādir b. Muḥammad b. Ibrāhīm al-Maqrīzī or Ibn al-Maqrīzī, the hadith scholar and historian, was born in Cairo in 766/1364–65 into a family of Ḥanbalī scholars originally from Baalbek.[1] It was

1 For the life of al-Maqrīzī, see Ibn Ḥajar al-ʿAsqalānī, *Inbāʾ al-ghumr bi-abnāʾ al-ʿumr*, ed. Ḥ. Ḥabashī, 4 vols (Cairo, 1969–72), vol. IV, pp. 187–88; idem, *al-Majmaʿ al-muʾassis bi'l-muʿjam al-mufahris*, ed. Y.ʿA.R. al-Marʿashī, 4 vols (Beirut, 1992–94), vol. III, pp. 58–60; Ibn Fahd, *Muʿjam al-shuyūkh*, ed. M. al-Zāhī and Ḥ. al-Jāsir (Riyadh, 1982), pp. 63–67; Ibn Taghrībirdī, *al-Manhal al-ṣāfī wa'l-mustawfī fī baʿd al-wāfī*, ed. M.M. Amīn et al., 13 vols (Cairo, 1984–2009), vol. I, pp. 415–20 (no. 221); idem, *al-Dalīl al-shāfī ʿala'l-manhal al-ṣāfī*, ed. F.M. Shaltūt, 2 vols (Mecca, 1983; reprint Cairo, 1998), vol. I, p. 63 (no. 217); idem, *al-Nujūm al-zāhira fī mulūk Miṣr wa'l-Qāhira*, s.n., 16 vols (Cairo, 1963–72), vol. XV, pp. 490–91; idem, *Ḥawādith al-duhūr fī madā al-ayyām wa'l-shuhūr*, ed. F.M. Shaltūt, 2 vols (Cairo, 1990), vol. I, pp. 39–41; al-Biqāʿī, *ʿUnwān al-zamān bi-tarājim al-shuyūkh wa'l-aqrān*, ed. Ḥ. Ḥabashī, 5 vols published so far (Cairo, 2001–), vol. I, pp. 109–10; al-Sakhāwī, *al-Ḍawʾ al-lāmiʿ ʿan ahl al-qarn al-tāsiʿ*, s.n., 12 vols (Cairo, 1934–36; reprint Beirut, 1992), vol. II, pp. 21–25; idem, *al-Tibr al-masbūk fī dhayl al-sulūk*, ed. N.M. Kāmil et al., 4 vols (Cairo, 2002–7), vol. I, pp. 70–78; idem, *Wajīz al-kalām fi'l-dhayl ʿalā duwal al-islām*, ed. B.ʿA. Maʿrūf et al., 4 vols (Beirut, 1995), vol. II, p. 580 (no. 1342); al-Ṣayrafī, *Nuzhat al-nufūs wa'l-abdān fī tawārīkh al-zamān*, ed. Ḥ. Ḥabashī, 4 vols (Cairo, 1970–89), vol. IV, pp. 242–44 (no. 536); ʿAbd al-Bāsiṭ b. Khalīl al-Malaṭī al-Ẓāhirī, *Nayl al-amal fī dhayl al-duwal*, ed. ʿU.A. Tadmurī, 9 vols (Sidon-Beirut, 2002), vol. V, pp. 150–51; idem, *al-Majmaʿ al-mufannan bi'l-muʿjam al-muʿanwan*, ed. ʿA.M. al-Kandarī, 2 vols (Beirut, 2011), vol. I, pp. 347–52 (no. 429); Ibn Iyās, *Badāʾiʿ al-zuhūr fī waqāʾiʿ al-duhūr*, ed. M. Muṣṭafā, 5 vols (Wiesbaden, 1960–75), vol. II, pp. 231–32; Ibn al-ʿImād, *Shadharāt al-dhahab fī akhbār man dhahab*, ed. ʿA.Q. al-Arnaʾūṭ and M. al-Arnaʾūṭ, 10 vols (Damascus-Beirut, 1986–93), vol. IX, pp. 370–71; al-Shawkānī, *al-Badr al-ṭāliʿ bi-maḥāsin man baʿd al-qarn al-sābiʿ*, ed. M.Ḥ. Ḥallāq (Damascus-Beirut, 2006), pp. 109–11 (no. 46); F. Bauden, 'al-Maqrīzī', in EMC, vol. II, 1074–76; *Mamlūk Studies Review* 7 (2003), *passim* (proceedings of the international conference *The Legacy of al-Maqrīzī [1364–1442]*, University of Notre Dame, September 28–29, 2001); Ḥ. ʿĀṣī, *Al-Maqrīzī Taqī al-Dīn Aḥmad ibn ʿAlī ibn ʿAbd al-Qādir al-ʿUbaydī (766–845 h.-1366–1441 m.), muʾarrikh al-duwal al-islāmiyya fī Miṣr* (Beirut, 1992); K. al-D. ʿI. al-D. ʿAlī, *Arbaʿa muʾarrikhīn wa-arbaʿa muʾallafāt min dawlat al-mamālīk al-jarākisa* (Cairo, 1992), pp. 157–239; idem, *al-Maqrīzī muʾarrikhan* (Beirut, 1990); S. ʿĀshūr, 'Aḍwāʾ jadīda ʿala'l-muʾarrikh Aḥmad ibn ʿAlī al-Maqrīzī wa-kitābātihi', *ʿĀlam al-fikr* 14 (1983), 165–210; J.-C. Garcin, 'Al-Maqrîzî. Un historien encyclopédique du monde afro-oriental', in *Les Africains*, vol. 9, ed. Ch.-A. Julien et al. (Paris, 1977), 195–223; F. Rosenthal, 'al-Maḳrīzī', in EI2; *Dirāsāt ʿan al-Maqrīzī* (Cairo, 1971); al-Ziriklī, *al-Aʿlām*, 8 vols (4th ed., Beirut, 2002), vol. I, pp. 177–78; C. Brockelmann, *Geschichte*

 | DOI 10.1163/9789004280687_009

his great-great grandfather Ibrāhīm, or the latter's father Muḥammad, who first settled in the Syrian town. It is not known where this ancestor originally came from but the area of Baalbek in which he chose to live, Maqāriza, meant his descendents came to be known under the name al-Maqrīzī, according to al-Maqrīzī himself.[2] Another possibility, although a more debatable one due to the nature of the source, is that the origin of this *nisba* could be from a certain Ibn Amqrīz, a Berber who belonged to the Kutāma tribe. One of his daughters may have married an ancestor of al-Maqrīzī and the family would thus have been known through this slightly altered form of the name.[3] Whichever is the case, it seems probable that the family must have originally been Shīʿīs, perhaps themselves related to the Fāṭimids, which would explain why al-Maqrīzī's ancestor opted for a family name which allowed him to blend into Baalbek when he settled in the city. Al-Maqrīzī, however, doubts a Fāṭimid origin for his family. Yet he did leave several clues which suggest that his family did have such a background, or at least that he believed this until a certain point in his life; this does not mean, however, that he was necessarily right or that he continued to believe until the end of his life what may have been a family legend.

It was al-Maqrīzī's grandfather, Muḥyī al-Dīn ʿAbd al-Qādir (born in 677/1278–79, d. 28th Rabīʿ I 732/29th December 1331),[4] who was the first to leave his home town and go to Damascus where he was, among other things,

der arabischen Litteratur, 2 vols (Weimar-Berlin, 1898–1926; 2nd ed. Leiden, 1943–49), 3 supplements (Leiden, 1937–42), vol. II, pp. 47–50, and S., vol. II, pp. 36–38; ʿU.R. Kaḥḥāla, *Muʿjam al-muʾallifīn*, 4 vols (Beirut, 1993), vol. I, pp. 204–5 (no. 1515). See also the introduction by M. al-Jalīlī to his edition of al-Maqrīzī, *Durar al-ʿuqūd al-farīda fī tarājim al-aʿyān al-mufīda*, 4 vols (Beirut, 2002), vol. I, pp. 13–39.

2 Ibn Ḥajar al-ʿAsqalānī, *al-Majmaʿ al-muʾassis*, vol. III, p. 59. The passage in question was approved by al-Maqrīzī himself, who reviewed and corrected his own biography in the autograph manuscript of Ibn Ḥajar al-ʿAsqalānī. See F. Bauden, 'Maqriziana IX: Should al-Maqrīzī Be Thrown Out With the Bathwater? The Question of His Plagiarism of al-Awḥadī's *Khiṭaṭ* and the Documentary Evidence', *Mamlūk Studies Review* 14 (2010), 159–232, pp. 221–23.

3 Ibn Fahd, *Muʿjam al-shuyūkh*, p. 64; Sibṭ Ibn al-ʿAjamī, *Kunūz al-dhahab fī taʾrīkh Ḥalab*, ed. Sh. Shaʿth and F. al-Bakkūr, 2 vols (Aleppo, 1996–97), vol. II, p. 267.

4 On al-Maqrīzī's grandfather, see al-Dhahabī, *Dhayl taʾrīkh al-Islām*, ed. M.S. Bā Wazīr (Riyadh, 1998), pp. 392–93; al-Ṣafadī, *al-Wāfī bi'l-wafayāt*, 30 vols (Beirut, 1993), vol. XIX, (ed. R. Sayyid) pp. 42–43; idem, *Aʿyān al-ʿaṣr wa aʿwān al-naṣr*, ed. N.A.ʿA. ʿAlī Abū Zayd et al., 6 vols (Beirut-Damascus, 1997–98), vol. III, pp. 119–20; Ibn Rajab, *al-Dhayl ʿalā ṭabaqāt al-ḥanābila*, ed. ʿA.R.S. al-ʿUthaymīn, 5 vols (Riyadh, 2005), vol. V, p. 29; al-Maqrīzī, *Durar al-ʿuqūd al-farīda*, vol. II, pp. 516–17 (a biography of his grandfather contained within the notice devoted by al-Maqrīzī to his own father); idem, *al-Sulūk li-maʿrifat duwal al-mulūk*, ed. M.M. Ziyāda and S.ʿA.F. ʿĀshūr, 4 vols (Cairo, 1934–73), vol. II, p. 365 (*sub anno* 733!). It is unclear whether members of the family remained in Baalbek during al-Maqrīzī's lifetime, but an older brother

responsible for teaching hadith studies at Dār al-Ḥadīth al-Bahāʾiyya, a leading institution for the subject.[5] While based in Damascus he also made an academic journey which took him to Cairo, Aleppo, and the two Islamic Holy Cities, almost certainly on pilgrimage. Al-Maqrīzī's father, ʿAlāʾ al-Dīn ʿAlī (d. 25th Ramaḍān 779/25th January 1378 in Cairo, at the age of almost 50), was born in the Syrian capital where he would both benefit from the social status his father had acquired and undertake all his training.[6] He does not seem to have made trips to any other places during this time, and instead he began working in Damascus, seemingly only departing that town when he left for Cairo, which was presumably an attempt to make his way through the ranks of the civil administration. His departure for Cairo cannot be precisely dated, but all indications suggest that it must have occurred before he was thirty years old.

Professionally, he was able to benefit in Cairo from the relations he cultivated with Sayf al-Dīn Āqtamur al-Ḥanbalī (d. 11th Rajab 779/13th November 1377), a Mamlūk emir who held a high position within the military government.[7] When Āqtamur became chief executive secretary (*dawādār*) he took al-Maqrīzī's father under his wing, enabling the latter to take a job at the chancellery (*dīwān al-inshāʾ*) as a secretary (*kātib*). He was thus able to quickly consolidate his position and his fortune.[8]

(born 668/1269–70) of his grandfather, named Ibrāhīm and described as a Sufi, died there in 737/1337. See Ibn Rāfiʿ al-Salāmī, *al-Wafayāt*, ed. Ṣ.M. ʿAbbās, 2 vols (Beirut, 1982), vol. I, p. 185.

5 This madrasa was founded by Bahāʾ al-Dīn Ibn ʿAsākir; see al-Nuʿaymī, *al-Dāris fī taʾrīkh al-madāris*, 2 vols (Beirut, 1999), vol. I, pp. 43–45.

6 On al-Maqrīzī's father, see al-Maqrīzī, *Durar al-ʿuqūd al-farīda*, vol. II, pp. 516–17; idem, *al-Sulūk*, vol. III, p. 326; Ibn Ḥajar al-ʿAsqalānī, *Inbāʾ al-ghumr*, vol. I, p. 166.

7 He was essentially chief executive secretary (*dawādār*) from 19th Rajab 769/10th March 1368 to 20th Ramaḍān 770/28th April 1369; viceroy (*nāʾib al-salṭana*) from 20th Rabīʿ I 777/19th August 1375 to 21st Ramaḍān 778/1st February 1377 and from 19th Dhu'l-Qaʿda 778/30th March 1377 to 25th Ṣafar 779/3rd July 1377; and then governor of Syria, a position he occupied until his death. See al-Maqrīzī, *al-Sulūk*, vol. III, p. 326; Ibn Ḥajar al-ʿAsqalānī, *Inbāʾ al-ghumr*, vol. I, pp. 245–46; Ibn Taghrībirdī, *al-Nujūm al-zāhira*, vol. XI, p. 191; idem, *al-Manhal al-ṣāfī*, vol. II, pp. 492–93. He must not be confused, as Ibn Ḥajar al-ʿAsqalānī, *Inbāʾ al-ghumr*, vol. I, p. 166, did, with Sayf al-Dīn Āqtamur min ʿAbd al-Ghanī al-Nāṣirī al-Turkī (d. 29th Jumādā II 783/20th September 1381), who held the post of lieutenant of the sultan in Cairo alternatively with his homonym. For the latter, see al-Maqrīzī, *al-Sulūk*, vol. III, p. 462; Ibn Ḥajar al-ʿAsqalānī, *al-Durar al-kāmina fī aʿyān al-miʾa al-thāmina*, 4 vols (Hyderabad, 1930–32; reprint Beirut, 1993), vol. I, p. 392 (no. 1008); idem, *Inbāʾ al-ghumr*, vol. I, pp. 243–44 (no. 12); Ibn Taghrībirdī, *al-Manhal al-ṣāfī*, vol. II, p. 493 (no. 498); idem, *al-Dalīl al-shāfī*, vol. I, p. 141 (no. 497); idem, *al-Nujūm al-zāhira*, vol. XI, pp. 178–79.

8 According to al-Maqrīzī, Āqtamur was so powerful as an chief executive secretary that he could issue documents in his own name without consulting the sultan, as stated on the

In the meantime, he had married Asmā' (born 21th Rajab 747/7th November 1346; d. 12th Rabīʿ I 800/3rd December 1397), the daughter of the famous Ḥanafī scholar Muḥammad b. ʿAbd al-Raḥmān b. ʿAlī b. Abi'l-Ḥasan al-Suʿūdī b. al-Ṣā'igh (d. 12th Shaʿbān 776/16th January 1375). Such a match was another way in which he increased his standing in society, through this union with a prominent family from the Cairo elite. ʿAlī al-Maqrīzī's father-in-law held many important positions, notably that of *Mufti* at the supreme court (*dār al-ʿadl*). One year after the marriage (in Muḥarram 765/October–November 1363) al-Maqrīzī was born. At least two other births followed, as al-Maqrīzī had two brothers named Muḥammad (772/1371–822/1419) and Ḥasan.[9] When al-Maqrīzī's father died around the age of fifty his eldest son had not yet reached his fourteenth birthday.

Although he came from a Ḥanbalī family al-Maqrīzī was educated according to the *madhhab* of his maternal grandfather, even though he was only ten when the latter died. His influence must have been a significant factor in this choice of Ḥanafism and, although his father did not oppose it, it seems that the latter could not have gone against the decision of his father-in-law. At just three years old al-Maqrīzī was present at his grandfather's lessons and at seven, having memorised the Quran, he was trained in the religious sciences for which he demonstrated a definite aptitude, particularly in hadith studies. Even by the age of five he could boast of possessing several transmission licences, issued by some of the greatest scholars of his age. Yet when he was twenty he decided to change to the Shāfiʿī *madhhab*. This choice, which he made well after the death of his maternal grandfather and his father, had its basis in his indifference towards the more conciliatory character of Ḥanafism, for which his aversion grew, as well as from concern over his career, as membership of the Shāfiʿī *madhhab*, which was followed by the majority in Egypt, constituted the quickest way by which he could climb the career ladder. While this change was justified by personal reasons, everything seems to suggest that in dogmatic terms al-Maqrīzī remained attached to the *madhhab* of his father: the various

---

documents issued. See al-Maqrīzī, *al-Mawāʿiẓ wa'l-iʿtibār fī dhikr al-khiṭaṭ wa'l-āthār*, 2 vols (Būlāq, 1853), vol. II, p. 221 = ed. A.F. Sayyid, 5 vols (London, 2002–4), vol. III, pp. 720–21.

9 This was Asmā''s second marriage: she had been married to Najm al-Dīn al-Muhallabī al-Ramlī at the age of twelve. After the death of al-Maqrīzī's father she married for the third and final time, and gave birth to another boy. See al-Maqrīzī, *Durar al-ʿuqūd al-farīda*, vol. I, pp. 394–97 (no. 319); idem, *al-Sulūk*, vol. IV, p. 1107; Ibn Ḥajar al-ʿAsqalānī, *Inbā' al-ghumr*, vol. II, p. 33. For al-Maqrīzī's maternal grandfather, see al-Ṣafadī, *al-Wāfī*, vol. III, 244; al-Maqrīzī, *Durar al-ʿuqūd al-farīda*, vol. III, pp. 255–60; idem, *al-Sulūk*, vol. III, p. 245; Ibn Ḥajar al-ʿAsqalānī, *Inbā' al-ghumr*, vol. I, pp. 95–96. There is no biography of al-Maqrizī's brother Ḥasan in the sources, and so nothing is known of him.

positions he took in his diverse writings demonstrate that he favoured a more literal interpretation which was characteristic of the Ḥanbalī *madhhab*. Thus, his profession of faith, *Tajrīd al-tawḥīd al-mufīd*, written towards the end of his life, is full of implicit references to the works of Ibn Qayyim al-Jawziyya (d. 751/1350), who was himself a disciple of Ibn Taymiyya (d. 728/1328).[10] His propensity for literalism led him to being accused of Ẓāhirism, a movement of thought which took its name from its founder Ibn Ḥazm (d. 456/1064), but the foundation of this accusation is very thin and seems to have been the result of a confusion of genres.[11]

In 783/1381 he performed the Hajj, the first of a number of times he did so,[12] and he profited during his sojourn in Mecca by studying under numerous scholars, an activity in which he would also engage during several future visits to the Holy City. His entry into working life came a little after this, and his first position was as a delegated judge and administrator of endowments. He then worked in the chancellery, following in the footsteps of his father by working there as a *kātib* alongside the famous al-Qalqashandī (d. 821/1418). His contacts with various emirs grew and he became noticed by the sultan Barqūq (r. 784/1382–791/1389 and 792/1390–801/1399) and, at the end of the latter's reign, al-Maqrīzī was appointed to the prestigious post of inspector of the Cairo markets (*muḥtasib*).[13] However, this gained him the enmity of many of his colleagues, including his fellow-historian al-ʿAynī (d. 855/1453), who

10 See al-Maqrīzī, *Tajrīd al-tawḥīd al-mufīd wa-yalīhi Taṭhīr al-iʿtiqād ʿan adrān al-ilḥād li-Muḥammad ibn Ismāʿīl al-Ṣanʿānī (t. 1182)*, ed. Ṣ.S. Šāhīn and M.I. al-Ṣanʿānī (Riyadh, 2005). It is not disinteresting to note that al-Maqrīzī's grandfather was buried near the tomb of Ibn Taymiyya, in Damascus.

11 See N. Rabbat, 'Who was al-Maqrīzī? A Biographical Sketch', *Mamlūk Studies Review* 7 (2003), 1–19, pp. 12–14.

12 In addition to his first stay, which lasted several months (he arrived at Mecca at the beginning of Ramaḍān 783/end of November 1381 and left with a pilgrim caravan which departed at the beginning of 784/Spring 1382), he went to Mecca in 787 (arriving in the middle of the year/August 1385, and remaining until the beginning of 788/Spring 1386), in 790 (arriving for the pilgrimage, which was at the end of the year 1388, he left at the beginning of the year 791/1389), in 825 (again to carry out the pilgrimage, at the end of 1422, leaving just after the beginning of 826/1423), in 834 (he arrived in the middle of the year, in March 1431, staying several months, departing for Cairo at the end of the pilgrimage, at the beginning of 835/Autumn 1431), and finally in 838 (arriving with the Cairene caravan at the end of the year/June 1435, he remained there until the beginning of the year 840/July–August 1436). These very precise dates are provided by Ibn Fahd, the Meccan historian, who met al-Maqrīzī during his final two stays; see Ibn Fahd, *Muʿjam al-shuyūkh*, p. 65.

13 For this office during the Mamlūk period, see K. Stilt, *Islamic Law in Action. Authority, Discretion, and Everyday Experiences in Mamluk Egypt* (New York, 2011).

repeatedly rivalled him for the position.[14] Barqūq's son, al-Nāṣir Faraj, who became sultan after his father (r. 801/1399–808/1405 and 808/1405–815/1412), confirmed him in his position. Al-Maqrīzī was also, by turns, preacher in the mosque of ʿAmr ibn al-ʿĀṣ in Fusṭāṭ, then inspector and imam of the mosque of al-Ḥākim, and so his power and influence continued to grow. He was even appointed Mamlūk ambassador to Tamerlane (d. 807/1405) by the sultan, before being replaced by the son of a Mamlūk emir. Al-Maqrīzī was also part of a group which accompanied the sultan on a trip to Damascus in 810/1407.

This journey was to mark the beginning of a new period in the life of al-Maqrīzī, as he stayed in the Syrian capital at regular intervals from 810/1407 to 815/1412. These years correspond to a politically difficult period in which the power of the sultan in Syria was severely tested. In Damascus, al-Maqrīzī held a number of different roles, although it seems likely that he did not remain in the town continuously and returned to Cairo each time the sultan did. During his final journey the sultan was assassinated, and it was in the company of the caliph al-Mustaʿīn bi-llāh, who also became sultan for several months in 815/1412, that al-Maqrīzī returned to Cairo. This return marks the beginning of a decline in his fortunes, as support from powerful patrons began to become rarer. From this point on he decided to retire from public life and to devote himself full-time to his passion for writing history, particularly that of his native country, Egypt. If al-Maqrīzī could afford to do this, it was because he had gained a fortune which partly came from his parents—both from the paternal and the maternal sides—and partly from his professional activities.

This choice was doubtless also influenced by the loss of most of his relatives. In 782/1381 he had married a young girl (she was 12) from a family who had their origins in Baghdad. This woman, Safrā bint ʿUmar b. ʿAbd al-Salām (or b. ʿAbd al-ʿAzīz) b. ʿAbd al-Ṣamad al-Baghdādī, gave birth to his son, Abu'l-Maḥāsin Muḥammad, in 786/1384. Repudiated several months later for unknown reasons, al-Maqrīzī married her again after a period of two years, when she bore him another son, Abū Hāshim ʿAlī, in 789/1388, but he died a few months after, in 790/1388.[15] Al-Maqrīzī also had a daughter named Fāṭima (born 798/1396; d. 826/1423), either from another marriage or by his concubine, Sūl (d. 824/1421). It is not known when all his children died, but Fāṭima was the last of his children to do so.

14 Al-Maqrīzī recovered his position in 802/1400, although he held it for less than three months, and again took it, at the insistence of the sultan, in 807/1405, this time for less than one month. See A. ʿAbd al-Rāziq, 'La *ḥisba* et le *muḥtasib* en Égypte au temps des Mamlūks', *Annales islamologiques* 13 (1977), 115–78, pp. 148–49 and 153.

15 See al-Maqrīzī, *Durar al-ʿuqūd al-farīda*, vol. II, pp. 98–99.

The only member of his family to outlive al-Maqrīzī was his nephew Nāṣir al-Dīn Muḥammad (born 801/1399, d. 867/1462), who was the son of his brother Muḥammad, and who seems to have supported him in his old age.[16] We know for certain that he accompanied al-Maqrīzī during his sojourn at Mecca between 838/1435 and 840/1436. The sole inheriter still alive at the time of al-Maqrīzī's death, Nāṣir al-Dīn took possession of all his manuscripts, among other things, as demonstrated by marks of possession signed in his own hand which can be found on the title pages of certain works written by his uncle. Al-Maqrīzī also owned a slave, Abu'l-Durr Yāqūt, who helped him during the last years of his life and participated in some of his master's teaching sessions.

Becoming a recluse in his home—which he seldom left except to perform his religious obligations and to make his final pilgrimage to Mecca (838/1435–840/1436)—and only receiving visits from scholars and disciples in search of his knowledge, he died on the 26th Ramaḍān 845/7th February 1442. He was buried in the Sufi cemetery, situated outside the city walls, beyond the Gate of Victory (*Bāb al-Naṣr*), the same place where both the great historian Ibn Khaldūn (d. 808/1406) and al-Maqrīzī's own father had been buried some decades before.

Al-Maqrīzī's Historical Writings

In the initial years of his studies, al-Maqrīzī had devoted himself to the prophetic tradition (hadith): the first attestation of his lectures appears in a work devoted to traditionists who were considered unreliable, of which he made a précis (dated 795/1393).[17] His interest in such material never dissipated, as evidenced by other summaries and autograph copies of works of the same genre which can be dated to the beginning of the ninth/fifteenth century. But it was his passion for writing history which occupied the majority of his scholarly activity after he reached around forty years of age. It is undeniable that his contact with the great Ibn Khaldūn, whom he greatly admired, had an influence on the direction of his historical writing. From the beginning of the ninth/fifteenth century he read and summarised various historical sources, such as *al-Mughrib* by Ibn Saʿīd (d. 685/1286), al-Musabbiḥī's (d. 420/1030) *Akhbār Miṣr*, and *al-Iḥāṭa* by Ibn al-Khaṭīb (d. 776/1374), all of which would prove useful for the works he was already planning on writing. The result of his indefatigable writing activity such as it appears to us today thanks to numerous copies

16 For details of Nāṣir al-Dīn's life, see al-Sakhāwī, *al-Ḍawʾ al-lāmiʿ*, vol. IX, p. 150.

17 See Bauden, 'Maqriziana II', p. 115 (number 8).

having been conserved—of which more than twenty are autograph volumes—is over thirty different titles. Some of these have multiple volumes, while others are comparable to treatises or pamphlets, and at least some of these were works written in response to a specific request.

His employment in the Mamlūk chancellery at the end of the eighth/fourteenth century inspired him to write two works focussed on two types of civil servants which he considered essential to guarantee good governance of the state: *Khulāṣat al-tibr fī kuttāb al-sirr*, which was written about chancellery secretaries (*kuttāb al-sirr*), and *Talqīḥ al-ʿuqūl waʾl-ārāʾ fī tanqīḥ akhbār al-julla al-wuzarāʾ*, dedicated to viziers. No copy of either of these two works has reached us and it is thus difficult to say precisely when they were written. However, it can be confidently suggested that he must have written them before he commenced his historiographical project which would focus on the land of his birth, Egypt, and consequently before the beginning of the second decade of the ninth/fifteenth century.[18]

The first work which he seems to have written that may be dated with certainty is a small socio-economic tract entitled *Ighāthat al-umma bi-kashf al-ghumma*.[19] Incorrectly identified as a treatise on famines by its first editors and by G. Wiet afterwards,[20] it actually addresses the multiple causes which led to the economic crises between the years 796/1394 and 808/1405, reaching their zenith in 806/1403–4.[21] Written in 808/1405 with the aim of fostering reforms, and particularly economic ones, which would reverse the crises, this pamphlet probably also had an ulterior motive: to draw the attention of the powers-that-be onto him and his abilities as market inspector (*muḥtasib*), a position which he occupied on many occasions, including up until a year after writing this piece. His ties with the sultan al-Nāṣir Faraj were to increase two years later, when he accompanied the latter in his various sojourns in Damascus, suggesting this aim may have been successful.

It was around this time that al-Maqrīzī developed a major project which would occupy him until his death and gain him fame during his lifetime even

18 For the first work on chancellery secretaries, information comes from a note added by al-Maqrīzī to an autograph copy of *al-Mughrib* by Ibn Saʿīd (MS Sūhāj—Maktabat al-Shaykh Aḥmad ʿAlī Badr, f. 105v), where he states that he was in the middle of writing this work when he read Ibn Saʿīd's book, that is, in 803/1400–1.

19 Ed. K.Ḥ. Farḥāt (Cairo, 2007).

20 Ed. M.M. Ziyāda and J. al-Shayyāl (Cairo, 1940); tr. G. Wiet, 'Le traité des famines de Maqrīzī', *Journal of the Economic and Social History of the Orient* 5 (1962), 1–90 (also published as a book the same year by Brill in Leiden).

21 English tr. by A. Allouche as *Mamluk Economics. A Study and Translation of al-Maqrīzī's* Ighāthah (Salt Lake City, 1994).

beyond the borders of the Mamlūk sultanate. The circumstances in which he decided to embark on this project remain obscure, but it is possible to make an educated guess. When he went to Damascus for the second time, in 811/1409, accompanying the sultan al-Nāṣir Faraj, al-Maqrīzī had come into the possession of a manuscript which would change his life: the text, partly in draft form and partly completed, was a historical topography of Cairo written by his friend and neighbour al-Awḥadī (d. 811/1408), to which the latter had devoted many years of his life. The text was far from being in a publishable state, but it served as a blueprint for al-Maqrīzī's own work which would, to a large degree, earn him his place in posterity: *al-Mawāʿiẓ wa'l-iʿtibār fī dhikr al-khiṭaṭ wa'l-āthār*—often shortened, as much by medieval authors as by modern, to *al-Khiṭaṭ*. Al-Maqrīzī increased the amount of material in al-Awḥadī's work by starting with the history of the town from the Muslim conquest and also considered, among other things, the history of other towns, as well as Jewish and Christian monuments. The subject matter of this work is not original: many authors preceding him produced works of this genre, as much in Iraq and Syria as in Egypt.[22] However, its chronological extent, the number of sources employed, and the combination of topographical data and historical elements make it a veritable encyclopaedia of the heritage of Cairo. His parallel projects, of a history of Egypt from the Muslim conquest until his time and of biographical dictionaries, all overlap with this first book in scope.

Although part of a family originally from Baalbek, al-Maqrīzī devoted the majority of his works to the land of his birth. At the beginning of the 19th century, when his writings began to be rediscovered, the output of al-Maqrīzī was related in these terms by the French Orientalist A.-I. Silvestre de Sacy:

> Si ces travaux de Makrizi, dont quelques parties manquent encore à nos bibliothèques, étaient réunis, on pourrait les regarder comme une espèce d'encyclopédie pour l'histoire de l'Égypte pendant les huit premiers siècles de l'hégire et la première moitié du neuvième. Makrizi n'est guère cependant autre chose, comme nous l'avons dit, qu'un compilateur; et s'il montre, parfois, un jugement sain et plus de critique que la plupart des écrivains de sa nation, il ne paraît pas plus réservé sur l'article du merveilleux.[23]

22 At the same time as al-Awḥadī, another author had become interested in the genre and had begun to write another work which remained, in part, only in draft form: Ibn Duqmāq (d. 809/1407), *al-Intiṣār li-wāsiṭat ʿiqd al-amṣār*, ed. K. Vollers, vols IV–V (Cairo, 1893).

23 A.-I. Silvestre de Sacy, 'Notice sur Abd-allatif', in idem, *Mélanges de littérature orientale, précédés de l'éloge de l'auteur par M. le Duc de Broglie* (Paris, s.d.), p. 118, note 1.

This critique by de Sacy concerning the character of the writer is undoubtedly too severe. If it is true that al-Maqrīzī had a special gift for unearthing sources which were, already in his time, rather rare, such as those relating to the Fāṭimid era, he also managed to extract the essence and restore the data intelligently, using an attractive style of writing. All the experts who have examined his outputs recognise that he managed to combine reports from differing sources in order to reconstruct the facts reported into a single narrative. It suggests that intense preparatory work—undertaken through diverse readings, notetaking and the preparation of summaries—was his *modus operandi*, as demonstrated by rare surviving volumes of his notebooks and some of his summaries.[24] It is thus undeniable that he had an exceptional ability to construct historical reports.[25] The influence which Ibn Khaldūn—who was also his teacher—and his works had on al-Maqrīzī is clear in many of the latter's writings, as much by the deep level of his reflections on history itself as by the wide-ranging nature of his interests.

Al-Maqrīzī could also employ other methods of working, such as borrowing from authors whose work was not published, such as the partially completed draft of the work of al-Awḥadī on the topography of Cairo, or using works which were difficult to get hold of, such as the encyclopaedia of Ibn Faḍl Allāh al-ʿUmarī (d. 749/1349) entitled *Masālik al-abṣār fī mamālik al-amṣār*, in a manner which often comes close to that which would be regarded as plagiarism today. In the former case, it has been proved that the autograph manuscripts of al-Awḥadī served as the basis for al-Maqrīzī's writing of the *Khiṭaṭ*, without at any time acknowledging his debt to his colleague and neighbour, not even citing his name. From the autograph fragment of al-Awḥadī's work conserved in the autograph draft of al-Maqrīzī, it can be determined that his personal contribution was essentially limited to the adding of biographies of the founders of the monuments examined.[26] In the latter case, it appears that al-Maqrīzī largely used the data provided by Ibn Faḍl Allāh al-ʿUmarī for many

24 See F. Bauden, 'Maqriziana I: Discovery of an Autograph Manuscript of al-Maqrīzī. Towards a Better Understanding of His Working Method. Description: Section 1', *Mamlūk Studies Review* 7 (2003), 21–68; idem, 'Maqriziana I: Discovery of an Autograph Manuscript of al-Maqrīzī. Towards a Better Understanding of His Working Method. Description: Section 2', *Mamlūk Studies Review* 10 (2006), 81–139; idem, 'Maqriziana II: Discovery of an Autograph Manuscript of al-Maqrīzī. Towards a Better Understanding of His Working Method. Analysis', *Mamlūk Studies Review* 12 (2008), 51–118.

25 See F. Bauden, 'Maqriziana XI. Al-Maqrīzī et al-Ṣafadī: Analyse de la (re)construction d'un récit biographique', in idem (ed.), 'Les méthodes de travail des historiens en Islam', *Quaderni di Studi Arabi* 4 (2009), 99–136.

26 See Bauden, 'Maqriziana IX'.

of his works and even, in one case, going so far as to knowingly alter the words of the latter for purely ideological reasons.[27]

However this may appear to our modern eyes, such an approach earned great renown for his works which themselves indelibly marked Islamic historical writing. The most important of these are: the *Khiṭaṭ*; his trilogy on the history of Muslim Egypt, of which only the last two components are preserved (*Ittiʿāẓ al-ḥunafāʾ bi-akhbār al-aʾimma al-khulafāʾ* for the Fāṭimid period, covering the fourth/tenth to the sixth/twelfth centuries, and *al-Sulūk li-maʿrifat duwal al-mulūk* for the Ayyūbid and Mamlūk eras, the sixth/twelfth to the ninth/fifteenth centuries); and to which he later added a biography of Muḥammad (*Imtāʿ al-asmāʿ li-mā liʾl-rasūl min al-anbāʾ waʾl-aḥwāl waʾl-ḥafada waʾl-matāʿ*), a history of humanity (*al-Khabar ʿan al-bashar*), numerous biographical dictionaries (*al-Taʾrīkh al-muqaffā al-kabīr*, which lists Egyptians and people who lived or passed through Egypt; and *Durar al-ʿuqūd al-farīda fī tarājim al-aʿyān al-mufīda*, which relates his contemporaries, that is, people who died or were born after the beginning of the decade of al-Maqrīzī's own birth [i.e. before 760/1358–59], and who he did not necessarily meet), and finally his booklets on other subjects (economics, metrology, numismatics, the history of Egyptian borderlands such as Abyssinia, gemology, religion, etc.).

For historians of the Crusades, the most important of these works, to varying degrees, are his chronicles covering the Fāṭimids (*Ittiʿāẓ al-ḥunafāʾ*) and the Ayyūbids and Mamlūks (*al-Sulūk*); the biographical dictionary of people who were born in or who lived in Egypt, known as *al-Muqaffā*; his history of humanity (*al-Khabar ʿan al-bashar*); and *al-Khiṭaṭ*.

Al-Khiṭaṭ

Al-Khiṭaṭ is extant in four manuscript volumes, two of which are autograph copies of the drafts while one is an autograph volume of the version published in the time of al-Maqrīzī.[28] First published in 1853–54 at the Būlāq press in Cairo[29] it was a great success upon its release during al-Maqrīzī's lifetime, as witnessed by its wide diffusion: more than 250 manuscripts have been

27 See F. Bauden, *Trusting the Source as Far as It Can Be Trusted: Al-Maqrīzī and the Question of the Mongol Book of Laws* (*Yāsa*) (*Maqriziana* VII) (Schenefeld, 2015).

28 MS Istanbul—Topkapı Saray Library E.H. 1405 and H. 1472, and MS Ann Arbor—Michigan University Library Isl. 605, respectively.

29 A new edition has recently been published: ed. A.F. Sayyid, 5 vols (London, 2002–4). On the quality of this edition, see the review by F. Bauden in *Mamlūk Studies Review* 11 (2007),

identified around the world. Known as an archaeological and monumental history of the city of Cairo, it was inspired by many other books of the same genre composed from the fourth/ninth century onwards. However, al-Maqrīzī's work renewed the whole genre by adding preliminary chapters on Egypt, including its description, position, history, and main towns. This means the book includes, for example, a description of the initiation rites into the Ismāʿīlī sect, information usually jealously guarded by its followers. He also provides an account of the history of Cairo from its foundation until his own day, including the Fāṭimid period, which is essential for understanding the development of the city. He then details the districts and buildings of the town which he categorises (as baths, mosques, madrasas, etc.), placing each building into its historical context by providing, among other things, biographical details about the people who founded them and why they did so.

The variety of the sources exploited by al-Maqrīzī is vast and reflects his capacity to locate texts which must have been difficult to access even in his own time. These included chronicles, annals, biographical dictionaries, Quranic commentaries, lexicographical works, scientific encyclopaedias and works of the same genre by his predecessors, and the overall number may be estimated at more than a hundred.[30] For many of them al-Maqrīzī prevented their contents from being lost completely, as many of them have not otherwise been preserved, particularly those dealing with the Fāṭimid era. In his introduction, he took the time to specify that he would be scrupulous in citing his sources:

> When I transmit a passage taken from scholars who dealt with different areas of study, I must indicate from which work it is taken, so I can be absolved of any responsibility and cannot incur blame.[31]

However, despite this laudable aim he did not follow it in every case; there are numerous passages in which al-Maqrīzī neglects to indicate his sources. This is notably the case with Ibn Faḍl Allāh al-ʿUmarī, whom al-Maqrīzī hardly seemed to appreciate, despite the fact that he happily pillaged al-ʿUmarī's encyclopaedic work *Masālik al-abṣār fī mamālik al-amṣār*.

169–76. A partial French translation is available: *Description topographique et historique de l'Égypte*, tr. U. Bouriant and P. Casanova, 2 vols (Paris-Cairo, 1895–1920).

30 See A.R. Guest, 'A List of Writers, Books, and Other Authorities Mentioned by El Maqrīzi in his Khiṭaṭ', *Journal of the Royal Asiatic Society* (1902), 103–25.

31 Al-Maqrīzī, *al-Khiṭaṭ* (Būlāq ed.), vol. 1, p. 4 = (Sayyid ed.), vol. 1, p. 8.

As has already been stated, al-Maqrīzī came up with the idea of writing the *Khiṭaṭ* after reading the partly-finished draft of his colleague and neighbour al-Awḥadī (d. 811/1408). The autograph volumes of the first version of the *Khiṭaṭ* demonstrate that the essence of the text was already written by 818/1415. It must have taken another few years and the discovery of new sources for the definitive version to finally be made available and published; the autograph volume of this version, recently discovered, allows it to be dated to slightly after 831/1427 and certainly before 834/1430–31.[32] However, al-Maqrīzī continued to add information to it until two years before his death.

The *Khiṭaṭ* provides only limited interest for crusade historians with the exception of a section devoted to the city of Damietta, which, situated on the mouth of the Nile, was the subject of numerous Frankish attacks.[33] In the section which al-Maqrīzī devotes to it, one finds a very accurate historical account of these attacks, although it provides only limited interest given that al-Maqrīzī does not cite his sources (although they can be guessed) and that the texts he used are now available, for the most part, in critical editions and, for some, in translation. This observation can be regarded as a general principle because it is equally valid for other works of al-Maqrīzī which will be mentioned later in this article.

This section on Damietta also had a separate life from the *Khiṭaṭ*: in the cadre of tracts describing the merits of towns (*faḍāʾil*),[34] it was circulated as an independent text to enhance the importance of the city of Damietta. No doubt this was the work of an inhabitant of Damietta who had access to the *Khiṭaṭ*.[35]

This section attracted the attention of the Dutch Orientalist Henri Arens Hamaker (1789–1837), who first edited it and translated it into Latin on the basis of manuscripts held in Leiden.[36] However he limited this work up to the year 618/1221, having found that the report of the Crusade of Louis IX was

32 N. Gardiner and F. Bauden, 'A Recently Discovered Holograph Fair Copy of al-Maqrīzī's *al-Mawāʿiẓ wa'l-iʿtibār fī dhikr al-khiṭaṭ wa'l-āthār* (Michigan Islamic MS 605)', *Journal of Islamic Manuscripts* 2 (2011), 123–31.

33 Al-Maqrīzī, *al-Khiṭaṭ* (Būlāq ed.), vol. I, pp. 213–26 = (Sayyid ed.), vol. I, pp. 580–611; *Description topographique et historique de l'Égypte*, vol. II, pp. 632–65.

34 On this literary genre, see R. Sellheim, 'Faḍīla', in *EI2*.

35 See, for example, MS Harvard—University Library, Houghton 357, ff. 1r–25r, entitled *Kitāb tarjamat thaghr Dimyāṭ wa-mā waqaʿa bi-hā min ʿahd Nūḥ ʿalayhi al-salām ilā ākhir dawlat al-Turk*.

36 *Takyoddini Ahmedis al-Makrizii, Narratio de expeditionibus, a graecis francisque adversus dimyatham, ab A.C. 708 ad 1221 susceptis*, ed. and Latin transl. H.A. Hamaker (Amsterdam, 1824).

based on the accounts of Ibn Wāṣil (d. 697/1298) and Ibn al-Furāt (d. 807/1405).[37] Al-Maqrīzī used, for the most part, Ibn al-Furāt, but preferred to go back to the sources used by this historian where he could. Hamaker was therefore correct when he identified Ibn Wāṣil as al-Maqrīzī's main source for events relating to the Crusade of Louis IX.

For the most part, the report of Damietta recounts the multiple Frankish attacks on it between the sixth/twelfth and the seventh/thirteenth centuries. The first of these is dated to the year 550/August 1155 and is attributed to William I of Sicily (r. 1154–66), the son of Roger II (Lūjīz ibn Rujjār).[38] This was followed by another in 558/1163, this time led by Amalric I (Murī), the Frankish King of Jerusalem, who besieged Cairo and imposed a tribute on it after having burned the area of Fusṭāṭ.[39] The third expedition was dated to 565/December 1169: according to al-Maqrīzī, more than twelve hundred Frankish ships brought troops who encircled the town. After a stand-off of 55 days, the Franks were driven back into the sea. This attack caused Saladin to reinforce the defences of Damietta in a number of ways: garrisons were placed in the two forts on either side of the Nile; the passage of boats was prevented by means of a chain reinforced by ships placed along its entire length; and a dam and ditches were constructed.[40] These attempts did not, however, stop the Franks from making another assault on the town during the Fifth Crusade (614/1217–618/1221). Al-Maqrīzī mentions the support of the Pope, Innocent III, for this expedition and he then narrates the events which took place during the attack against Damietta, the fall of the city (25th Shaʿbān 616/5th November 1219) after a siege of sixteen months and 22 days, and its occupation until the 19th Rajab 618/8th September 1221, over a period of 22 months and 24 days.[41] Al-Maqrīzī gives an extremely detailed report of these events, and particularly highlights the conditions for the inhabitants of Damietta during the siege. He reports that his source for these details was *al-Muʿjam al-mutarjam*, a dictionary of authorities, considered lost, by the Egyptian scholar al-Mundhirī (m. 656/1258), who relates the eyewitness account of one of his teachers who was in Damietta during the time of the siege. These details highlight the difficult living conditions of the inhabitants trapped in a city where the price of food had

37 *Ibid.*, p. 5.

38 Al-Maqrīzī, *al-Khiṭaṭ* (ed. Būlāq), vol. I, p. 214; *Description topographique*, vol. II, p. 635.

39 *Ibid.*

40 Al-Maqrīzī, *al-Khiṭaṭ* (ed. Būlāq), vol. I, pp. 214–15; *Description topographique*, vol. II, pp. 635–36.

41 Al-Maqrīzī, *al-Khiṭaṭ* (ed. Būlāq), vol. I, pp. 215–19; *Description topographique*, vol. II, pp. 636–46.

skyrocketed. He also mentions the strategems developed by the Muslim inhabitants of the surrounding area to secure food for their co-religionists who were trapped in the city, such as stuffing the belly of a camel's carcass with produce before throwing it into the Nile to be recovered by the besieged inhabitants.[42] The final victory of the Muslim troops is seen by al-Maqrīzī as a salvation for Islam, since the Mongols had by that time made themselves rulers of a number of regions in the East while the Franks were on the point of seizing Egypt.

Al-Maqrīzī also gives a report of the Crusade of Louis IX in Egypt (646/1248–648/1250).[43] This summarises a number of unnamed sources, and presents the events in a continuous narrative. He reports that the Ayyūbid sultan al-Ṣāliḥ II (r. 637/1240–648/1250) received a messenger sent by the Emperor Frederick II, information he can only have taken from Ibn Wāṣil, who was in contact with the envoy in question and from whom he received direct testimony,[44] and al-Maqrīzī also cites extracts from the correspondence between Louis IX and the Ayyūbid sultan. The account continues with some detail about the battles between the two armies, and al-Maqrīzī enhances his account through the use of interesting anecdotes, such as that of the watermelon. All methods were acceptable, he affirms, to capture Franks, and the following strategem was employed by a Muslim fighter in order to seize one of them: he hollowed out a watermelon which he then placed on his head, and entered the water making for the Franks. One of them, thinking that it was an actual watermelon, entered the water in order to take it, but was captured and taken to the Muslim camp.[45] Al-Maqrīzī concluded his account of Louis IX's Crusade with the request for safe-conduct (*amān*) made by the French king and his subsequent captivity, while also mentioning the red and scarlet riding hood (*ghifāra*) of the French king, covered with squirrel fur, which was sent by the new Ayyūbid sultan al-Muʿaẓẓam Tūrānshāh to his deputy at Damascus. Some verses of added poetry help glorify this event and heap further derision onto the French king. The events which follow this in the text are the brutal fall of al-Muʿaẓẓam Tūrānshāh (r. 648/1250–650/1252) and the accession to the throne of Shajar al-Durr, during whose rule Louis IX negotiated the evacuation of Damietta and received assurances that his brother, his wife, and all those who were prisoner with him would gain their liberty. Escorted along the bank

42 Al-Maqrīzī, *al-Khiṭaṭ* (ed. Būlāq), vol. I, p. 217; *Description topographique*, vol. II, p. 642.

43 Al-Maqrīzī, *al-Khiṭaṭ* (ed. Būlāq), vol. I pp. 219–24; *Description topographique*, vol. II, pp. 646–59.

44 For this, see E. Blochet, 'Les relations diplomatiques des Hohenstaufen avec les sultans d'Égypte', *Revue historique* 80 (1902), 51–64, pp. 61–64.

45 Al-Maqrīzī, *al-Khiṭaṭ* (ed. Būlāq), vol. I, p. 221; *Description topographique*, vol. II, p. 652.

of the Nile, they all set sail for Acre. Al-Maqrīzī cannot resist the urge to further celebrate this victory over the Franks by citing poems which celebrate the débâcle of Louis IX at Tunis and his sad and rather pathetic demise.

The Trilogy on the History of Egypt

It was when he was writing the initial version of the *Khiṭaṭ* that al-Maqrīzī must have conceived of the projects of both a great history of Egypt running from the Muslim conquest until his own day and his two biographical dictionaries, and the numerous preparatory readings carried out in order to write the *Khiṭaṭ* must have led him to the conclusion that he could write these works. His history of Egypt was drafted gradually. Being a triptych, it was composed of three parts, each devoted to a precise period: *ʿIqd jawāhir al-asfāṭ fī akhbār madīnat al-Fusṭāṭ* for the period covering the Muslim conquest of Egypt to the end of the Ikhshīdid dynasty (in the middle of the fourth/tenth century), *Ittiʿāẓ al-ḥunafāʾ bi-akhbār al-aʾimma al-khulafāʾ* for the Fāṭimid period and, finally, *al-Sulūk li-maʿrifat duwal al-mulūk* for the Ayyūbid and Mamlūk dynasties.

Of the first part, practically nothing is known except that al-Maqrīzī started writing the second, *Ittiʿāẓ al-ḥunafāʾ*, after he had completed it. No copy has been preserved, which suggests an extremely limited circulation; it may be that only one copy ever existed and that was the autograph.[46] It seems to have still been accessible a few years after his death because a later witness claims that the work consisted of one volume.[47]

Ittiʿāẓ al-ḥunafāʾ

The next part of the trilogy, however, has been well preserved. *Ittiʿāẓ al-ḥunafāʾ* is devoted to the history of the Fāṭimid dynasty, which ruled Egypt and parts of Syria in the period 358/969–567/1171. In devoting a work to this Shīʿī Ismāʿīlī dynasty, al-Maqrīzī departed significantly from his predecessors and his contemporaries. While certain historians of the Mamlūk era did write the history of this period, it was often done within a much larger historical work, and consequently al-Maqrīzī was something of a pioneer when he wrote his history of

46 Al-Maqrīzī's colleague, Ibn Ḥajar al-ʿAsqalānī, had been able to examine it before 829/1426. At this time, the work was called *al-Ightibāṭ bi-aḥwāl al-Fusṭāṭ*. Al-Maqrīzī changed its title sometime before 824/1421.

47 See Ibn Fahd, *Muʿjam al-shuyūkh*, p. 66.

the dynasty. His sympathy for it, doubtless caused by his family's probably fanciful genealogical links with it, is undeniable. In more ways than one, this work is a fundamental source for the history of the Fāṭimid period: al-Maqrīzī had access to sources which are now lost, written as much by Shīʿīs as by Sunnīs, not to mention the works written by members of the Ismāʿīlī sect itself.[48]

The writing of this work came at a time when al-Maqrīzī was still occupied writing the first version of the *Khiṭaṭ* (between 811/1408 and 816/1413–14): one finds, at the end of *Ittiʿāẓ al-ḥunafāʾ*, a reference to the fact that al-Maqrīzī would deal with their government in the *Khiṭaṭ*.[49] It is also known that he only had access to one of the main sources for this period, Ibn Muyassar (m. 677/1278), from 814/1411 at the earliest, the date at which he prepared a summary of this source, the only trace of this text which is today preserved.[50] Thanks to this, it has been established that *Ittiʿāẓ al-ḥunafāʾ* was written between 814/1411 and 818/1415 since the notes taken from Ibn Muyassar and inserted into the draft autograph volume of the *Khiṭaṭ* figure in the body of the text and not in the margin or on the rapportés sheets.[51] A *terminus ante quem* can also be fixed for the end of the redaction: in the preserved autograph volume of *Ittiʿāẓ al-ḥunafāʾ* al-Maqrīzī added some information in a marginal note which he took from *al-Fihrist* by Ibn al-Nadīm (d. 385/995 or 388/998). Here too, the manuscripts show us that al-Maqrīzī would have had access to this source only in 824/1421.[52] By this time, the manuscript must have already been finished, even if al-Maqrīzī continued to add further information over time.

According to the account of a contemporary, the work had only one volume,[53] and of this an autograph part, corresponding to the first 58 folios, has been preserved[54] and was edited very early.[55] A number of years passed before a complete copy based on the autograph before it was split was

48 See P.E. Walker, 'Al-Maqrīzī and the Fatimids', *Mamlūk Studies Review* 7 (2003), 83–97.

49 Al-Maqrīzī, *Ittiʿāẓ al-ḥunafāʾ bi-akhbār al-aʾimma al-fāṭimiyyīn al-khulafāʾ*, ed. J. al-Shayyāl and M. Ḥilmī, 3 vols (Cairo, 1967–73; reprint Cairo, 1996), vol. III, p. 344.

50 MS Paris—BNF ar. 1688. This copy was made using the autography copy of al-Maqrīzī.

51 See Bauden, 'Maqriziana XII. Evaluating the Sources for the Fatimid Period: Ibn al-Maʾmūn al-Baṭāʾiḥī's *History* and Its Use by al-Maqrīzī (with a Critical Edition of His Résumé for the Years 501–515 A.H.)', in B.D. Craig (ed.), *Ismaili and Fatimid Studies in Honor of Paul E. Walker* (Chicago, 2010), 33–85.

52 See Bauden, 'Maqriziana II', p. 118, n. 200. Al-Maqrīzī added a note in the manuscript which he consulted detailing that he had taken from it a summary of the year in question.

53 Ibn Fahd, *Muʿjam al-shuyūkh*, p. 66.

54 MS Gotha—Forschungs- und Landesbibliothek, Ar. 1652.

55 Al-Maqrīzī, *Kitāb ittiʿāẓ al-ḥunafāʾ bi aḫbār al-aʾimma al-khulafāʾ* (*Fatimidengeschichte*), *zum ersten Mal herausgegeben nach dem autographen Gothaer Unikum*, ed. H. Bunz

discovered in Istanbul[56] and could be fully edited.[57] It was, however, not without numerous mistakes which Claude Cahen did not fail to highlight as two of his students had prepared an edition which had been pre-empted by the Cairene editor.[58] Recently a new edition has been published by Sayyid.[59] With the exception of this Istanbul copy and the partial autograph version, no other copy has yet been identified, which suggests that the work had little success and did not capture the attention of many scholars. It can thus be supposed that al-Maqrīzī's study of this Shīʿī dynasty was not highly regarded.

Al-Maqrīzī records in his introduction that after he had completed writing the first part of his trilogy, *ʿIqd jawāhir al-asfāṭ*, which recorded the history of al-Fusṭāṭ from the Muslim conquest to the arrival of the armies of the Fāṭimid caliph al-Muʿizz li-Dīn Allāh in 358/969 and the foundation of Cairo which ensued, he developed the desire to write a history of the caliphs who had reigned from the city. The title which he gives in the introduction, *Ittiʿāẓ al-ḥunafāʾ bi-akhbār al-aʾimma al-khulafāʾ*, clearly demonstrates the ideas al-Maqrīzī had about the legitimacy of their power, as he recognises the titles of caliph and imam.[60] Al-Maqrīzī was not unaware that the genealogy of the Fāṭimids had been the object of denigration, particularly by eastern scholars, and his work thus begins with a number of chapters whose only aim is to establish the merits of their genealogy and, consequently, of their descent from Muḥammad via his daughter Fāṭima and his cousin and son-in-law ʿAlī, thereby disproving the views of scholars who did not believe the truth of these claims.[61]

These elements having been clarified in the eyes of the author, he retraced the beginnings of the Shīʿī dynasty in Tunisia (Ifrīqiya) from its first representative, ʿUbayd Allāh, up to the conquest of Egypt, the foundation of Cairo and the installation of the caliphal seat in the Egyptian capital. The internal structure of the work is based on the reigns of the caliphs and within each reign it follows an annalistic structure; several short obituaries are sometimes added

(Leipzig, 1909). Another edition of the same manuscript was prepared by J. al-Shayyāl and M. Ḥilmī (Cairo, 1948).

56 MS Istanbul—Topkapı Saray 3013.

57 Ed. J. al-Shayyāl et M. Ḥilmī (see above, note 49).

58 C. Cahen and M. Adda, 'Les éditions de l'*Iṭṭiʿāz* [*sic*] *al-ḥunafāʾ* (Histoire fatimide) de Maqrīzī par Aḥmad Hilmy, Sadok Ḫunī (Khouni), Fātiḥa Dib et Peter Kessler', *Arabica* 22 (1975), 302–20.

59 Al-Maqrīzī, *Ittiʿāẓ al-ḥunafāʾ bi-akhbār al-aʾimma al-khulafāʾ*, 4 vols, ed. A.F. Sayyid (Damascus-London, 2010). A critical edition with an English translation is in preparation by P.E. Walker, which will appear in the series *Bibliotheca Maqriziana*, published by Brill.

60 Al-Maqrīzī, *Ittiʿāẓ al-ḥunafāʾ*, ed. al-Shayyāl and Ḥilmī, vol. 1, p. 4.

61 Al-Maqrīzī, *Ittiʿāẓ al-ḥunafāʾ*, ed. al-Shayyāl and Ḥilmī, vol. 1, pp. 5–34.

to the end of a year, but in no systematic order. The distribution of the material is rather unbalanced since the events of one year can be related, in some cases, over a number of pages while, at other times, on only half a page. The work ends with the removal of the last caliph in 567/1171, followed by a plea from the author on behalf of the dynasty and an account of the fate of their descendants after the beginning of the Sunnī Ayyūbid dynasty. In his plea, al-Maqrīzī shows once more his general sympathy for the dynasty, although he does criticise some of its members, such as the caliph al-Ḥākim (r. 386/996–411/1020). It is also in this section that he demonstrates that he is a historian concerned with weighing up his sources, calling the reader's attention to the fact that certain other historians present the facts in a biased manner, which recalls the words of Cicero (*Non numerentur sed ponderentur*): 'Make a distinction between the information [you receive] as you do for good money'.[62]

The sources used by al-Maqrīzī must have been numerous and may be guessed at from reference to those cited in the *Khiṭaṭ*, because he did not take the trouble to systematically note them in *Ittiʿāẓ al-ḥunafāʾ*. Among those which he does specifically cite, particularly for the years corresponding to the first volume of the edition, there are as many Sunnī sources as Shīʿī, because, as has been demonstrated, it is undeniable that he had access to the latter.[63] Among the former, he seems to have often had recourse to Ibn al-Athīr (d. 630/1233)—whose position with regard to the Fāṭimids he harshly criticises—Ibn Zūlāq (d. 386/996)—for the first years of the Cairene caliphate—al-Musabbiḥī (d. 420/1030), Ibn Muyassar (d. 677/1278) and Ibn Saʿīd (d. 685/1286). Among the Shīʿī authors, he cites the works of Ibn al-Maʾmūn (d. 588/1192) and Ibn Abī Ṭayyiʾ (d.c. 625–30/1228–33), to only mention historians. A recent study has proved that al-Maqrīzī cited Ibn al-Maʾmūn by the intermediary work of Ibn ʿAbd al-Ẓāhir (m. 692/1292), but that he managed to find a copy of the original work later in his life, which allowed him to correct the indirect citation and to complete his work.[64] The importance of this is in how it highlights al-Maqrīzī's working method: to try to go back to the sources closest to the events they are describing.

For the history of the Crusades, it is the third volume of the printed work which is of most interest, although it must be emphasised that this is almost exclusively limited to Egypt. Unlike Ibn al-Athīr, who wrote a history of Islam and who reports occurrences from across the Islamic world and principally, at least for the crusading period, the Near East, al-Maqrīzī has an Egyptocentric

62 Al-Maqrīzī, *Ittiʿāẓ al-ḥunafāʾ*, ed. al-Shayyāl and Ḥilmī, vol. III, pp. 345–46.

63 See Bauden, 'Maqriziana II', pp. 65–67.

64 See Bauden, 'Maqriziana XII'.

view of events. Taking, for example, the year 507/1113–14, Ibn al-Athīr concentrates his account on the attack led by the Muslim forces assembled by the rulers of Mosul, Sinjār and Damascus in response to actions undertaken the previous year by Baldwin I of Jerusalem around Damascus, which had led to a rise in prices of essential commodities.[65] Al-Maqrīzī, on the other hand, focuses on the reinforcements of men and supplies which were sent to Tyre by an Egyptian fleet, which contributed to a reduction in prices there. He also reports the conclusion of a treaty between Baldwin I and Masʿūd, the governor of Tyre, at the request of the former, an event that Ibn al-Athīr seems to have ignored.[66] In addition, no events are reported for the year 510/1116–17—even though al-Maqrīzī was prepared to add new information, as he left three folios relating to this year blank in his autograph text—while Ibn al-Athīr relates a number of events which took place in the East.

While information on the Franks occurs regularly between 492/1099 and 514/1120, it is rarer thereafter. Mention is made of the release of Baldwin II, king of Jerusalem, in 517/1124 after he had been made prisoner by the ruler of Aleppo, Balak ibn Bahrām, for a ransom of 80,000 dinars and 30 Muslim prisoners, a report which is at odds with some Syrian sources, which insist that Baldwin II had managed to escape through the connivance of the Muslim army.[67] The loss of Ascalon, the last Fāṭimid bastion in Palestine, in 548/1153, appears in the assessment al-Maqrīzī gives of the reign of the Fāṭimid caliph al-Ẓāfir, where it is embellished by a commentary on the immoderate tastes of this caliph for entertainment and fun in the company of his concubines, thus highlighting the consequences of such a depraved lifestyle.[68]

From 552/1157 until 554/1159 references are lengthier and occur more often, as these years correspond to a renewal of Fāṭimid attacks against the Latin states in the Levant.[69] This is also the case during the account of the end of Fāṭimid rule, during the rise to power of Shīrkūh and Saladin and the forfeit of the country by the vizier Shāwar, who made an alliance with Amalric I of Jerusalem and allowed the Franks right into the heart of Egypt.[70] The year 564/1169 is presented by al-Maqrīzī as one where the Franks took possession of Egypt and imposed a tyrannical government on it, so that the people were

65 Ibn al-Athīr, *al-Kāmil fī'l-taʾrīkh*, ed. A.F.ʿA.A. al-Qāḍī and M.Y. al-Daqqāq, 11 vols. (Beirut, 1987–2003), vol. IX, pp. 149–50.

66 Al-Maqrīzī, *Ittiʿāẓ al-ḥunafāʾ*, ed. al-Shayyāl and Ḥilmī, vol. III, p. 52.

67 Al-Maqrīzī, *Ittiʿāẓ al-ḥunafāʾ*, ed. al-Shayyāl and Ḥilmī, vol. III, p. 106.

68 Al-Maqrīzī, *Ittiʿāẓ al-ḥunafāʾ*, ed. al-Shayyāl and Ḥilmī, vol. III, p. 209.

69 Al-Maqrīzī, *Ittiʿāẓ al-ḥunafāʾ*, ed. al-Shayyāl and Ḥilmī, vol. III, pp. 230–37.

70 Al-Maqrīzī, *Ittiʿāẓ al-ḥunafāʾ*, ed. al-Shayyāl and Ḥilmī, vol. III, pp. 262–318.

convinced that no-one was able to protect them. The description of these events is highly detailed and is derived, for the most part, from the works of ʿUmāra al-Yamanī (d. 569/1174) and Ibn Abī Ṭayyiʾ (d. 625–30/1228–33).[71]

Overall, al-Maqrīzī, unsurprisingly, presents the Franks in a negative light, and their mention is often accompanied by curses against them. With regard to the Fāṭimids, his writing is more positive, and he tries to highlight the multiple efforts led by them and their viziers to attempt to stem the losses of territory in Palestine in the first decades of the Frankish presence.

Al-Sulūk

Barely had al-Maqrīzī completed writing the second part of the trilogy than he began preparations for the third and final part which, as he indicated in the introduction, would examine the history of the Kurdish Ayyūbid and Turkic and Circassian Mamlūk dynasties who ruled Egypt from 567/1171 until his own day. The precise date at which he began to work on these annals is unknown: it is thought that he began to acquire material for it during the course of the years when he was working on the *Khiṭaṭ* and the first two volumes of the trilogy being described. However, the date can be surmised, taking into account that *Ittiʿāẓ al-ḥunafāʾ* was probably finished by 818/1415. Another factor is that by 820/1417 he had already written the whole part covering the years 567/1171–791/1389, the equivalent of three volumes, as there is a comment that a practice which he described is still current at the time he wrote the passage, that is to say the year 820/1417.[72] Thus, it cannot have taken more than a few more years to write to his own time, and he then continued to add the events of the years through which he lived, a practice which he continued until a few months before his death: the work ends with the final month of 844/April 1441. It can therefore be assumed that he wrote the events of each year at the end of it, which would explain why we have no information about the year of his death (845/May 1441–February 1442). But as early as 828/1425 the work's reputation had already crossed the frontiers of the Mamlūk empire: that year, a Tīmūrid

71 ʿUmāra al-Yamanī, *al-Nukat al-ʿaṣriyya fī akhbār al-wuzarāʾ al-miṣriyya*, ed. and tr. H. Derenbourg, 3 vols (Paris, 1897–1904); Ibn Abī Ṭayyiʾ, *Maʿādin al-dhahab fī taʾrīkh al-mulūk waʾl-khulafāʾ wa-dhawī al-rutab* (numerous extracts preserved in Ibn al-Furāt, *Taʾrīkh al-rusul waʾl-mulūk*).

72 Al-Maqrīzī, *al-Sulūk*, vol. III, p. 639.

embassy arrived in Cairo with the aim, amongst others, of obtaining a copy of *al-Sulūk* for the library of Shāh Rukh, the son of Tīmūr.[73]

After the death of al-Maqrīzī the work was hugely successful, as demonstrated by the large number of manuscripts preserved in libraries across the world. According to his contemporary, the Meccan historian Ibn Fahd (d. 885/1480), *al-Sulūk* consisted of five volumes,[74] and this comment is likely to be accurate since this author consulted the autograph version only one year after al-Maqrīzī's death.[75] However, nowadays most of the copies made on the basis of the autograph are in four volumes.

When al-Maqrīzī began writing *al-Sulūk* he had already been in a state of worldly withdrawal in his home for a number of years. His contacts with the Mamlūk elites were rare and he did not receive visitors apart from his colleagues, friends and followers. He did not write these annals tracing the events which took place under the rule of his former patrons the Mamlūks in an effort to get closer to the centre of power; al-Maqrīzī's comments about certain sultans are not devoid of acerbic criticism, demonstrating that he was not afraid to express himself freely and that he was not interested in sycophantically praising the current rulers. No copy made from the autograph is attested during al-Maqrīzī's lifetime (the oldest dates from 847/1443–848/1444); the autograph must therefore have been the only copy and it was without doubt kept with him, which may explain the freedom with which al-Maqrīzī criticised certain sultans in his assessment of them, or the actions of certain influential emirs. However, many of the extant copies were made to satisfy the wish of various Mamlūk emirs to possess an example of these annals in their library. Among these, at least one bears the name of its sponsor, the emir Yashbak min Mahdī, the executive secretary under the sultan Qā'itbāy (r. 872/1468–901/1496).[76] Thanks to these copies it is known that the work was widely appreciated, despite its open criticism of the ruling Mamlūks.

Of the autograph work, only the first volume has reached us.[77] However, it furnishes us with unique information on the author's working method and his

73 Al-Maqrīzī, *al-Sulūk*, vol. IV, p. 818 (year 833/1429).

74 Ibn Fahd, *Muʿjam al-shuyūkh*, p. 66.

75 MS Istanbul—Süleymaniye Kütüphanesi, Yeni Cami 887, f. 3 (consultation note dated 846/1442–43).

76 MS Istanbul—Fatih Kütüphanesi 4383. On this emir as bibliophile, see Z. Tanındı, 'Two Bibliophile Mamluk Emirs: Qansuh the Master of the Stables and Yashbak the Secretary', in D. Behrens-Abouseif (ed.), *The Arts of the Mamluks in Egypt and Syria: Evolution and Impact* (Göttingen, 2012), 267–81.

77 MS Istanbul—Süleymaniye Kütüphanesi, Yeni Cami 887.

aims. As al-Maqrīzī explains in his introduction, in a note added *a posteriori* in the margin, he did not intend to add obituaries at the end of each year for the simple reason that he had already undertaken to write a separate biographical dictionary.[78] Although he does not name this it is possible to infer, from a passage in the year 733/1332–33, that he means *al-Taʾrīkh al-kabīr al-muqaffā*. However, this approach seems to have been forgotten afterwards since *al-Sulūk* contains a section of obituaries, listing important people who died during that year, along with the exact date of their death, although these only appear from the reign of Shajar al-Durr (r. 648/1250) onwards, the time which can be said to mark the transition of power from the Ayyūbids to the Mamlūks. The autograph reveals that the decision to add these obituaries from this date onwards was late: they all appear either on slips of paper pasted at the right place, or in the body of the text written on quires of a smaller size than the rest of the manuscript, which indicates that these sections were rewritten by al-Maqrīzī, thus allowing him to integrate them directly into the body of the text. The reason for this reversal is perhaps to be found in the criticism of a colleague who had learnt of his decision, or al-Maqrīzī's realisation that the majority of his predecessors and contemporaries had adopted this system. Another contribution of the autograph concerns how it is possible to understand the author's working method: al-Maqrīzī made a number of revisions to his text, no doubt because he discovered new sources who were better informed. Consequently, marginal additions, deletions and rewritten sections are legion.

In its design, *al-Sulūk* is the successor of the two previous works, written in an annalistic form.[79] It is thus logical that its internal organisation would be identical: a year by year presentation and, when a new sultan ascended the throne in a given year, a sub-section including information about his life before he became sultan and the circumstances which led to his taking power. Furthermore, in the year of his death there is a general review of his reign.

After the traditional introduction, composed of a doxology and an explanation of the reasons which drove al-Maqrīzī to embark on writing this book, the work begins with a series of small chapters which have no other goal but to explain how power passed into the hands of representatives of those who were not Arabs. The first chapter gives an overview of the religious situation before the appearance of Islam; this is followed by another which details the caliphs who ruled between the death of the Prophet and the establishment of the

78 See below, p. 191.

79 This is at least the case for *Ittiʿāẓ al-ḥunafāʾ*. For *ʿIqd jawāhir al-asfāṭ* it is pure conjecture, but there is no reason to believe that the internal organisation would have been any different from that of the two other parts of the trilogy.

ʿAbbāsid caliphs in Cairo under the aegis of the Mamlūk sultans. Al-Maqrīzī then devotes two chapters to the Būyids, Persian emirs, and to the Seljūq sultans who had unquestionably been the real holders of power in the East, to the detriment of the caliphs of Baghdad who had been confined to their palace. This allows him to make the transition with the arrival of Saladin in Egypt and the establishment of the Ayyūbid dynasty. These introductory chapters to *al-Sulūk*, taken together and placed in the context of the two other parts of the trilogy and the works which followed (*Imtāʿ al-asmāʿ* and *al-Khabar ʿan al-bashar*), allow us to discern the true intention of al-Maqrīzī: to highlight the ephemeral character of power and the divine will which makes and destroys rulers, seemingly on a whim. His introduction is unequivocal about this subject:

> Praise be to God […] who humiliates the vanity of the powerful and the rich, who elevates the humble and obscure man, who demeans the powerful and noble, who glorifies the one who is despised and reviled, who hides the fugitive from the sight of men who pursue [him], who abases those who are armed with inexorable laws or who have many soldiers, those who hold above their heads banners and flags, and those who control the armed forces and troops. He gives his strength to the one who has nothing, whose fathers and ancestors are unknown, but who conforms in his conduct to the wish of his Master and who is good to his neighbor, whom people hate and for which no one has any care, who cannot make himself useful to himself or anyone else, who is incapable of avoiding the evil and the calamities which fall on him because of his weakness and the obscurity in which he lives. He removes the empire to those who the worst of people fear because of their trickery, to those before whom warriors, despite their hardness and cruelty, humble themselves, at the feet of whom the bravest soldiers prostrate themselves.[80]

It is also possible to infer here an expression of the wish that the Arabs should be the holders of power and that the caliph, who should come from the family of the Prophet (the Banū Hāshim), should regain his rightful power.

The importance which al-Maqrīzī gives to each of the two historical periods which are the object of *al-Sulūk* varies: the section on the Ayyūbids only occupies 93 folios of the first volume of the preserved autograph, while that devoted to the Mamlūks holds the lion's share. This difference may be explained by the evidence he had to work with, but only partly. All signs seem to indicate that

80 Al-Maqrīzī, *al-Sulūk*, vol. 1, p. 7.

al-Maqrīzī knew that he could not produce an original work for the events of which he had not been a contemporary and for which he was therefore limited to providing a synthesis, as full as possible, but nonetheless limited in space. As in his other works, al-Maqrīzī was largely reliant on his sources which were both numerous and of various genres, although, as for the majority of his other works, he neglects to directly cite them, so the modern historian is thus reduced to having to make comparisons with extant sources which he may have employed; such efforts have been carried out for the Mamlūk era.[81] Modern studies have demonstrated that al-Maqrīzī provides originality, as he manages to give accounts which are not to be found in any extant sources, although al-Maqrīzī's synthetic approach is not without its problems in certain cases.[82] For the Ayyūbid period, detailed study of this kind is still lacking, although it can be determined that al-Maqrīzī made extensive use of the works of his predecessors: Ibn Wāṣil, Ibn Abī Ṭayyi', Ibn al-Athīr, al-Mundhirī, al-Qāḍī al-Fāḍil (d. 596/1200), Bahā' al-Dīn Ibn Shaddād (d. 632/1245), Sibṭ Ibn al-Jawzī (d. 654/1256), Abū Shāma (d. 675/1276), and al-Nuwayrī (d. 732/1331).

The contents of *al-Sulūk* first gained the attention of historians of the Crusades at an early stage, in 1761, when Denis Dominique Cardonne (1721–1783), the holder of the Chair of Turkish and Persian at the Collège Royal in Paris (from 1750) made a translation of extracts relating to Louis IX.[83] Yet it was only half a century later that the work received the attention that it merited, when the Orientalist Étienne Marc Quatremère (1782–1857), a disciple of Antoine-Isaac Silvestre de Sacy (1758–1838) and holder of the Chair of Hebrew and Syriac at the Collège de France (from 1819), published for the first time a translation of the part relating to the Mamlūk dynasty which covered the years 648/1250 to 708/1309. This translation was a milestone in the history of oriental studies not only for its quality but also for its detailed annotations

81 D.P. Little, *An Introduction to Mamlūk Historiography: An Analysis of Arabic Annalistic and Biographical Sources for the Reign of al-Malik an-Nāṣir Muḥammad ibn Qalā'ūn* (Wiesbaden, 1970), pp. 76–80; S. Massoud, *The Chronicles and Annalistic Sources of the Early Mamluk Circassian Period* (Leiden, 2007), pp. 48–53, 112–15, 158–62.

82 See also R. Amitai, 'Al-Maqrīzī as a Historian of the Early Mamluk Sultanate (or: Is al-Maqrīzī an Unrecognized Historiographical Villain?)', *Mamlūk Studies Review* 7 (2003), 99–118; S. Massoud, 'Al-Maqrīzī as a Historian of the Reign of Barqūq', *Mamlūk Studies Review* 7 (2003), 119–36.

83 D.D. Cardonne, 'Extraits des manuscrits arabes, dans lesquels il est parlé des évènements historiques relatifs au règne de S. Louis', in *Histoire de Saint Louis par Jehan Sire de Joinville* (Paris, 1761), 525–45.

explaining the numerous technical terms.[84] In order to do this, Quatremère used numerous sources which in his time were still only available in manuscript form. In his introduction, he explained that his intention was to translate the part dealing with the Ayyūbids and to publish the result of his work in the *Collection des Historiens des Croisades*, but circumstances outside his control prevented him from achieving this aim.[85] Ultimately, it was Edgar Blochet (1870–1937), keeper of oriental manuscripts at the Bibliothèque Nationale de France, who realised the wish of Quatremère. Between 1898 and 1902 he published his translation which covered the whole of the Ayyūbid dynasty and so completed Quatremère's work,[86] although Blochet's translation is generally regarded as being of inferior quality to that of Quatremère. While this work was, nonetheless, accessible in French, an English translation was still lacking until Broadhurst published his translation in 1980 in the collection *Library of Classical Arabic Literature*.[87] Between these two publications the first Arabic critical edition of the text appeared; the first two volumes were prepared by the Egyptian scholar M.M. Ziyāda, who only had time to publish these two,[88] and his work was taken up by another Egyptian scholar, Saʿīd ʿAbd al-Fattāḥ ʿĀshūr, several years later, although this work does not match the critical quality of his predecessor.[89]

As it is in the form of annals, it should be obvious that the Crusades are not treated separately from other events. The main disadvantage of the presentation of events on a yearly basis is that the reader only gets a global vision of them after having read all of the years concerned. In order to achieve this in his writing, al-Maqrīzī therefore had to summarise and synthesise sources where their authors may have used a different methodology.

In general, it seems that al-Maqrīzī refrained from passing judgement on the actions of both Franks and Muslims. Occasions when the name of the Franks is accompanied by curses are almost non-existant in his writing. Even with regard to the infamous Reynald of Châtillon, al-Maqrīzī remains sober

84 É.M. Quatremère, *Histoire des sultans mamlouks de l'Égypte*, 2 vols (Paris, 1837–45).

85 *Ibid.*, vol. 1, p. xviii.

86 E. Blochet, 'Histoire d'Égypte de Makrizi. Traduction française accompagnée de notes historiques et géographiques', *Revue de l'Orient latin* 6–11 (1898–1908). This collection of articles was reprinted as a book under the same title in 1908 (Paris).

87 R.J.C. Broadhurst, *A History of the Ayyūbid Sultans of Egypt* (Boston, 1980).

88 Al-Maqrīzī, *al-Sulūk li-maʿrifat duwal al-mulūk*, ed. M.M. Ziyāda (Cairo, 1934–58), vols. 1–2 in 6 parts.

89 Al-Maqrīzī, *al-Sulūk li-maʿrifat duwal al-mulūk*, ed. S.ʿA. al-F. ʿĀshūr (Cairo, 1970–73), vols. 3–4 in 6 parts. There is another, non-critical edition, recently prepared by M.ʿA.Q. ʿAṭā, 8 vols (Beirut, 1997).

in his judgement. The latter's attack against the Ḥijāz in 578/1183 is reported neutrally, with al-Maqrīzī content to report that a Christian had never before even approached the Holy Cities.[90] The only examples where he does alter this approach are when he writes that a Muslim victory was granted by God to the true faith, thereby highlighting the religious fallibility of the Franks. As for the Muslims, al-Maqrīzī sometimes takes the part of a critic, such as his assessment of the decision to destroy the walls and buildings of Ascalon in 594/1198; for al-Maqrīzī, the destruction of this town was the result of the sultan's inability to repel the Franks by force of arms. Had he been stronger, the Muslims would not have been reduced to razing the city out of fear that it would be re-taken by the Franks.[91]

The historian of the Crusades needs to know which sections of *al-Sulūk* dealing with events surrounding the Franks and the Latin states between 1171 and 1291 are original. It is undeniable that for a long time the work was considered one of the principle sources for the history of the Ayyūbid and Mamlūk periods, and numerous modern historians, including P.K. Hitti, H.A.R. Gibb and F. Gabrieli, put great significance on al-Maqrīzī's writings.[92] This esteem, no doubt merited at the time these historians were writing, has now been lessened, for the simple fact that many of the sources used by al-Maqrīzī have been discovered and published since then. If *al-Sulūk* still possesses some interest for historians of Ayyūbid and Mamlūk times, this is primarily due to al-Maqrīzī's ability to unearth sources which were often difficult to access, even in his own time, and which are no longer extant. Whatever judgement is brought to bear on his working method in the future, he will remain an essential source for the period he writes about, although he was not a witness and still less an actor in the events which he reports; he is thus entirely dependent on his sources, while the accounts he gives of the events also reflect the subjective level of importance he gave to them. For the Ayyūbid era, the reader will find evidence for events throughout the Crusades, especially during the reigns of Saladin and al-Kāmil. The reigns of other sultans are dotted with brief reports concerning Palestine, but these contain little new information compared to contemporaneous sources.

However, certain events which made a deep impression on the people who lived through them and which are regarded as key moments in the Muslim reconquest receive only limited attention from al-Maqrīzī. Unlike other historians who were witnesses of these events, al-Maqrīzī knew the outcome of the struggle with the Franks, and so they no longer constituted a threat from his

90 Al-Maqrīzī, *al-Sulūk*, vol. 1, pp. 78–79; Broadhurst, *History*, p. 70.

91 Al-Maqrīzī, *al-Sulūk*, vol. 1, pp. 141–42; Broadhurst, *History*, pp. 124–25.

92 See Broadhurst, *History*, pp. xvii–xviii.

point of view and so Muslim victories against them are of less significance for him. Thus, the famous battle of Ḥaṭṭīn (583/1187) receives only a very brief mention in *al-Sulūk*: there is just a summary paragraph containing the main pieces of information (the date of the battle, the opposing forces, the death of Reynald of Châtillon and others from the Frankish forces),[93] immediately followed by the siege of Acre. Unusually for *al-Sulūk*, al-Maqrīzī embellishes his report with an account he took from an eyewitness, ʿAbd al-Laṭīf al-Baghdādī (d. 629/1231–32), concerning the market which accompanied Saladin's army when he was encamped opposite Acre.[94] Al-Maqrīzī's notebook reveals that he did not have direct access to this source, but that he cited the extract in question from another author whose work is considered lost: al-Yaghmūrī (d. 673/1274). The extract found in the notebook was added by al-Maqrīzī in the margin of the autograph of *al-Sulūk*,[95] which suggests that he discovered this source after he had already written this part of his work.[96]

The alliance concluded by al-Kāmil and the German Emperor Frederick II which led to the return of Jerusalem to Frederick in 626/1229 also garners little comment from al-Maqrīzī. In contrast, the behaviour of Frederick II when he entered Jerusalem, giving favourable position to the Muslims and respect to their places of worship, is reported positively.[97] Moreover, when al-Maqrīzī gives his assessment of al-Kāmil at the time of his death, he makes no mention of the handover of Jerusalem, choosing instead to portray him as a good politician.[98]

On the other hand, al-Maqrīzī reports many details concerning the sale of arms and other military equipment to the Franks who were allowed to visit Damascus by the ruler al-Ṣāliḥ Ismāʿīl in order to purchase them in the year 638/1240–41. He provides valuable information on the reactions of Muslim scholars who judged the permissibility of this and cites the prayer which was recited in the Great Umayyad Mosque of Damascus on this occasion.[99] Overall, although al-Maqrīzī's references to the treaties concluded between

93 Al-Maqrīzī, *al-Sulūk*, vol. I, pp. 93–94; Broadhurst, *History*, pp. 82–83.

94 Al-Maqrīzī, *al-Sulūk*, vol. I, p. 94; Broadhurst, *History*, pp. 82–83. This passage does not appear in ʿAbd al-Laṭīf al-Baghdādī, *The Eastern Key. Kitāb al-ifādah wa'l-iʿtibār*, tr. with a facsimile of the Arabic autograph by K.H. Zand and J.A. and I.E. Videan (London, 1965), as in this book the author gives a report of his stay in Egypt in 588/1192–589/1193.

95 MS Istanbul—Süleymaniye Kütüphanesi, Yeni Cami 887, f. 26.

96 Bauden, 'Maqriziana I/2', pp. 119–21.

97 Al-Maqrīzī, *al-Sulūk*, vol. I, pp. 221–22 and 230–32; Broadhurst, *History*, pp. 198 and 206–9.

98 Al-Maqrīzī, *al-Sulūk*, vol. I, pp. 258–60; Broadhurst, *History*, pp. 229–31 ('he was deeply politic').

99 Al-Maqrīzī, *al-Sulūk*, vol. I, pp. 303–4; Broadhurst, *History*, pp. 262–63.

the Ayyūbids and the Franks are numerous, quotations of extracts from these treaties remain rare, as is the case for correspondence between the sultans and various Frankish rulers. One rare example is a letter sent by Louis IX a little after his landing in Egypt and the response which was drafted by the Ayyūbid chancellery; the extracts cited are sufficiently long to give an idea of their overall contents.[100]

Al-Maqrīzī's taste for good stories and anecdotes can be seen in his reference to a Genoese merchant, whom he named William the Frank (Kilyām al-Firanjī), who arrived in Egypt in 607/1210–11. According to al-Maqrīzī, he managed to win the trust of al-ʿĀdil by offering him sumptuous gifts. The sultan made him a member of his entourage despite warnings from his advisors that he was a spy giving information to the Franks. The sultan gave little heed to these words and, the following year, William accompanied him to Damascus.[101] Unfortunately, al-Maqrīzī makes no mention of what happened after that.

One other fairly characteristic element of al-Maqrīzī in his capacity as a historian appears in his appreciation of curious coincidences (*ittifāqāt gharība*).[102] His account of the capture of Ascalon (587/1191) is embellished by an eyewitness account which he took from *al-Muʿjam al-mutarjam* by al-Mundhirī, mentioned above. This recounts how there was an inscription found in the tower of the Templars which indicates that the tower in question had been built by a certain Khuṭluj during the Fāṭimid era. The author notes the incredible mirroring of events in this case, as the name of the person who was in charge of its destruction was also Khuṭluj and the time at which it took place (the month of Shaʿbān) was the same as that of the completion of its construction.[103]

In light of what has been said about the Egyptocentrism of the majority of al-Maqrīzī's work it is hardly surprising that it is events relating to this country which receive the most exhaustive treatment on the part of our author. Those which receive the most detailed accounts are the Fifth Crusade and the Crusade of Louis IX, both of which led to occupation of part of the country for a time, although it should be noted that these reports differ little from those in the *Khiṭaṭ*.

From the thirteenth century onwards al-Maqrīzī was aware, like his predecessors, that the danger the Franks represented for Islam was limited and that there was instead a different threat to the whole of the Muslim East: the Mongols. It is no coincidence that the victory of al-Kāmil over the Fifth

100 Al-Maqrīzī, *al-Sulūk*, vol. I, pp. 333–35; Broadhurst, *History*, pp. 288–89.

101 Al-Maqrīzī, *al-Sulūk*, vol. I, p. 173; Broadhurst, *History*, p. 154.

102 See Bauden, 'Maqriziana I/2', p. 134.

103 Al-Maqrīzī, *al-Sulūk*, vol. I, p. 106; Broadhurst, *History*, p. 94.

Crusade is presented by al-Maqrīzī as a victory announced across the world but, at the same time, it is placed alongside the news of the appearance of the Mongols in the East.[104]

With the advent of the Mamlūk dynasty the presentation of events varies somewhat from reports from the preceding period. For this section, al-Maqrīzī is heavily reliant on al-Nuwayrī even if, as is usual, he does not limit himself to just one source. Mentions of sieges conducted against fortresses remaining in Frankish hands are more frequent, even if these events by this time really only affected Palestine. References to more northerly lands, such as Cilicia and Armenia, are even more sporadic, but treaties signed between the Mamlūk sultans and the Frankish rulers are frequently cited. Although certain details related to the conditions of these treaties are provided by al-Maqrīzī, the texts themselves are almost never mentioned.

He does, however, provide a detailed narrative for the most important Mamlūk conquests of Frankish strongholds. This is the case for the fall of the fortress of Arsūf (663/1264), where very precise details are given for the role played by Baybars, who actively participated in the work of sapping and mining the place, and by the deep religious fervour which prevailed in the Muslims camp where wine was prohibited and where virtuous women carried drinks and participated in the work.[105]

The fall of Acre in 690/1291, which marked the end of the Frankish presence in Palestine, is, however, only recorded in a summary occupying little more than a page. It is preceded by numerous lines reporting preparations, but the report of the siege—which lasted forty days—and the fall of the town receive only very limited attention. Instead, the event is given the merit it deserves through citations of poems which were composed for the occasion.[106]

Thus, the interest of *al-Sulūk* for scholars of the crusading period is undeniable, and not just because the parts dealing with this period are available in English and French translation. Events concerning Egypt in particular receive significant attention from al-Maqrīzī and his account of these events has the advantage of being based on sources written by contemporary historians about events which occurred in Egypt during their own lifetime. For Palestine, it is clear that the interest of his account is somewhat lessened by the numbers of extant Syrian sources which have been brought to light in the second half of the twentieth century but it is also true that, for a good number, they are not

104 Al-Maqrīzī, *al-Sulūk*, vol. I, p. 210; Broadhurst, *History*, p. 188.
105 Al-Maqrīzī, *al-Sulūk*, vol. I, pp. 527–29; Quatremère, *Histoire*, vol. I/2, pp. 8–10.
106 Al-Maqrīzī, *al-Sulūk*, vol. I, pp. 763–67; Quatremère, *Histoire*, vol. II/1, pp. 121–129.

available in translation, and so al-Maqrīzī remains extremely useful for this period.

Al-Muqaffā

The idea of collecting data for a biographical dictionary devoted to Egyptians who left their mark on history in some way must have started when al-Maqrīzī examined the sources which would serve him when writing the *Khiṭaṭ*. However, it is likely that he only conceived of writing it after beginning drafting his annals of the Ayyūbid and Mamlūk sultans (*al-Sulūk*) because, as noted above, the only preserved autograph of the completed version of these annals, that of the first volume, carries a marginal note by al-Maqrīzī where he writes that he will not deal with biographies and obituaries, having already devoted a biographical dictionary to this material. Even though he does not name this work, it is easy to guess that al-Maqrīzī is here referring to *al-Taʾrīkh al-kabīr al-muqaffā li-Miṣr*, more often known under the shortened title of *al-Muqaffā*.[107] He must only have added this marginal note after he was well advanced in his writing of this dictionary, to which he had not yet given a title. The events relating to the year 733/1332–33 must be examined to obtain more detail:

> Our great book which is a continuation (*al-muqaffā*) [of *al-Sulūk*] is a work of biographies and obituaries just as this book (*al-Sulūk*) is a work of events and occurrences.[108]

The first mention of its title which can be fixed in time appears in a marginal note which al-Maqrīzī added to a volume of the encyclopaedia of Ibn Faḍl Allāh al-ʿUmarī, called *Masālik al-abṣār*, which may be dated with precision to 831/1427–28.[109] By this time, al-Maqrīzī must already have been well advanced in his writing and it is not rare to find references to this dictionary on the pages of many of his autograph volumes.

---

107 In his edition of *al-Sulūk* (vol. I, p. 9, n. 3), Ziyāda put forward the idea that it could also have referred to al-Maqrīzī's other biographical dictionary, *Durar al-ʿuqūd al-farīda*, which he devoted to his contemporaries. This is impossible given that al-Maqrīzī's idea for this text was to include data on the biography of people who had died after the beginning of the decade during which he was born, i.e. 760/1358–59. *Al-Sulūk* treated the Ayyūbid period similarly.

108 See *al-Sulūk*, vol. II, p. 365.

109 See Bauden, *Trusting the Source*.

By the time of his death, this dictionary extended to sixteen volumes, but al-Maqrīzī informed some of his visitors that, if he had had enough time to work on it, it would have run to 80. Of these sixteen volumes, it is known that four have been preserved in their autograph form while the whole of the first part, comprising the letters *alif-khāʾ*, exists only in a copy made from another part of the autograph which had been considered lost until 1978,[110] when the library of Leiden University took the opportunity to purchase an autograph volume of *al-Muqaffā*. While this discovery was essential for the textual history of the work and the study of the author's working method, it was less so in terms of content as it roughly corresponds to the Istanbul manuscript: only 20 more biographies were discovered when compared to the Istanbul version.[111]

Of the sixteen autograph volumes available on the death of al-Maqrīzī, five have been identified so far (totalling around 1,550 folios). They have just over 3,600 biographies encompassing the letters *alif*, *bāʾ*, *tāʾ*, *thāʾ*, *jīm*, *ḥāʾ*, and *khāʾ*, part of the letters *ṭāʾ* and *ʿayn*, a tiny part of the letters *kāf* and *lām*, and finally the letter *mīm*. The unevenness of the spread of these letters is evident from a comparison of them: for the first seven letters of the alphabet there are a total of 1,401 notices, while for the single letter *mīm*, where the name Muḥammad is the most popular, for obvious reasons, and where Maḥmūd also often appears, there is a total of 2,062. From this, it is possible to get a sense of the scale of the project and its state upon the death of its author. It can be calculated that the autograph manuscripts represent 9.6 volumes of the 16 originals,[112] which means that *al-Muqaffā* contained around 6,000 biographies. This also means that, if al-Maqrīzī had been able to complete his project, it would have contained around 30,000, making it one of the most complete biographical dictionaries of the history of Egypt ever written.

Studying the autograph manuscripts allows historians to understand how al-Maqrīzī developed his biographical dictionary. He worked by using a system of notes, the contents of which were then written up as drafts at a time

---

110 The autograph volumes are: MS Leiden—University Library, 1366a, 1366c, 3065 (= 1366b) and MS Paris—BNF arabe 2144. The copy made using part of the autograph is in Istanbul: MS Istanbul—Süleymaniye Kütüphanesi, Pertev Pasha 496.

111 The incredible history of this acquisition is reported by its principal participant, the curator of oriental manuscripts at that time, J.J. Witkam. See J.J. Witkam, *Inventory of the Oriental Manuscripts of the Library of the University of Leiden, vol. 15: Manuscripts OR. 14.001–OR. 15.000* (Leiden, 2007), pp. 242–44. The announcement of this acquisition was made the following year: J.J. Witkam, 'Discovery of a Hitherto Unknown Section of the *Kitāb al-Muqaffā* by al-Maqrīzī', *Quaerendo* 9 (1979), 353–54.

112 J.J. Witkam, 'Les Autographes d'al-Maqrīzī', in A.-Ch. Binebine (ed.), *Le manuscrit arabe et la codicologie* (Rabat, 1994), p. 96.

when al-Maqrīzī believed he had amassed enough material to constitute a full work. However, he knew that this work could only continue to increase in size. Additions were introduced in various ways: at the end of one biography if a blank space remained, written on extra sheets inserted into the quires if the notice was brief, or, for larger biographies, full quires of a smaller format could be added to the original. It is therefore unsurprising that biographies generally begin at the top of a page and are sometimes followed by other notices added *a posteriori*. As for all of his works, al-Maqrīzī continually revised his text and made corrections, additions and deletions.

The text of *al-Muqaffā* was noted very early by Orientalists. The first partial edition was that of Michele Amari (1806–1889) in his famous *Biblioteca arabo-sicula*, an anthology of sources dealing with people who were born, lived or died in southern Italy or Sicily.[113] These extracts were then translated by the same scholar into Italian.[114] This first effort was not followed by a complete edition of the work, probably because the only four autograph copies which were known before the second half of the twentieth century (three volumes have been in Leiden since the eighteenth century while one volume is in Paris) are considered defective, so scholars preferred to wait until more complete copies were discovered. Thus, it was not until 1987 that another partial edition was published, this time limited to the records of people from the Fāṭimid era, by an expert on the Fāṭimids, the Tunisian scholar Muḥammad al-Yaʿlāwī.[115] He stated that it was his intention to undertake a full critical edition of the preserved manuscripts, including that in Istanbul, and this was finally published in 1991.[116] However, he was unable to consult the autograph manuscript acquired in 1978 by the University of Leiden (Or. 14533), as it was being restored for several years around this time. As the Istanbul manuscript covers the same material as that of Leiden, the editor decided to rely on it in the meantime. Since then, it has come to light that the Leiden manuscript contains a few additional records; thus, the editor published a new revised, corrected and enlarged edition in 2006.[117] It should be noted here that al-Yaʿlāwī did not realise that dozens of notices were added in the autograph manuscripts of the

113 M. Amari, *Biblioteca arabo-sicula ossia raccolta di testi arabici che toccano la geografia, la storia, le biografie e la bibliografia della Sicilia* (Lipsia, 1857), pp. 661–69.

114 M. Amari, *Biblioteca arabo-sicula, versione italiana*, 2 vols (Turin, 1880–81), vol. II, pp. 572–87.

115 Al-Maqrīzī, *Kitāb al-muqaffā al-kabīr* (*tarājim maqhriqiyya wa-maghribiyya min al-fatra al-ʿubaydiyya*) (Beirut, 1987).

116 Al-Maqrīzī, *Kitāb al-muqaffā al-kabīr*, ed. M. al-Yaʿlāwī, 8 vols (Beirut, 1991).

117 Al-Maqrīzī, *Kitāb al-muqaffā al-kabīr*, ed. M. al-Yaʿlāwī, 8 vols (Beirut, 2006).

work, probably after al-Maqrīzī's death, by his friend and colleague Ibn Ḥajar al-ʿAsqalānī. They therefore should not have been edited in the body of the text of al-Maqrīzī, but rather placed in an appendix, since they were not written by him. This is but one of the many flaws of this edition.

The title chosen by al-Maqrīzī for his biographical dictionary is not without its problems and the absence of an introduction, explained by the evolutionary nature of the book, complicates our understanding of the author's true intention. The word *al-muqaffā* is derived from the root (Q-F-W) which means neck and, by extension, the sequel to something. It is rarely attested in Arabic book titles—only one example can be found, that of the 'chronicle' of al-Birzālī (d. 739/1339), which is a continuation of the work of Abū Shāma (m. 665/1267)[118]—and it does not correspond to what may be expected, as it is not a continuation of the work of an earlier historian. Rather, its meaning seems to be closely linked to the overall aim of al-Maqrīzī's historical project: *al-Muqaffā* is the continuation of his many other histories. Al-Maqrīzī sometimes calls it *The Great History of Egypt* (*al-Taʾrīkh al-kabīr li-Miṣr*), and in the notes he made on title pages or inside his manuscripts he refers to it most often as *The Great History* (*al-Taʾrīkh al-kabīr*). I suggest that the aim of the dictionary was to list the maximum number of biographical notices of persons who had had links—sometimes firm, sometimes tenuous—with the land of Egypt. In al-Maqrīzī's eyes, to be included in *al-Muqaffā* it seems to have been enough simply to have seen Egypt. Thus, it not only contains notices on people who were born and who lived much of their life there: the spectrum is much broader and, given Egypt's position as a gateway between the East and the West of the Islamic world which had to be traversed if travelling overland between those regions, huge numbers of people were eligible for inclusion. Some of the most extreme examples include the grandson of Muḥammad, al-Ḥusayn, who never set foot in Egypt, but nevertheless receives a long notice for the simple fact that his head was brought to Cairo by the Fāṭimids (where it is still located), and even Idrīs I, who passed through Egypt when moving to the far West to establish his dynasty in Morocco. In addition, the time period was immense: from Abraham until the time of al-Maqrīzī; consequently, eighty planned volumes does not seem to have been an overestimation.

As with the majority of his writings, al-Maqrīzī used an impressive number of sources, although these are often the same as those he used for his chronographical works. Yet in contrast to the methodology he developed for the *Khiṭaṭ*, al-Maqrīzī refrains from citing them in most cases. The historian is

118 Al-Birzālī, *al-Muqtafī ʿalā kitāb al-rawḍatayn al-maʿrūf bi-taʾrīkh al-Birzālī*, ed. ʿU.A. Tadmurī, 4 vols (Sidon, 2006).

therefore reduced to guessing through comparison—when the relevant source is preserved—or speculating without possibility of corroboration. This work of identifying sources, which any serious scientific text editor should carry out, is unfortunately lacking in the only complete edition available to date. Footnotes regarding innumerable facts, and references to places, people and objects are also seriously lacking in the edition.

As al-Maqrīzī's main geographical area of historical interest is Egypt, it is unsurprising that there is consequently limited detail on the Crusades in *al-Muqaffā*, although it must be borne in mind that the book has survived in an incomplete and deficient form. Nevertheless, al-Maqrīzī did devote a biographical notice to Baldwin I[119] because of the latter's incursion into Egyptian soil. This fairly brief entry (occupying half a folio), begins with the name of the King of Jerusalem using the system of alphabetical classification employed throughout the dictionary: Baghdawīn ibn […]. Al-Maqrīzī took the trouble to vocalize the first three letters (B-GH-D), thus indicating the pronunciation of the name according to him. Unaware of the name of Baldwin I's father, he left the space blank in the hope of being able to complete this information should he discover it somewhere later. In its brevity, the record provides little new. Al-Maqrīzī deals with the main facts of Baldwin's life after the death of his brother Godfrey (*K.N.D.F.RĀ*): his arrival in Jerusalem in the company of 500 knights and infantry; the victory of the Egyptian army sent against him at Ramla in 495/1102 (neglecting to mention, in passing, the victory of Baldwin in the same place against the same enemy the previous year); his escape from the reeds which were set ablaze by Muslim troops; the fire which caused burns that left marks on parts of his body; and his capture of Acre in 497/1104. His march against Egypt in the year 512/1118 is reported, as is his conduct in al-Faramā (Pelusium), which led to the destruction of much of the city—in the words of al-Maqrīzī, it was there that God decreed his death.[120] According to the historian, Baldwin's comrades hid the death of the King for fear of what the reaction might have been, doing so by keeping his body hidden after it had been emptied of its entrails and filling the hole with salt when they brought it back to Jerusalem. Al-Maqrīzī here reveals a detail that is unknown in any other preserved source: Baldwin's entrails were buried in an area of salt marsh located near the city of al-Warrāda which was still known in al-Maqrīzī's time

119 Al-Maqrīzī, *al-Muqaffā* (ed. 1991), vol. II, p. 440 = (ed. 2006), vol. II, p. 254. The title added to the notice (*Baghdawīn ṣāḥib al-Quds* ['Baldwin, lord of Jerusalem']) has been added by the editor and does not appear in the manuscript.

120 In *Ittiʿāẓ al-ḥunafā'*, ed. al-Shayyāl and Ḥilmī, vol. III, pp. 53 and 56, al-Maqrīzī puts his death both in the year 509/1115–16 and 511/1117–18!

under his name (*sabkhat Bardawīl*).[121] This place was the subject of a *damnatio memoriae* rite practiced by the common people of the area: the stoning of the burial place of Baldwin I's entrails.[122] Such detail from al-Maqrīzī is unsurprising given that our author liked to gather such data concerning Egyptian sites. As Baldwin I had the honour of receiving a biographical sketch in *al-Muqaffā*, it is extremely likely that Louis IX would also have been included in the same way, due to his presence on Egyptian soil during the first of his crusades. Yet, if that was the case, his record has not survived.

In addition to a few scattered references in various notices, the only other noteworthy passage is the capture of the city of Acre (690/1291) at the end of a siege that lasted 44 days, according to al-Maqrīzī. As may be expected, this comes as part of the death notice of the Mamlūk sultan al-Ashraf Khalīl, who led the Muslim armies against that last Frankish stronghold.[123] This report matches, *grosso modo*, that which al-Maqrīzī gave in his annalistic work, *al-Sulūk*.[124]

Al-Khabar ʿan al-bashar

When he went to Mecca on pilgrimage in 834/1431 al-Maqrīzī expressed a wish to transmit part of his biography of the Prophet (*Imtāʿ al-asmāʿ*) which he had begun to write in 832/1429. In Mecca he was able to transmit the first four volumes that he had already finished, before completing two more volumes during the subsequent four years,[125] and he carried out his wish to transmit

121 Al-Warrāda was situated on the route linking Egypt and Syria. In the thirteenth century it was surrounded by sand dunes. It may be significant that the lake situated in this area of the northern Sinai is still, today, called *Baḥr Bardawīl* ('Baldwin's Lake'). See Yāqūt al-Rūmī, *Muʿjam al-buldān*, 5 vols (Beirut, 1977), vol. V, p. 369; al-Maqrīzī, *al-Khiṭaṭ* (ed. Būlāq), vol. I, p. 184 (where this episode is not reported); M. Ramzī, *Al-Qāmūs al-jughrāfī li'l-bilād al-Miṣriyya min ʿahd qudamāʾ al-Miṣriyyīn ilā sanat 1945*, 6 vols (Cairo, 1953–54, reprint 1994), vol. I, pp. 124–25.

122 Cf. al-Nuwayrī, *Nihāyat al-arab fī funūn al-adab*, ed. M. Qumayḥa, 33 vols (Beirut, 2004), vol. XXVIII, pp. 178–79.

123 Al-Maqrīzī, *al-Muqaffā* (ed. 1991), vol. III, pp. 794–96 = (ed. 2006), vol. III, pp. 452–54.

124 Al-Maqrīzī, *al-Sulūk*, vol. I, pp. 763–67; Quatremère, *Histoire des sultans mamlouks*, vol. II, pp. 121–29. Al-Maqrīzī follows, for the most part, al-Nuwayrī, *Nihāyat al-arab*.

125 The sixth and final volume has the date of the 10th Shawwāl 836/30th May 1433. See MS Istanbul—Fazıl Ahmad Paşa 1004, f. 919. For the first complete edition, see al-Maqrīzī, *Imtāʿ al-asmāʿ bi-mā li'l-nabī min al-aḥwāl wa'l-amwāl wa'l-ḥafada wa'l-matāʿ*, ed. M.ʿA.Ḥ. al-Numaysī, 6 vols (Beirut, 1999).

it entirely in the Holy City during the last pilgrimage he made to Mecca in 838/1435–840/1436. The idea for this biography of the Prophet came to him after completing his trilogy, although he still added material to all his works, notably *al-Sulūk*, which he continued writing until a few months before his death. Having completed this new book, al-Maqrīzī hoped to write another allowing him to terminate his historical writings and thus complete the historical cycle to which he had devoted most of his life as scholar *ab orbe condito usque ad dies nostros*: thus, the project of a history of humanity (*al-Khabar ʿan al-bashar*) was born, one which would serve as an introduction (*madkhal*) to *Imtāʿ al-asmāʿ*. If al-Maqrīzī had succeeded in completing it, his total *œuvre* would have included pre-Islamic history, the life of the Prophet, and the history of Egypt from the Muslim conquest until his own time. He began to work on this in 836/1433, as soon as he had finished *Imtāʿ al-asmāʿ*, and he seems to have worked hard on it until the end of his life. It was divided into six volumes and five autograph volumes corresponding to the fair copy have been preserved. Thanks to them, we know that the third volume was completed in 844/1441, nine months before his death, meaning that the following three were started by al-Maqrīzī during the last months of his life.[126]

The first of the six volumes is the introduction to the whole book. It includes a section on the Creation, followed by a geographical presentation of the world according to the traditional division into seven climes, after which there are a number of remarks on chronology. Al-Maqrīzī then moves onto the inhabitants of the earth and the appearance of the first human being and its offspring, which brings him to the ancestors of the Arabs, followed by the Yemeni kings and finally the different Arab tribes. Volumes 2, 3 and 4 are devoted to the pre-Islamic Arabs, including their genealogy, customs, religion, and institutions in Mecca. In volume 5, al-Maqrīzī divided the material into four sections: the first is devoted to poet-brigands and the days of the Arabs (*ayyām al-ʿArab*); the second to the Persians before Islam; the third to the Jews and the last to the Greeks and other related peoples. The final volume deals with the history of the prophets (biblical and others).

Al-Maqrīzī's initial aim, writing what he knew would be his last book, is clearly explained in the introduction: to write something which would serve as an introduction to his biography of the Prophet (*Imtāʿ al-asmāʿ*) with the

---

126 MSS Istanbul—Süleymaniye Kütüphanesi, Aya Sofya 3362 (vol. I); Fatih 4338 (vol. III); Fatih 4339 (vol. IV); Fatih 4340 (vol. V); Fatih 4341 (vol. VI). See also F. Tauer, 'Zu al-Maqrīzī's Schrift *al-Ḫabar ʿan al-bašar*', *Islamica* 1 (1925), 357–64. The text has recently been published as *al-Khabar ʿan al-bashar fī ansāb al-ʿArab wa-nasab sayyid al-bashar*, ed. Kh.A.M. al-Suwaydī and ʿĀ.ʿA. al-Ghanī, 8 vols (Beirut, 2013).

history of humanity since the beginning of the Creation until the appearance of the Arabs and their division as its subject. The aim of this was to highlight the importance of the Arabs who had been singled out by God, demonstrated by the fact that He elected His Messenger to be from the Banū Hāshim, of the Quraysh, which was, itself, one of the Arab tribes; the Arabs thus deserve affection, respect, and glory. However, al-Maqrīzī realised after beginning his work that he had accumulated enough material that he could make an independent book, one he chose to entitle *A History of Humanity*.[127]

Chronologically therefore, al-Maqrīzī reversed what many of his fellow historians did: instead of writing a universal history as his first work, al-Maqrīzī began with a history of Egypt since the Muslim conquest until his time and only after completing this did he write a biography of the Prophet and followed it with a history of humanity. Behind this method an ideological, if not a political, programme can be discerned: al-Maqrīzī intended to highlight the Arabs at the expense of other peoples, bringing to the forefront the question of power in Islam which he thought should only be in the hands of the Quraysh. The true aim of al-Maqrīzī can thus be seen in the background of this work; he always underlined the central role which the ʿAbbāsid Caliphs played. It is therefore not surprising that the Turks and the Mongols, peoples who embraced Islam and dominated much of the eastern Islamic world for centuries, are absent from this story of humanity.

At the end of his life, al-Maqrīzī had accumulated enough material for this book to be a final example of the scale of his ambitions and of his curious mind. The sources he used are numerous, and many of them are currently unpublished, lost or little known. In addition to Muslim sources, al-Maqrīzī also employed Christian sources such as Paul Orose (d.c. 418 A.D.) and Ibn al-ʿAmīd (d. 673/1273), Arabic translations of the Gospels of Matthew and Luke, and a Synaxarion. In the light of these sources, the interest of this book is significant.[128]

It is in the fifth volume that al-Maqrīzī devotes space to the Franks. The fourth section (ff. 233r–64v), which contains descriptions of the Greeks, Byzantines, Latins and Goths, also includes a description of the Franks which gives a history of their conquests since the beginning of the *Reconquista* until the end of the Crusades (f. 260v). Their arrival in the Middle East is interpreted as the result of a weakening of the power of the Arabs and of the ʿAbbāsid Caliphate. Al-Maqrīzī recounts the journey of the First Crusade from Constantinople into

127 MS Istanbul—Süleymaniye Kütüphanesi, Aya Sofya 3362 (vol. 1), ff. 4v–5r.

128 For the question of the idols of Mecca, see M. Lecker, 'Idol Worship in pre-Islamic Medina (Yathrib)', *Le Muséon* 106 (1993), 331–46. This work was recently edited (see bibliography), but the collection will be a part of the *Bibliotheca Maqriziana* project and many sections are in the course of being edited.

Muslim territory, the initial refusal of the Byzantine Emperor to let them go, the changing of his mind by the Franks with the promise to hand over the city of Melitene (Malaṭya) to him if they conquered it, their penetration into Seljūq territory up to the fall of Antioch, and the installation of Bohemond of Taranto (Bīmand) as prince of the city. The story continues with the capture of Jerusalem by Godfrey of Bouillon (Kandafrī), the first king, who was succeeded by his brother Baldwin (Baghdawīn). Al-Maqrīzī also mentions events surrounding Raymond of St.-Gilles' (Ṣanjīl) operations at Tripoli and gives the list of the places taken by the Franks in the years that followed. He goes on to report (f. 261) events which took place in Constantinople at the time of Roger II of Sicily (Rujjār)—such as attacks by his admiral George of Antioch (Jirjā ibn Mikhāʾīl)—the creation of the Latin Empire of Constantinople after 1204 and that of the Empire of Nicaea under the ruler Lascaris (Alashkarī). He then recalls the Muslim resistance to the Franks, their expulsion from the Middle East, the attempt of Louis IX on Egypt, and his death in Carthage in 668/1270, which al-Maqrīzī also chronicled in *al-Sulūk*.

In his eyes, it was from this time on that the power of the Franks weakened and their territories became limited to the north of the Mediterranean and some islands they occupied. He details (ff. 262–263v) the Frankish states which remained at the time of his writing, from those of Venice in the East to Iberia in the West. This part is of considerable interest because of the details al-Maqrīzī provides on the political systems in force in each of these states. From these it appears he was well informed, even if the complexity of certain systems, such as that of Venice, for example, escaped him. The historical facts reported about the crusader states and the names of the rulers are also accurate. From this, we can infer that his source of information was certainly oral and of European origin, and the date at which he collected his information may be located around 814/1411, a time when he went frequently to Damascus; it is not impossible that he was in direct or indirect contact with a merchant whose origin was the Italian peninsula.

Conclusion

In conclusion, the Egyptocentric nature which marks much of al-Maqrīzī's production results in this historian being especially attentive to events that have a direct connection with that country in which he was born. Those Crusades which had a direct impact on Egypt (specifically the Fifth Crusade and the Crusade of Louis IX) are therefore treated in some detail in several of his works, while those which were directed against Palestine and Syria receive less attention from our author; operations against Muslims and their cities here are mentioned little and when they are it is in relation to the actions of Ayyūbid and Mamlūk sultans. Despite this, his books still have much interest for crusade historians despite the significant amount of time elapsed between the end of the Latin presence and the time of writing, mainly due to the ability of al-Maqrīzī, an ardent worker with great energy, to find sources which, at least in part, have disappeared, even though he rarely cites these sources within his works.

A Bibliographical List of al-Maqrīzī's Major Works Available in Standard Editions and Translations

Ḍawʾ al-sārī li-maʿrifat khabar tamīm al-dārī, ed. and English tr. Y. Frenkel (Leiden, 2014).

Al-Dhahab al-masbūk fī dhikr man ḥajja min al-khulafāʾ wa'l-mulūk, ed. and English tr. J. Van Steenbergen (Leiden, forthcoming).

Durar al-ʿuqūd al-farīda fī tarājim al-aʿyān al-mufīda, ed. M. al-Jalīlī, 4 vols (Beirut, 2002).

Ighāthat al-umma bi-kashf al-ghumma, ed. K.Ḥ. Farḥāt (Cairo, 2007); English tr. A. Allouche (Salt Lake City, 1994).

Al-Ilmām bi-akhbār man bi-arḍ al-Ḥubsh min mulūk al-Islām, ed. F.Th. Rinck (Leiden, 1790); tr. G.W.B. Huntingford (s.l., typescript, 1955).

Imtāʿ al-asmāʿ bi-mā li'l-nabī min al-aḥwāl wa'l-amwāl wa'l-ḥafada wa'l-matāʿ, ed. M.ʿA.Ḥ. al-Numaysī, 15 vols (Beirut, 1999).

Ittiʿāẓ al-ḥunafāʾ bi-akhbār al-aʾimma al-khulafāʾ, ed. A.F. Sayyid, 4 vols (Damascus-London, 2010).

Al-Khabar ʿan al-bashar fī ansāb al-ʿArab wa-nasab sayyid al-bashar, ed. Kh.A.M al-Suwaydī and ʿĀ.ʿA al-Ghanī, 8 vols (Beirut, 2013).

Al-Mawāʿiẓ wa'l-iʿtibār fī dhikr al-khiṭaṭ wa'l-āthār, ed. A.F. Sayyid, 5 vols (London, 2002–2004).

Al-Nizāʿ wa'l-takhāṣum fī-mā bayna Banī Umayya wa-Banī Hāshim, ed. Ḥ. Mu'nis (Cairo, 1988); tr. C. Edmund Bosworth (Manchester, 1980).

Shudhūr al-ʿuqūd fī dhikr al-nuqūd, ed. and French tr. D. Eustache, 'Études de numismatique et de métrologie musulmanes, II', *Hespéris Tamuda* 10 (1969), 95–189.

Al-Sulūk li-maʿrifat duwal al-mulūk, ed. M.M. Ziyāda and S.ʿA.F. ʿĀshūr, 4 vols (Cairo, 1934–73); English tr. R.J.C. Broadhurst (Boston, 1980); French tr. É. Quatremère, 2 vols (Paris, 1837–45).

Al-Taʾrīkh al-muqaffā al-kabīr, ed. M. al-Yaʿlāwī, 8 vols (Beirut, 2006).

Tajrīd al-tawḥīd al-mufīd, ed. Ṣ.S. Shāhīn and M.I. al-Ṣanʿānī (Riyadh, 2005).

Index

'Abbāsid caliphate/caliph 6, 12, 20, 23, 30, 45, 54, 60, 69, 85, 86, 184, 198
'Abd al-Laṭīf al-Baghdādī 188
'Abd al-Mun'im al-Lu'ayba al-Ḥalabī 129
'Abdallāh b. 'Abd al-Raḥmān Ibn al-'Ajamī 130
Abi'l-'Alā' al-Ma'arrī 116
Abu'l-Durr Yāqūt, slave of al-Maqrīzī 167
Abu'l-Fatḥ Naṣr Allāh Ḍiyā' al-Dīn, brother of Ibn al-Athīr 56
Abū 'l-Fażl-e Bayhaqī 42
Abu'l-Fidā' 160
Abū Ḥanīfa 93
Abū Hāshim 'Alī, son of al-Maqrīzī 166
Abu'l Ḥusayn, Sufi ascetic 123
Abu'l-Maḥāsin Muḥammad, son of al-Maqrīzī 166
Abu'l-Maḥāsin b. Salāma Ibn al-Ḥarrānī 132
Abū Qudāma 88–89
Abu'l Sa'ādāt al-Mubārak Majd al-Dīn, brother of Ibn al-Athīr 55, 71
Abū Shāma 4, 16, 69, 101, 142, 143, 147, 148, 150, 152, 154, 185, 194
Acre 49, 143, 155, 170, 195
 Fall of (1291) 190, 196
 Siege of during the Third Crusade 39, 54, 188
Adab/adīb 7–8, 55–56, 68, 71, 93
Al-'Āḍid, last Fāṭimid caliph 53, 60
Al-'Ādil, brother of Saladin 37, 39, 40, 54, 65, 71, 90, 91, 151, 156, 189
Al-'Ādil II 112, 113, 153
Al-Afḍal, son of Saladin 45, 56
Al-Afḍal Shāhanshāh, Fāṭimid vizier 22, 23
Aḥdāth 8, 9
Aḥmad ibn Marwān, governor of Antiochene citadel 130
'Alā' al-Dīn 'Alī, father of al-Maqrīzī 163
'Alam al-Dīn Qayṣar 137, 143
Alan of al-Athārib 122
Aleppo 12, 53, 54, 56, 57, 69, 87, 92, 101, 109–12, 114, 117, 119–22, 125, 128, 131, 133, 134, 139, 142, 143, 146, 153–56, 163, 180
 Besieged by Franks and Muslims 122, 128, 131
Alexandria, attacked by Sicilians 83
'Alī 93, 178
'Alī b. 'Abdallāh Ibn Abī Jarāda 129
Amalric I/Amaury, King of Jerusalem 74, 174, 180
Amalric II, King of Jerusalem 151
Amari, Michele 193
Amedroz, H.F. 14
'Amīn al-Dawla, vizier 91
Al-Āmir, Fāṭimid caliph 22
Al-Amjad 90
'Amq 133
Al-Andalūs 39, 60, 63
Andalusia 63
Anṭarṭūs 133
Antioch 15, 18, 63, 67, 74, 121, 123, 129, 131, 133, 143, 146, 153–56
 Captured by the Franks 69, 130, 199
Apulia 142, 144
Aq Sunqur al-Bursuqī 122, 129
Aqsīs, Turkish military strongman 62
Arab Conquests 59
Arabs 183, 184, 197–98
 Pre-Islamic 5
Al-'Arīsh 24
Aristotle 105
Armenia 71, 190
Armenian kingdom 1, 146, 153–56
Armenian texts 1
Armenians 82, 122, 130, 131, 133
Arsuf 190
Ascalon 101, 180, 187, 189
Ash'arī 32
Al-Ashraf Khalīl, Mamlūk sultan 196
'Āshūr, Sa'īd 'Abd al-Fattāḥ 186
'Assemblies of Exhortation' (*Majālis al-wa'ẓ*) 33, 84, 88
Astronomy 122, 139
Al-Athārib 122, 131
Autobiography 4, 35
Al-Awḥadī 169, 170, 173
Aybak 140
'Ayn Jālūt, battle of 144
Al-'Aynī 120, 165
'Ayntāb 112

Ayyūb 38, 79, 146
Ayyūbid era 9, 41, 97, 116, 125, 139, 140, 143, 144, 150, 159, 171, 185
Ayyūbids 39, 52, 54, 56, 84, 86, 87, 90, 92, 104, 106, 116, 119, 133, 134, 142, 146, 147, 157, 171, 179, 181, 183, 184, 186, 187, 189, 191, 200
  Defeat Franks at Manṣūra 64, 104
  Overthrow of 105
ʿAzāz 131
Al-ʿAẓīmī 10, 129
Al-ʿAzīz, Ayyūbid ruler 57, 65, 112, 115, 124, 158
Al-ʿAzīz, murdered uncle of ʿImād al-Dīn al-Iṣfahānī 30, 33, 34, 35, 38, 43

Baalbek 25, 90, 143, 153, 161–63, 169
Bāb al-Azaj madrasa 86
Badr al-Dīn Lu'lu', vizier of Zengid Mosul 54, 56, 58, 68
Badriyya madrasa 87, 92
Baghdad 14, 19, 23, 30–37 *passim*, 45, 54, 56, 57, 63, 82, 85–86, 90, 113, 122, 136, 142, 148, 184
Baghrās 133
Bahā' al-Dīn Ibn al-Khashshāb 132
Bahā' al-Dīn Ibn Shaddād 4, 43, 50, 122, 128, 132, 133, 134, 147, 148, 150, 185
Bakās 132
Al-Bākharzī 34
Balak ibn Bahrām 180
Balāṭ, battle of 101, 131
Baldwin I of Jerusalem 61, 83, 101, 180, 195–96, 199
Baldwin II of Jerusalem 18, 67, 122, 128, 180
Al-Balkhī 11
Bāniyās 67, 133
Banu'l-Abī Jarāda 109
Banu'l-ʿAdīm 109, 110
Banu'l-ʿAjamī 110
Banu'l-Bārizī 136
Bar Hebraeus 65, 68
Baʿrīn 83, 152, 153
Barqūq, Mamlūk sultan 165
Baybars, Al-Malik al-Ẓāhir 140, 190
Bayt Lihyā, Mosque of 11
Beirut 58, 65
Berbers 60, 162
Biographical Dictionaries 55, 57, 98, 107, 117–18, 125, 129, 165, 170, 171, 172, 176, 183, 191
Biography 4, 76, 77, 93, 94, 98, 99, 121, 125, 172, 191–96
Al-Birzālī 5, 194
Blochet, Edgar 127, 186
Bohemond of Taranto (I of Antioch) 199
Bohemond III of Antioch 74, 128, 133
Bohemond IV of Antioch 154–56
Boṣrā 143
Broadhurst, R.J.C. 2, 186
Al-Bundarī 101
Burhān al-Dīn Ismāʿīl Ibn Abi'l-Damm 136
Būrids 9, 11, 13, 16, 19–22, 67
Burzey 132
Būyids 184
Byzantine Emperor 199
Byzantine Empire 1, 150
Byzantines 23, 72, 82, 130, 198 (see also Greeks)

Cahen, Claude 2, 14, 15, 67, 96, 97, 121, 154, 178
Cairo 23, 39, 53, 54, 58, 60, 69, 110, 113, 114, 116, 122, 136, 139, 141, 157, 161, 163–66, 169–74, 178, 182, 184, 194
Camel, food stuffed inside 175
Cardonne, Denis Dominique 185
Carolingian Empire 72
Carthage 199 (see also Tunis)
Charles of Anjou 150
Christian historians, medieval 1, 5, 198
Christianity 47, 105, 159
Christians 72, 103, 131, 187
  As polytheists 16, 47
Chronography 4, 10, 57, 98, 100, 194
Church of al-Qusyān (Antioch) 123
Cicero 179
Cilicia 190
Conrad III, German Emperor 72
Constantinople 198, 199
County of Tripoli 90, 143, 144, 151, 153, 154, 155
Crusaders 11, 45, 48, 53, 60, 72, 150
Crusades 1, 3, 4, 5, 16, 63, 69, 96, 121, 126, 127, 141, 142, 147, 179, 186, 187, 195 (see also Latin East)
  'Arabic Historiography of' 2
  Fifth Crusade 62, 64, 89, 90, 102, 106, 134, 150, 157, 174, 189, 199

First Crusade 60–62, 72, 101, 126, 198
Of Frederick II 89, 97, 102, 103, 105, 134, 135, 150, 157–59, 160, 188
Of Louis IX 98, 102, 104, 105, 106, 108, 141, 148, 150, 160, 173–76, 189, 196, 199
Modern study of 1, 3
Second Crusade 10, 16, 17, 22, 28, 63, 69, 71, 72, 97, 99, 102
Third Crusade 54, 157
Cyprus 130, 155

Dahhān, S. 114, 124, 125
Damascus 7–28 *passim*, 29, 31, 39, 56, 57, 63, 67, 69, 71, 72, 82, 84, 87–92 *passim*, 97, 99, 102, 105, 106, 121, 122, 139, 141, 143, 147, 159, 162, 163, 166, 168–69, 180, 188, 189, 199
Intellectualism and politics within 11–12
Damietta 62, 64, 104, 106, 150, 157, 173–76
Dār al-Ḥadīth al-Bahā'iyya 163
Dār al-Islām 59–61, 72, 76, 83
Darbasāk 133
Al-Dargazīnī, vizier 30
Ḍayfa Khātūn 112, 113
Défrémery, C. 58, 127
Al-Dhahabī 10, 16, 95, 120
*Dhimmī*s 65, 72
Diplomacy 24, 49, 101, 142–44, 151–57, 188–89
Dom Berthereau 52, 126
Dubays b. Ṣadaqa 82, 121, 122, 131
Dysentery, suffered by Franks 102

Eddé, Anne-Marie 2
Edessa 26, 128
Fall of 25, 53, 71, 122, 131
Egypt 15, 23, 24, 39, 53, 54, 60, 62, 71, 79, 83, 86, 100, 112, 114, 118, 119, 124, 135, 136, 140, 150, 170, 175, 176, 180, 181, 189, 190, 191, 195, 197
El-Hibri, Tayeb 6
English, translations of Arabic into 2, 4, 58–59, 97
Euclid 149

Al-Fāḍil 38, 39, 43, 45, 46, 50, 56, 132, 185
Fagnan, Edmond 58
Fakhr al-Dīn 104
Fakhr al-Dīn al-Rāzī 138
Al-Faramā 195
Fāṭima, daughter of al-Maqrīzī 166
Fāṭima, daughter of Muḥammad 178
Fāṭimids 12, 16, 23–24, 53, 60, 69, 101, 162, 170–72, 176–81, 189, 193–94
Field of Blood, battle of – see Balāṭ, battle of
Al-Findalāwī 99, 100, 108
Fifth Crusade 62, 64, 89, 90, 102, 106, 134, 150, 157, 174, 189, 199
First Crusade 60–62, 72, 101, 126, 198
Food 21, 63, 65, 116, 174–75
France 150, 185–86
Frankish attacks on Islamic lands 60–62
Frankish pilgrims 49
Frankish women 47–48
Franks *passim*
Frederick II, German Emperor 94, 97, 102, 103, 105, 107, 108, 134, 135, 142, 143, 149, 150, 157–60, 175, 188
Freitag, G.W. 126
French, translations of Arabic into 2, 4, 58–59, 69, 96, 126, 186, 190
French Revolution 126
Fulk, King of Jerusalem 101
Fusṭāṭ 166, 174, 178

Gabrieli, Francesco 1, 52, 78, 97, 98, 103, 160, 187
Gaza 62
George of Antioch 199
German, translation of Arabic into 126
Germans 72, 149
Germany 150
Gesta Francorum 5
Al-Ghazālī 11
Ghazna 63
Ghūr 63
Gibb, H.A.R. 14, 67, 78, 187
Godfrey of Bouillon 72, 195, 199
Gospels 61, 198
Goths 198
Grand Mosque of Aleppo 111
Great Seljūqs 12, 13, 23 (see also Seljūqs)
Great Umayyad Mosque 11, 12, 88, 89, 103, 109, 151, 156, 188
Greek texts 1, 32
Greeks 197, 198 (see also Byzantines)
Guy of Lusignan 48, 49

Hadith 30–32, 55, 56, 66, 84–87, 93, 95, 110, 115, 117–19, 124, 137, 161, 163, 164, 167
Al-Ḥākim, Fāṭimid caliph 166, 179
Al-Ḥallāwiyya madrasa 111, 113
Ḥamā 83, 110, 121, 136–39, 141–44, 146, 149, 151–55
Hamaker, Henri Arens 173–74
Ḥamdān al-Athāribī 5, 122, 129
Ḥanafī(s) 11, 31, 91, 93, 109–12, 134, 164
Ḥanafiyya madrasa 87
Ḥanbalī(s) 31, 91, 161, 164, 165
Al-Harawī, Abū Sa'd 12, 77
Ḥarbiyya, battle of 108, 141, 149
Al-Ḥarīrī 43
Ḥaṭṭīn, battle of 48, 54, 74, 188
Al-Ḥaẓīrī 34
Hebron 87, 92
Henry VI, German Emperor 65
Ḥijāz 187
Hilāl al-Ṣābi' 14, 15, 102
Hillenbrand, Carole 103
Ḥiṣn al-Akrād 151, 152, 155
Ḥiṣn Kayfa 139
Historiography, Islamic 5–6, 63, 76–78, 98–100, 103, 107, 123, 133–34
Hitti, P.K. 187
Hohenstaufens 136, 143, 150
Holy Lance 74
Holy Roman Empire 150
Holy Sepulchre 47
Homs 90, 143, 144, 153, 155
Hospitallers 48, 151–52, 153, 154 (see also Military Orders)
Humphreys, R.S. 90, 106
Ḥusām al-Dīn al-Hadhabānī 139, 140, 141, 144
Al-Hūta 113

Iberia 199
Ibn 'Abd al-Ẓāhir 179
Ibn Abī Ṭayyi' 128, 132, 179, 181, 185
Ibn Abi'l-Wafā' al-Qurashī 120
Ibn al-'Adīm 66, 68, **109–35**, 139, 147, 154, 158
  Aims in writing 123–24
  Career of 111–14
  Interests of 115
  Life of 110–14
  Material possessions of 113
  Methodology in writing 118
  Sources used by 118–19, 125
  Sponsor of 124
  Studies of 110
  Views of Franks 128
  Writings of 115–35
    Historical value of 121–23, 128–33
Ibn al-'Amīd 5, 198
Ibn Amqrīz 162
Ibn 'Asākir 7–8, 9–10, 12, 66, 117
Ibn al-Athīr 2, 16, **52–83**, 99–103, 106, 130, 148, 152, 154, 155, 157, 158, 179, 180, 185
  Divine will in the writings of 82–83
  Life of 52, 56–57
  Quality of his writings 68
  Sources used 67–68
  Style of writing 62–66, 69, 79
  Views of Fāṭimids 60
  Views of Fifth Crusade 62
  Views of First Crusade 60–62
  Views of the Franks 71–76
  Views of Frankish religion 74–76
  Views on Saladin 78–83
  Writings of 57–83
  Zengid sympathies of 52, 69–71, 78–83
Ibn al-Azraq 100
Ibn al-Dawadarī 95
Ibn Faḍl Allāh al-'Umarī 170, 172, 191
Ibn Fahd, Meccan historian 182
Ibn al-Furāt 67, 95, 160, 174
Ibn al-Ḥājib 139
Ibn al-Ḥanbalī 121
Ibn Ḥajar al-'Asqalānī 68, 194
Ibn Ḥazm 165
Ibn Hubayra, vizier 36, 85, 86
Ibn al-'Imād 120
Ibn al-Jawzī 85–86, 98, 101
Ibn Kathīr 87, 95, 112
Ibn al-Khaṭīb 167
Ibn al-Khaṭīb al-Nāṣiriyya 121
Ibn Khaldūn 65, 160, 167, 170
Ibn Khallikan 14, 55, 56, 57, 120
Ibn al-Khayyāṭ 11
Ibn Jubayr 4, 50
Ibn al-Ma'mūn 179
Ibn Muyassar 177, 179
Ibn al-Nadīm 177
Ibn al-Nafīs 138

Ibn al-Qalānisī 7–**28**, 67, 100, 101, 129, 130, 131
as *adīb* 7–10
as *raʾīs* 8–9
Dhayl taʾrīkh Dimashq of 13–28
Image of Būrids in 19–22
Image of Fāṭimids in 22–24
Image of Franks in 16–19
Image of Zengids in 24–28
Source material for 14–16
Intellectual and political context of his life 10–13
Ibn Qayyim al-Jawziyya 165
Ibn Saʿīd 167, 179
Ibn al-Ṣalāḥ, Damascene 11
Ibn al-Ṣalāḥ, associate of Sibṭ Ibn al-Jawzī 90
Ibn Shākir al-Kutubī 115, 120
Ibn al-Shiḥna 120
Ibn al-Ṣuqāʿī 112
Ibn Taghrībirdī 95, 120
Ibn Taymiyya 138, 165
Ibn Wāṣil 68, 102–7, **136–60**, 174, 175, 185
And jihad 142–43, 147–48
Knowledge of European politics 142, 149–50
Scholarly interests 137–39
Transregional career of 139–45
End of, in Ḥamā 140–41
Writings of 145–60
Ayyūbid politics in 150–60
Ibn Zūlāq 179
Ideal Rule 20, 28, 76–78, 146–47
Ifrīqiya 60–63, 178
Il-Ghāzī 131
ʿImād al-Dīn al-Iṣfahānī 2, **29–51**, 67, 68, 100–1, 132, 147, 148, 150
Belief in Frankish degradation 47–50
Career in Syria and Egypt 37–41
Economical with the truth 45–46
Education of 30–33
Frankish women in the writings of 47–48
Gains lifelong madrasa chair in Damascus 32
Life of 29–41
Literary production of 33–35, 41–51
Moral dualism in the writings of 42–43
Moves to Syria 37
Poetry and 31, 34–35
Sense of his own value and his mission 35, 40, 51
Writing style of unappreciated 43–44
Al-ʿImādiyya 82
Inab, battle of 15, 18, 27
India 32, 60
Iraq 12, 15, 31, 59, 62, 63, 98, 100, 109, 118, 134, 169
Iran 118, 134 (see also Persia)
Isfahan 29, 30, 34, 35
Italian, translations of Arabic into 2, 97, 193
Italy 136, 138, 142, 143, 149, 193
Situation for Muslims in 149
ʿIzz al-Dīn al-Afram 140
ʿIzz al-Dīn Ibn Shaddād 120
ʿIzz al-Dīn Kay Kāwūs, Rūm Seljūq sultan 156
ʿIzz al-Dīn Masʿūd I, ruler of Mosul 53, 54, 55
ʿIzz al-Dīn Masʿūd II, ruler of Mosul 54, 68, 69
ʿIzz al-Dīn Mawdūd, ruler of Aleppo 80
ʿIzz al-Dīn al-Sulamī 156–57

Jabal Samʿān 113
Jabala 72, 133
Jackson, Peter 97, 105, 106, 160
Jaffa 54, 65, 151 (see also Treaty of Jaffa)
Jamāl al-Dīn Aydughdī 140, 141
Jamāl al-Dīn Muḥammad, son of Ibn al-ʿAdīm 110
Jamāl al-Dīn Muḥammad, uncle of Ibn al-ʿAdīm 110
Jazīra 31, 38, 52, 54, 59, 70, 71, 78, 112, 114, 131 (see also Mesopotamia)
Jazīrat Ibn ʿUmar 53, 55, 56
Jerusalem 12, 40, 48, 61, 62, 74, 75, 80, 87, 92, 105, 108, 110, 123, 136, 139, 149, 188
Captured by Franks of the First Crusade 12, 101, 145
Handed over to Frederick II 89, 97, 103, 105, 107, 108, 134, 135, 158
Holiness of in Christianity 47, 49
Latin Kingdom of 54, 143, 153, 156
Jewett, J.R. 97
Jews 145, 197
Jihad 11, 17, 19, 20, 22, 24–28, 46, 53, 54, 61, 63, 70, 73, 81, 83, 88–89, 104, 129, 142, 143, 147–48, 151, 153, 154–55

Joscelin I of Courtenay (I of Edessa) 128
Joscelin II of Edessa 25
Jubayl 17

Kafarṭāb 121
Kalām 32, 138
Kamāl al-Dīn ʿUmar Ibn al-ʿAdīm – see Ibn al-ʿAdīm
Kamāl al-Dīn ʿUmar al-Tiflīsī 114
Kāshān 30
Kawkab 133
Kaykhusraw II, Seljūq sultan of Rūm 112
Kayqubād, Seljūq sultan of Rūm 112
Kerak 91, 136, 137, 141, 143
Kerboghā of Mosul 74, 131
Al-Khaṭīb al-Baghdādī 117
Al-Khawābī 155
Al-Khūnajī 137, 138
Khurāsān 82
Al-Khusrūshāhī, ʿAbd al-Ḥamīd b. ʿAlī 137, 138
Khuṭluj 189
Khwārazmians 135, 142
Kutāma, Berber tribe 162

Lascaris 199
Latin, translation of Arabic into 126, 173
Latin East 1, 3, 5, 69, 147, 180 (see also Crusades)
Latins 72, 198
Lattakia 130, 133
Le Tourneau, Roger 14
Leon II, Armenian ruler 154–56
Levant 1, 3, 5, 16, 28, 50, 69, 73, 102, 106, 107, 180
Louis IX of France 98, 102, 104, 106, 108, 141, 148, 150, 160, 173, 175–76, 185, 189, 196, 199
Lucera 142
Lydda 151

Maʿarrat Miṣrīn 113, 121, 122
Maʿarrat al-Nuʿmān 121, 131
Madrasa(s) 30, 31, 32, 36, 37, 39, 40, 84, 87, 91, 92, 98, 110, 113, 134, 139 (see also individual madrasas)
Maghrib 39
Al-Mahdī 60
Al-Mahdiyya 63
Maḥmūd of Ghazna 77
Maḥmūd b. Masʿūd b. Arslān Shāh 56
Majālis al-waʿẓ, see 'Assemblies of Exhortation'
Majd al-Dawla, ruler of Rayy 77
Majd al-Dīn ʿAbd al-Raḥmān, son of Ibn al-ʿAdīm 110, 113
Al-Malik al-Ashraf 90, 93, 112, 115, 158
Al-Malik al-Kāmil 54, 86, 89, 97, 103, 112, 135, 143, 157–59, 187–89
Al-Malik al-Manṣūr 138, 141, 152, 153
Al-Malik al-Muẓaffar 152
Al-Malik al-Ẓāhir Ghāzī 54, 56, 77, 115, 119, 124, 133, 153, 154–56
Mālikī(s) 31
Mallāḥa 15
Ma'mūniyya madrasa 86
Mamlūk era 9, 41, 124, 136, 140, 143, 171, 176
Mamlūks 105, 113, 140–44, 146, 163, 168, 171, 176, 181–87, 190, 191, 200
Manfred, German Emperor 136, 138, 142, 143, 149, 150, 159, 160
Manṣūra, battle of 64, 104
Manzikert, battle of 102
Maqāma genre 43
Maqāriza 162
Al-Maqrīzī, Taqī al-Dīn Aḥmad 2, 95, **161–200**
  Family history of 161–64
  General writings of 167–71
  Historical writings of 171–200
  Life of 164–67
  Methodology in writing 170–71, 182–85, 192–94, 197–98
  Sources used by 172, 179, 194–95, 199
Mardin 122, 123, 142
Marqab 133
Masʿūd, Fāṭimid governor of Tyre 180
Masʿūd b. Muḥammad b. Malikshāh, Seljūq sultan 32, 36, 63
Al-Masʿūdī 68
Matthew Paris 5
Mazyadids 82
Mecca 56, 68, 92, 111, 139, 140, 165, 167, 182, 196–97
Medicine 32, 122, 139
Medina 89
Mediterranean 72, 199
Meisami, J.S. 6

Melitene 199
Mesopotamia 45, 144, 147 (see also Jazīra)
Micheau, Françoise 2
Military Orders 133, 134 (see also Templars, and Hospitallers)
'Mirrors for Princes' 77, 78, 107
Miskawayh 77
Mongols 55, 60, 62, 64, 81, 113, 114, 120, 124, 134, 135, 141, 148, 175, 189, 190, 198
Mosul 12, 38, 52–58 *passim*, 59, 60, 67–71, 77–79, 87, 92, 106, 122, 131, 142, 180
Mount Qāsiyūn 10, 88, 92
Mouton, Jean-Michel 67
Al-Muʿaẓẓam ʿĪsā 89, 90, 91, 93, 151
Al-Muʿaẓẓam Tūrānshāh 106, 139, 141, 145, 175
Muḥammad 5, 17, 57, 59, 75, 84, 93, 94, 117, 128, 171, 178, 194, 196–97
Muḥammad b. ʿAbd al-Karīm, father of Ibn al-Athīr 55
Muḥammad b. ʿAbd al-Malik Ibn Abī al-Jarāda 129
Muḥammad b. Maḥmūd b. Muḥammad, Seljūq sultan 36
Muḥtasib 165, 168
Muḥyī al-Dīn, son of Ibn al-Jawzī 86
Muḥyī al-Dīn ʿAbd al-Qādir, grandfather of al-Maqrīzī 162
Muʿīn al-Dīn Unur 22, 23, 100
Al-Muʿizz li-Dīn Allāh, Fāṭimid caliph 178
Muʿizz al-Dīn Sinjār Shāh, son of Sayf al-Dīn Ghāzī II 55
Mujāhid al-Dīn Buzān 15
Mujīr al-Dīn Ābaq 11
Müller, J.J. 126
Al-Mundhirī 174, 185, 189
Al-Musabbiḥī 167, 179
Muslims, in Italy 149
Al-Mustanjid, caliph 82
Al-Mustaʿīn bi-llāh, Mamlūk-era caliph 166

Nablus 89, 107
Najm al-Dīn, son of Ibn al-ʿAdīm 110
Najm al-Dīn Aḥmad, father of Ibn al-ʿAdīm 110, 111
Al-Nāṣir Daʿūd 89, 141
Nāṣir al-Dīn Maḥmūd, ruler of Mosul 54
Nāṣir al-Dīn Muḥammad, nephew of al-Maqrīzī 167
Al-Nāṣir Faraj 166, 168–69
Al-Nāṣir Yūsuf II 112, 113, 124, 137
Naval power, Egyptian 23
Nicaea, Empire of 199
Niẓām al-Mulk 78
Niẓāmiyya madrasa 32, 36, 37
Nizārīs 12, 20, 22, 144, 155, 156
Normandy 150
Northern Syrian Alliance System 146, 151–57
Nūr al-Dīn Arslān Shāh I, ruler of Mosul 54, 55, 57, 69, 71
Nūr al-Dīn Arslān Shāh II, ruler of Mosul 54
Nūr al-Dīn Maḥmūd 12, 13, 18, 24, 26–28, 30, 37–40, 53, 54, 63, 70, 71, 73, 79, 81, 83, 108, 123, 126, 134, 147 (see also Zengids)
  Aims to restore Sunnism in Syria 53
  Besieges Damascus in 546/1151 27
  Defeated by Franks 15
  Image of in chronicles 26–28, 78
  Takes Damascus 9–11, 24, 27
Al-Nuwayrī 4, 68, 185, 190

Oghuz 82
Orderic Vitalis 5

Pagans 17
Palestine 151, 180–81, 187, 190, 199
Papacy 150 (see also Pope)
Patriarch of Jerusalem 75
Paul Orose 198
Perfume 116
Persia 12, 29, 30, 31, 100 (see also Iran)
Pilgrims, Frankish 49
Poetry 8–10, 30, 31, 34–36, 41, 44, 68, 87, 100, 109, 115–16, 125, 129, 132, 133, 138, 175
Pope 74, 149, 157, 174 (see also Papacy)

Qāʾitbāy 182
Al-Qalqashandī 165
Al-Qaysarānī 11
Qayṣariyya 112
Qilij Arslān 73
Qizoghlū b. ʿAbdallāh, father of Sibṭ Ibn al-Jawzī 85
Quatremère, Étienne Marc 185–86
Al-Quḍāʿī 60
Quran 17, 30, 32, 47, 84, 85, 87, 93, 110, 117, 128, 164, 172

Quraysh 198
Qūṣ 140
Quss ibn Sāʿida 45
Quṭb al-Dīn Mawdūd, ruler of Mosul 53, 55
Quṭuz, (future) Mamlūk sultan 113

Raʾīs 7, 13, 20
Ramla 151, 195
Rāshidūn 5
Raymond, son of Bohemond IV of Antioch 155
Raymond of Antioch (of Poitiers) 18, 74
Raymond of St. Gilles (I of Tripoli) 73, 199
Raymond III of Tripoli 46, 74
Reinaud, J.T. 58, 127
Religious Conversion 123
Reynald of Châtillon 46, 48, 49, 74, 128, 186–87, 188
Richard the Lionheart 49, 54
Richards, D.S. 2, 58
Riḍwān of Aleppo 121, 131
Rodinson, Maxime 116
Roger of Antioch 131
Roger I of Sicily 61
Roger II of Sicily 174, 199
Röhricht, G.R. 126

Saʿd Allāh b. Wāṣil 137, 144
Ṣafad 133
Al-Ṣafadī 95, 120
Safi, Omid 6
Ṣāfitā 152
Safrā bint ʿUmar b. ʿAbd al-Salām b. ʿAbd al-Ṣamad al-Baghdādī, wife of al-Maqrīzī 166
Ṣafwat al-Mulk 24
Ṣāḥib al-shurṭa 9
Al-Sakhāwī 94, 120
Saladin 30, 31, 37–40, 44, 46, 51, 54, 56, 67, 69, 70, 78, 81, 83, 108, 109, 132, 133, 134, 143, 147, 155, 174, 180, 187
  Conquers Jerusalem 75, 80, 149
  Financial problems of 157
  Kills Reynald of Châtillon 46, 48, 49
  Massacres Military Orders after Ḥaṭṭīn 48
  Takes Damascus 80
  Takes power in Egypt 53, 86, 184
Al-Ṣāliḥ Aḥmad 112
Al-Ṣāliḥ Ayyūb 86, 104, 113, 139, 141, 142, 145, 150, 156
Al-Ṣāliḥ Ismāʿīl, Ayyūbid ruler of Damascus 156, 188
Al-Ṣāliḥ Ismāʿīl, *nāʾib* 90
Al-Samʿānī 57
Sarmāniyya 133
Sayf al-Dawla, tenth century ruler of Aleppo 125
Sayf al-Dīn Āqtamur al-Ḥanbalī 163
Sayf al-Dīn Ghāzī I, brother of Nūr al-Dīn 53, 63
Sayf al-Dīn Ghāzī II, nephew of Sayf al-Dīn Ghāzī I 53
Second Crusade 10, 16, 17, 22, 28, 63, 69, 71, 72, 97, 99, 102
Seljūqs 6, 8, 19, 30, 32, 53, 54, 62, 69, 121, 135, 184, 199 (see also Great Seljūqs)
  Takeover of Syria 102
Seljūqs of Rūm 27, 112, 146, 156
Shādhbakhtiyya madrasa 111
Shādī 38
Shāfiʿī(s) 31, 32, 37, 110, 114, 139, 141, 164
Shāh Rukh 182
Shajar al-Durr 175, 183
Shams al-Khilāfa 101
Shams al-Mulūk Ismāʿīl 13, 21
Sharīʿa 82, 103, 107–8, 149
Shāwar, Fāṭimid vizier 180
Shibiliyya madrasa 87, 91
Shihāb al-Dīn Ibrāhīm Ibn Abiʾl-Damm 136–37, 139, 142
Shihāb al-Dīn Maḥmūd, Būrid ruler of Damascus 24
Shiḥna 9
Shīʿīs 12, 23, 60, 77, 93, 118, 132, 162, 176–7
Shipping, Byzantine 23
Shipping, Frankish 23
Shirkūh 38, 53, 72, 79, 180
Shughr 132
Shuhda, daughter of Ibn al-ʿAdīm 110
Sibṭ Ibn al-ʿAjamī 120
Sibṭ Ibn al-Jawzī 16, 68, 84–108, 142, 151, 159, 185
  And attacks on Franks 89–90
  Conversion to Ḥanafism 91–92, 93
  Left Baghdad 87
  Life of 84–92, 102
  Preacher 87, 88–90, 103–4, 159

Relations with Ayyūbids 87, 90–91
Travels outside Damascus 92
View of history 94
Written works of 92–108
Criticisms of 95
Impact on later Arabic historiography 95
Methodology of 98–99, 107–8
Originality of 102–3
Sicilians, attack Alexandria 83
Sicily 61, 193
Sijilmāsa 60
Silvestre de Sacy, Antoine-Isaac 126–27, 169–70, 185
Sinjār 53, 180
Siyāsa 82, 107
Sufism/Sufis 32–33, 41, 60, 77, 123, 167
Sūl 166
Al-Sulamī 11, 81, 129
Sunnī Islam 28, 31, 53, 82, 85, 93
Sunnīs 12, 22, 23, 60, 107, 109, 118, 177, 179
Al-Su'ūdī, Muḥammad b. 'Abd al-Raḥmān b. 'Alī b. Abi'l-Ḥasan 164
Al-Suyūṭī 120
Synaxarion 198
Syria 8, 15, 24, 39, 53, 54, 56, 59, 62–64, 67, 71, 73, 76, 84, 100, 118, 124, 134, 135, 136, 140, 199
Syriac texts 1

Al-Ṭabarī 59, 66, 77, 100
Tāj al-Mulūk Būrī 12, 19, 23
Talmon-Heller, Daniella 89
Tamerlane 120, 166
Tell Bāshir 128
Templars 48, 104, 152, 189 (see also Military Orders)
Al-Tha'ālibī 34
Theobald of Champagne 156
Thiqatiyya madrasa 32
Third Crusade 54, 157
Tīmūrids 181
Timurtāsh, ruler of Mardin 122
Toledo 61
Tornberg, C. 58
Trade 50, 74
Treaty of Jaffa 40, 54, 135
Trinity 17
Tripoli 12, 143, 144, 151, 153, 154, 155, 199
True Cross 47, 74, 75
Ṭughril 82
Ṭughril Shihāb al-Dīn, Atabeg 57
Ṭughtegīn 12, 19–20, 23
Tunis 176 (see also Carthage)
Turkmen 21, 25
Turks 13, 60, 91, 133, 198
Tyre 23, 54, 60, 80, 180

'Ubayd Allāh, first Fāṭimid representative in Cairo 178
'Ulamā' 5, 84, 88, 90, 98, 99, 100, 103, 104, 107–8, 113, 118, 139
'Umar ibn al-Khaṭṭāb 80
'Umara al-Yamanī 181
Umayyad era 125
Umma 60, 62, 150
Al-'Urayma 63
Usāma b. Munqidh 4, 8, 129

Venice 199

Walter the Chancellor 5
Al-Warrāda 195
Watermelon, used to capture Franks 175
Wilken, F. 126
William the Frank 189
William I of Sicily 174
William of Tyre 5, 42
Women, Frankish 47–48

Al-Yaghmūrī 188
Yaghrā 63
Al-Ya'lāwī, Muḥammad 193
Yāqūt al-Rūmī 65, 113, 115, 119
Yashbak min Mahdi, Mamlūk emir 182
Al-Yūnīnī 68, 95, 96, 114, 120

Al-Ẓāfir, Fāṭimid caliph 180
Zakkār, Suhayl 8, 14
Zengī, 'Imād al-Dīn 11, 13, 21, 24–26, 53, 70, 73, 83, 122, 131, 132 (see also Zengids)
Captures Edessa 25, 71, 122
Image of in chronicles 24–26, 70
Zengids 12, 16, 24–28, 52–58 *passim*, 69–71, 78, 80, 106, 143, 146
Ziyāda, M.M. 186

... a welcomed addition to the existing texts and monographs on this field and certainly accomplish the goal to be an important and appreciated reference work for those who are interested in the study of the narratives of Muslim historians and chronicles of the crusading period.

– Robert Celestre in: *Eurasian Studies*, 13 (2015)

This is a very useful book. [...]. *After an introduction by the editor, we have contributions by Niall Christie on Ibn al-Qalānisī, Lutz Richter-Bernburg on ʿImād al-Dīn al-Iṣfahānī, Françoise Micheau on Ibn al-Athīr, Alex Mallett on Sibṭ Ibn al-Jawzī, Anne-Marie Eddé on Ibn al-ʿAdīm, Konrad Hirschler on Ibn Wāṣil and, finally, Frédéric Bauden on al-Maqrīzī. Each essay discusses the life of the author, the scope of his writings, the earlier and current editions and translations of the texts and the attitudes of the historians to the Franks. Anyone embarking on the study of the Crusader states in the Levant will find this a helpful guide. For the non-Arabist, it will provide background and context for works which are otherwise only names in footnotes.* [...]. *This volume is an excellent introduction...*

– Hugh Kennedy in: *EHR*, cxxxi. 550 (2016)

www.ingramcontent.com/pod-product-compliance
Lightning Source LLC
Chambersburg PA
CBHW021946290426
44108CB00012B/976
* 9 7 8 9 0 0 4 7 3 3 4 3 5 *